Searching for Peace

'Very interesting ... a particular pleasure to read something not only sensible but even hopeful on methods for moving towards some decent outcome under what appear to be almost hopeless situations ... [a] very good read.' **Noam Chomsky**

'I read [the book] with absorbing interest. The sections on conflict resolution are especially perceptive. So is the discussion on the war culture. Thank you for a fine contribution to peace science.' **Anatol Rapoport,** *Professor Emeritus, University of Toronto*

'Fascinating! This highly condensed and powerful overview of the past and present realpolitik of peacemaking during continuing historical struggles between national identity and state integrity opens up major new ways to think about the seemingly intractable problems of state–nation interface. The Transcend method takes its place as a highly significant strategy in the rich array of peacebuilding techniques. This book is a must-read for scholars, practitioners, policy makers and peace activists.' **Elise Boulding,** *Professor Emerita, Dartmouth College / former Secretary-General of the International Peace Research Association*

'Our world yearns for peace and the reduction of violence. This book provides a creative, constructive contribution to peacekeeping and peacemaking.' **Project Ploughshares network,** *Canada*

'While challenging peacekeeping and peacemaking approaches in past conflicts and analysing the emergent conflict dynamics that threaten the 21st century, this book focuses on the TRANSCEND approach to peacebuilding, aimed at including all participants in the peace dialogue.' *Oxfam Review of Journals*

'Galtung's writing always provides succinct and important insights ... The book has appropriate and important targets: it seeks to uncover the general truth among the particular complications; it does not draw back from proposing courses of action; it confronts serious tasks.' *Ethnic Conflict Research Digest*

'In the face of the impacts of the conflict formations discussed here, the creative and stimulating thinking evident in this book is to be congratulated.' *Millennium*

'*Searching for Peace* takes the reader from global conflict patterns and big power strategic partnerships down to the personal level in peace negotiations, and even into the Freudian tradition of the sub-conscious.' *Journal of Refugee Studies*

'This wonderfully wide-ranging, multi-faceted book provides a comprehensive approach to achieving peace. The authors draw from their many years of experience as analysts, consultants, and trainers around the world, and from that of colleagues in the global TRANSCEND network. In this second edition, the authors demonstrate the value of their approach, incorporating diagnosis, prognosis, and therapy, by applying it to understanding and responding to the events of September 11, 2001. They present challenging insights from a global perspective.' **Louis Kriesberg**, *Maxwell Professor Emeritus of Social Conflict Studies, Syracuse University*

'Offers an inspiration that challenges and a beacon that braves the fossilized indifference of the world in the face of recurring and ever-intensifying conflicts. Especially pertinent is the manner in which it holds up this special mirror of tools and codes to the faces of African scholars, institutions, policy makers and civil society and says: "This is your moment to make that difference".' **Catherine A. Odora Hoppers**, *peace and development activist, Unesco expert, and Professor of Education, University of Pretoria*

'A provocative and practical resource for those interested in war, violence, and building peace in the current era. Through the book, TRANSCEND offers a new narrative – peace by peaceful means – to guide peace action that challenges older narratives – those of just violence/war, and intervention on the side of justice. Through their rich analyses the authors drive the reader to embrace alternative ways of thinking about and practicing peace. Overall, the book is a must-read for all seeking to understand, or practically influence the building of peace around the globe.' **Erin McCandless**, *Co-Executive Editor, Journal of Peacebuilding and Development*

Searching for Peace

The Road to
TRANSCEND

Johan Galtung, Carl G. Jacobsen
and **Kai Frithjof Brand-Jacobsen**

Pluto  Press

LONDON • STERLING, VIRGINIA

in association with

TRANSCEND

First published 2000
Second edition published 2002 by Pluto Press
345 Archway Road, London N6 5AA
and 22883 Quicksilver Drive,
Sterling, VA 20166–2012, USA

www.plutobooks.com

British Library Cataloguing in Publication Data
A catalogue record for this book is available from the British
Library

ISBN 0 7453 1929 7 hardback
ISBN 0 7453 1928 9 paperback

A catalogue record for this book is available from the
Library of Congress

10   9   8   7   6   5   4   3   2   1

Designed and produced for Pluto Press by
Chase Publishing Services, Fortescue, Sidmouth EX10 9QG
Typeset from disk by Stanford DTP Services, Towcester
Printed in the European Union by
Antony Rowe, Chippenham, England

Dedicated to Carl Gustav Jacobsen
1944–2001
in loving memory

Contents

Series Preface

Peace by Peaceful Means

(Edited by TRANSCEND – A Peace and Development Organization for Conflict Transformation by Peaceful Means)

> 'Peace is a revolutionary idea; peace by peaceful means defines that revolution as nonviolent. That revolution is taking place all the time; our job is to expand it in scope and domain. The tasks are endless; the question is whether we are up to them.' Johan Galtung

To work for peace is to work against violence; by analysing its forms and causes, predicting in order to prevent, and then acting preventively and curatively since peace relates to violence much as health relates to illness. Of particular concern is genocide, or massive category killing, across the fault-lines in human society: nature (between humans and their environment), gender, generation, race, class, exclusion, nation, state. Whether as direct violence or as the indirect slow, grinding violence of social structures that do not deliver sufficient nutrition and health at the bottom of world society, enormous suffering is the effect. To work for peace is to build liberation, wellness in a world with peace with nature, between genders, generations and races, where the excluded are included but not by force, and where classes, nations and states serve neither direct, structural nor cultural violence. In such a world they would all pull together for a better livelihood for all. That would be true globalization, unlike the present reduction of that term to represent only state and corporate elites in a handful of countries.

Drawing upon more than 45 years of experience working in the fields of peace-building and development, *Peace by Peaceful Means* brings together some of the world's leading scholars-practitioners to address the major challenges and conflicts of our time, while offering constructive and viable proposals for what can be done. Intended for the enquiring reader, social and political activists, researchers, students, and peace and development workers from the North and the South, the book combines creative and critical analysis, going to the roots of today's conflicts and violence in the world, with practical therapy and strategies for conflict transformation by peaceful means. Spanning peace research, conflict, gender and development studies, international relations, political economy, ecology, philosophy and sociology, *Peace by Peaceful Means* brings forth the challenge for a theory and practice of peace for the twenty-first century.

Preface

TRANSCEND: A Philosophy of Peace – And One Way of Enacting It

To work for peace is to work against violence. We analyse its forms and causes, we predict in order to prevent, and we act preventively and curatively – all medical terms, since peace relates to violence much as health does to illness. Particularly important are the pandemics of violence, *genocide*, or *massive category killing*, across the eight fault-lines in the human condition: nature, gender, generation, race, class, exclusion, nation and state. Whether as direct violence or as the indirect violence of social structures that do not deliver sufficient nutrition and health at the bottom of world society, enormous suffering, *dukkha*, is the result.

To work for peace is to build *sukha*, liberation, wellness in a world of peace with nature, peace between genders, generations and races, where the excluded are included but not by force, and where classes, nations and states serve neither direct nor structural violence. In such a world they would all pull together for a better livelihood for all. That would be true *globalization*, unlike the present 'globalization' that benefits only state and corporate elites in a handful of countries. The best instrument of true globalization would be an improved United Nations, with a UN People's Assembly for global democracy, without any veto power for privileged countries, located where most people live – somewhere in the Third World, for instance in Jerusalem or Hong Kong.

An improved UN would also build on civil society actors – non-governmental organizations (NGOs) and local authorities (LAs) – and transnational corporations (TNCs), an underutilized peace actor. The overutilized state system, from the Westphalia 'peace' of 1648, even gives states a 'right of war' (except Japan: Constitution Article 9 denies Japan that right). An improved UN would also have to learn to build on nations striving for autonomy and not privilege states only.

States were not created to bring peace to the world, but to satisfy 'national interests' as defined by their elites, if necessary by war. Peace has a lower priority, as seen clearly when we compare the size of their establishments for peace and war. Some states are predators and see their interests located outside their own territory – euphemistically called their 'sphere of interest'. When states pretend to work for peace it is very often as a way of solidifying their sphere of interest. And even if the effort is honest, it is usually painfully clear how little they know and how amateurish their endeavours. Nothing of this, however, prevents them from claiming a monopoly on peace, as also on war.

From this it does not follow that non-states in the world civil society, whether NGOs and as LAs, TNCs and individuals, are necessarily competent. Nor does it follow that states cannot be improved, nor that states cannot often be excellent peacemakers across the other divides, defined by nature, gender, generation, race, class and exclusion; often in ways codified by that major instrument of peace, *human rights* (universal, indivisible), protected by the institutions of *democracy*. But these two institutions are far from culturally neutral and not necessarily practised in inter-nation and inter-state relations, the macro-level of human construction, where state and alliance egotism seems to dominate, often supported by democratic majorities.

Hence the rise early in the twentieth century (but with forerunners in the high Middle Ages) of *non-state actors working for peace*. There are at least three generations of such approaches so far.

To understand them better, TRANSCEND's definition that *peace = the ability to handle conflict with empathy, non-violence and creativity* may be useful, since so much violence is due to mishandling conflict, allowing it to fester, like a deep wound.

Conflict = Attitudes + Behaviour + Contradiction – the ABC triangle. At the root of the conflict is a *contradiction*, incompatible goals. Hateful/apathetic *attitudes* and *behaviour* often come later, all three corners stimulating each other. After some time it all crystallizes and polarizes around friend/Self and foe/Other, the former being surrounded by increasingly positive, and the latter by increasingly negative attitudes/behaviour. Friend and foe images become megalomaniac in their inability to include anything negative in the former, and paranoid in their inability to include anything positive in the latter. We can talk about personal and social pathologies bordering on collective psychoses, as we would classify an individual with similar character traits. Rationality evaporates, deep culture, with ready-made polarization, takes over. Violence is not far away. The Cold War was such a case until forces in civil society had a depolarizing effect. So are conflicts in and around Yugoslavia, and between terrorists and state terrorists.

We can use the ABC triangle to identify *deep attitudes*, *deep behaviour* and *deep contradictions*. They steer or influence the surface level of what people say they feel or think, the behaviour we can observe and the incompatible goals. 'Deep' means subconscious, hidden, beneath the surface. We identify these three with *deep culture*, *basic human needs* and *deep structure*, the last based on all eight fault-lines in the human condition, and not only Marxism's class, feminism's gender or realism's state.

We then get peace approaches by trying to change all six, the attitudes, behaviour and contradictions, at the surface level and deeper. That gives us three *generations of peace approaches*:

The first generation of peace approaches, up to the Second World War:

A-oriented: *peace movements*, advocating, demonstrating;
B-oriented: *war abolition*, eliminating war as social institution;
C-oriented: *global governance*, globalizing good government.

The three were related, with people expressing themselves through their movements, with governments searching for regional and global harmonization and for the abolition of war through mechanisms of democracy, human rights and regimes. The motto for this generation:

> *Peace is too important to leave to the generals.*

Second generation of peace approaches, after the Second World War:

A-oriented: *peace education/journalism* for more knowledge;
B-oriented: *non-violence*, fighting, but *non-violently*;
C-oriented: *conflict transformation*, solving conflicts *creatively*.

The three are related, evolving from the first generation. People start doubting that peace ranks high among the interests pursued by governments, and doubt their capability, watching them stumble, on the brink of the abyss, through the Cold War. People start demanding research and education for peace, and come out on the streets to fight, inspired by Gandhi and Martin Luther King Jr., Nelson Mandela, Desmond Tutu. Patterns of people's NGO diplomacy begin to emerge to solve conflicts rather than waiting for governments to do so. The motto for this generation:

> *Peace is too important to leave to states.*

Third generation of peace approaches, after the Cold War:

A-oriented: *peace cultures*, going into deep cultures if needed;
B-oriented: *basic human needs*, as non-negotiable pillars;
C-oriented: *peace structures*, repairing fault-lines like gender.

A search for foundations for peace beneath the surface, generalizing Freud/Jung (needs and culture) and Marx (needs and structure). The motto:

> *Peace is too important for shallow approaches.*

The first generation was *a reaction against war*. People demanded peace through governmental cooperation, transcending nations and states. The second generation is a *reaction against governments*. People become increasingly sceptical and want to work for peace themselves. In the third generation there is a reaction against simplistic peace approaches, realizing how deep-rooted – and linked to development = satisfaction of basic needs – these problems are.

There is also another, and more dynamic, way of using conflict as a point of departure to understand peace approaches.

Conflicts have life cycles. Conflicts pass through phases. We can use violence, outbreak and cease-fire, as cut-off points:

Phase I: *Before violence*: Peacemaking = conflict transformation, and Peace-building = depolarization
Phase II: *During violence*: Peacekeeping; Peace Zones
Phase III: *After violence*: Reconciliation (with Reconstruction)

This can only be done by cooperating with states. Non-states do not necessarily contest state monopoly on violence, but do contest any state monopoly on peace action. Cooperation is needed for all five approaches above. Non-state actors may be able to transform conflicts; states may follow and formalize an outcome as a treaty. Peace-building is essentially the antidote to polarization, with the individual and social pathologies mentioned, used preventively in Phase I, and curatively in Phases II and III. Peacekeeping and Peace Zones (models of normality) can best be done by the military, police and civilians working together. And reconciliation (= healing the traumas of violence + bringing about closure of the conflict) has to include state actors if they have resorted to violence. Reconciliation between Serbs, Croats and Bosniaks in Bosnia-Herzegovina, and between Serbs and Albanians in Kosovo/a is necessary, and so is reconciliation with French and Dutch UN peacekeeping forces, with NATO, US and UK bombers, Austrian and German protectorate chiefs.

How do peace research/peace studies come into this? They have to cover all the fault-lines and approaches, and more; be applicable to the *micro-* (intra/inter-personal), *meso-* (intra-social), *macro-* (inter-nation, inter-state) and *mega-* (inter-civilization, inter-region) levels of human organization. The old model of one term or summer courses will have to yield to treating peace studies like health studies, with its own university faculty, and 4–5 years' study with practice, preparing for professional activity.

The following 14 approaches combine to make a model for a peaceful world:

1. *Peace movement*: extend this concept to include a commitment to peace on the part of all states and corporations, accountable to peace programmes.
2. *Abolition of war*: treating offensive arms like hard drugs, outlawing research, development, production, distribution, possession, use of them.
3. *Global governance*: democratizing the United Nations through direct elections to a People's Assembly, and abolition of the veto power.
4. *Peace education*: to be introduced at all school levels like civics, hygiene, sex education, knowledge of own culture.
5. *Peace journalism*: that all decent media focus on ways out of conflicts, building a solution culture, not a violence culture.
6. *Non-violence*: that non-violent ways of fighting for a cause and defending own integrity = basic needs become part of common skills.
7. *Peacemaking/conflict transformation*: that conflict handling knowledge and skills become parts of civic education anywhere, like hygiene.
8. *Peace culture*: that people start exploring their own culture, what can be done to make it more conducive to peace, and then do it.
9. *Basic needs*: that respect for the basic needs of everybody, and especially the most needy, become a basic guideline for politics.
10. *Peace structure*: from exploitative and repressive structures with nature, genders, races, classes, nations, states to equity, parity.
11. *Peace-building*: develop good *and* bad rather than good *or* bad images of the world's actors, and positive links in all directions.
12. *Peacekeeping*: with minimum violence becomes a protection for the defenceless, and a protective barrier against the violent.
13. *Peace zones*: starting with yourself as a peace zone of one person based on the ideas above, constructing archipelagos of peace.
14. *Reconciliation*: learning to apologize and to accept apologies, to ask for forgiveness and to forgive, to heal and to close conflicts.

More can be added and will be when we now turn to TRANSCEND as an effort to enact this. Does the model stand any chance, or is it only a *fata morgana*, a desert mirage overheated by the excessive violence, not to mention the threats, of the twentieth and twenty-first centuries (the little we have seen so far). It can be argued that humanity has been through much worse; and that increasingly military and civilians, politicians and people will do all of this together, given more knowledge, skill and will.

TRANSCEND: A Network for Peace and Development consists of invited, cooperating individuals working for peace by peaceful means, development by developmental means and the environment by environmental means. The mission statement reads:

> To bring about a more peaceful world by using action, education/training, dissemination and research to handle conflicts creatively and non-violently.
>
> Members (by invitation) include about 200 invited scholars and practitioners from over 50 countries, working on 20 programmes:

     I.   *Peaceful Conflict Transformation*
    II.   *Peace Building and Empowerment*
   III.   *Peace Pedagogy*
   IV.   *Peace Journalism*
    V.   *Peace Zones*
   VI.   *Peace Keeping*
  VII.   *Peaceful Reconciliation*
 VIII.   *Peace Business*
   IX.   *Development Subsistence, Equity and Sustainability*
    X.   *Peace, Deep Culture, Cultural Violence and Dialogue*
   XI.   *Nonmilitary Approaches to Security and War Abolition*
  XII.   *Human Rights, Democratization and Self-Determination*
 XIII.   *Global Governance*
 XIV.   *Peace, Women and Men*
  XV.   *Peace and Development Analysis*
 XVI.   *Peace and the Arts*
 XVII.   *Peace Museums*
XVIII.   *Peace Tourism*
 XIX.   *Peace at the Personal Level*
  XX.   *Peace, Deep Structure and Structural Violence*

Some new approaches have been added to the 14 outlined above:

> *Peace business*: how could business not only benefit from peace and development and a clean environment, but also contribute to them?
>
> *Peace, women and men*: in the present circumstances women are leading the way guided by basic needs. How can that inspire men?
>
> *Peace and development analysis*: not all intellectual tools are adequate for peace and development; what should our methodology be?

Peace and the arts: arts are very powerful means of communication, how have they been used for peace and how can they be developed further?

Peace museums: museums, like text-books, monuments, street names, are guardians of our collective memory, how can they serve peace?

Peace tourism: tourism as the world's biggest industry could become a giant peace-building activity; how can tourism serve peace?

Peace at the personal level: all conflicts are born equal and have the same right to be transformed, at micro-, meso-, macro- and mega-levels!

TRANSCEND is based on four pillars/modes of activity: *action, education/training, dissemination, research*. Take peace museums: Action is to stimulate or build a peace museum. Education/training would include participants who want to know more about peace museums or work in them. Dissemination would inform about existing and future peace museums. Research would explore artifacts to exhibit in a peace museum and investigate the causes and consequences of peace museums.

Action will always be the most important pillar. So far activity has above all focused on peaceful conflict transformation, using the TRANSCEND method based on extensive dialogues with all parties, individually, to stimulate their creativity about possible outcomes and processes leading to those outcomes. This is then written up as a 'conflict perspective', posted on the TRANSCEND web-site, <www.transcend.org>, and updated. The reader can find out more about this mediation process over the last 45 years by reading about it in this book introducing TRANSCEND, the second edition of Johan Galtung and Carl Gustav Jacobsen eds., *Searching for Peace: The Road to TRANSCEND* (London: Pluto, 2000). The 45 conflicts attempted are on the web-site and in this book. Here we shall list only the most important ones.

Hawai'i-Pacific, Sri Lanka, Colombia, China, Rwanda, Korea, Ulster, Japan/Kuriles–Okinawa, Euzkadi, Japan/Korea–China–US, Yugoslavia, North–South, Development Crisis, Israel/Palestine/Middle East, East–West/US–Eurasia/Cold War II, Caucasus, Christianity and Islam, Afghanistan, Globalization, Kashmir, Sustainable Development

And indeed the conflict between and within countries after 11 September 2001.

Considerable expertise has been developed around these conflicts. However, it should be emphasized that TRANSCEND's focus is on therapy/transformation/solution rather than on diagnosis/prognosis.

By mid-2001 TRANSCEND had carried out about 200 such workshops for more than 4,000 participants in 31 countries, in dialogue groups in many languages; about conflict transformation using the UN/DMTP manual, and peace-building and empowerment, peace journalism, democracy and human rights, nutrition rights, peace pedagogy, peace analysis, dialogue, reconciliation and non-violent approaches to security. Participants have included ambassadors/diplomats, professors, NGO workers, students, journalists, psychiatrists, peace researchers, social workers and international civil servants. Countries: Argentina, Australia, Austria, Azerbaijan, Bulgaria, Canada, Colombia, Denmark, France, Georgia, Germany, Hungary, Italy, India, Japan, Jordan, Macedonia, North Korea, Norway, Pakistan, Philippines, Romania, Russia, South Korea, Spain, Sweden, Switzerland, Thailand, UK, US, Yugoslavia.

TRANSCEND and Future Development

TRANSCEND is already launching:

For peace action:	**TRANSCEND Conflict Service** (TCS)
For peace education:	**TRANSCEND Peace University** (TPU), and Training
For peace dissemination:	**TRANSCEND Media Service** (TMS)
For peace research:	**TRANSCEND Research Institute** (TRI)

TRANSCEND largely draws on 45 years of *research* experience, from when peace research started becoming institutionalized at the end of the 1950s, and *practice*, having worked to transform peacefully 45 major conflicts internationally. In a sense TRANSCEND is an effort to put all of this intellectual activity into conflict transformation, peace and development practice. But in so doing the need for new research arises, stimulated by practice. Thus, there is a need for a summary of much available information, in index form, such as:

War Participation Index (WPI), measuring the extent to which a state historically has been involved in war;

Early Warning Index (EWI), measuring the inclination of a state (and other actors) to engage in wars, based on the tendency to do so (WPI) and the levels of structural and cultural violence. **Conflict Transformation Index (CTI)**, measuring the transformation level in a given conflict, facilitating comparisons of the same conflict over time, and with other conflicts, and pointing to missing efforts as a guide to action.

Research is important to guide successful action, but it must not become an end in itself. We would find it unacceptable if the medical profession limited itself to describing disease, without making any effort to heal patients and relieve their pain. It is equally unacceptable for social science to limit itself to studying human misery without seeking to alleviate it.

Conflict Intervention: Some TRANSCEND Guidelines

To give more depth and precision to the general philosophy of peace, here are some guidelines for outside conflict intervention:

Arguments in favour of conflict intervention: the conflict parties are unable to transform the conflict so as to avoid violence; keep violence under control; handle post-violence resolution/reconstruction/reconciliation.
Arguments against conflict intervention: the conflict and any solution is the joint property of the conflict parties; outside parties will never understand the uniqueness of the conflict; outside parties also enter with their own agendas.

As there is some truth to these arguments, the general principle would be *to proceed with caution*, which might be interpreted, at a minimum, to mean:

1. *Reversibility*: you have a right to propose and act, but only that which can be undone: *you may be wrong*. Hence, no or minimal violence; UN Chapter 6 (Sun Tzu), not Chapter 7 (Clausewitz).
2. *Reciprocity*: only engage in conflict intervention, peacemaking, peacekeeping, peace-building if you are sure that you yourself are willing to be intervened, peace-made, peace-kept, peace-built by others, letting that question inform your action.
3. *Universality, but with care*: do not always do unto others what you would like them to do unto you; *their tastes may be different*.

Even if electoral democracy and individualist human rights are good for you, they may not be to others.

4. *Empathy with others*, obtained through deep dialogues. Be sure you are able to identify what drives the other parties in the way they agree with, not necessarily the way you agree with.

5. *Empathy with self*, obtained through inner dialogues (meditation). Be sure you are able to identify the driving forces in yourself, beyond helping the parties to transform the conflict and to undo damage, in a creative and non-violent way.

6. *DPT consistency*: be sure that you know what the problem is before you suggest a solution to it, so that you do not always suggest a panacea solution simply out of habit. Be willing to have dialogues with all parties about diagnosis–prognosis–therapy.

7. *Encourage intervention by the Other*: organize dialogues about their situation by the conflict parties themselves.

8. *Seek participation*: do not fall into the temptation of seeking solutions as seen by leaders only; search for a broader basis.

9. *Seek acceptability*: meaning an outcome not agreed out of fear of punishment or the desire of reward (stick and carrot incentives), but because the outcome comes through as right.

10. *Seek sustainability*, meaning an outcome that does not have to be propped up artificially from the outside, but generates its own support by speaking to the conditions of all parties.

Conflict Transformation: A TRANSCEND Code of Conduct

To give some guidance for the conflict worker in the field, here is a code of conduct for conflict transformation that can apply to micro-, meso- and macro-levels of conflict:

A. *Mission statement: peace by peaceful means*
By *peace* we mean the capacity to transform conflicts constructively and without violence; a never-ending process.

By *transforming conflicts* we mean helping bring about a situation so that the parties can proceed in a participatory, mutually acceptable, and sustainable manner.

By *constructively* we mean channelling conflict energy towards new, innovative ways of satisfying basic human needs for all.

By *without violence* we mean that this process should avoid:

- any threat or use of direct violence that hurts and harms,
- any use of structural violence that demobilizes the parties.

B. *The relation between the conflict worker and him/herself*
1. Your motivation should be to help the parties transform the conflict, not your own promotion, materially or non-materially.
2. You should have the skills or knowledge for the task and use the conflict to develop them further, not to acquire them.
3. Do not have a hidden agenda beyond conflict transformation, for yourself or for others; have nothing to conceal.
4. Your legitimacy is in your skills, knowledge, creativity, compassion and perseverance and ability to stimulate the same in the conflict parties; not in any mandate or in any organization.

C. *The relation between the conflict worker and the parties*
5. Do not enter a conflict if you yourself have an unresolved conflict with any one of the parties or bear deep grudges.
6. Empathy/dialogues with *all* parties, overcome dislikes.
7. Do not manipulate; play with open cards, say what you do.
8. Respect demands for confidentiality, do not attribute.
9. Do not receive honoraria, gifts, etc. from the parties beyond ordinary hospitality.
10. Communicate between the parties only with their permission.
11. Speak with one tongue, not one version for one party and another for the others, granted that the focus may be different.
12. Be open to new ideas; do not become a prisoner to any plan.
13. Never propose any outcome or any process that cannot be undone – you may be wrong.

D. *The relation between the conflict worker and society*
14. Do not seek personal or organizational credit.
15. Withdraw from the conflict when no longer needed.
16. Plans for conflict outcomes and conflict processes belong neither to you, nor to the parties, but to the public.
17. Share your skills, knowledge, experience with others; try to contribute to a general conflict transformation culture.
18. Do not receive direct funding from past, present or future conflict parties who have used, use or may use your services.
19. Conflict work is a job and the reward is a job well done.

All conflicts are born equal and have the same right to transformation, no conflict is 'higher level' than another.

Johan Galtung   Dietrich Fischer   Kai Frithjof Brand-Jacobsen
Director   Co-Director   Co-Director

INTRODUCTION

A Bird's Eye View

CHAPTER I.1

Conflict, War and Peace: A Bird's Eye View

Johan Galtung

A Bird's Eye View

There is a standard natural history, with many variations and sub-types, leading to violence and war, that is, organized group violence, which indicates how violence can be avoided or at least reduced. That prototype includes two stages preceding the violence.

The first stage is a *conflict* (parties with contradictory goals), a ubiquitous phenomenon in human and social reality, a major driving force. Or, more correctly: *unresolved conflict*, leading to frustration because of blocked goals, and a potential for aggression against parties perceived as standing in the way.

The second stage is *polarization*, the reduction to two groups, Self and Other, with positive interaction within and negative interaction between the groups. Under extreme polarization Other is dehumanized, satanized and Self exalted as supreme, sacred or secular. This prototype is as much a part of human reality as high exposure (pathogens) + low resistance (immunity) leading to disease. Like disease, violence is caused by the preceding stages in the prototype; like disease violence can be prevented by removing the cause(s). Conflict is removed as a cause by *transformation* so that the conflict can be handled by the parties non-violently, creatively, empathically. Polarization is removed as a cause through *depolarization*, peace-building, flattening the gradient from Self to Other, relinking. As violence is polarizing, violence should be minimal. By transforming the conflict the 'bellogens' frustration + aggression are removed; depolarization adds to this a 'paxogen' corresponding to the immune system.

In UN jargon these two activities are known generically as *peacemaking* and *peace-building*. In medical jargon they are similar to primary and secondary prophylaxis, removing pathogens and strengthening the self-healing capacity of the body.

Then there is *peacekeeping*, which aims at controlling violence, reducing it, possibly even removing it to the point called cease-fire. In medical jargon that would be curative therapy, removing the symptoms of disease, as distinct from the two types of preventive therapy mentioned above. In peace as in health the total therapy is in the package, not in any one part of it.

The flow chart would look like this:

CONFLICT	→	POLARIZATION	→	VIOLENCE/WAR
incompatible		dehumanization		hurt/harm body
goals		Self–Other gradient		mind or spirit
contradiction		*attitude*		*behaviour*
		deep structure/culture		*basic needs*

We have added some explanatory categories: conflict has to do with *contradictions* among incompatible goals, polarization has to do with attitudes which may be translated into behaviour like a prejudice, but can also start as behaviour like discrimination. Violence is a form of avoidable behaviour – physical, verbal or both (body language) – which hurts/harms. Direct violence can be mapped on a sentence with subject (the perpetrator), verb (the action) and object (the hurt/harmed victim). With no subject we would talk about indirect or structural violence.

Beneath are the deeper levels of explanation: the deep, more long-lasting structures and cultures defining long-lasting contradictions and attitudes and the basic human needs defining more permanent behaviour (in medical theory deep = generic/genetic).

Let us now have a second glance, reviewing the prototype.

Basic question: are these antecedents (if that is what they are) necessary causes, sufficient causes, both or neither? Do they really explain violence?

Let us start with 'necessary'.

Is there always an unresolved conflict underlying violence? The imperial powers were extremely violent in their overseas conquest. But they had no prior conflict with those peoples, they did not even know them, they 'discovered' them. The conflict was over the unlimited submission required of them (by the papal bull *Inter Caetera*) as subjects, economically as labour, culturally as converts. If they submitted, they could be admitted as slaves (today: second-class citizens); if they did not, military power, violence or war was used against them.

Suggestion: if violence is the smoke, conflict is the fire. Search and you'll find.

Is polarization always underlying violence? Polarization means social distance, horizontally (like countries separated by borders), vertically (like classes separated by unequal power), or both. Social distance means human distance. Even the most violent bully probably has somebody he (usually a he) would not harm or hurt. He recognizes a common identity = identification. The bully has a buddy even if the family is not exempt from his violence. Somebody is untouchable, protected by identification. For Gandhi identification includes all humanity; for Buddhism all sentient life (capable of experiencing a *dukkha–sukha* gradient, from suffering to well-being). Romans spoke of *homo res sacra hominibus*. Needless to say, the less polarized will employ the more polarized for the dirty job of violence, the riff-raff of any society, and on top of that train them to kill. Scratch the surface and you will find elements of polarization.

The 'sufficiency' part is much more problematic.

Will an unresolved conflict with the frustration of goals unattained for one or all parties always lead to aggression, violence? In a *basic conflict*, with basic needs among the goals, aggression is more likely. But even so there may also be *suffering in silence*, seeing the predicament as an unavoidable part of the human condition, dwelling in human nature.

This holds particularly for structural conflicts, built into the social structure between those high up who want to remain on top, and those lower down who do or do not reconcile themselves to their fate: the dangerous classes, 'dangerous' because they may one day wake up and see reality. But in actor conflicts, where there is a very concrete actor on the other side (and real conflicts are mixes of the two) the subject standing in the way is easily identified, and 'what can we do about It' becomes 'what can we do about Him'.

Will polarization always lead to violence? Of course not, it can go on for ages, as between countries with no ties. And between classes the polarization is already structural violence if those lower down are really hurt/harmed, that is, their basic needs are molested or at best left unsatisfied by the structure.

Will direct violence be added? If basic needs are deeply insulted, yes. But states and nations have kept apart for ages without violence, as have class structures, between peoples, between countries. Moreover, can we ever be close to everybody?

What has to be added for unresolved conflict + polarization to lead to violence? One answer (and that is enough, we are dealing with sufficiency here) would be a *culture of violence*, making violence seem natural/normal, lowering the threshold.

One such culture of violence is provided by the hard reading of the *Book*, the *kitab* of the Abrahamitic religions, the Old Testament (but also the Christian New Testament, although there the focus is more on faith and the Kingdom of God in heaven and/or inside us than on acts and Zion for the Jews).

Conflict is seen as dual, between *two* parties, like God and Satan, one good, one evil, fighting over *one* issue. It can end in only one way, in a massive, violent encounter, possibly with Evil triumphing over Good on Earth, but Good continuing in Heaven.

We refer to it as the DMA syndrome: Dualism–Manicheism–Armageddon. If a conflict is constructed as a contradiction between two parties, one worthy of survival and the other not, predestined to meet in a major battle, then this 'natural law of violence', its DMA inevitability, becomes a self-fulfilling prophecy, as in Marxism; embedded in the deep culture.

The dangerous sufficiency mix, the nitrate–carbon–sulphur mix, would include a violent culture turning an actor frustrated by an unresolved conflict into a bad actor, a bully; a violent structure already pre-polarizing society; and some kind of precipitating event, the hammer blow on the dangerous mix. Bad actor + bad culture (violent) + bad structure (polarized) = violence.

That now gives us four components in a preventive therapy:

1. Identify the bad actors (e.g. by past behaviour) and arraign them in court, hold them in detention, incapacitate them.
2. Change a violent culture into a peace culture.
3. Change a violent structure into a peace structure.
4. Be on guard against precipitating events.

But violence-prone actors and precipitating events there will always be. Better build on peace cultures and structures.

The First Narrative: Just Violence/War

This is a mainstream narrative, following the arrows.

In the beginning is not the word, but an issue between two or more goals held by one or more parties. A goal can be put in words, but they may not convey the intense emotions of hopes and fears fuelling the pursuit of the goal, be it positive, something to attain, or negative, something to avoid. And the more so the more the goals are related to the *sine qua non* of human existence: the basic needs, survival, well-being, freedom, identity.

Polarization enters because other parties are seen as standing in the way of goal-attainment. A social/human distance is created for such parties. At the root may be the problem of legitimacy. My goal-attainment is legitimate; his is not, even if he says it is. Projecting on him hidden, evil goals makes his proclaimed goals a cloak, and I have won the first round by constructing not only his goals but also him as evil/illegitimate.

Evil-doers should be incapacitated, depriving Other of the capability to enact his evil motivations. But the problem with violence is that it molests the most basic of basic human needs, survival itself. There will be a *reactio* to a violent *actio*.

One possibility is that violence makes Other see himself as at least partly evil, amends his ways and gives up the goal. This is the rationale for the legal use of punishment = violence.

A second possibility is escape; Other becomes unavailable.

A third possibility is for Other to suffer violence with no resistance, common when violence is institutionalized, direct or structural; possibly with extermination at the end of the road.

A fourth approach is violent resistance by Other; *revenge*.

And a fifth approach is non-violent resistance by Other.

Violence introduces a conflict after the root conflict, a *meta-conflict* between molest! and remain unmolested!, which then leads to a *meta-polarization* and feeds into the root conflict in the well-known vicious circle of violence breeding violence. In the first three cases Self gets what he wants; and so he does if he wins, overcoming violent or non-violent resistance. This is called a 'military solution', i.e. a lull before next round.

Again, the key element is probably legitimacy. The beaten Other may draw the conclusion that he was wrong, illegitimate; and that provides the happy ending for Narrative 1 for Self.

But Other may also draw the conclusion that his goal in the root conflict was legitimate and demand a *revanche*, a new deal.

And/or, Other may draw the conclusion that his goal in the meta-conflict – survival – was legitimate and demand *retribution*.

This is where the narrative makes a loop via deep culture for legitimacy feedback, and the next round gets a fresh start.

The narrative now becomes drawn out if the capacities to incapacitate are relatively equal, the 'equal playing field'; more likely to serve, as in sports, the goal of fairness in identifying the winner than deterrence, abstaining from playing. The archetype is the duel/battle for individual/collective decision-making in conflict according to 'the winner takes all'. There is an underlying meta-narrative identifying being victor with being legitimate. Watching that violence/war unfold is watching justice at work, according to this narrative.

Violence, war, is a morality play. God is on the side of the winner. Or if not God, then Evolution. Or, in globalization, the Market is on the side of the winner. He who loses deserves to do so. Justice has been done.

The more equal the playing field, the higher the suffering.

What, then, makes a fully fledged war with conflict and meta-conflict, polarization and meta-polarization and meta-meta come to an end? Remember that a war presupposes capability, motivation and targets of incapacitation, so why end the game?

The first scenario is *incapacitation* of one side; both being incapacitated is unlikely. The winner dictates the terms.

The second scenario is *capitulation* by one side short of inca-pacitation; simultaneous capitulation being unlikely. But he may be suspected of saving capabilities for revenge/revanche; hence better make the capitulation unconditional.

The third scenario is *cease-fire by mutual agreement* because the costs are too high and incapacitation/capitulation is not in sight. The question is, who demands it from a position of strength, and who from weakness?

The fourth scenario is *choking the violence/war* by running out of targets (or making them unavailable), by running out of capabili-ties (arms, ammunition, money, food), by running out of motivation. Simultaneous choking is unlikely, but the choking point does not have to be the same for the parties.

The fifth scenario is in occidental *deep narrative*: a war is mono-climactic, the end comes after the climax. Male orgasm as metaphor. With both parties driven by this narrative a climax ushers in one of the scenarios above and a victor is declared.

The narrative attributes justice to violence/war. The war is not only mutual carnage; it has a function. If God sides with the winner, then the war makes God reveal His will. If Evolution by definition sides with the winner/the fittest, then war makes Evolution reveal its arrow. If some float to the top, buoyed by the Market, and some sink, then so be it. It is what they deserve.

The Second Narrative: Intervention on the Side of Justice

But imagine there is *no end in sight*; the war is protracted. Or worse: the party on the side of God (read: our side), or higher on Evolution (read: having democracy), or more embodying the Market (read: access, privatization) is not winning. Time has come to open a second narrative: *intervention* by outside, so-called third parties. To mingle in the strife they have by definition to be big powers lest they get badly hurt. Even so they may limit interven-tion by doctrines of 'force protection'.

Being now parties to the conflict the question is: what goals do they have, and are the goals legitimate? Being big they may be suspected of having big, even ulterior goals. 'Humanitarianism' provides formulas for legitimacy, but is hardly sufficient to allay suspicions of ulterior goals. A conflict, and particularly a violent conflict, shakes any system. There may be loose bits and pieces floating around, morsels for outside parties to pick up. Big powers may be suspected of doing that: reconstruction, even reparation contracts, trade privileges, political clientelism, cultural cloning, military bases/allies.

We are now entering the narrative of the conflict between the intervenor and the intervened. The narrative will probably be that they enter on the side of justice to level the playing field, helping the righteous side to a righteous victory over the unworthy, and in addition reducing innocent suffering. Basically they have to embody the three principles of legitimacy around which these morality tales are spun: the three selectors, God, Evolution and the Market. They have to enter so that God can make His choice, Evolution can run its course by rewarding the most evolved, the most ready to embody Market principles.

For what follows, see above. It all hinges on the ability of the intervenor to be seen as legitimate and not just as one more party with a 'what is in it for me?' motivation. *For that reason it is essential to enter late enough to give the parties a chance, also to exhaust each other so that the military risk to the intervenor is less, yet before the evil side is winning.* If the good side is winning, there's no problem. If not, and with good timing, the scenarios may combine into victory for the intervenor who dictates the terms of a cease-fire, of how to depolarize and the terms of conflict resolution (in favour of the Good party).

The third possibility is almost too horrible to contemplate, but it does happen: the evil side wins not only over the just side, but also over the intervenor in the name of justice. The narrative dissolves in a nightmare. At stake is not only the justice of Good overcoming Evil. Good, being too weak, could not win alone. But if Good, reinforced by super-Good, cannot win either, then what is the moral? That we live in the worst of all worlds and the End is nigh? Possibly, and that would be compatible with the Armageddon metaphor.

But there are at least three other interpretations.

First, *bad*, could it be that the intervention was self-choked, having insufficient capability, or motivation, or that they ran out of targets? There was lack of nerve, lack of will?

Second, *worse*, could it be that the credentials of the intervenor, as catalyst in this justice-revealing activity, were not good enough? Worse still, could it even be that they were negative, that the intervenor was on the side of Evil?

Third, *worst*, could it be that the use of war to serve justice, to obtain political-cultural goals, is basically flawed?

The Third Scenario:
Transformation–Depolarization–Peace

The first narrative (Clausewitzian) was about the quick or slow, but successful, pursuit of a political goal, the conflict goal, by military means. For that purpose instant polarization may be used, trusting that violence itself is polarizing and will overcome bonds of economic ties, neighbourhood, friendship even kinship. The process will bypass deep polarization, go straight from unresolved conflict – unresolved because the other party refused to submit – to violence and war, and then pass through some loops of meta-conflict and meta-polarization to victory.

The second narrative was about the quick or slow but successful intervention into protracted warfare. It better be by 'overwhelming force' lest the three nagging problems at the end of the preceding section should surface.

Is there a third narrative hidden somewhere in this prototype? Certainly, and like the first narrative it starts in the conflict end of the story, but unlike the second narrative it does not start with violence. It may be called *the peace by peaceful means narrative*, and has less backing in our deep culture, being more recent. But it is not entirely without archetypal backing. Jewish prophets, the words of Christ and of the Prophet are rich in proposals for conflict resolution. But there is a tendency for such proposals to be of the 'or else' variety, ultimately backed up by the wrath of the Almighty.

The narrative does not exclude a peacekeeping prologue to reduce the violence, if possible down to zero, but not 'peace enforcement' to help one party win. But peacekeeping is not necessarily done by military force. 'Overwhelming non-violent force' may also be a formula, leaving no room for violence.

The first chapter in this narrative is *an image of an outcome for the conflict* so compelling that the parties say, 'This is much better than what the first and second narratives have to offer, especially given the suffering and the revenge/revanche factor that may follow in their wake.'

The second chapter is *the story of peace-building*, in other words depolarization, stitching torn tissue, substituting new tissue. This is much broader than 'confidence-building measures', which may also be cosmetic if not internalized in hearts and minds and insti-tutionalized in the structures. Truth for the minds and reconciliation for the hearts!

The third chapter is *peacekeeping by non-violent or very soft violent means*, e.g. police forces, similar to the prologue mentioned above. But there is also another scenario for the third factor. An image of conflict solution would make violence look irrelevant, misplaced, out of step. Weapons become dis-targeted, 'decommissioned'. They may start 'withering away'.

We say 'chapter', but they are to be read simultaneously. And the 'reading' has to be aloud, in public, and massively so, based on solid knowledge of the texts.

Has this narrative ever had an empirical counterpart? Oh yes, but the two preceding narratives are read so loudly in the media that they tend to overwhelm public consciousness. The collective subconscious, the belligerent deep culture, has war reporting as a major conveyor belt. Empirically the third narrative is so frequent that it is not even told but taken for granted. This is the normal way things are settled. An image of a viable = acceptable + sustainable future emerges. People move from imaging to fantasizing to living it. And that's it.

The Peace Narrative: Four Cases

The white/black conflict over desegregation in the US South did not lead to a major war (although there was violence), with intervention (although there were elements of that) and a *diktat* (although there were and are elements of that in the schools). There was and is an *image* of a one person-one vote democracy, a colour-blind society. The image gains in acceptability, as can be seen in the countless desegregated facilities in the South, including restaurants, toilets, recreation areas. There was and is increasing depolarization of blacks and whites simply practising a future of togetherness, highly provocative for segregationists, but in the longer run irresistible. Crucial peacekeeping was non-violent until the process became to a large extent self-sustaining. And it all happened in a surprisingly short period of time. No doubt it mattered who propagated the conflict outcome image: the US Supreme Court, on 17 May 1954. The image negated the old 'separate but equal', in favour of 'desegregated and equal'.

The white/black conflict in South Africa did not lead to a major war either, only exchanges of violence between terrorism and state terrorism, nor to a major intervention to put an end to the violence and settle the conflict. People increasingly bought into the compelling image of one-person, one-vote democracy, with human rights. There was a major depolarization at the top: the Mandela–de Klerk tight, cooperative relationship. No doubt it was helpful that US desegregation had preceded the abolition of apartheid with no major backlashes of any kind. It is good to live in a virtual image; quite another to have a real case sufficiently similar to make the image really compelling. No doubt a peaceful Rhodesia-Zimbabwe next door was also useful.

But the end of the Cold War is even more impressive as a case for the third narrative, the peace narrative. True, we have pointed out that the antecedents to violence/war are not sufficient causes, not even when unresolved conflict and heavy polarization combine with an arms race into a cold war. And the underlying conflict was massive: over interests, *who is the master in Eastern Europe*; and over values, *what is the good society* – multi-party/capitalist or single party/socialist? Enacting the first narrative would have been catastrophic as seen in the places it was partly enacted, Korea and Vietnam. And: no powerful intervenor would have been available. Fortunately, what happened followed the third narrative.

There were the images of outcomes projected by the two parties: all that is needed is that you become like me. This is not known as an acceptable solution but as imposition, victory.

Then the idea of convergence started to take root, with social democracy or democratic socialism (the first ideology of Solidarnosc) as an obvious meeting ground. This was not to be, however, because of internal processes in the US consistently moving to the right politically relative to, say, the New Deal, and the Soviet Union, consistently moving towards demoralization and implosion because of its inability to overcome many contradictions.

But there was another compelling image coming out of the peace movement and the dissident movement: no more danger of nuclear war/human rights, and democracy for all. The movements practised the future by depolarizing different and complementary segments of a heavily polarized East–West system. The resistance against nuclearism and post-Stalinism was done non-violently and successfully so. The Berlin Wall fell. We all knew it was over.

The fourth case has a different flavour because of the time span between the first and second narratives, and the third. The Spanish civil war of 1936–39 between the Loyalists (to the democratically elected Popular Front government of republicans, socialists, communists, anarchists and nationalists in Catalonia and the Basque Country) and the Insurgents (under Franco, supporting and supported by *los poderes fácticos*, the real powers, land-owners, military, clergy) was also based on a massive conflict between two very different images of the good society. Put simply: communist (but with strong anarchist elements) versus fascist, the *falange*. Narrative 1 was enacted through many loops in a cruel war with massive polarization and one million dead. Narrative 2 came with much military aid to the Insurgents from Germany and Italy, and an International Brigade and a trickle of aid from the Soviet Union for the Loyalists.

Who won? In the short run Franco, of course, enacting his image in an unstable, deeply traumatized society. But who won in the longer run? Neither one nor the other. A very compelling image was in the air from the Second World War, often twisted, thwarted: multi-party democracy, human rights, self-determination for minorities. Both sides gradually bought into this image, travelled abroad, lived it, received testimony from visitors. But time, say one generation, was needed to overcome the most acute phase of the traumas. And that coincided roughly with the life of Franco. When he died in November 1975, lamented by few, no night of long knives was in sight. And the successors to the Loyalists and the Insurgents met in a multi-party endeavour to construct, successfully so far, non-fascist/non-Stalinist Spain, with only one small backlash: the Tejero incident of 23 February 1981.

Why doesn't this work in the Basque Country, in Ulster, in the Middle East/Israel–Palestine? Why is there no peace process, except as a propaganda term, with no real peace in sight, only some breaks in Narrative 1 violence? And enactment of Narrative 2 by Spanish and English police and military in the first two cases, and a denial of Narrative 2 by Israel in the third lest the playing field becomes level?

First answer: for lack of a compelling image of the future. General autonomy for the Basque Country in Spain is less than what is wanted; moreover, it does not include the French Basques. In Northern Ireland the Good Friday Agreement does not provide for symmetry in arms. The IRA is up against the British Army + the Police Service for Northern Ireland (formerly the Royal Ulster Constabulary) (made up of about 93 per cent Protestants) + the para-military Ulster Defence Forces. And there is no serious image of how two states, Israel and Palestine, could live side by side, bearing in mind that any image has to be symmetric in such basics as the right to have a state (and a capital and a right of return).

Second, a negative answer: the ritualistic demand for a cease-fire, even disarmament, only then depolarization around the table, only then conflict solution. Why should they do that when there is no light at the end of the tunnel, not even an image as an anchor for trying out of that outcome, virtually? Even if they are not planning any major violence, arms have at least a nuisance value. Why should they give that up?

Rather much more can be said, but let this suffice. The basic conclusion is this: The first narrative leads to demands for revanche and revenge. The second puts the cart before the horse by demanding that people do at the beginning what they will only do at the end. The peace narrative is more promising.

Which does not mean that it is infallible. Moreover, like natural medicine it cures without doing harm but needs more time than violent antibiotics. People have to engage in virtual tests of a concrete peace proposal. Much psychological mobility is needed; hence a need for something 'compelling', 'irresistible'. The proposal has to be so good that the time factor can be considerably shortened. It defies reason to believe that such creative proposals should emerge from a 'table' accommodating people who have been in a tunnel killing each other according to Narratives 1 and 2. How can they suddenly switch to Narrative 3?

Ancient and not-so-ancient history speaks to us through Narratives 1 and 2. We sense primitive society using rituals of violence to settle conflicts. We sense traditional society adding God's finger and His chosen instruments, the kings. We sense modern society with the state as successor to the kings for the execution of these atavistic rituals, adding the social darwinist idea of evolution, now with democracy-cum-market as the crowning achievement, The End of Evolution/History.

There is more than the power of the most powerful state(s) at stake. There is a whole syndrome of interconnected beliefs down there in the collective subconscious with 'bringing to justice', in the battlefield and ultimately in the court room, as connecting elements. And we sense how subversive the idea of peace is, the third narrative, cutting out the atavism of violence, going straight to the solution, then solidifying it through depolarization and as much non-violent control of violence as possible. Peace becomes left-wing not because left-wing people are more pacifist, but because they believe less in the rest of the narrative. May it spread and be shared by all.

And What Do Mainstream Journalists/Politicians Make of This?

1. *They leave out the unresolved conflict and polarization,* and focus only on violence, which then looks irrational, autistic.
   Example: 'Terrorism' (see Chalmers Johnson's *Blowback*).
2. *They confuse conflict arena – where the violence/'action' is – with conflict formation* the parties with a stake in the outcome.
   Example: The focus in Ulster is only on violent parties, not on 85 per cent of the population who want peace by peaceful means.
3. *Dualism, reducing the number of conflict parties to 2 and the number of issues to 1 as dominant discourse.* not looking for hidden parties presenting themselves as mediators and issues.
   Example: Omitting Germany as major conflict party in Yugoslavia, with her own goals (see Matthias Küntzel, *Der Weg in den Krieg*); omitting class and gender as major issues in Yugoslavia.
4. *Manicheism, presenting one party as evil and the other as good,* (re)enforcing polarization, denying the 'evil' a voice.
   Example: The standard image of Serbia, Indonesia, Saddam Hussein; taking sides, usually same as their nation-state government.

5. *Armageddon, presenting the violence as something inevitable* omitting alternatives, blaming evil party of autism.
   Example: NATO's war against Yugoslavia (Serbia), omitting the many alternative causes of action, denying their existence. It is worth noting that dualism/Manicheism/Armageddon are basic elements in occidental, Judeo-Christian/Islamic, deep culture.

6. *They omit structural conflict/polarization and violence,* like ghettos, refugee camps, reporting only the direct violence.
   Example: 100,000+ dying from hunger and disease daily.

7. *They omit the bereaved,* easily ten per victim and their desire for revenge and revanche, fuelling spirals of violence.
   Example: Almost any conflict, except 'our' prominent bereaved.

8. *They fail to explore the causes of protraction and escalation,* and particularly the role of the media in keeping violence going.
   Example: Arms supplies to the parties, e.g. in Sri Lanka.

9. *They fail to explore the goals of intervenors,* how big powers tend to move in when the system is shaken loose by conflict and violence, picking up morsels, gaining footholds.
   Example: The 'international community' in Yugoslavia, missing the Camp Bondsteel story, the German protectorate policy.

10. *They fail to explore peace proposals and compelling images*
    Example: Omitting the Pérez de Cuéllar proposal of December 1991 for the Yugoslavia conflict; ignoring citizen groups.

11. *They confuse cease-fire and conferences with peace* and hold exaggerated expectations when 'warlords' meet for peace, following the standard government agenda: cease-fire–negotiation–peace.
    Example: Afghanistan, with no regard for peace images.

12. *They leave out reconciliation,* basic for depolarization.
    Example: any conflict, e.g. Ethiopia–Eritrea.

CHAPTER I.2

Peace: The Goal and the Way

Kai Frithjof Brand-Jacobsen

Conflicts exist at all levels, within and between individuals, communities, countries and cultures. Conflicts are natural. They are experienced by people of every background, culture, class, nationality, age and gender every single day. What is important, is not whether conflicts themselves are *good* or *bad*, but how we deal with them.

War culture and *war-provoking* responses to conflicts focus on *conflict the destroyer*. Conflicts are seen as a struggle between good and evil, black and white, zero-sum, where the victory of one is based upon the defeat of the other, and one actor's gain comes only at the expense of another actor's loss. What peace researchers, peace workers and others have worked over several decades to promote is an alternative culture, and an alternative approach to dealing with conflicts – one based on *conflict the creator*, recognizing the positive, constructive and creative opportunities available in any conflict situation.

The distinction can be likened to that between *dukkha* and *sukha* in Hinduism. *Dukkha* is suffering, destructive, negative, damaging – a state of violence/disease – while *sukha* is bliss, perfect happiness, nirvana – a state of peace/health. A further illustration can be taken from the Chinese symbol for crisis, itself a combination of two other symbols: danger and opportunity. Crisis, or conflicts, can be understood as containing both possibilities: a) the deterioration of a situation or relationship to a negative, destructive dynamic bringing harm to one or all of the actors involved, and/or b) an opportunity to reach towards a higher, more constructive, positive goal, working to transcend and overcome contradictions within a system, relationship or culture.

Another assumption often made is that 'conflict' and 'violence' are one and the same. This stems from the belief that conflict and violence are indistinguishable, that violence is the only (and/or best) method of addressing conflicts, and that the only way to deal with confrontation or difference is to 'win', 'destroy' or 'beat' 'the other', and to 'take revenge' when one has been wronged. The recognition that there are different ways of dealing with conflicts, and that violence is only one possible approach, one based on a *war culture* and *violence-provoking* response to difficult situations, is vital if we are to search and find more creative, more constructive and more viable approaches to dealing with conflict which seek to address and transcend the underlying contradictions which are often at the root of conflicts between individuals, communities, countries, cultures, and within every single one of us.

A difficulty which results from automatically associating *conflict* with *violence* is that people may assume that, if there are no direct or open acts of violence, there must be no conflicts. This leads to journalists, politicians, 'experts' and others waiting until violence has broken out before focusing on or trying to find a solution to a conflict. If a conflict has already reached the point of violence, this is perhaps the clearest sign that it has been mismanaged, poorly addressed or simply ignored until the situation has deteriorated to a destructive level.

For this reason, the 'violence triangle' was developed by Johan Galtung, pointing to the distinction between three separate types or forms of violence, all of which are closely interrelated.

The first of these, *direct violence*, refers to *physical acts of violence* such as a man beating his wife, children fighting at school, or soldiers going to war. One of the clearest and most obvious types of violence, beamed into our homes and brought to us daily in many different forms, *direct violence* is itself only one possible form of violence. In one of its most extreme forms, *war*, direct violence has resulted in the deaths of 40 million people since 1990, nearly equal to the number of those killed in the Second World War. If we were to add to this the number of people killed in the world in the last decade through direct *intra*-personal (suicide) and direct *inter*-personal (murder, infanticide) violence, the number would be at least two or three times as high. Direct violence also includes such categories as abuse, rape, battery.

The second corner of the violence triangle, *structural violence*, can often be far more difficult to recognize and understand. This is the violence built into the very social, political and economic systems that govern societies, states and the world. It is the different allocation of goods, resources, opportunities, between different groups, classes, genders, nationalities, etc., because of the structure governing their relationship. It is the difference between the possible/optimum, and what is. Its relationship to *direct violence* is similar to that of the bottom nine-tenths of an iceberg, hidden from view, while only the tip juts out above the waterline.

Examples of structural violence are apartheid, patriarchy, slavery, colonialism, imperialism, the former state authoritarian regimes of Eastern Europe, and today's global imperialism/capitalism (frequently termed globalization, globalism). In terms of lives lost, misery and human suffering, *structural violence* is by far the more devastating and destructive of the two forms of violence explored so far. The approximately 30 million people killed each year from hunger are only one of several extreme expressions of structural violence. The US$1 trillion spent each year on the production of armaments and weapons (the equivalent of US$2 million per minute), instead of on schools, health, nutrition, social infra-structure and development, is itself the result of a structure of violence (and clear political decisions by corporations and governments) which favours the production of instruments of death over investment in the creation or improvement of life.

The third form (or aspect) of violence is *cultural violence*. On one level, this can be taken to be those aspects of a culture that *legitimize* or make violence seem an *acceptable* means of responding to conflict. That violence is 'normal', 'OK' or even 'macho' is an expression of *cultural violence*. The degree to which violence has begun to pervade almost every aspect of our cultures – particularly music, television and a great deal of popular literature – is an expression and a form of *cultural violence* (and not simply a reflection of 'the world we live in' as is often suggested).

At a deeper level, however, the concept of *cultural violence* is important in understanding how a community or individuals view themselves in relation to themselves, to 'others', to their community, and the world, and how this may affect our responses to conflict. Whether or not a nation or group believes itself to be 'chosen' (by God, History, Race, Nation, Civilization, Gender or the Market), superior to 'the Other', viewing the world as black or white, a struggle of good against evil, zero sum, with only one possible outcome, win/lose, will affect whether it chooses to respond violently or constructively when faced with conflict. 'Dehumanization' of the Other, making them seem somehow 'less', 'unworthy', and ascribing to them entirely negative, self-serving or even 'evil' motives are also components of cultural violence. Racism, xenophobia and the cultures of imperialism, patriarchy and neoliberalism are all expressions of this (though often also the result of insecurities and fears on the parts of those who promote them). The Dualism–Manicheism–Armageddon formula expresses this well. A further indicator can be found in a community or nation's 'collective memory', focusing upon shared myths, together with moments of trauma or glory, which are celebrated in its history.

No culture is entirely black or white, entirely violent or peaceful. Just as there are elements of *cultures of violence* within almost every culture in the world, so there are elements of *peace culture*. Rather than black/white, the Chinese symbol of yin and yang is more appropriate for this conception of the relationship between *cultures of peace* and *cultures of violence*. When applied to religion, this can help us recognize that the differences between the *hard* (a wrathful, revengeful, *God the destroyer*, together with judgement, excommunication, and wars against infidels and heretics) and *soft* (the meek shall inherit the earth, turn the other cheek, kingdom of heaven on earth and within every single one of us, do unto others as you would have done unto yourself, he/she who walks with peace, walk with him/her) aspects *within* a religion are often greater than the differences *between* different religions (or even cultures).

As a side-note, the distinction between ideology and cosmology is important. Ideology can be understood as those systems of thought and frameworks of understanding consciously constructed and adhered to in order to formulate our understanding(s) and interpretation(s) of the world (or our community or Self), how it is, and how it should be. Cosmology, however, exists at a deeper level. Again, the nine-tenths of the iceberg beneath the surface, out of sight, is an appropriate metaphor.

Cosmology is akin to our 'collective subconscious', to borrow from Freud and extrapolate from the individual to the community. Cosmologies, also known as *deep cultures*, are made up of those 'assumptions' and unquestioned beliefs passed on to or inherited by people as members of a community. They are our underlying values, which provide the soil from which our 'conscious' values are developed/expressed. Some of the examples provided above when exploring cultural violence can be taken as clear expressions of assumptions which often fall under the category of a people's or community's *cosmology*. Making these assumptions clear, and understanding how they affect and influence our actions and decisions, is a precondition for being able to change them and an important step in working to promote peaceful and constructive approaches to the transformation of conflicts.

These three categories, *direct*, *structural*, and *cultural*, can also be useful when thinking about peace, helping us to identify:

1. direct acts in support of peace and conflict transformation such as dialogue, active non-violence and non-violent struggle, and the refusal to surrender to or to allow injustices, oppression, and violence/cruelty to take place;
2. structures that provide for the needs of all members of a community, providing opportunities for individuals and groups to develop to their full potential, not exploiting, oppressing, or denying rights to any one or group of individuals; and
3. cultures of peace which promote peace as a value, which respect and celebrate differences and which protect/promote the political, civil, social, economic, and cultural rights of all *individuals, communities, and groups, and which are inclusive* (by

choice and dialogue rather than by force), *rather than exclusive in vision*.

These are only some examples. Dialogue and further reflection can provide many more.

Another important tool for understanding conflicts, also pioneered by Johan Galtung, is the *conflict triangle*. This time, the three points of the triangle are A (attitudes), B (behaviour) and C (contradiction).

Attitudes refer to how parties to a conflict *feel* and *think*, how they perceive 'the Other' – with respect and love or contempt and hatred – their own goals, and the conflict itself. Behaviour refers to how parties to the conflict *act* in the conflict – seeking common interests and constructive, creative action or seeking to inflict loss and pain on 'the Other'. Contradiction refers to the actual issue(s), and what the conflict is about. Perceptions of the contradiction or issues at the root of the conflict often differ between parties to the conflict. More often than not, they are almost entirely obscured and hidden, as parties and actors – including the media – on all sides prefer to focus upon *attitudes* and *behaviour*, either their own (usually portrayed in a positive light) or the Other's (usually portrayed in a negative light).

In discussions with participants and parties to conflicts in dialogues and training programmes around the world, some of the *attitudes* (both cognitive and emotive) which people often describe themselves as having when in a conflict include: blaming the Other, seeing their actions as the 'cause', and feeling 'fear', 'hatred' or 'insecurity'. Behaviour in conflicts, particularly where structural and cultural violence are rife, is often violent, seeking to reach a desired goal or goals through force, or to enforce/impose one's views upon another. This is further promoted through most mainstream or 'realist' interpretations of the concept of power, the ability to force another to act in a certain way. Power *with* or power *for* are completely ignored or excluded, as a war culture focus on *power over* (and with it, the concepts of domination – physically, socially, economically, and discursively – control, rule by force and 'might is right') is accepted as normal. The contradictions underlying conflicts, and what the conflicts are actually about, are (or at least can be) numerous, with any one conflict often involving several contradictions or issues, and with several conflicts often overlapping and intertwining within any one space or time. What is important – indeed, what is crucial if any approach to peace-building and constructive conflict transformation is to be successful – is that the issues and contradictions be identified and addressed in a way that leaves all parties feeling included in the solution, and which doesn't deny, ignore or reject the basic needs of any involved.

Ideologies and philosophies have developed which address each of these different 'points' of the conflict triangle.

In a simplified form:

The Liberal Focus – on attitudes/belief systems. The answer to conflicts lies in getting people to love each other, making parties/actors more 'civilized', enlightened, reasonable.

The Conservative Focus – on behaviour/action, seeking to suppress action seen as negative, threatening to the system, through law, imprisonment, by putting more police on the streets, and more 'criminals' into jail.

The Marxist Focus – on structures, seeing the solution to conflicts in transforming structures of violence, injustice and exploitation.

The problem that may arise: exclusivity, focusing on any one of the corners to the exclusion of the others. One possible solution/approach: both/and rather than either/or, a good approach for conflicts and peace in general. This is done by organizations such as TRANSCEND, the ICL/Praxis for Peace, and the Peace, Action Training and Research Institute of Romania, amongst others, which recognize that conflicts can (and do) arise at any of the three points, and can be reinforced, escalated and also transformed and diminished, at any of the three points. Constructive and lasting transformations of a conflict must address all three corners of the triangle – attitudes, behaviour and contradiction – if they are to have any chance of success.

A basic formula for *peace by peaceful means*:

- for attitude(s): *empathy*
- for behaviour(s): *non-violence/peace struggle*
- for contradiction(s): *creativity*

There's a problem with this: our education and upbringing often do not equip us for the task. History classes focus on wars, violence and the history of elites (emperors, kings, queens, generals, presidents) and treaties (often to end wars started by emperors, kings, queens, generals and presidents); the media focus on violence and decisions taken by elites, and often those supporting war or labelled 'extremists', denying a focus to alternative visions, options, choices, proposals to transform the conflict(s) peacefully and those working for peace rather than violence, and structures and cultures which (re-)enforce hierarchy, the power of elites (generally middle-aged men), exploitation, inequality, militarism, and violence.

The challenges are certainly there, and may often be daunting, even overwhelming (leading to apathy, pessimism, disempowerment, and the belief that 'I/we can't do anything about it'). The history of wars in recent years, decades, centuries provides ample evidence of what occurs when these *contributors to violence* are left unaddressed, unchallenged. What is necessary, therefore, is to address them, to *transcend* violence-provoking and violence-enhancing approaches to conflict/life, and to equip ourselves, to *empower people* ('I/we can!') with the tools, skills and knowledge, not to mention structures (or lack of them) and cultures to promote peace.

Conflict the creator over *conflict the destroyer*.

An important tool for this: Diagnosis–Prognosis–Therapy. Borrowed from health/medicine, emphasizing the relationship between health and peace – the desired goal – with disease/violence – that which is to be avoided, prevented, transcended. *Diagnosis* involves analysis and mapping of the situation/conflict. Who are the actors? What are their goals/needs/interests? This should be done for all the actors/parties; no one should be excluded. This also involves analysis using the A–B–C triangle – attitude, behaviour, contradiction – for all the actors involved in the conflict, and the D–S–C triangle – direct, structural and cultural violence – for the conflict itself. What is important? That the mapping of the conflict be as thorough and complete as possible. Complexity rather than simplification is preferred, with the more actors and interests involved the greater the opportunity to come up with a creative approach to transforming the conflict. Go beyond the simplistic, war-culture/textbook explanation of conflicts, which tends to:

1. reduce the number of actors to 2: A and B;
2. reduce explanatory factors to 1: the 'bad' side's evil or strategy;
3. reduce attitudes to 'white'/'black', 'good'/'evil';
4. present a Manicheistic vision of the struggle: Good vs. Evil;
5. reduce the 'Other': dehumanization, demonization;
6. personify the conflict: Iraq to Saddam Hussein
   Somalia to Mohamed Farah Aideed
   Yugoslavia to Slobodan Milosevic
   Romania's problems to Ceauşescu
   Terrorism to Osama bin Laden
7. reduce methods of struggle/dealing with conflict: to violence (D, S, C)
8. reduce the possible outcomes: win/lose; either/or.

A good diagnosis should contain as complete a mapping as possible of a) the conflict *formation*, and b) the conflict *history*, or the life of the conflict. The first, the conflict *formation*, should include all actors and parties to the conflict, not just those within a country/conflict zone. An analysis of the wars in Bosnia which focuses only on the Serbs, Muslim, and Croats, without addressing the involvement of outside powers (the US, Germany, EU, Russia, Iran, etc.), is simplistic and cannot lead to a full understanding and analysis of the conflict or what pushed it in the particular directions (i.e. violence) that it took. Analysis of the conflict formation, therefore, should include all parties and actors involved in the conflict. This also means *peace actors*, and those affected by the conflict, not simply those *fighting* or using violence to pursue their goals. *Peace actors* should be identified, as well as *violence actors*, with groups/individuals in one category often in the other as well – with those using violence potential actors for peace, and those working for peace potentially party to violence. Conflict *history* involves the entire history or life of the conflict, not simply the beginning and ending of violence. What are the roots of the conflict? What is its history? How did it reach the stage it is at now? It is important that *how parties to the conflict view the conflict history* be respected and understood, though it should not lock the peace worker into or prevent looking at different interpretations/analysis. What matters is that the parties/actors to the conflict do not feel that their perspectives/opinions have been dismissed, something all too common in most conventional approaches to 'peace'-making.

Prognosis – Where is the conflict going? What might happen? Given our diagnosis of what the situation is, what are the possible futures, outcomes? This can be important for recognizing both the potential damage/devastation which can be caused by not addressing a conflict constructively, as well as visions, ideas and possibilities for conflict outcomes.

Therapy is, in many ways, the most important and the greatest challenge. For a particular therapy or therapies to the conflict to be successful, they must be based upon good *diagnosis* and *prognosis*. Just as in health, good therapy, what should be undertaken to return to or go towards health/peace, must be based on good diagnosis of what the disease/cause of violence is, or what is preventing, or standing in the way of, health. Therapy is the proposals, ideas, suggestions for how to transform the conflict creatively, non-violently and constructively, to secure the needs of all actors/parties to the conflict. They are the strategy/vision or road map, of how to get from here (violence, conflict, non-peace), to our desired goal, *peace*. Therapies, however, cannot be imposed upon a conflict from above (leaders, elites, politicians, generals) or outside (outside leaders, elites, politicians, generals). They must be based upon developing real and concrete proposals that will be meaningful to those involved in the conflict and those living in communities affected by conflict. Part of successful therapies must be to *make peace practical*, to develop strategies/actions to transform the conflict which will be meaningful for people in their everyday lives, which will be based upon participation, mobilization and empowerment for peace, rather than simply serving to reinforce structures of domination and control by elites. Therapy, therefore, must be creative, and appropriate to the conflict.

One of the best ways to arrive at this is through dialogue, or rather, not just one dialogue, but thousands, at every level of society, repeated over and over again, coming up with as many ideas, and actions, for peace as possible. What is then needed is to act, and to keep acting, building, working, to empower ourselves, our communities, and the world, for the promotion of peace by peaceful means, refusing to surrender to the logic of violence, to accept violence, or to practise violence against others. A struggle in which peace is both the goal and the way.

PART 1

Towards a Theory and Practice of Peace
by Peaceful Means

Peacemaking as Realpolitik, Conflict Resolution and Oxymoron: the Record; the Challenge[1]

Carl G. Jacobsen with Kai Frithjof Brand-Jacobsen

The 1990s brought a near-tenfold increase in the frequency of UN and UN-sanctioned peacekeeping interventions, when set against its 1945–90 record – though, remarkably, the majority of current conflicts remain untouched by UN scrutiny or action. The concomitant growth in NGO conflict mediation and resolution efforts has been even more dramatic. From 'third party' interventions to training programmes in peace-building and conflict transformation and efforts to support and empower local capacities for peace, the scale and diversity of activities have never been greater. This extraordinary activism has paralleled and to some extent spawned a profusion of theoretical work, some drawing on and developing the vastly expanded data accumulated by traditional strategic and conflict studies research, some collating the lessons and experiences of more recent initiatives.

War Culture vs. Peace Culture – the Gorbachev Challenge

John Vasquez' *The War Puzzle* develops the lessons of the 'Correlates of War' project (an immense compilation of data on post-Napoleonic nineteenth- and twentieth-century armed conflicts, which caused 1,000 or more battle deaths) and other conflict analysis research.[2] His summary conclusion posits an essentially European experience-derived 'war culture', epitomized by the Cold War's zero-sum adage, according to which advantage for one equals disadvantage for the other. Its corollary is delegitimization and dehumanization of the 'enemy', often to the point that negotiation or mediation becomes all but impossible.[3] It was a culture that had already spawned its antithesis, though synthesis would remain frustratingly elusive.

'Gaming', modelling and simulation techniques were originally developed as advantage-optimizing tools, adjuncts of the 'war culture' that defined prevailing dogma. But their development and increasing sophistication soon brought fundamental intellectual challenges to this culture, and its underlying premise(s). The 'Prisoners' Dilemma' game indicated that, under conditions of long-term interaction, mutual advantage was not only possible, but, if pursued consistently, would ensure greater benefits to both (or all) protagonists than could be secured through zero-sum approaches. This insight, long ignored by traditional defence establishments, became the lynchpin for ever-more rigorous academic 'peace studies' – a cross-discipline whose early contributors included mathematicians and psychologists, sociologists and anthropologists, and, over time, a growing number of defectors from traditional strategic, national security and conflict studies constituencies.[4] The UN Palme Commission's embrace of the concepts of 'mutual security' and 'common security' marked the discipline's emergence from academic ghettoization.[5] The presence on the Commission and as witnesses or presenters to the Commission of past and future advisers to Mikhail Gorbachev, soon-to-be CPSU General Secretary, would generate a wider and more remarkable impact.

After he came to power in 1985, Gorbachev proceeded to cut the Gordian knot of apocalyptic Sino-Soviet and East–West confrontation through unilateral disarmament measures. These ignored the realist theologies of zero-sum (you win/I lose, and vice versa) and the equal-or-superior status dogmas, which resulted in so many ritualized, formal arms control negotiating fora ending in stalemate – most notoriously, perhaps, the never-ending Mutual and Balanced Force Reduction talks in Europe. Convinced of the irrelevance of most such arguments and postures in a world of manifestly superfluous superpower nuclear weaponry, and persuaded by the arms control research that imbued the Palme Commission's embrace of mutual security (we can both win or both lose), 'sufficient security' (you only die and can only kill once) and the transcendent, individual, non-state-centred concept of 'common security', he compelled others' agreement by granting them their primary demands – demands that were essential to their security cultures, yet now irrelevant to his.[6] How ironic that the state/UN-sponsored peacekeeping initiatives of the 1990s would revert to the prescripts of earlier, failed theologies, repeatedly following tradition-defined great power *diktats* rather than the prescripts of and for longer-term conflict amelioration or transcendence – dousing the flames of conflict, but leaving their embers glowing.

Vasquez' work has been followed by a burgeoning literature on the disjuncture between proclaimed and actual state conflict approaches and *modus operandi*.[7] Mary B. Anderson's *Do No Harm:*

Supporting Local Capacities for Peace through Aid collates data and derives lessons from 15 case-studies of NGOs' involvement in 14 violence-plagued societies.[8] Louis Kriesberg's *Constructive Conflicts: From Escalation to Resolution* and John Paul Lederach's *Building Peace: Sustainable Reconciliation in Divided Societies* provide valuable insights into the constructive transformation of conflicts and building peace by peaceful means.[9] These studies are complemented by a number of other ambitious review and prescription efforts, not least those produced by Jan Oeberg and the Transnational Foundation for Peace and Future Research (TFF),[10] Kai Frithjof Brand-Jacobsen's International Correspondence League (ICL/Praxis for Peace)[11] and Johan Galtung's TRANSCEND conflict-transformation and peace-building networks. Galtung's UN training manual, *Conflict Transformation by Peaceful Means: The Transcend Method* (1999) and his earlier *Peace by Peaceful Means* (1996) are seminal examples of this work; their further elaboration and refinement are two of this book's primary concerns.[12]

The new approach and focus of peace research and analysis reflected and reinforced the emergence of complementary training facilities and aspirations. The work of John Burton, Herbert Kelman and Edward Azar, for example, from the 1970s to the 1990s, played a pioneering role in interactive conflict resolution and problem-solving workshops and seminars. Simon Fisher's 'Responding to Conflicts and Working with Conflict' training programme at Selly Oak Colleges, Birmingham, also played an early role through the 1990s and continues today, in its attempt to train facilitators and nurture 'local capacities for peace' to build dialogue, resist oppression and heal wounds, from Guatemala to Rwanda, Afghanistan to Cambodia.[13] In 2001, Diakonhjemmet International Centre in Oslo, Norway, and the Peace Action, Training and Research Institute of Romania (PATRIR) began offering one- and two-week intensive courses in peace-building, conflict transformation, peace journalism, and peace and religion with some of the leading practitioners and scholars in the world. At Eastern Mennonite University, John Paul Lederach explored the dynamics and processes of conflict, differing approaches to peace-building and the transformative potential of active peace work. The European Peace University in Schlaining/Burg, Austria, designed according to Galtung's precepts and the recipient of UNESCO's Peace Prize, established a Certificate and advanced Masters programme, while Bradford University in England maintained the largest and oldest peace studies department in the world. In 2000/2001, initiatives were under way to launch new undergraduate and MA degree programmes in peace studies in Canada (in particular at McMasters University, Hamilton), the

United States, Norway (at the University of Tromso with Vidar Vambheim), Romania, South Africa and elsewhere. By the late 1990s vocational training programmes, most notably those run by TFF, EMU, PATRIR and TRANSCEND (now UN-embraced), dramatically expanded the accessibility – and hence potential impact and ramifications – of this essentially new profession, or professions. The realm of the peace worker necessarily encompassed a wide spectrum of expertise, extending to the training of peace correspondents (as antidote and corrective to the too late/reactive concerns of journalism's traditional war correspondents).[14] As work began following meetings in Budapest and London in 1999 for TRANSCEND to launch the first global, advanced MA in peace and development studies through distance learning over the Internet and at its 20 TRANSCEND centres around the world, and for the first TRANSCEND Summer Peace Institute to be held in Romania in the summer of 2002, peace research, peace education and training in peaceful conflict transformation seemed to be reaching a new stage.

A juxtaposing of recent peacekeeping/peacemaking practice and related, accumulating and developing theory highlights a number of fundamental problems – most importantly, the fact that some of today's acclaimed conflict-resolution prescriptions contain disturbing and probable future conflict-enhancing features. A critical précis of the Gulf War, the Oslo Accords and the Dayton Agreement, when set against theory's lessons from past conflicts and current attempts at conflict management, appears to support this conclusion. So does a review of today's Caucasian and other conflict dynamics, not least NATO's disastrous (in human terms) war against Yugoslavia – the bookend to a violent century. As the first major war of the twenty-first century began with US bombs raining down on Kabul and no evidence in sight of serious efforts to transform the underlying dynamics and causes of the 11 September attacks, Tacitus's description of the Romans seemed to return to haunt us, an apt portrayal of the world's current state-centred approaches to peace-building and conflict transformation: '*They have created desolation, and call it peace.*' As the new century dawned, any hope of *glasnost* (openness) and *perestroika* (reconstruction) on a global scale had been succeeded by the realities of *naglost* (brazen insolence) and *perestrelka* (shoot-outs).

From Peacekeeping to Peacemaking

The dramatic increase in the 1990s of UN and UN-sanctioned activism rested on a fundamental revision of mandate and purpose. Restricted previously to inter-state conflicts wherein both (or all) parties agreed to invite UN cease-fire and/or other conflict-resolution monitors or observers, the UN's mandate and purpose were now extended to intra-state conflicts and conflicts-in-progress, and relieved of any requirement to be invited or approved by the combatants, be they state or non-state. But problems of definition and implementation loomed.

The unprecedented scope of interventionary activity masked its exclusivity. UN and UN-sanctioned interventions were still directed at less than half of similarly definable conflicts, and not always at the worst or most intractable. Selectivity driven by superpower interests and agendas threatened to undermine UN credibility, throwing into question the goals and objectives behind the new wave of 'humanitarian' interventions. This highlights the problem of choice. Why the intervention in Somalia and not neighbouring Sudan, whose civil war was and remains, if possible, even more bestial? The easy answer, obviously, is the CNN's presence in Mogadishu and its transmission of images of Audrey Hepburn cuddling a starving child – though emergent oil interests clearly focused minds behind the scenes. More profoundly, the problem reflects the absence of a reliable, neutral intelligence collection and evaluation capacity, and the UN's consequent reliance on the partisan and self-interested data proffered by its core member states.

Another set of problems had an impact on the UN's ability to manage either grey areas or transitions from peacekeeping to peace-keepers' licensed response to endangerment to peacemaking. The Security Council's options might now more closely resemble that envisaged by the UN's founders, but the Secretariat's means of implementation did not. Some of the more ludicrous dissonance between mandate and means – such as the absence of duty officers in New York that so frustrated the early Bosnia peacekeepers when faced with weekend or evening emergencies – was later rectified.[15] But HQ military staffing remained inadequate, and independent stand-by force/reinforcing potential – to which a number of lesser-power members such as Norway and Canada were willing to commit – remained effectively vetoed by the more dominant members. Where and when member troops were accepted, on a case-by-case basis, they mirrored their nations' strategic cultures and concerns. National contingents consequently often worked at cross-purposes, effectively identifying or being identified with different partisan local combatant agendas (thus becoming *de facto* parties to the conflict rather than 'neutral' arbiters), with little effective coordination. Further, they lacked serious grounding or training in conflict transformation and its problematics.

The fiscal crisis occasioned by UN debtors (notably, the United States) compounded these problems, forcing the diversion of already inadequate intervention funds to day-to-day housekeeping accounts. The UN peacekeeping budget remained, at its height, a mere 0.3 per cent of global military expenditures. By the mid-1990s the cumulative crisis had compelled a new pattern of interventionary responsibility delegated to regional organizations, and through them to regional hegemons, whose partiality and purpose were questionable – to NATO, with its US/German dominance, in Europe; to the CIS, with its Russian preponderance, in former Soviet areas; to the Organization of African Unity, with Nigeria's odious Abacha regime long providing the primary military clout, in Africa; and to other such constellations. As violent conflicts multiplied and humanitarian catastrophes worsened, the success and viability of UN peacekeeping and peacemaking missions fell into doubt. With the UN increasingly sidelined and prevented from playing a meaningful role (except that of cleaning up afterwards with funds nowhere near those required for the task), global militarism and militarization and the resort to violence to 'solve' conflicts gained ground.

The record of achievement was and remains mixed. Peacekeeping's humanitarian appendage (now dramatically expanded) was in many cases extraordinarily successful, saving lives in conflict zones as disparate as Somalia, Bosnia and Cambodia. Yet in some cases, most notably in Central Africa in the mid- and later 1990s, but also in Somalia, Bosnia and elsewhere, both UN-directed humanitarian and complementary NGO aid efforts became hostage to combatants' whim and *diktat* – as well as outside party interests.

More restrictively interpreted, peacekeeping was also in many cases successful. But here too success proved hostage to combatants' acquiescence. The Somalia mission collapsed when a US directive to capture and prosecute a recalcitrant warlord (General Aideed) failed, after incurring politically unacceptable casualties. An embarrassing retreat to a non-partisan posture proved a prerequisite for the resumption of even minimalist humanitarian aid activity. UN-mandated, funded and supervised elections in Cambodia and Angola were successfully conducted, but when electoral losers later disregarded the results, there was no effective penalty. Conversely, when the OSCE, the delegated election guarantor in Bosnia in 1996, documented the fact that Alija Izetbegovic's plurality win rested on fraud so extensive as to presuppose that past wars had caused no deaths, his 'win' was nevertheless confirmed.[16] But, then, this instance is more properly classified as belonging to the category of enforced settlement.

Peacemaking – Enforced Settlements

The brutally swift Gulf War, the Oslo Accords chartering Israeli–Palestinian peace negotiations and the Dayton Agreement, which 'ended' the Yugoslav successor wars, were UN-sanctioned dominant power (that is, US-imposed) conflict-resolution prescriptions, which each secured short- and perhaps medium-term US interests, but at possible jeopardy to longer-term considerations (so also with the calamitous NATO war ending the decade; see below). Stark criticism has been levelled at each of the prescriptions, and these illuminate core problems of past and current great power conduct. But they divert attention from the realist arguments and success criteria that shaped them, and from the future problems that they embed.[17] Some of the criticism illuminates the under-appreciated truism of any approach to war or otherwise forced policy prescription. Such approaches have always been accompanied by determined efforts to manufacture consent through media manipulation.[18] But while mendacity in these matters has an ancient lineage, today's media technologies, concentrated ownership and reach offer unparalleled opportunities. In the approach to the Gulf War Saddam Hussein's (not wholly unjustified) ogre appellation was cemented through an utterly cynical PR campaign orchestrated by two of Wall Street's leading firms, Ruder Finn and Hill & Knowlton. The campaign was typified by the utterly false presentation to Congress by the daughter of Kuwait's Ambassador to Washington, who professed to be a nurse who had witnessed Iraqi soldiers throwing babies out of incubators, to die.[19] In the approach to the Oslo Accords no equivalent Wall Street connection is known to this author. But the *New York Times* led the establishment US and allied media's near-systemic ignoring of near-universal (bar Washington and Tel Aviv) and thus international law – suggestive UN resolutions, affirming Palestinians' right to a state as *quid pro quo* for Israel's right to exist, the rights of those occupied to resist an occupier, and the rights of refugees to return – all explicitly countermanded by various clauses of the Oslo 1 and Oslo 2 Accords.[20] The Yugoslav wars saw the open return of Ruder Finn and Hill & Knowlton, now hired by Croatia's government (and later the Bosnian Muslim government), with a particularly scurrilous anti-Serb campaign that outspent the Coca Cola and Pepsi advertising budgets combined. It set the moral parameters, justified the chosen course and still reverberates in the War Crimes Tribunal's focus on a Serb killing field and a Serb internment camp, with much less attention paid to Croat and Muslim killing fields and camps (see also NATO war coverage, below).[21]

The campaigns did not only demonize the opponents; they also sanitized the allies. Feudal Saudi and Kuwaiti oligarchs were presented as democrats (the subsequent election in Kuwait enfranchised an all-male 6 per cent of the population to vote for a legislature without decision-making powers). Croatia's President

Tudjman became a democrat, notwithstanding his embrace of Croatia's Nazi-allied past (his historiography has Jewish guards responsible for death camp victims); so also Izetbegovic, whose advocacy of fundamentalist Islam won him the friendship and financial – and later military – support of Ayatollah Khomenei and his successors; and the Kosovo Liberation Army, promoted to freedom fighters despite Europol-documented Mafia and drug ties, and ruthlessness second to none. Israel's systemic flouting of Geneva Convention standards, most blatantly in its collective punishment and interrogation torture policies (Israel's was the world's only legal system that gave formal sanction to the use of torture until the law was struck down in late 1999) and effective *carte blanche* for special forces' death squads were similarly deemed irrelevant to her democratic assertion.[22] As the manufacture of consent increased in quantity and importance, George Orwell's 'Newspeak' was made mainstream discourse: war is peace, control is freedom, and an 'eye for an eye' is 'conflict resolution' and 'peacemaking'.

This partisan demonizing/sanitizing phenomenon was accompanied by a reaffirmation of the malleability and great power-dependent status of international law – never absolute, never generic. Its appellation to Iraq's (re-)conquest of Kuwait, her erstwhile 16th province, was not extended with the same consequences to others' less historically defensible and also UN-condemned regional occupations, such as Israel's and Syria's occupations of Lebanon, and Israel's continuing occupations of Gaza, the West Bank and the Golan Heights (see below). The ignoring of commonly accepted international law strictures by the Oslo Accords was referred to above. Far from granting *quid pro quo* regional autonomy, they deny the Palestinian Authority the rights normally confirmed by statehood (which cannot be reversed even if the status is later granted, *pro forma*) and the rights accorded to occupied peoples. They reserve most lands, resources and ultimate security authority to Israel, make the Palestinian police a dependent appendage of Israeli security policy and restrict Palestinian authority to residual, isolated enclaves with less autonomy than that once granted to South Africa's Bantustans.

The precipitate recognition of seceding Yugoslav and Soviet republics, with a denial of similar secession rights to dissenting minorities and regions, defied all previous notions of international law – as well as the warnings of then UN Secretary-General Pérez de Cuéllar. The US, typically, had opposed all secessions, whatever their democratic mandate, since its own civil war against secession. The only international convention of relevance, the Helsinki Final Act, sanctified then-existing European borders – that is, those of federal Yugoslavia and the USSR. And international law interpretations would soon be reversed again, when the international community rallied around Canada's position that the right to self-determination was automatic only in colonial contexts – and her fallback assertion that if Canada could nevertheless be partitioned, then so could Quebec. But this posture would of course also be reversed for Kosovo (a one-off exception?).

The problem arose from the fact that most internal federation boundaries defied notions of statehood; they were indeed often designed to *preclude* statehood, through the inclusion of groups alienated from the dominant majority. Quebec's northern two-thirds, populated by Cree and Inuit nations, were given to it after Confederation, for reasons of temporal and political calculations, devoid of any thought to the break-up of Canada. Krajina and other Serb lands were Nazi gifts to Croatia, confirmed by Broz Tito. (Both feared Serb nationalism and sought to contain it through the tactic of divide and rule.) Stalin gave ancestral Polish lands and Wilno/a, now Vilnius, to Lithuania, and non-Romanian Trans-Dniester to Romanian-majority Moldova. He gave Abkhazia and other smaller-nation lands to Georgia, Armenian-populated Nakichevan and Nagorno-Karabakh to Azerbaijan, and Tashkent and other Tajik regions to Uzbekistan. Khrushchev gave Russian Crimea to Ukraine, in return for fidelity to (his) Moscow. The resultant conundrums were exemplified when Quebec's separatists lost a referendum vote by less than 1 per cent in 1996, with the Cree and Inuit voting almost unanimously to remain in Canada.

Quebec's separatists, like Croatia's separatist President Tudjman, Georgia's, Azerbaijan's and indeed all new-state regimes, insisted that their rights to secede from unwanted super-structures would not extend to their own, now disaffected regions. And they could all, and did and do, invoke international law's 1991 permutation as both sanction and licence, while their separatists find solace in its always logical and (for Canada only?) now confirmed next-step permutation. The resultant civil war in Croatia was finally resolved through the single largest (pre-1999 NATO war) ethnic cleansing of the Yugoslav wars (sanctioned through Milosevic's acquiescence). Other resultant conflagrations, such as between Trans-Dniester and Moldova, Abkhazia and Georgia, Ossetia and Georgia, and Nagorno-Karabakh and Azerbaijan are contained by fragile cease-fires, only loosely guaranteed by Russian peacekeepers, and may yet re-ignite (as in Chechnya). Yet others may self-ignite or be ignited elsewhere.

The Oslo Accords and the Dayton Agreement may be particularly vulnerable to future unravelling, as evidenced by the explosion of violence and descent into war following Ariel Sharon's September 2000 visit to the Temple Mount, and the worsening situation, with escalation of violence on all sides, following 11

September 2001. The Oslo Accords' extreme fine-print concessions, underlined by Israel's subsequent assertiveness, clearly alienate most Palestinians. Similarly, most Serbs, who interpret Dayton against the backdrop of the lost lands of Krajina and western and eastern Slavonia, clearly view it as unjust and unjustly imposed (most Bosniaks are also alienated by the fact that Dayton in its essence mirrors the agreement that US Ambassador Zimmerman dissuaded them from signing before the wars – and thus also the wars' futility). One recalls Bismarck's prescient warning to the Kaiser after the Franco-Prussian war of 1870, that annexing Alsace-Lorraine would cement French enmity. The Kaiser's shortsighted hubris was echoed in the Allies' *diktat* at Versailles after the First World War, which fatefully fuelled the Nazis' later rise. But in this case the greater immediate danger threatened to flow from the resurrection of Muslim maximalist aims wrought by the US decision to placate their allies' sensibilities with a sharply stepped-up, destabilizing arms and training programme.[23] NATO's 1999 war against Serbia/Yugoslavia and its aftermath, with the continued ostracism of Belgrade, reinforced suggestions of the Balkans again divided along lines imposed by outside hegemons, and enforced by an external military presence designed to protect others' interests – always a recipe for future conflict.

The second cause for jeopardy derives from the peculiar dynamics driving both Arafat's and Milosevic's willingness to agree to the proffered deals. Arafat, in exile in Tunisia with most of the PLO leadership, saw his authority in Palestine threatened by the growing popularity of Hamas-led resistance. The Oslo Accords may well have appeared his last chance to assert his leadership – his last chance to return. Milosevic, a later and more opportunistic convert to ethno-religious exclusivity than either Tudjman or Izetbegovic, similarly later found himself outflanked by nationalism's newer and older disciples – not least Bosnian Serb and Krajina leaders (and now championed 'democratic' leader Vuk Draskovic). His vilification of these leaders, his (negotiated) betrayal of Krajina and his (pre-negotiated) acceptance of the NATO air war and Dayton Agreement terms can be explained in part by reference to his consequent need for political repositioning. The spectre of a second front unleashed by separatist Kosovo/a Albanians provided a legitimizing pretext and rationale. Finally, if Arafat's and Milosevic's signatures derived from constellations of particular, peculiar weaknesses, the converse motivation spurring Tel Aviv's and Washington's agreement was surely an appreciation of the extraordinary opportunity for maximalist deals. Kaiserian over-reach?

Peace-securing/enhancing

The realist approach to peacekeeping and peacemaking, so characteristic of US, German, Russian and indeed Chinese, Nigerian and others' *modus operandi* in these matters, reflects the war/deterrence lessons and the more general hierarchical/elitist decision-making legacy ingrained by the war culture of modern Europe/US. The approach and its prescriptions in fact have singularly poor records in terms of peace preservation; their longer-term outcomes mark them as war-conducive rather than war-preventive. But if the realist approach rests on dangerous folklore, as Vasquez concludes, the alternative NGO/idealist route of attempting to nurture and expand nodules of peace culture (and there have indeed been such societies in the past, societies of sometimes extraordinary longevity), is often pursued with dangerous, conflict-encouraging naïveté.

As noted, NGO and UN humanitarian aid activities often fall victim to local and international power dynamics. To reach at least some intended recipients they often have to work through, and thus reinforce the power status of, local warlords – which also, of course, means that the recipient list may be skewed. Conversely, attempts to defy and operate independently of local warlords are often seen as a threat to their power, leading to direct or indirect attacks, which may force aid workers to withdraw and suspend all delivery aspirations.

NGO/UN activities have also at times been infiltrated, used and manipulated, with or without consent, by outside, interventionist actors. In Bosnia, for example, a number of Red Cross drivers were later identified as CIA operatives. NGO and UN vehicles have also been used by both local and outside actors to smuggle arms and other goods, thus extending one or the other side's war-making and war-prolonging capacity. The money associated with aid and humanitarian operations, and the above-local norm salaries of employees, have in some cases been subject to coercive, partisan extortion schemes, and in others have had corrosive, corrupting and lasting negative consequences for the local economy, creating a profit-generating, war-related aid economy, and hence vested interest in the perpetuation of conflict. Several international 'NGOs' have even gone so far as to cooperate actively with foreign governments and intelligence agencies in funnelling weapons and funding to warlords and paramilitary death squads, as in Afghanistan, Colombia, Mexico and elsewhere.[24]

Prescriptions for nurturing peace cultures, or local capacities for peace, are often persuasive, if not compelling. Thus *Do No Harm*'s summary of past experience, which acknowledges many of the problems outlined above, with notes on how they have sometimes been creatively circumvented, emphasizes the need to create non-controversial scope for conflict diffusion and opposing *voice, space* and inter-communal *initiatives*. Similarly, other efforts have argued for the need to remove enemy images and conflict-provoking assumptions about the other ('they can't be trusted'; 'they'll just take advantage ...'), and to replace them with trust-building dialogue and an emphasis on similarities, complementarities and mutually enriching alternatives.

Invariably, some prescriptions are too theological in terms of own-culture political correctness, and sometimes naively impatient. Thus, *Do No Harm* makes the (re-)establishment of inter-faith and inter-ethnic harmonies an immediate priority, evincing little appreciation of or understanding for history's lesson that, in the aftermath of inter-communal war, some separation may be a pre-requisite for reconciliation. A sullen Germany forced into European Union in 1945 may well have proved a cancer at its core, whereas the confident, reconstructed nation that later sought membership is arguably its strongest pillar and most committed defender. Similarly Bosnia, wherein enforced togetherness amidst the cauldron of horrific memories promises only to embed and exacerbate paranoias. Separation accompanied by substantial non-partisan developmental aid would be far more likely to develop forward-looking leaderships to replace the warriors of yesterday, and to instil a sense of security that alone might give scope for other logics to unfold – the ultimately reconciling logics of geography and economics. So also in Afghanistan and other communally-riven conflict zones. Where ethno-religious memories are too traumatized, impatient prescriptions may reinforce paranoias, reinforce the legitimacy of warriors and Massada-type complexes, and retard or thwart the realization of other visions, and the unfolding of other logics.

The greatest problem, however, is inadequate knowledge and inadequate, independent intelligence about local conflicts' histories, cultures, courses and dynamics. Counter-war culture advocates are often perversely crippled by the fact that their premises derive from the very war culture they strive to replace. The most serious problem with own-culture political correctness is the extent to which that political correctness is moulded by partisan interests. Peace workers are often subconsciously imbued with parameters established for partisan purpose.[25]

Do No Harm illustrates this. Warlords, arms merchants and profiteers are excoriated, with little appreciation of the facts of, reasons for or consequences of (their) foreign sponsors. There is no appreciation of the causal dynamics and ramifications of, say, US support for former Georgian President Ghamsakhurdia, Croatia's Tudjman and Bosnia's Izetbegovic, Russia's support for separatist leaders in Georgia, Azerbaijan and elsewhere, or France's support for the Hutu extremists of Rwanda – orchestrators of our generation's worst genocide.

There is little appreciation of donors' preconceptions and inculcated assumptions of guilt and blame (on which history is never as unequivocal as contemporary combatants' and their allies' professed judgement), and scant questioning as to what or whose information underlies particular judgements. There is an appreciation of the fact that aid more often makes conflict worse, yet no realization of the single most important reason for this: namely, that aid is rarely distributed according to non-partisan criteria. This invariably gives encouragement to the ambitions of one side and fuels the paranoia of the other. It is also ahistorical. There is the hubris assumption that the aid providers know the truth, though history invariably affirms more truths and less single-hued truths.

The problem of donor-directed and often less than locally optimal priorities is compounded by donor-derived time horizons. Programmes are often aborted or wasted as their funding source is exhausted and the agency on the ground is forced to turn to differently focused and often other-region/other-donor priorities. Thus it is not enough to nurture 'local capacities for peace'; they need to be made self-sustainable – and therein lies the greatest challenge.[26]

Appreciation of the need for a period of separation between contending groups as between contending individuals, of the need for respect for the germs of truth and the causes that underlie every paranoia (this does not necessarily mean agreement or sympathy), and of the need for non-coercive patience and creatively suggestive but never overbearing or enforced counselling, are among the most compelling features of Johan Galtung's Transcend Method.

This author (like Galtung) was a course section designer, lecturer and workshop leader to two contingents participating in the Norwegian government and Red Cross-funded Yugoslav reconciliation project conducted through the Nansen Academy in Lillehammer. The first, in September 1996, involved a cross-section of combatant communities. They, perhaps in deference to the presumed hopes of their hosts, but also echoing earlier cooperative memories, nurtured hopes of reconciliation, though there were discordant notes. The second, in February 1997, perhaps because it was more self-reinforcingly one- and to a lesser extent two-sided, rather than three- or more sided – or perhaps because of the impact of partisan aid disbursement (military, humanitarian and developmental) – encouraged pessimism and fears of renewed warfare. It dramatically reinforced the point that what you see as opposed to what you don't see matters enormously. So also do the presumptions of both circumstance and sponsor, which dictate where you go and whom you meet. When steeped in the horrors of one side only, it is easy to be blinded to the depth and scale of the horrors of the other.

While Galtung's approach admirably incorporates the self-evident but all too often under-appreciated need for patience and the avoidance of *diktat* if true reconciliation is to be fostered, its mandated nurturing of a genuine peace culture also entails and demands a time-frame and perseverance of effort that seems well beyond the gratification needs of state and also NGO policy realms. On the other hand, Galtung himself insists that final solution definitions (including 'peace') should be avoided. The focus should be on understanding the structural and cultural causes of violence, and on understanding the problems of moving from conflict modes (attitude–behaviour–contradiction) through outcome alternatives (withdrawal–compromise–transcendence) to future prevention (empathy–non-violence–creativity). The prescriptions for early warning and prevention, conflict transformation, complementary, no deadline dialogues for peace venues (never insist on face-to-face negotiations between those not yet ready or comfortable with them) and overlapping and reinforcing peaceful transformation mechanisms are both generic and exhaustive.

This author and Galtung were invited to present proposals to various fora in Georgia, Armenia and Azerbaijan in June 1997. (Galtung was on a Transcend Method dissemination tour, which encompassed dispute locales from the Basque regions to Taiwan, Okinawa and Zaire-Rwanda.) A select proposals summary may be useful for purposes of comparison, elucidation and example.[27]

1. A consideration of dual/multiple/joint sovereignty – a peace/cooperation zone some kilometres in size, donated by each for a trial period at the tri-border intersection for, ultimately, an expandable free trade joint-venture zone with a regional airport and highways to each capital. It would be a possible site for a pan-Caucasian Parliament or Council, an NGO/professional associations meeting/negotiations building, and a conflict mediation/resolution centre. Initially, it might be a site for youth/ecumenical meetings and festivals. (Galtung)
2. Re. Nagorno-Karabakh (N-K), the separatist Armenian enclave in Azerbaijan which, after a brutal civil war, now controls the Lachin corridor and adjacent regions that separate it from Armenia proper. Azerbaijan demands restoration of sovereignty (assigned by Stalin) and the return of displaced persons, while N-K and Armenia demand recognition of the new status quo – recipes for non-resolution and possibly renewed warfare. If the presumed minimalist demands of both, namely *pro forma* return of Azerbaijan sovereignty and refugee return, and satisfaction

of N-K's security demand for contiguity with Armenia, are the focus, then a compromise adjoining Lachin to N-K with guaranteed autonomy within Azerbaijan might outline a viable compromise. (Jacobsen)

3. Re. Abkhazia, the (non-recognized, Russian peacekeeper cease-fire monitored) 'independent', formerly autonomous Georgian region (given to her by Stalin): a multi-point plan based on analogous principles. (Galtung)

4. Re. Abkhazia, Ossetia (another Georgian breakaway province) and possible/aspiring other separatist potentials (Georgia contains 26 distinct 'nations'), and addressed to Azerbaijan and Armenia as well: discard the new-state liturgy of monolingualism and embrace multi-ethnic, multilingual tolerance, affirmed initially through locally elected and responsible school board directors. (Galtung and Jacobsen)

5. A Caucasian Council, perhaps modelled on the Nordic Council, with distinct representation (guaranteeing voice, though perhaps not the vote) for sub-state ethnicities/nations, would have coordinating, confidence-building potential. Ultimately, a Caucasian Parliament, perhaps with a Second House of Nationalities, might reinforce and embed cooperative dynamics. (Galtung and Jacobsen)

6. Current power-political alignments (Azerbaijan–Georgia–Turkey–perhaps Ukraine vs. Russia–perhaps Abkhazia–Armenia/N-K–Iran) perpetuate, justify and legitimize outside power involvement; pan-Caucasian cooperation, internally focused and externally non-threatening, would best serve both short- and long-term economic and security interests. (Galtung and Jacobsen)

1998–99 gave reason for both hope and despair, reaffirming the potency of Gorbachevian flexibility and the enduring non-flexibility and self-focused partisanship of great power 'conflict management'. The first – what might be termed the Gorbachevian rebirth (though intellectual credit should probably be ascribed to Johan Galtung, whose decades-long advocacy for sovereignty sharing or obfuscation as conflict solvents heralded the eventual success recipes, and to Joe Camplisson and other community initiative champions who provided early building blocks) – was evinced in the Northern Ireland agreement, the Ecuadorian–Peruvian conflict compromise, and the resolution of the decades-long Bear Island dispute between the USSR/Russia and China.

The Northern Ireland Good Friday Agreement finessed the irreconcilables of Catholic demands for Irish unity and Protestant demands for British indivisibility through the creation of overlapping bodies that cut the Gordian knot by effectively serving both purposes. The Ecuador–Peru formula followed a similar path – 'transcending' agreement-precluding dogmas.[28] Their ideas echo in and clearly helped chart the final accords. So also with the Bear Island Resolution, which ended the last Russian–Chinese border dispute. It granted Russian sovereignty over the island (covering the southwestern confluence of the Amur and Ussuri rivers, its sensitivity derived from the buffer space it provided for Khabarovsk, on the immediately opposite northern bank of the Amur), but in the context of economic co-dominion.[29]

The grander end-of-decade, turn-of-the-century conflict response and 'resolution' initiatives, however, were devoid of nuance. The early 1998 build-up to enforce Iraqi compliance with US-interpreted UN resolutions, the September strikes against Bin Laden's 'terrorist' camp in Afghanistan and Sudan's 'chemical-biological weapons' facility, the October assembly of a sea- and land-based air armada (including six B-52s) threatening Serbia/Yugoslavia, and December's devastating attacks on Iraq by US and British forces, all drew justification from asserted moral cause. Yet, in each case, the sufficiency of the moral cause was questioned, even by NATO members; in no case did the Security Council authorize strikes. Western ambassadors and specialists visiting the plant in Sudan found no evidence of non-legitimate production. The personalized animosities that animated the other cases, though accepted by many, were thought by others to skew judgement and set a dangerous precedent. The October build-up, for example, was seen by some as a vendetta-like response to anti-Dayton hard-line victories in the preceding Bosnian elections (others noted that the build-up/strike announcements coincided with revelations from the Starr investigation into President Clinton's affairs), while the threat's singular focus on Serb terror implicitly condoned the arguably precipitating terror of the Albanian- and Iranian-sponsored Kosovo Liberation Army. The 200 missile strikes that bombarded Iraq (as the House of Representatives voted for Clinton's impeachment) appeared similarly vindictive and strategically non-coherent, in that they targeted 'mass destruction weapon sites' not found by UNSCOM's intrusive inspection regime, visiting horror on the populace, but leaving Saddam Hussein secure and UNSCOM *persona non grata*. Washington and London continued to find cause for near-daily strikes through the following months. Yet Saddam remained in power. The lowest UN estimate for Iraqi children dead since 1991 from the bombing's carnage stands at almost one million.

Washington's and London's declaration of just cause and willingness to proceed without UN and, if necessary, without NATO sanction, in October 1998 (as they did in December, and again in 1999) brought the Russian riposte that the precedent would legitimize analogous action (for example, attacks on Turkey for its brutal suppression of Kurd separatists) by others, and eviscerate the UN – as unilateralist Japanese, Italian and later German foreign agendas emasculated the League of Nations in the 1930s. Moscow also let it be known that it had provided targeting upgrades for Serbia's surface-to-air missiles, and threatened more deliveries and an end to its 'strategic partnership' with NATO. The threatened strike was ultimately averted through an apparent eleventh-hour agreement that Yugoslav army and special forces units deployed for the offensive would withdraw, with verification to be provided by 2,000 civilian OSCE observers and unarmed aerial overflights. Western aid to victims and refugees would also be permitted. Viewed against the size of the assembled armada, Milosevic's concessions were minimal. Serbia's government had already declared victory and the withdrawal of its armed forces before the threat was assembled; a willingness to reinstate local autonomy provisions had already been announced; lesser-scope foreign aid agencies and NGO (and Western embassy and media) observers were in place and tolerated; the more extensive aid and observation presence now decreed arguably relieved Belgrade of reconstruction costs and burden; while the acceptance of Serb and Yugoslav sovereignty effectively extended the verifiers' duty to monitor KLA re-assembly efforts, thwart its resupply ambitions (the presence also of OSCE contingents sympathetic to Serbia would dictate a degree of non-partisanship) and/or legitimize Serb counteractions.

Indeed, by January 1999 the initial failure of the first, US-led OSCE contingent to limit KLA activities became the pretext for Serb mini-offensives – and yet more tragedies. Another Serb-attributed atrocity, and disregard for the fact that the KLA had wrought 'more deaths during the cease-fire than the Serbian security forces', brought a renewed NATO threat against Belgrade (as the Senate impeachment trial of President Clinton formally opened).[30]

Then came 'NATO's' war against Yugoslavia, driven by ultimatums designed to legitimize and indeed force a war bereft of legal or UN sanction; a war, like the First World War, that brought horrors far worse than those it purported to forestall. Its launch denied the most fundamental dictates of diplomacy. Milosevic's regime had in fact accepted all the principal ('G-8') demands, including the deployment of an armed, international peacekeeping force.[31] The war was launched at least in part because US Secretary of State Albright and others insisted on NATO rather than UN helmets, and because they naively believed that 'if you whack him, he'll cave'.[32] They foresaw a two-day 'demonstration', with scant thought given to the horrors and destruction that would ensue if they were wrong. The most elementary principle of strategy – a clearly thought-out end warranting the means (that is, deaths and casualties) needed to attain it – was ignored.

The proclaimed moral agenda was a charade. Why, otherwise, no intervention in conflicts that had caused more victims by orders of magnitude, such as Rwanda, the Sudan, Kurdestan or Tibet? Were the answers, respectively: racism, racism, 'Turkey is our ally' and 'China has nuclear weapons' (in which case, the message implied was clearly: 'go nuclear')? And why no intervention, but instead US/German arms and training to Croatia when it 'cleansed' 650,000 Serbs from Krajina and Slavonia less than four years earlier – Serbs who remain refugees, living in squalor, disregarded by the media and without aid, denied any and all rights of return?

NATO's/Washington's real agendas lay elsewhere. One derived from hundreds of billions of dollars' worth of Middle East investment and Gulf War reconstruction projects, oil and gas fortunes and arms sales prospects; all dictated denial of Saddam's potent charge that the West would target Muslims only. Washington clearly also wanted to cement its position as *the* global security arbiter. Another motivator was the need to expunge the Monica Lewinsky legacy, which haunted President Clinton, and the similar legacy enveloping Britain's Foreign Secretary, Robin Cook. This was complemented by Albright's Thatcher-like macho posturing, her mindset's 'post-Munich' need to appear Churchillian, 'decisive', regardless of the consequences. Finally, there was the trigger-releasing consensus that Russia's political and economic crises made her impotent – though her reaction in breaking off relations with NATO, warnings of missile re-targetability, the sending of a naval intelligence vessel to the Aegean and a swelling tide of anti-American sentiment (more virulent than any seen through 74 years of Soviet existence), all bode ill.

A small-scale insurgency/counter-insurgency struggle was transformed into an incalculably larger horror zone. NATO's 'murderous bombing' (in the words of Pope John Paul and Patriarch Teoctist) legitimized extremist, secessionist KLA horrors, thereby legitimizing also Serb nationalist fanaticism and no-holds-barred 'forced deportations' (again to quote John Paul and Teoctist) such as had found no legitimacy before.[33] (The cleansing also arguably had military justification: to thwart cellphone and other communication to NATO bombers and 'clear the battlefield'.) 'Forced deportation' is all too common in history: the US did it to millions of native Americans and encouraged it when done to millions of Polish and Czech Germans after the Second World War, and to 900,000 Palestinians. Tragic and outrageous, yes, but morally could it be said to justify or legitimize 'murderous bombing'?

Within weeks, 'precision munitions' dropped from over 15,000 feet to avoid surface-to-air missiles had 'accidentally' killed thousands of innocent Serbs and Kosovars, in factories, schools, trains, buses, convoys, hospitals and embassies. Diminishing supplies promised ever-less 'precise' munitions, ever-more civilian horror. Noxious chemicals from bombed petrochemical and pharmaceutical plants seeped into ground water and rivers, polluting not only Serbia but also neighbouring countries. Depleted uranium munitions left a deadly legacy, making this, in effect, a low-level nuclear war.

Traumatized Kosovar refugees found health care, shelter, food and security; Serbs and Kosovars in Serbia/Kosovo remained under constant threat, with no electricity, often no water, little or no food, no medicines, surgery cut short by blackouts, and their neurological and maternity wards bombed.

Milosevic a bogeyman? Never mind that demonization of the antagonist, always a numbing of intellect, is an inevitable conflict corollary. This author has long since advocated the international law and tribunal that might indict him, though pointing out that such law and such a tribunal would also have to indict Croatia's Tudjman, Bosnia's Izetbegovic and other world leaders who, with or without foresight, order or condone analogous atrocities (including NATO's). If not, it would be little more than a show-trial.

In fact, Milosevic was under political pressure at home before the bombs began to fall. But the bombs delegitimized his opposition. He had stood as a symbol of past failures; now he symbolized Serb defiance. His democratic (and other) rivals accepted the need for national unity. With a compromise and the bombing halted, Serb opposition would again be legitimate, and probably successful. Yet the bombing continued, blindly, with preparations for a ground war (against a partisan-trained populace, in ideal guerrilla terrain), perpetuating both his power and legitimacy.

A vendetta to destroy a politician on the verge of losing power – for that a country, a civilization, was reduced to rubble? In the words of Canada's former ambassador and pre-eminent Yugoslav specialist, it was 'imbecilic ... barbaric!'[34]

The NATO 'war party' ignored the pope and patriarch; the Washington and London-beholden 'War Crimes Tribunal' indicted Milosevic in blatant partisanship, ignoring also the 'unprecedented and barbaric attack' judgement rendered against NATO by the 20 judges of Greece's Supreme Council of State, and others' judgements. When Milosevic did cave in, after 79 days of up to 1,000 sorties a day, leaving legacies of lasting despair in

Kosovo and the rest of Yugoslavia, the terms of 'victory' largely repeated Milosevic's previously offered compromise (rejected by more nationalist Serbs). In contrast to NATO's initial 'non-negotiable' demands, it restricted the international force to Kosovo proper; mandated no future Kosovo independence referendum; and, crucially, stipulated that the force be UN-sanctioned and legitimized, with significant Russian and non-NATO participation, with the latter stationed in the Serb-dominated northern regions, presaging the (officially denied) option of future partition.

With the devastation wrought so catastrophic, the 'victory' could be sold politically. Yet the Yugoslav Army remained astoundingly intact (having seen out the onslaught in Kosovo's caves and tunnel systems); partisan prospects in partisan terrain clearly worried military ground war planners. That, and the fact that opinion polls in the US, Germany and France now showed opposition to the war and doubt on a steadily rising curve, were presumably relevant to the *dénouement*.

The 'victory' has left a lethal legacy for generations to come. The question is whether it leaves wider-ranging legacies, precedents as fateful to the dawning century as the First World War did to the twentieth. The sanctioning of vigilante 'justice', a haunting echo of the 1930s, clearly defined the reigning 'world order' in non-sustainable terms.

The calamity simultaneously unfolding in East Timor, soon to climax in an even more grotesque bloodbath, was of a different order, and perhaps an even more emphatic testimony to the perfidy of prevailing 'morality'.[35] The 24 years since Indonesia's genocidal invasion had each seen more killings than the worst months of Kosovo carnage, yet moral opprobrium (never mind intervention) was routinely set aside in the interest of preserving the Suharto regime's strategic relationship with Washington, Canberra and London, and lucrative investment, trade and still continuing arms sales contracts. Only when students' and others' protests toppled Suharto did his less entrenched successor, B.J. Habibie, succumb to finally emergent Western media and consequent political pressure to permit a UN-supervised independence referendum. The orgy of army-sponsored militia killings unleashed in the run-up to the vote, with or without his approval, clearly designed to suppress independence aspirations and compel a majority vote for the alternative of autonomy within Indonesia, was defeated by an 80 per cent pro-independence vote – an extraordinary testimony to courage. The 'final solution' that ensued, of murders, arson and destruction, a 'lesson' to other secession-minded provinces, left East Timor a wasteland, while West and East stood aside, now professing adherence to an 'international law' that precluded intervention without Jakarta's consent. Only when that consent came, with the lesson and warning delivered with unambiguous finality, did Western/UN intervention proceed – still swearing fealty to transitional Jakarta authority!

Kosovo and East Timor, joint exclamatory bookends to a century which ended as bleakly and as ominously as it began. They stand as graphic testimony to the compelling need for a redefinition of purpose and redirection of approach.

This book is dedicated to that task; to the charting of a different course.

*

There may be conflict zones, Kosovo/a included, that require Western or others' intervention and aid if underlying issues are to be resolved – assuming UN, and thus more general, 'legal' sanction – but such purpose requires even-handedness. Embedded conflicts rarely reflect simple morality tales of good versus evil. Single-group victim identifications may serve outside as well as local agendas, but they are caricatures. They may 'legitimize' imposed solutions, but they do not address a conflict's root causes, and are counter-productive to conflict resolution and reconciliation.

But if official peacekeeping still seems mired in older, self-serving 'realist' constructs, and if alternative non-governmental efforts sometimes fall prey to the influence and consequences of such constructs, New Thinking was clearly not lost with Gorbachev's fall from power. The findings of *The War Puzzle*, the essential, core ideals of *Do No Harm, Building Peace, Peace by Peaceful Means*, the *Transcend Manual*'s exhaustive recommendations and the work of ICL/Praxis for Peace all summon weighty historic and contemporary testimony to the benefice of the clarion calls of New Thinking and Creativity. While reaffirming the absolute necessity of pursuing that task, they also effectively affirm it as the always necessary Task Eternal. Cultural change is not amenable to quick-fix solution.

In the end, it is perhaps not the dreary familiarity of great power arrogance, hubris and sometimes bungling unilateralist instincts on which one should focus, but rather the increasing maturity and suasion of the intellectual challenge, and the Ulster, Ecuador–Peru and Bear Island precedents. They reconfirm history's all-too-often forgotten lesson: that imposed, punitive peace is a prescription for future war; a peace that addresses the grievances and minimum demands of both is far more likely to endure. Thus, Albright's and Blair's theologies notwithstanding, the most sustainable Kosovo/a prescription would probably give Kosovo Polje (Serbia's 'Alamo') and pro-Serb northern and northwestern regions to Serbia/Yugoslavia; then sanction a greater Albania (joined by majority Kosova and, perhaps, Albanian-dominated western

Macedonia) *and* a larger Serbia (joined by Srpska, Bosnia's Serb republic, but bereft of Krajina, Croatia's now cleansed Serb province) – complementing previous sanctions accorded a Muslim Bosnian space and greater Croatia.[36]

As a new century dawns these principles could make final conflict resolution in East Timor and Chiapas – and Kosovo/a – at least somewhat more likely. They most surely do not suffice to negate the inertia and continuing ramifications of our still dominant 'war culture'. But they shift the parameters of the conceivable, plausible and possible, and they do so in a direction that can only be welcomed.

Beyond Mediation: Towards More Holistic Approaches to Peace-building and Peace Actor Empowerment

Kai Frithjof Brand-Jacobsen, with Carl G. Jacobsen

War, like oppression, is a paper tiger. What is needed is to recognize it as such.

The goal of overcoming war is not a new one. It has been the central focus of many peace researchers and activists over the last 40–50 years and has roots reaching back long before that. Since the end of the Cold War the need to transcend war as an institution and to transform the underlying structures and cultural pathologies which legitimize and reinforce war and violence at all levels of society has not diminished. In fact, in many ways it has grown stronger.

The end of the 1980s was suffused with the promise of a new era in international relations, based on cooperation between the two superpowers rather than confrontation. The counter-culture logic of disarmament and peaceful conflict resolution promoted in the work of peace researchers and activists, and adopted at the strategic-political level in the UN Palme Commission's embrace of mutual and common security, offered the hope of a less violent future. Its contrast to the arms races and ever-present threat of a nuclear holocaust was resounding.

Encouraged by the possibility of reducing Cold War tensions and moving beyond the zero-sum (win/lose) mindsets that had stalemated previous attempts at disarmament and weapons reductions (seen as necessary precursors to the longer-term goals of détente and cooperation), Mikhail Gorbachev, then the new Soviet leader, proceeded unilaterally to slash military spending and reduce military force deployments from Eastern Europe to the Sino-Soviet border. As this new logic, *novoe politicheskow myslenie*, took hold and spread, a gradual reduction in conflict, at both the global and regional levels, could be seen around the world.

Today, this has been reversed. Now the world is confronted with a dramatic rise in intra- and inter-state conflicts on almost every continent, and a concomitant increase in global militarism and

militarization in the expansion of NATO/AMPO/TIAP, world
military expenditure approaching US$1 trillion and the proposed
new Star Wars defence system. The implosion of the Soviet Union
and the end of the Cold War brought not the realization of the
promise of *perestroika* and *glasnost*, but the dreary, familiar reality
of great power hegemony and realpolitik, and 'new world order'
heralded by the raining of bombs on Baghdad. More than ten years
later, the bombs are still falling, while the sanctions put in place
after the Gulf War have left a legacy of 1.9 million dead – in the
name of peace.

The dream of a world free from the scourge of war is seen by
many as naive and utopian, if not dangerously unrealistic, against
a logic that dictates that violence must be met with violence and
that peace is achievable only through the use of arms.

Yet this image is false. As noted time and time again throughout
history, violence begets violence: 'An eye for an eye will leave the
whole world blind' (Ghandi). The limited vision of those states
and ideologues able to identify only the act of violence and not its
roots, to respond with violence and not with alternatives and to
perpetuate the very acts they seek to condemn presents the world
with the spectre of an ever-worsening spiral of warfare and violence,
spreading to affect more and more regions around the globe. The
belief that these wars will be limited in scale and involve only those
countries in the poorer, 'developing' world is simply unrealistic.
There is no such thing as a purely intra- or inter-state conflict. The
nodes and networks linking actors across state boundaries dictate
that any conflict is likely to involve more parties than those fighting
directly on the ground, and far more than those normally
recognized in most media coverage. With the five major powers of
the UN Security Council responsible for more than 85 per cent of
the entire world's arms trade, most armies today are supplied by
the very governments that claim to stand for peace. While weapons
alone do not cause wars, they do enable them to ignite and spread,
making ever-increasing levels of violence more and more likely.
Rhetoric and Newspeak aside, political, economic and military
elites that speak in the name of peace and justice are often those
supporting or carrying out the worst crimes against humanity,
propping up structures and cultures of violence that bring
incredible destruction to people around the world.

Against this trend lies the growing recognition that humanitarian catastrophes and the structural and cultural violence underlying
them are at the core of many of today's wars. In addition, racist
mindsets and the belief that 'others' are somehow inferior and less
worthy are some of the most frequent assumptions leading to and
fuelling war. Historical legacies and memories of glory and trauma
quite often provide the fuel for future periods of expansion and

conflict. The need to develop early and effective mechanisms for violence prevention, to identify patterns and to transform the underlying structures and causes of violence is gaining increasing recognition. Yet today's approaches to conflict 'resolution' are in most cases conflict-enhancing, providing short- and medium-term solutions responsive to power interests, while threatening longer-term destabilizations and escalation. Conflict mediation, not peace-building or conflict transformation, is the dominant approach, accepted by states, peace researchers and NGOs alike.

Mediation: The Dominant Approach to Conflict Resolution – War-enhancing or Peace-building?

Setting the Stage

Mediation has long been accepted as the dominant approach to conflict resolution by peace researchers and practitioners in Western Europe and North America. It has been practised at many different levels and in many different settings, from worker–employer disputes to international trade agreements. It has been used, in one form or another, to settle conflicts between families, as well as those that arise between, or within, states. In most cases the basic approach, and the philosophy underlying it, is much the same: bringing parties together and working with them to find a solution acceptable to both/all sides.

At the same time, the rise of 'mediation experts' and the increasing participation of NGOs in conflict resolution have led to the 'marketing' of mediation. More and more mediation is put forward as a package of skills and exercises, a universal toolkit for solving conflicts. Pamphlets and training manuals expounding the benefits of one form of mediation over another abound. The message, constantly repeated, is that the skills and tools necessary to solve conflicts exist; all that is left to do is learn them and put them into practice. Yet while numerous books and essays have been written about the different approaches to mediation and its history of successes and failures in different settings and conflicts, one aspect has remained largely overlooked. Mediation, though practised around the world and in many different contexts, is predominantly a Western approach to conflict resolution. It is the product of a specific culture and psychological/ideological cosmology, which affect the way conflict is viewed and the tools we develop in response to it. The progeny of the environment in which it has been developed, it suffers from both the positive and negative aspects of its inheritance.

One of the aims of this chapter is to explore mediation from this new perspective, looking at it as the product of a specific psycho-social environment, and exploring the psychological and ideological assumptions inherent in its basic approach. A broader aim is to go beyond mediation as a tool of conflict resolution and suggest alternative approaches to understanding conflict and the methods and tools of conflict transformation which go with them. In order to do this, we will critically analyse *mediation in practice*, looking at the role of mediation in three conflicts: Israel–Palestine; the former Yugoslavia (including Kosovo/a); and Afghanistan. The limitation inherent in the Western, neoliberal perspective on conflict and conflict resolution will be explored in light of non-Western cultural perceptions and cosmologies related to conflict and its transformation. What is hoped is that by providing a broader framework in which to understand mediation and conflict, we will be able to take one step further in developing more holistic approaches to the peaceful transformation of conflicts and the structures, attitudes and cultures underlying them.

Mediation as a Tool for Conflict Resolution

As noted earlier, mediation is largely a Western/North American approach to the resolution of conflicts. The very belief that conflicts can or should be resolved is based on assumptions prevalent in Western understandings of conflict (with other cultures and approaches pointing more to the need to 'heal', 'transform', 'transcend' or 'go beyond'). Though much recent literature has indeed 'gone beyond' this concept, developing new terminologies such as conflict 'management' or conflict 'transformation', the basic assumptions underlying most approaches to mediation is that the result of the entire process is the *resolution* of conflict.

In most cases conflict is seen as the incompatibility (real or perceived) of goals between two or more parties or actors, giving rise to a contention, contradiction or dispute. The focus is on conflict *between* actors rather than *within* them. The process of mediation works to reframe the context of the conflict, to move actors away from positions of incompatibility and opposition towards a dialogue focusing on interests, similarities and goals. The role of the mediator is to serve as a *medium*, helping to facilitate dialogue, to *go between* the parties to the conflict, and slowly to bring them towards some kind of resolution. Increasing awareness has recognized that the solution to be found must be one that comes *from the parties to the conflict themselves*, and cannot be forced on them by the mediator or any other outside party. The extent to which this has been accepted by mediators or in the international arena, however, is open to question.

The focus of mediation is on the *actors*, and away from *relations* and *structures*. Its orientation is towards individuals or, more specifically, towards leaders and those in power. This is one of the main reasons why the vast majority of interactive conflict resolution and problem-solving workshops developed by conflict mediators, from the US and UK, focus almost exclusively on addressing attitudes and behaviours of the parties to a conflict, nearly always neglecting the context and contradiction in which a conflict occurs.

In most cases, and in almost all international mediation, it is a top-down and elitist approach. A significant drawback that results from this is the failure of mediation to work *in conjunction with* outside approaches and methods of conflict transformation. When this occurs in a setting outside Western Europe and North America (and arguably even within those settings) traditional and cultural approaches to conflict transformation and peace-building are marginalized, weakening a community's own ability to transform conflicts non-violently and discouraging participation. Thus peace actor empowerment, strengthening local resources and actors at a community and grass-roots level, plays very little role in traditional approaches to mediation and conflict resolution.

The basic assumption underlying this approach to conflict resolution at the top level is that in order to bring about the 'resolution' of a conflict it is necessary first to identify the representative leaders and get them to agree. Emphasis is placed on 'getting them to the table', synonymous in Western thinking with bringing them together in order to reach an agreement, but perhaps foreign to those who do not share this understanding. Too great a focus in bringing parties together is often based on a failure to recognize that time and healing may be needed before dialogue can begin and before an effective peace process can be implemented. At the same time, dialogue between the conflict or peace worker and the parties to the conflict may be a useful and sometimes necessary step before actually bringing opposing parties together. Often, this earlier stage can be useful in helping parties to understand the importance of recognizing the interests and needs of the other actors in a conflict and to focus on the conflict as a shared problem to be overcome, rather than as a force splitting them apart.

The all too frequent focus on leaders assumes not only that the appropriate representatives can be identified, but that they will articulate and advocate the interests of those they are meant to represent. The fact that parties to a conflict might feel left out and neglected if not invited to participate in the process is real, and may lead to destabilization and threats to the process by those so excluded. The desire to reach an agreement and punish those seen as guilty or extremists often leads mediators to focus on moderates, ignoring those perceived as 'hard-liners' or 'war criminals' and refusing to involve them in the mediation. The effect may be to dismiss the needs, concerns and fears of those the 'hard-liners' represent, leading certain segments of the populations involved to feel neglected and ignored, fuelling a sense of dissatisfaction and alienation from the process. In the case of the Oslo Accords between Israel and the PLO, the failure to involve the 'hard-liners' on all sides led to the assassination of Yitzak Rabin, then Israel's prime minister, increased car bombings and suicide attacks, the election of a right-leaning government which threatened to (and essentially did) destroy the entire process, and the eventual re-explosion of war following Ariel Sharon's visit to the Temple Mount in September 2000 and Ehud Barak's provocative and massive deployment of overwhelming force.

In Ireland similar difficulties have been experienced, further complicated by the fact that one of the parties acting as a 'neutral' mediator is the former colonial master against whom one of the sides has been struggling.

A further difficulty often overlooked is the belief that those in leadership positions will be able to guarantee compliance to the agreement and deliver the support of their respective communities. The problems faced by parties involved in mediation in 're-entering' and convincing their constituencies to support the deal are often enough to break an agreement even before it has been implemented. Resistance to peace can sometimes be strong, as those who have a vested interest in maintaining the conflict, as well as those who believe that their fundamental needs and fears have not been addressed, mobilize to protect their interests. The belief that those involved in the mediation have sold out to the other side and betrayed those they were meant to represent may be exacerbated if again the parties to the conflict have been excluded from the beginning.

What mediation most often fails to address, however, are the underlying causes and structures which generate conflict. Also ignored are the residual traumas, psychological and physical suffering, and the enemy perceptions generated and enforced by conflict and violence. While bringing leaders together for an agreement may be sufficient to bring about a cease-fire or peace agreement, it does not deal with the damaged relationships or the human suffering which conflicts engender. The capacity of one conflict to create new conflicts, of pain and suffering to form the basis of lingering hatred, fear and enmity and to explode into further violence, is left untransformed. In this context 'peace' agreements are often simply the continuation of war by other means.

Mediation to a large extent assumes the replication of Western structures of hierarchy, social 'governance' and 'free market' economic systems, while overlooking, marginalizing and neglecting other structures and communities. Where these are lacking, the ability of leaders to guarantee acceptance of an agreement is called into doubt. Rather than focusing on the restoration of damaged relationships, on healing and reconstruction, both physical and emotional/psychological, mediation focuses on getting an agreement. It often neither addresses nor even recognizes the changed structures and relations, the polarization and enmity, which conflict gives rise to. Where mediation (when successful) is useful is in bringing an end to fighting, a clarification of the positions and interests of both sides and the necessity to go beyond conflict as a destructive and damaging relationship. At best it can create the space for future healing, the restoration of broken and damaged relationships, and an understanding of the positive, generative, constructive forces of conflict. Mediation alone, however, cannot bring peace, and agreements reached between top leaders may often result in the outbreak of future conflicts and wars.

Where Theory Meets Practice

In order to understand mediation *as it actually happens* we need to look at the role of mediation in practice. So far we have focused primarily on mediation as a concept and an approach. Later, we will concentrate on the psychological assumptions about conflict that underlie this approach, while introducing several other perspectives and the approaches that they generate. The focus now, however, will be locating mediation in the real world of conflict and conflict transformation.

To do so we will look at three conflicts: Israel–Palestine; former Yugoslavia (including Kosovo/a); and Afghanistan. Each of these are conflict nodes that have weighed and will continue to weigh heavily in defining the new world order – because that threatened and threaten potential escalation, drawing in regional and other actors; because they embroil crucial issues of international law and governance; and because of the extensive external state and non-state involvement.

What is presented here is a critical analysis of the 'solution' brought about by mediation and general lessons from the failures and successes of top-level mediation and peace agreements arrived at from above, or imposed from outside, rather than generated by those party to a conflict, which induces not just state actors and other elites, but groups, organizations, individuals and social networks at every level of society. The experience gained from these examples points to the need to go beyond mediation as an approach to conflict resolution and to deepen peace-building efforts by working to promote more extensive involvement in peace work by actors at a number of different levels. Rather than focusing solely on specific actors involved in the mediation and the mediation process itself, we shall attempt to locate them within the broader narrative of the general conflict dynamics and more specifically to look at how the agreements arrived at affect the deeper structures and processes of the three conflicts and contributed or failed to contribute, towards the promotion of peace.

Israel–Palestine: The Oslo Accords Peace Agreement or Occupation?

At the time they were announced, the Oslo Accords were seen as one of the most promising developments in the new world order. The product of a series of secret meetings between Israeli and Palestinian negotiators in a cottage outside Oslo, the Accords were heralded as a breakthrough in a conflict that had lasted since shortly after the end of the Second World War. Both the Israelis and the Palestinians, long-term adversaries and sworn enemies, promised to put down their guns and work together towards peace. For Norway, it was a testament to the role middle-level powers could play on the world stage and the victory of mediation where guns and bombs had failed. Less focused on were the reasons why the negotiations were held in the first place, or what real and lasting contribution would be made in transforming the conflict on the ground towards peace. An agreement between leaders. What was left was to see how it would be implemented.

With the *Intifada*, Israel was faced with the first large-scale popular opposition to its occupation of Palestine since it began in 1948.[1] Increasing awareness of and sympathy for the plight of the Palestinians was leading to widespread condemnation and criticism of Israel. Repeated UN Resolutions censured Israel and were opposed only by the US and Israel itself and, on one occasion, Dominica, acting as a faithful US colony. Rising numbers of Israeli youth began to refuse military service in the occupied territories and a few were sent to jail for refusing to serve altogether. Those who did serve often returned with first-hand experience of the brutality of Israeli rule. The stories they told their families helped make them more aware also.

A well-organized movement on the part of the Palestinians, popularly supported and participated in, together with increasing international support for an independent Palestine and criticism of Israel and a slowly forming body of dissidents in Israel who opposed their government's policy of occupation and annexation, encouraged the government to recognize the necessity to look for a way out of the situation, which was beginning to look less favourable.[2] At the same time, the Palestinian economic boycott of Israel was becoming increasingly painful to Israeli businesses, and the need to transform the Israeli economy to more high-tech industries with a large service sector led to increasing support for the peace process from members of the Israeli elite and corporate sectors.

Meanwhile, the PLO, in exile in Tunisia, was finding itself marginalized and faced the threat of losing contact with the realities on the ground in Palestine. Having failed to provide any meaningful support for the *Intifada*, it had wasted its resources in continuing negotiations in Cairo, negotiations that appeared ever more futile in the face of Israeli intransigence. Both within the PLO and without calls were being made for the democratization of the PLO.

As corruption within the PLO became more evident, those within Palestine were less willing to lend it their support. An ageing leadership drawn largely from the elite of Palestinian society-in-exile risked being replaced by younger leaders, many of whom had risen up from the strong grass-roots organization of the *Intifada*. The necessity of linking the organizational and international structure of the PLO to the popular movement of the Palestinian people was recognized and called for, threatening to sideline Yasser Arafat and the traditional leadership in favour of more democratic forces.

The Oslo Accords represented a way out for both the Israeli and PLO leaderships. Through the Accords, Israel was able to enter negotiations with a weakened opposition in the form of the PLO's representatives (still damaged by their support for Saddam Hussein in the Gulf War), rather than with the grass-roots movement of the *Intifada*. For the PLO the Accords represented a means of fulfilling their promise to the people of Palestine and returning to Palestine as liberators and heroes. The reality of the Accords, however, was a reversal of what the Palestinians had been able to achieve over the previous five decades. No mention was made of the Palestinians' right to a state, something that numerous UN Resolutions had demanded. A loose timetable was laid down for Israeli withdrawal from some Palestinian territories, with no provision for enforcement or for checking that it was being kept.

Significantly, the Oslo agreement was not a peace process between two peoples or states, but an agreement between the Israeli government and the PLO. By recognizing the West Bank and Gaza Strip as 'disputed' territories, both sides having an equal right, Arafat effectively legitimized Israeli claims to the land, something decades of occupation had failed to do.[3] The future map envisaged by the Accords was a fragmented Palestine surrounded on almost all sides by Israeli territory and economically dependent on Israel. To further this process, the right of Israel to build an interlinking network of roads and highways connecting its various colonies and dividing Palestine still further was guaranteed in the Accords. More critical analysts have pointed to the interests of Israeli business in turning Palestine into a service sector and market for the Israeli economy.

Thus the Oslo Accords failed in almost every way to lay the foundations for a stable and lasting peace. They did not deal with any of the questions most relevant to the conflict or the underlying structures and mindsets. The issue of water distribution, of vital concern to all the countries of the Middle East, was not even touched on. Support and cooperation between the political and governmental levels at which the negotiations were carried out, and the network of grass-roots organizations and institutions throughout Israel and Palestine, were virtually non-existent (and remain so today). The suffering, traumas and enemy images developed as a result of one of the longest-lasting occupations in postwar history were left unresolved. Instead, promises of 'self-governance' and an independent Palestine *in some form* if not a state were issued, while how to build peace, to make it meaningful for the millions of people in Israel and Palestine, was left for the future. That even those promises would be betrayed as the rate of Israeli settlements and colonization of the occupied territories increased, was soon obvious. As events unfolded, it became clear that the Oslo Accords were no more or less than the 'peace' to end all peace.

A Note on the Wye River Agreement

Building on the process entrenched in Oslo, the Wye River Agreement significantly reduced the amount of territory (from 30 per cent to 13 per cent) to be placed under Palestinian control. Since Oslo, more than 600 Palestinian homes have been demolished and 140,000 dunums of Palestinian land confiscated, reflecting Israel's continuing determination to grab as much land as possible before a final settlement is reached.[4]

Significantly, the major issue dealt with in the Wye River Agreement is security. Palestinian responsibility to 'combat terrorism and fight violence' is repeatedly attested to, while no analogous responsibilities are given to Israel. This is all the more startling in light of the fact that, according to B'Tselem, a leading human rights organization in Israel, many more Palestinians than Israelis have been killed since the signing of the Oslo Accords (up to October 1998: 356 Palestinians; 251 Israelis). Palestinian responsibility for prosecuting terrorist suspects is emphasized, while 'there continues to be almost total impunity for unlawful killings of Palestinians' (Amnesty International). Since Oslo, and resulting from the frequent Israeli 'closures', the 'Palestinian standard of living has fallen by nearly 40 per cent, with 30 per cent of the

workforce unemployed and 40 per cent of the population living at
or below the poverty line'.[5]
The Oslo process and the Wye River Agreement marked the
continuation of occupation, not its abatement. Through them,
Palestine is left with less autonomy than South Africa's Bantustans
under apartheid. The interim period allowed for in Oslo was not
used to build trust, but to consolidate Israeli domination of the
occupied territories. The Wye River Agreement and the Oslo
Accords before it put in place a Palestinian façade allowing for
continued Israeli rule, with Israel following the traditional model
of neo-colonialism and establishing local gendarmes to keep order
in its place. A year after Oslo, Israel's control of West Bank land
reached about 75 per cent, up from 65 per cent when the Accords
were signed, while water supplies to Gaza have been halved.[6] In the
West Bank, for every litre of water available to one Palestinian,
one Israeli settler consumes 876 litres.[7] Since then, the situation
has deteriorated further, with continued seizures of Palestinian
land and flagrant violations of the Oslo Accords. The farcical
charade now being played out in the Middle East leaves little or no
hope that the process begun in Israel can lead to the establishment
of a real and lasting peace in Israel/Palestine. Instead, the 'peace
process' itself, in grand Orwellian fashion, has been transformed
into a cover for continued expansion and expropriation of land
and denial of even the most basic human rights to the Palestinian
people. A process that fuels violence, not peace.

Update, 2001

Discussions and analysis of recent events in Israel/Palestine by area
specialists, political leaders, peace workers, journalists, human
rights activists and others have been cause for both encouragement
and a great deal of concern. The situation in Israel and Palestine
and throughout the Middle East is alarming, but in no way
surprising. From Cairo to Oslo, to Wye River, Paris and back to
Cairo and Camp David, the peace process of the past decade has
addressed none of the underlying causes of the conflict. It has
promoted solutions which themselves further enforce the structure
of violence, and has sought to ensconce the hegemony and
domination of one of the parties to the conflict. Anger and
frustration at one of the most oppressive and exploitative structures
of violence in the world has exploded into war, exacerbated by the
use of violence on all sides. The cycle of violence, recrimination,
fear and anger is growing and, given the complete absence of any
real attempts at peace on the part of the leadership of either the
Israelis or the Palestinians can be expected to continue. Following
the attacks on the World Trade Center and the Pentagon on 11

September, the Israeli government and military have taken advantage of the fact that the attention of the world has been distracted elsewhere to launch massive military attacks and interventions into the occupied territories. Terrorism on both sides is increasing. Any 'peace' which would be accepted today on the terms put forward by the Israeli government and the US would not be peace; nor would it be a solution to the causes and structures of the conflict in Israel–Palestine. Instead, it would be a continuation of war by other means.

To protest against the violence that has now exploded in Israel–Palestine, to seek to come up with creative and non-violent ways of transforming the conflict, and to work actively for the promotion of peace are necessary and vital. To do this, without trying to understand what really lies behind the conflict, or without trying to address any of the injustices or inequalities behind the violence, is to perpetuate a war, which has continued in one form or another for over 50 years. Peace must be inclusive. It must be open to participation by all actors and all parties, and include recognition of the basic humanity and dignity of all involved. But it cannot be blind.

This is a call for direct, non-violent action and solidarity between those working for the promotion of peace and to transform the conflict through peaceful means, based on the recognition that:

- Peace will be brought about only through honest attempts to address the underlying dynamics and structures of the conflict and through recognition of the needs and human rights of all Palestinians and Israelis.
- No meaningful peace can be brought about that is based on exploitation, annexation, continuing occupation or the use of terror.
- Support for peace also demands direct and sustained action in support of peace, echoing Edward Said's call for mass non-violent struggle in Palestine and welcoming true solidarity between Israelis and Palestinians committed to building peace on the formula 'no exploitation, no surrender', the catchwords of Ghandi's struggle for *swaraj*.
- Israelis and Palestinians both have the right to live in security, have access to water and land, to the same basic social, economic, cultural, political and civil freedoms, freedom of movement, worship and travel.

What is necessary is an end to Newspeak, to the culture of violence and racism, the propaganda and the belief that one or the other side is 'less than human', which has so often been at the heart of war – whether fought through economic or military means. Peace is a struggle. Peace by peaceful means defines that struggle as non-violent. It is not something that will simply fall into our laps or appear because we close our eyes and wish the violence would go away. For too long our eyes have been closed. This is why we are seeing the violence that is exploding today. One question we must all ask ourselves, as experts, journalists, politicians and 'peace workers' fill the pages of newspapers and journals with their articles and analysis, is why has it taken this long? Why did we wait, why did we ignore the violence, the daily killing of Palestinians over so many years, the destruction of homes, the situation in the refugee camps? Why did we wait, and how can we now believe ourselves to be satisfying our conscience because we respond to the sight of children being shot, buildings blown up and stones being thrown? The number of Palestinians that have died since Oslo because of lack of access to medicines, because of poor health and economic collapse in the occupied territories, because of the slow death of structural violence, exceeds the number of those killed in the latest outbreak of war. Were their deaths any the less horrific; were their lives any less worthy or sacred, because they weren't captured on the evening news? This is a question we must be willing to ask ourselves, for the people of Palestine and of Israel, because if we truly believe, as we should, that Israelis and Palestinians have the right to live in peace, not to fear car bombs and 'terrorism', then we must recognize that this can only happen if Israelis and Palestinians are willing to work for a true, just and honest peace, and if outside powers stop intervening to prevent it. We cannot be satisfied with being silent. If we are, we are only helping the war to continue.

Former Yugoslavia: The Dayton Agreement – Enforced 'Peace'

The Dayton Agreement marked the continuation of the post-Cold War, essentially war culture-driven approach to conflict resolution heralded by the Oslo Accords. It bore testament to the continuing movement away from the less rigid, more creative, Gorbachevian alternative which brought an end to the Cold War by addressing the underlying causes and structures of conflict and 'untying the Gordian knot', and a return to the essentially power-driven aspirations of realpolitik and its concomitant embrace of enforced peacemaking.[8] An excellent cease-fire though a lousy peace agreement, the Dayton Agreement laid the foundations for a state between non-peace and non-war, accompanied by re-arming and remilitarization of the federation and troops placed along the internal demarcation line between the Federation and Republika Srpska, solidifying the divide, rather than along the country's borders. Thus Bosnia was divided into a state with two entities and at least three nations, and made the only state in the world to exist with no prefix, just a geographical name. To call Dayton a 'peace' agreement is to mix terminology, to cover over its underlying faults and contradictions and to hide from view the structures and foundations it is built on.

The imposition of 'great power' *diktat*, brought on by NATO air-strikes against Serbian positions (in 1995), ignored other policy prescription alternatives and instead laid the foundations for a 'Cold War' peace, which ended the fighting by placing a layer of concrete, in the form of NATO troops, on otherwise unresolved conflicts and traumas. The devastation and destruction brought about by the war, not least to the lives and relationships of the people of Bosnia-Herzegovina, remained only insufficiently addressed. Forgotten by the negotiations in Dayton were the victims of the war, not only those who died, but those who survived, the *people* from *all* sides as opposed to the media-portrayed images/caricatures of suffering Muslims and evil Serbs (and less frequently mentioned Croats). The victors of peace were those who had risen to power through the war and/or earlier, through the promotion of xenophobic, ethnocentric and exclusive visions which both gave rise to and formed its course. The rush to hold early elections immediately after the fighting had stopped and before any time for healing had been given, led to a freezing of the situation and acceptance of the political forces born in the war, now given greater, quasi-democratic legitimacy through election results. The government then established was based on a federative state with no source of direct income, in which the assembly of Bosnia-Herzegovina is to be consulted by 14 Serbian, 14 Bosnian-Muslim and 14 Croatian representatives, preventing Serbs from voting for Croats, Croats for Bosniaks, Bosniaks for Serbs and vice versa, and forcing 9.2 per cent of the population who are not Croat, Serb or Muslim to choose between them.

By forcing the people of Bosnia-Herzegovina together without allowing the time and space necessary for healing to take place and the natural restoration of relationships which would go with it, the architects of Dayton effectively prescribed a recipe for continuing fears and uncertainties. Dramatically skewed distribution of aid, with the overwhelming majority of humanitarian and postwar reconstruction assistance going to the Muslim-Croat Federation (in 1996–97 the numbers were 98 per cent to the Federation and 2 per cent to Republika Srpska, with only slight improvements since then) was accompanied by massive shipments of arms to and military training for the Bosnian government (predominantly Muslim) forces.[9] Lack of concern for the realities on the ground, or for the trauma and sufferings experienced by people on all sides, was reflected in the imposition of *peace by force* as embodied in the 60,000-strong I-FOR and later S-FOR contingents. Military build-ups and a hardening of conflict lines, instead of disarmament and reconciliation, are the main legacies of Dayton.

The most significant shortcoming of the Dayton Agreement, however, was in its failure to solve, or even address, any of the underlying conflicts involved in the wars in former Yugoslavia. While it did stop military activity by the major actors involved on the ground, the *theoretical, conceptual, structural* and *practical* failures of decision-makers to deal with the *roots* of the conflict has left the region with the potential for a future bloody sequel to a war which, at many levels, never ended. The apportioning of blame by the War Crimes Tribunal in the Hague, and the extremely lopsided distribution of aid has served to institutionalize and deepen the structural divide between the 'two' sides, promoting hostilities and distrust rather than serving to overcome them.

In such instances, as in most postwar situations, aid can be a powerful tool. If, rather than seeking to punish the Serbs and apportion to them collective responsibility and guilt for the war, the countries providing aid had sought to invest heavily in reconstruction, physical and psycho-social, with programmes developed to assist all parties, and aid provided on a massive scale, reminiscent perhaps of the postwar Marshall Plan for Europe, connections and ties between the communities could have been established much more easily, with peace growing up from within as well, rather than simply enforced on the contestants from abroad. *A force-based* or *imposed peace* or 'cease-fire', such as the one reached between Milosevic, Izetbegovic and Tudjman in Ohio in 1995, may end the fighting, but it cannot in and of itself bring peace. In the end, it may even prove a recipe for war.

Rambouillet – Peace or Imperialism?

This latest approach to great power mediation had little (if anything) to do with creating peace for the suffering people of Kosovo/a. At best it could be seen as the latest example in a long series of interventions and gunboat diplomacy by the world's last remaining superpower (from Iraq, Haiti, Somalia, former Yugoslavia, Afghanistan, Sudan, etc). At worst it showed the brutal manipulation of Serbs and Albanians alike while the so-called international community waited for the conflict to become violent before intervening to impose a 'solution' so distasteful as to be unacceptable to all sides. In the end, it became an excuse by which the existence of a local authoritarian regime was used as a justification by 19 'democracies' to promote authoritarianism on a global scale, placing NATO countries above and beyond the authority of the UN Charter and Security Council, and NATO *diktat* beyond the realm of international law.

Rather than lending support to the non-violent strategies of Ibrahim Rugova, or the dissidents and citizens' organizations calling for democracy in Belgrade, Western mediators, statesmen and decision-makers ignored the warnings of hundreds of peace researchers and area specialists for more than ten years, waiting until hard-liners and war-promoting policies were entrenched on all sides before becoming involved. As Jan Oeberg of TFF points out: 'if peace in Kosovo or the wider Balkans had been the real aim, we would have witnessed a completely different approach leading up to Rambouillet.'[10] To argue therefore that there were no alternatives, or that the choice was one between bombing and sitting back and doing nothing, is to falsify the reality of what actually occurred and to promote a simplifying of policy beyond all recognition.

Unlike former Yugoslavia in 1991–92, it is impossible to say that the events that unfolded in Kosovo/a were 'unforeseen'. For more than ten years, anyone with even the slightest knowledge of the region could have predicted the possibility of a violent explosion if the underlying structures and causes of the conflict – including grinding poverty, extensive repression and police brutality, and deep mistrust and fear on both sides – were ignored. Dozens of peace organizations, not the least of which are TRANSCEND, TFF and the ICL/Praxis for Peace, warned repeatedly of the possibility of escalating violence. The problem was not a lack of early warning, but a lack of listening, combined with a completely different agenda on the part of those in power.

Granted the miserable posturing and policies of the 'international community' to the Federal Republic of Yugoslavia and its province of Kosovo/a *before* the current outbreak, what can explain the state of diplomacy *now*, before, during and after Rambouillet and the war that followed it? Why is it that those presented as mediators and self-proclaimed 'conflict workers' singularly failed to put forth any creative and viable alternatives to the bloodshed capable of winning the confidence and support of both sides? Why this reliance on the menacing presence of NATO troops, warships and fighter planes to the detriment of good policy and sound reasoning? While NATO commanders and government spokespeople claim to have learned the lessons of Bosnia – giving voice to the memory and horror of Srebenica and other massacres as justification and illustration of the need to intervene – the same mistakes, the same apportioning of blame and failure to address the structures and causes of the violence, and the fear and suffering generated, are evident. As Dayton's shortcomings and the legacy of conflict mismanagement led to the war in Kosovo and the 79-

day bombing campaign, so would the failings of Rambouillet and the end of that war lead to the explosion of violence and a near-civil war in Macedonia only a short while later.

If the powers at Rambouillet had been seriously interested in peace, they would have started supporting alternative voices and visions within Serbia and Kosovo/a long before the outbreak of violence. The would have suggested the more acceptable alternative of a UN-led and UN-mandated peace force (possibly as an extension of the recently cancelled UNPREDEP and concomitant OECD missions in Macedonia) to monitor the region at the invitation of Belgrade, rather than presenting the Serbian government with the humiliating spectre of NATO occupation. (Or, as suggested by the then leader of the Nordic battalions serving in Macedonia, they could have extended UNPREDEP's mission to the Kosovo/a–Albanian border and halted the flow of arms into the region.)

They would have worked to promote a wide-based and extensive dialogue between Serbs and Albanians geared towards developing viable alternatives, which would have been acceptable to both sides, and encouraged LDK (League for a Democratic Kosova) and dissidents in Serbia to unite to promote democracy and the human rights and freedoms of all the people in the region, laying the foundations for a wider, regional approach to peace-building and security by promoting cooperation with other groups in the region.

They would have lent far more support than they did to free media and independent journalism within Yugoslavia which could have prevented a more complex and objective picture of the grievances and concerns of both Albanians and Serbs, rather than repeated portrayals of black/white, good vs. evil, so often found in the media of both sides, and internationally as well. And they would have done away with the policies they have supported for the last ten years which have served to strengthen the position of hard-liners and nationalists on all sides, promoting punishment and condemnation of those perceived as 'evil' (applied not only to individuals, but entire peoples), and embraced more open, creative and multi-layered approaches to peace-building and peace actor empowerment, based on extensive and far-reaching cooperation with actors on all sides.

But the mediators and 'conflict workers' at Rambouillet were not interested in peace, nor were they interested in working to resolve the underlying structures and causes of the conflict in Kosovo/a. The goals lay in their own interests and great power pursuits, in their imposition of their vision of how the Balkans should look, and in the build-up and stationing of a massive force of NATO soldiers in Kosovo/a, enlarging from Italy, Hungary, the Adriatic, Bosnia, Albania and Macedonia and on to Greece and Turkey.

As pointed out by Jan Oeberg: 'with US/NATO influence in Turkey, Greece, Georgia (and Azerbaijan?) and in Croatia, Bosnia, Albania, Hungary and Serbia, the goal of connecting NATO West and NATO East becomes more reachable, leading to a longer perspective, to more control with the "devilish triangle" of the Balkans, Middle East and the Caucasus – the end stations of which are a) permanent containment of Russia and b) access to the oil in the Caspian Sea region.'[11] In this picture, the existence of US Camp Bond Steel just outside Pristina, the largest military base built anywhere in the world outside the US in the last 30 years, takes on increased significance.

What was in Rambouillet presented as mediation and an opportunity for peace between the parties to the conflict was in reality, and in the words of Henry Kissinger, an 'ultimatum', which was not meant to be accepted. For NATO, the false dichotomy between bombing and doing nothing was based on a 'moral' argument in which an entire population was bombed and terrorized and where the object of NATO attacks was not the Yugoslav Army or leadership, but the citizens of Yugoslavia. After 79 days of bombing, begun on 24 March, only a third of the targets were of a military nature, with less than 5 per cent of the 2,000–3,000 bomb victims participants in the war in Kosovo/a. To this can be added the many tens of thousands killed in fighting between Serbs and Kosovars, and the nearly one million Kosovar Albanians forced from their homes by the terror that followed, including ethnic cleansing and destruction of houses and entire villages by the Serbian military and paramilitary forces – now given licence by NATO that they did not have before.[12]

However, even if we accept the arguments and logic of the NATO forces (those condemning large-scale ethnic cleansing and terror against Kosovsar Albanians deserved support, of course), in order to accept this principle there must be at least a modicum of generalization, so that if one country is to be treated in a certain way, other countries should be treated the same way for the same action. (In the case of Croatia, which had done the same thing to the Serbs in Krajina in 1996, and in the case of Turkey, whose treatment of the Kurds is, if anything, worse, nothing was done.) To be against the bombing campaign, therefore, is not the same as being in favour of the terror and repression imposed by the Serb forces, and the KLA (Kosovo Liberation Army) in Kosovo/a, but to recognize that alternatives did and do exist, and that the victims of the bombing were both Serbs and Albanians, people on all sides, not simply military targets, as NATO spokesmen suggested.

NATO bombing not only violated the UN Charter, it also violated NATO's own constitution, as well as those of three NATO members (Italy, Germany and Greece). By conducting an offensive war against a country which had not already attacked them, and without explicit support from the UN Security Council, NATO opened the way for future 'peacekeeping' and 'peace-enforcing' missions against any country it feels violates the interests and concerns of NATO member countries. With 'humanitarian intervention' as a fig-leaf, the devastation and destruction brought to the entire region by NATO bombing and the war on the ground derailed any chance of peace and escalated the fighting far beyond anything that could otherwise have been foreseen. The scale of the fighting that followed created the very conditions that the bombing was intended to prevent.

With an estimated US$50–100 billion in damages, Yugoslavia now faces the awesome task of reconstruction in a society in which half the workforce is unemployed. The cleavages and traumas caused by the fighting and terror, both from the air and on the ground, have all but extinguished the possibility that the Serbs and Albanians can live together in peace in the near future. While NATO prepares to keep its forces in Kosovo/a for a minimum of three years, the violence and tensions on the ground continue to escalate and threaten further destabilization. Continuing a recent donors' meeting in which development and reconstruction aid for the Balkans, excluding Serbia, was discussed, will only reduce the chances for a real and sustainable peace. The treat of a possibly violent civil war in Serbia or of increased conflicts between Serbia and Montenegro loom. After 79 days of one the largest bombing campaigns in history, it was the roots of violence, not the roots of peace, which were planted in the Balkans. Macedonia bears witness to this.

Afghanistan – The Promise and Failure of Global *Perestroika* and the Geneva Accords

The approaches to conflict resolution and the ramifications of the Afghan conflict in the wider, international setting are interesting for a number of reasons. First, Afghanistan represented one of the bloodiest confrontations of the Cold War. It involved massive expenditures (economic, military, political) on all sides, and potential escalation, threatening to destabilize Afghanistan's neighbours and hardening lines of conflict and confrontation. On the other hand, it confronted the Soviet Union with the spectre of a continuing war which could not be won – although it was not lost – and led to the search for alternative solutions to conflict transformation, solutions that would affect the resolution of conflicts in a number of settings, and not only in Afghanistan.

In 2001, however, Afghanistan would once again come into the world's focus: 1) for harbouring Osama bin Laden, suspected by the US of masterminding the 11 September attacks; 2) as the first target of the US 'war on terrorism'; and 3) as the conflict arena of the first major war in the twenty-first century. All these the legacies of a decade of neglect and complete conflict mismanagement. Throughout the 1990s the only major external involvement in Afghanistan, beyond pathetically small amounts of aid, by regional powers (most noticeably Pakistan, but also Iran, Tajikistan, Uzbekistan), UNOCAL (one of the US's largest oil companies), Russia and the US was to contribute negatively to the further exacerbation of the conflict and the partisan support for one or other of the warring factions. The US (UNOCAL)–Pakistan (ISI)-backed Taliban were, at the start of the twenty-first century, to become the primary targets of the world's only superpower as it failed to develop any meaningful policy to root out and destroy the 'terrorism' it had done much to create, sponsor and support. In more ways than one, Afghanistan represents the tragic failure of post-Cold War *war culture*-driven approaches to conflict (mis)management and the continuing legacy of that failure in the twenty-first century.

The change in strategy implemented by Gorbachev and the Soviet Union in bringing an end to the war and their occupation of Afghanistan heralded the promise of a new era of international cooperation. The Geneva Accords were characteristic of a more dramatic change taking place on the world stage. Their failure, and the failure of all subsequent attempts to mediate a settlement in Afghanistan, point to the inadequacies of great power mediation and imposed conflict resolution and to the disturbing developments brought about since the end of the Cold War. In addition, and perhaps more importantly, they outline the road and the challenges that lie ahead.

Like all conflicts looked on from above, the war in Afghanistan involved (and continues to involve) extensive interference and intervention by outside parties. Its 'resolution' (though not ultimately successful), and the process that led to it in the form of the Geneva Accords, was hailed a success for the UN and opened the way for the 'resolution' of a number of other regional conflicts – from Nicaragua, El Salvador, Cambodia, Angola to the Iran–Iraq War in the Middle East.[13] It represented a rise in the authority and prestige of the world's only truly global body with extensive experience and background in a number of different conflict settings around the world and opened the way for great power cooperation rather than confrontation. In a February 1988 speech, Gorbachev recognized Afghanistan as virtually the first regional conflict to inspire the US and USSR to approach a cooperative settlement.

The impact of the Soviet Union's involvement in Afghanistan on internal Soviet politic, something commonly overlooked by analysts, played a vital role in breaking the mould of Brezhnev's Moscow and opening the way to new challenges and new ideas embodied in Gorbachev's policies of reform and reconstruction. Just as the work of peace researchers and activists from the 1950s to the 1980s – brought into mainstream political and strategic discourse through their confirmation in the Palme Commission's embrace of mutual and common security – had been vital in providing the intellectual foundations and inspiration for Gorbachev's later reforms, the war in Afghanistan, more than any other conflict, served to discredit the established norms and values of great power rivalry and *Realpolitik* which so characterized the Cold War. Cooperation, dialogue and trust-building were proposed as alternatives to zero-sum rivalries and win/lose scenarios, or the more common reality of lose/lose in which both parties suffer – even the one claiming to have won.

The devastation of the war on the social and physical infra-structure of Afghanistan, leading to more than 1.5 million dead over the past two decades, was the price paid for ending the Cold War and the promise of a new age of international cooperation. The subsequent defeat of that promise is perhaps the greatest betrayal of the people of Afghanistan and can be seen in the legacy of Afghanistan's civil war, as well as the other approaches to conflict resolution discussed above. It is also the root of the war in and over Afghanistan in 2001–02.

The impact of Afghanistan on the Soviet Union was vital. One need not look far in history to see that nearly every major policy change in Russia has been preceded by a defeat in war. Failure in the Crimea served as a catalyst for the reforms of the 1860s, including the abolition of serfdom, and it was defeat in the Russo-Japanese War and virtual defeat and catastrophe in the First World War, which led respectively to the revolutions of 1905 and 1917. Similarly in Afghanistan, extensive Russian losses, in terms of a significant loss of international goodwill (particularly from the 'Islamic' and 'developing' world), huge military and aid expenditures – representing a tremendous drain on much needed resources for the conversion of military to civilian economy and production of consumer goods – and the high cost of human lives and worsening morale in the army discredited hawks and military hard-liners and opened the way to far more creative and flexible thinking. The failure of the 40th army to secure military victory (although it did succeed in securing cities and bases) served to discredit high-ranking political and military personnel who had risen to prominence under Brezhnev, and opened the way for a new generation more sympathetic to the goals and ideals of the new Soviet leader, Mikhail Gorbachev.

As early as 17 October 1985, in a Politburo meeting in Moscow, Gorbachev made clear his intention to withdraw Soviet forces from Afghanistan and had this message conveyed to the leadership of the PDPA in Kabul. This was stated even more emphatically by Gorbachev on 20 July 1987 when he called a high-level Afghan delegation to meet him face to face: 'You had better be ready in twelve months because we are going whether you are ready or not. You must strengthen your political base.'[14] On 13 November 1986, the Politburo had secretly decided to withdraw Soviet troops by the end of 1988 and encourage the replacement of the 'communist' PDPA with a broader coalition, a regime of national reconciliation. Continued dedication to a military solution by Washington/Reagan and failure to perceive the sincerity of Gorbachev's attempts to transcend the mutually defeating rivalry of the Cold War, impeded resolution.

While representative of the gradual embrace of a new era of cooperative politics and international conflict resolution, the Geneva Accords also suffered from the number of significant failings, which prevented their eventual realization. The mediations were essentially conducted by parties foreign to the traditional and cultural social structures in Afghanistan, that is, the PDPA and the government of Pakistan, supported respectively by the USSR and US. Failure to include representatives of the *mujaheddin* or the resistance parties, or traditional and local leaders, discredited the UN in Afghanistan and left out the major forces of opposition to the government in Kabul. Failure to confront or present alternatives to the growing war economy, the lack of adequate support and involvement from people *inside* Afghanistan, and the continued flow of arms from abroad – all served to destabilize and eventually destroy what had been gained through Geneva.

The UN mediators' dual-track approach, with the first track aimed at resolution of the international dimensions of the dispute – the presence of Soviet troops, external aid to anti-government forces and the flight of Afghan refugees to neighbouring countries – while the second, discrete track discussed the future Afghan government, failed to make adequate provisions for continued intransigence by both outside and internal parties to the conflict. The support structure and implementation process was extremely weak, not least because it was based on traditional, state-driven mediation techniques in a context in which the entire language and discourse of the state had little meaning in the traditional 'Western' state. It was a means for the disentanglement of the

Soviet Union and the US, allowing them to direct their attention elsewhere. What it failed to do, however, was to generate the foundations for a lasting and viable alternative to the war by addressing the *internal* effects of the war on *Afghan* society and social relations. *transformation story (Bush. Folger)*

As a treaty to end the Cold War and lay the foundations for peaceful cooperation and coexistence between two superpowers it was a success. As an imposed solution to end the war in Afghanistan, it was a failure. While it removed the 'cancerous' growth of the Afghan conflict from the limelight of international affairs, it failed to remove it from the social and physical reality of Afghanistan. The war continues unabated. The promise heralded by Gorbachev's reforms of *perestroika* and *glasnost* have been turned into a mockery, replaced by the resounding noise of bombs and the levelling of threats, the tools of conflict resolution so often embraced by the world's one remaining superpower as it attempts to discipline 'recalcitrant children' and heads of state. Instead of an age of peace and cooperation on an international level, the last ten years of the twentieth century saw the explosive rise of intra-state conflicts, together with rising levels of poverty, both within states and internationally. There is no better example of this than Afghanistan.

The Islamabad and Tashkent Meetings – Fire in the Lake

The Islamabad meetings of April 1997, and the Tashkent meetings of July 1999, represent the failure of Western approaches to mediation and conflict resolution in the Afghan conflict. Riddled with contradictions and conundrums, they involved none of the necessary ingredients to work towards a lasting peace. The first conference was preceded by a Taliban assault on positions held by the Northern Alliance, and in the context of continued arms transfers into Afghanistan from abroad, while the second conference was followed almost immediately by a Taliban assault on Panjshir Valley, the last stronghold of Ahmad Shah Masoud and the remnants of the army of the former government of Burhanuddin Rabbani, toppled by the Taliban in 1996. While talking of peace and condemning the Taliban for their record on human rights, external actors continued to lend assistance and fuel the dynamics of the conflict. With Pakistan and several Arab states aligned behind the Taliban, Masoud gained support from Russia and a number of Central Asian countries. Though the fighting remains localized in Afghanistan, it has become the epicentre of several regional fault-lines and divisions, and the point at which the heart of Asia is torn by bloody conflict. Any future, larger framework for regional security and economic and social

cooperation in Central Asia, or between Central Asia and the subcontinent and China and the Middle East, will be dependent on
an eventual resolution of the conflict in Afghanistan; it is in these
countries' own interests to support efforts towards peace and an
end to the fighting.

As a result of the war against Soviet occupation, alternative
structures of authority were built up around *mujaheddin* warlords
within Afghanistan and the resistance political parties without.
Traditional structures of village authority were marginalized,
weakening local mechanisms for conflict transformation and establishing social authority around the violence of the war. While 98
per cent of the people of Afghanistan long for peace, the professional warriors and fighters, perhaps 2 per cent of the population,
remain like a layer of oil on water. The imposition of externally
supported warriors and fighting parties keeps the fires of the lake
alive. The removal of the Taliban from power through combined
US bombing raids and Northern Alliance–US-supported ground
assaults, has served only to return that layer of professional warriors
and warlords to power. Peace remains elusive. The possibility of
continued fighting and the division and re-division of Afghanistan
according to the interests of outside parties is all too real.

The negotiations then (1997, 1999) and now (2002) concentrated on competition for power and control over the capital and
the political state of Afghanistan, in a society in which most people
identify themselves along alternative forms of identity other than
citizenship. It was based on an essentially realist approach to power
relations and counted on those dependent on war to lay the
foundations for peace. It focused on bringing to the table a conflict
in which tables have little relevance to those on the ground. At the
same time, by simply bringing the two/four+ sides (1997/1999:
the Northern Alliance and Taliban; 2001: the Northern Alliance,
King, Pashtun leaders from the south and east, and defectors from
the Taliban) together it held out some hope that resolution might
be possible. However, in a society in which the state has collapsed,
where the non-war economy has been destroyed and where drug
trafficking, smuggling and war are the main currencies, mediation
alone is not enough of an approach to peace-building to provide
any meaningful alternatives to war. While a political solution to
the conflict is necessary, the roots for transformation and transcending lie in the social fabric and social capital of Afghanistan and
its people, not in Accords or negotiated settlements. This process
can be supported from abroad, but it cannot be imposed. However,
while arms and support continue to flow into the country, and as
long as regional and other powers seek to pursue their own interests
at the expense of the people of Afghanistan, peace will at best be
a dream, as unattainable today as it has been for the last 20 years.

Beyond Mediation: Analysis and Suggestions (not Solutions)

What the examples above and in chapter 1.1 have served to illustrate is that mediation *as it is practised* has abandoned the challenge of Gorbachev and the work of peace researchers and activists throughout the last half-century, to search for cooperative approaches to peace by going beyond the structures and causes of conflict and returned instead to a simplistic process of conflict resolution based on elitist structures and *war culture-driven* approaches to conflict. Often 'mediation' has served as no more than the pursuit of power and interests by outside parties and actors, serving to fuel the dynamics of the conflict and deter resolution and transformation.

The belief that wars occur because there is nothing to *prevent* them is no longer adequate. Today's challenge is not only to come up with mechanisms and the institutions to prevent war, but to develop the creativity and imagination necessary to come up with viable alternatives, transcending all forms of direct, structural and cultural violence, and empowering people and communities for peace by peaceful means. What is needed is to take up the challenge and search for alternatives that can offer the hope of a future in which violence will no longer be seen as a legitimate response to conflict. This means addressing not only the attitudes and behaviours of the parties, that portion of the iceberg that appears above the surface, but going deeper and transforming the deep cosmologies and structures, the moments of glory and trauma, of memories of expansion and memories of contraction, which form the bedrock of war and violence and the beliefs and mindsets that sustain it.

The alternatives proposed in this book go far beyond the transformations brought by Gorbachev and those put forward by most dominant approaches to peace research. The aim here is to build a practice of peace that goes beyond states and even beyond NGOs, and works to build resources and capacities for peace-building amongst a wide variety of actors. It is a practice based on empowerment of civil society, of groups, organizations and individuals at every level of society, and of the traditional networks and social structures of cultures around the world so often excluded from most modern approaches to conflict resolution. It is practice and theory, action and reflection, drawing on a wide variety of experiences and approaches to conflict, and coming together to form a *praxis for peace*.

What was pointed out at the beginning of this chapter is that mediation is one possible approach to resolution/transformation. What too often happens, however, is that this one approach is seen as the only approach, leading to the marginalization of neglect of peace-building on wider scale. Thus in Northern Ireland, while more than 85 per cent of the population can be seen to support the peace process, almost all efforts directed towards resolving the conflict are aimed solely at the 15 per cent who favour the continuation of violence. This is a product of both our approach to conflict resolution and our approach to social governance and leadership from the top. This is not meant to contradict the point made earlier that 'hard-liners' and those resisting transformation should not be ignored, but emphasizes instead the importance of involving a variety of social actors in the transformation of conflict, and of building peace from all levels, from the grass roots up. Failure to develop creative and viable approaches to conflict transformation involving the participation of a large number of actors at a variety of social levels is the product of conflict illiteracy and is essentially war culture-driven, meta-conflict-provoking approaches to conflict resolution.

To promote approaches to conflict 'resolution' that focus only on top-level leaders and interests without addressing the underlying structures and causes of the conflict not only fails in 'bringing' peace, but often lays the foundations for the outbreak of future wars. It was the treaty that ended the Franco-Prussian War and Prussia's seizure of Alsace-Lorraine that laid the foundations for the First World War, and the Treaty of Versailles at the end of the First World War that laid the foundations for the Second. Each attempt at conflict 'resolution' looked at above is reminiscent of this earlier legacy, of war-provoking 'peaces', great power conferences and peace by *diktat*, rather than the counter-culture promise brought out in the work of peace researchers and activists, of Gorbachevian cooperative, rather than conflict-producing, conflict resolution. They are the products of approaches to conflict resolution embedded in a state-centred paradigm focusing on leaders and elites rather than structures and causes, reinforcing the processes and dynamics of conflict rather than opening for their transformation. Top-down approaches to peace-building, peace imposed *from above* or *from abroad*, are *conflict-provoking*, leading to a reduction in options, locking in the conflict and blocking the room for alternatives generated from a variety of actors. What is necessary is not only to go beyond the zero-sum approaches and win/lose to 'we can both win or both lose', but to ground peace work and peace-building in a process which engages *social*, rather than just *elite*, resources for peace.

The attempts at conflict mediation analysed above have pointed to the failures of mediation as an approach to conflict resolution when practised in a void and not reinforced by other, parallel peace-building efforts. Developing holistic approaches to peace-building is not about excluding approaches to peace-building at the top level, but about introducing new approaches, new levels, emphasizing complementarity and mutually reinforcing processes; of both/and rather than either/or solutions. Where mediation fails is in its inability to locate itself within a *process* of conflict transformation. The focus on 'reaching an agreement', 'bringing parties to the table' and on coming to a 'solution' or a 'conclusion' of the conflict neglects the many levels at which the structures and dynamics of the conflict are reinforced. Yet mediation, as it is practised, fails in other areas as well.

Too often, in the case of former Yugoslavia and Kosovo/a, mediation can become the cover for great power *diktat* and *resolution by force* or the threat of force. In other cases, as in Israel–Palestine, mediation can be a process to guarantee the position of leaders/elites who feel threatened by the changing dynamics of the conflict, rather than an attempt to address those conflicts at their roots and transcend them through alternative visions and realities.

By limiting mediation as a top-level approach, as conflict resolution *between leaders*, it reinforces the hierarchical divide between those identified with the power to take and implement decisions, and those treated as objects or the victims of conflict. Conflict resolution at this level not only fails to empower actors at the grass roots and middle levels of society, but casts them in the role of spectators, promoting feelings of helplessness and apathy, of resignation and acceptance, and serving to estrange people from the peace process, reducing faith in the possibility of peace as an alternative to war. On another level, mediation may also prove a means for withdrawing from a conflict without necessarily bringing an end to it, as in the case of Afghanistan and the Soviet withdrawal.

What is important to recognize is that it is not only the agreements reached, but the process of mediation itself that generally prevents, rather than promotes, more authentic approaches to peaceful conflict transformation. It is not enough to come up with 'better solutions' or 'better peace agreements' to end a conflict. Even the best peace agreement is insufficient to guarantee a good *peace process* unless it is based on widespread support and *involvement* by large numbers of people at every level of society. Mediation's focus on negotiated 'peace' necessarily involves only a few people, heads of state, party leaders, paramilitaries, etc. The alternatives, of transcending mediation in favour of dialogue, of moving from one dialogue to 1,000, and then replicating it at every level of society, is all too rarely embraced.

While there is a greater number of 'peace NGOs' today than at any other time in history, what is lacking are the *grass-roots social organizations* and *movements* (*Satyagraha*) for peace capable of bringing the fundamental shift from cultures of war to cultures of peace, and from the belief that 'I/we can't do anything' to 'I/we can'. The Ghandian view of conflict as a challenge to be shared by the parties, demanding the resources and skills of both/all in order to be transcended/overcome, is another crucial element all too often dismissed and more often not understood, as conflict is viewed as a competition in which only one party can come out on top.

'Elitization' and monopolization of 'peace' by governments and NGO leaders alike is not only insufficient for 'bringing' peace, it is often damaging. As a parallel process, the transformation of peace and NGO work into a business not only threatens to delegitimize outside actors, but makes NGO efforts largely dependent on governments as a key source of funding. Where NGOs often criticize governments for their 'suits and limousines' approach to conflict resolution, it is worth remembering that in many conflict areas, the NGOs themselves are the ones in 'suits and limousines', driving around in Range Rovers and with salaries far beyond those available to most living in a conflict area, and often with little or no knowledge or understanding of the underlying dynamics of the conflict. The rise of interactive conflict resolution and problem-solving workshops from 1970s to the 1990s saw an increase in 'purchasing' conflicts, by which individual universities or organizations would purchase a conflict in order to practise their ability to resolve it – meanwhile guaranteeing themselves several books and publications, whether or not they were successful, as they used the opportunity to test out knowledge and theories with regard to conflict and human relations. This is not to say that 'experts' and organizations from the outside cannot make a positive contribution to the transformation of a conflict, but rather that we must be humbler in our approach and aims, and work to promote greater cooperation between efforts, and greater support for indigenous forces and capacities for peace, rather than attempting to steal the conflict from those experiencing it.

A peace culture, and the force necessary to confront the dynamics and structures of violence and transform them towards peace, cannot be found in institutions and organizations coming from above or abroad. It can only be found in broad social involvement in building peace. This is as true in those countries experiencing extreme forms of violence as it is in those countries experiencing other forms of violence, direct and structural, such as large numbers of homeless, increasing poverty and malnutrition, and denial of the right to education to certain groups and peoples. Delegitimizing and outlawing war is one solution, one that is being proposed by a growing number of NGOs around the world. What is more necessary is the development of creative and viable approaches to conflict transformation promoting positive rather than purely negative peace. Building peace and outlawing war are not necessarily the same thing, just as forbidding and creating are two entirely different processes. The yardstick for a culture of peace is its ability to transform conflict constructively and non-violently, emphasizing the role of *conflict the creator* above that of *conflict the destroyer*.

To transcend conflict, dialogue is vital, inviting participation and insight from a variety of actors and drawing on their own knowledge and experiences of conflict and conflict transformation rather than importing it from abroad. Only when dialogue, as the foundation on which peace is to be built, is brought together with peace theory and peace action – involving *conscientization, organization, mobilization* and *empowerment* (COME) of individuals and organizations at every level of society – does an authentic peace process develop. Dialogue (between parties, between parties and an outside mediator, conflict worker, peace worker (*satyagrahi*), etc. and between actors and parties at all levels (vertical/vertical, horizontal/horizontal, horizontal/vertical, vertical/horizontal) + theory (creativity, capacity to come up with 'solutions'/alternatives/ideas for transforming the conflict, knowledge and understanding for the conflict-particular or conflicts-general and approaches to peaceful conflict transformation and peace actor empowerment) + action (listening, empowerment of peace actors, *satyagraha*, active peace work, resistance to violence, promotion of dialogue and theory in practice, building/healing relationships and structures and strengthening/creating constituencies for peace) = *peace praxis*. What is crucial is *process*: how, where, when, why and who/what. What is needed is – *to start!*

Violence has a negative cause: conflict illiteracy and lack of creativity. More violence, bombings, threats of force, military build-up – in the Gulf, Afghanistan, the Balkans, etc (with North Korea and Colombia as possible future areas) – is the product of this same illiteracy. Creativity, and the ability to develop and search for alternatives and the organizations, processes and movements capable of implementing them, is one answer. From *meta-conflict*, about winning, only one outcome, one party prevails, fought with physical means (violence, war) usually leading to victory for one party and defeat for the other, to *meta-peace*, with peace as a *process* and a goal, creative and viable alternatives to violence, mutually enriching outcomes/visions, open/ended, non-linear from one victor one vanquished to all victors.

For this, *confianza* ('trust' or 'confidence', assuring sincerity, reliability and support), *cuello* (literally meaning 'neck' or network of resources and people) and *coyuntura* ('a metaphor for the unique and mostly unconscious human endeavour of placing ourselves and experience in the fluid stream of time and space', 'timing') are vital.[15] To these should be added *ubuntu* (South African) and *sho* (Indian): 'I am who I am because of you/a person is a person because of other persons', opening for empathy, solidarity. Indigenous empowerment, peace action based on *communidades de base*/grass-roots communities, the cultural relevance of conflict transformation and long-term commitment on the part of those working to build peace and transform the conflict constructively, are crucial, as are *solidarity* and *alliances*, between those committed to and working for peace and the transformation of violence.

Those working for peace (not only as an alternative to violence, but as an end and a process in itself) must remember not to lock themselves in any one particular 'solution'/approach, or to over-extend themselves in one direction to the neglect of others. Proposals/solutions/processes should always be reversible, allowing for new proposals, new solutions, new processes and a willingness to start again at the beginning should it be necessary. Whereas mediation is usually a single activity, sometimes repeated if necessary, dialogue is a constant process. What is important, however, is to treat each dialogue as the *first* dialogue, never bringing presumptions, conclusions from another dialogue with another party, into a new dialogue with a new party. People in dialogue must be willing to enter into a new process, to 'start again from the beginning' each time.[16] Parties to a dialogue are companions. The moment one person starts leading, it is no longer a dialogue.

The road to transcending, to developing a praxis for peace, is through transforming the underlying structures and causes of a conflict by promoting a plurality of visions, alternatives and voices, and by building peace work on the search for creative and viable alternatives to violence, drawing on the background and experiences of actors at every social level. It does not neglect traditional and cultural approaches to conflict resolution, but seeks to build on them, learning from them, strengthening them and generating new approaches and new visions. If people are to become active, they must not only see the possibility of constructive action, but also what they as individuals can do to help to solve the problem. Many people would like to do more, but may feel inhibited by lack of knowledge of the range of alternatives available for what can be done, or the possibility that conflicts can be transformed, even in the face of overwhelming opposition, constructively and non-violently. What is important: to learn about other struggles, experiences and practices, to look deeper into our own and build concrete skills and knowledge for conflict transformation by peaceful means. This is one of the greatest challenges for the peace movement, peace researchers, peace educators and all those working for peace today. The promise of viable peace work can be found in peace praxis as a fundamentally dynamic force/process which seeks not only to resolve conflict but also to lay the foundations for a viable and lasting peace built on dialogue, learning and practice, making peace meaningful and practical to those living in the conflict area by building it on their own experiences and expectations, going beyond utopia and rooting it in the possible, that is, *making peace possible*. It answers the challenge to creativity and peace based on transcending the structures and causes of violence, which mediation fails to do.

Some Psychological Assumptions about Conflict – Actors; Structures; Relationships

In order to understand the relevance of any one tool to the transformation or resolution of conflicts in a given society, it is necessary to understand how that society views conflict. Whether it is seen as destructive and evil, *conflict the destroyer*, ruining what exists and threatening development, or whether it is viewed as a challenge, something to be overcome, transcended, with the potential to invigorate relations and social structures, mixing the new with the old and going beyond, *conflict the creator*. Essential to this is an understanding of psychological and ideological assumptions/perspectives, the way in which relations between people, including relations between people and themselves and people and the environment, are conceptualized.

Often, the relationship between people, cultures and their environment is crucial in forming the perspective and response to conflict. In the rich, fertile valley of ancient Egypt where life was directly linked to the cycle and flow of the Nile, chaos, *Ogdoad*, was seen as a life-giving and creative force, both friendly and cooperative, giving birth to the creator, the Sun. The gods of ancient Egypt were powerful but not excessively violent, and conflict between gods and mortals, or between competitors, rivals and foes (within Egypt and amongst their neighbours), were generally handled through peaceful assimilation. In contrast, in Mesopotamia chaos was viewed as a dangerous force, a power of incredible profusion, of both good and evil, threatening life and the established order. Tiamat, the Great Mother and force of chaos, was ferociously attacked and destroyed, just as rivals and competitors were bloodily defeated and annihilated. Marduk, the defender and champion of rugged, windswept Mesopotamia, had to fight a desperate struggle for the survival of his land and people.[17] Different lands, different experiences and different cultures can often result in fundamentally different ways of dealing with conflict.

Whether human beings are considered as part of a community, of an interlinking network connecting all members of a society, or whether they are viewed as individuals, with no responsibilities or obligations towards others, can dramatically affect the different ways in which conflict can be, and is, approached. Generally, the reality lies somewhere in between, with actors seen as both individuals and as social creatures. By looking at how society and individuals are viewed from a number of different perspectives and discussing the possible contributions which these different perspectives may make to our understanding of conflict, it may be possible to come up with more holistic and varied approaches to conflict transformation, benefiting from the experiences of a variety of cultures/perspectives. Of relevance to our investigation is how different ideologies/perspectives view existence, whether they are homo- or nature-centred, whether humans are seen as existing in a web, or in isolation. From this we may better be able to develop responses to conflict that draw on a variety of perspectives and understandings, rather than limiting our conceptual repertoire to one discourse to the exclusion of others.

1. Liberal, Enlightenment, Euro-American, Protestant

Society is perceived as a whole, an organism, often portrayed as a body, with the leaders at the head, the army and police the arms, and the workers and peasants the legs.[18] Conflicts that arise within society come from competing interests and goals, and are not the result of conflicts between different groups, classes (whose existence is denied), etc. or generated by underlying structures and social inequalities. The individuals and his/her behaviour are the focus, not society – a focus on knots rather than webs. Therefore, responsibility lies with the individual. Economic and social differences are the responsibility of the individual, with success coming from hard work and initiative, and failure from laziness and an inability to work. The world divided: good vs. evil; right vs. wrong. Solution: salvation, prayer; separation of the spiritual from the 'practical'. Time is linear, reaching from creation to judgement, and beyond (?).

2. Socialist Critique (Primarily 'Utopian' Socialists)

Society is a pyramid, not a whole. The wealthy and powerful are at the top, the poor, exploited and oppressed at the bottom, and the middle classes in between. Critical of the liberal, Enlightenment, Protestant model which allows for the benefit and luxury of the few while leaving the 'masses' to live in misery. Two demands arise from this: 1) a return to a pre-industrial society, involving the idealization of early, pre-modern, 'communist' society; or 2) including keeping the pie, but making it bigger and giving everybody a more equitable share. Reflected today in many critiques of 'Western' societies, often leading to withdrawal and separation, or transformation through reform (without altering the underlying structures – distribution of power rather than production).

3. Marx and Early Marx (not the same as Soviet or Marxian)

Keeps the pyramid, but focuses on the structures, the relations, that give rise to it. Opens the way for understanding the systems, and explains social and economic inequalities as resulting from differences in control of the means of production. As long as these differences exist, conflict along class lines will continue. Marx's concepts of alienation, exploitation and inequality emphasize 'structural violence', not just direct, personal. Solution: socialization of the means of production, eliminating class differences and founding society on social, economic, civil and political equality, allowing for the freer development of a more human society based on scientific principles Early Marx (not necessarily separate from later Marx): critiques liberalism and bourgeois society for separating man's civil and political existence from his social and economic reality. Man as a social being, existing in relationships with objects both outside *and* inside himself; that is, man's relations to man, man's relation to other men, man's relation to his environment and man's relation to his species being. Emphasis on relationships, therefore: structure *and* web, not just structure as is commonly presented. Conflict is viewed as natural, part of history, with conflict resolved conflict won, the victory of antithesis over thesis.

All Three

Man, homocentric, conflict the destroyer over conflict the creator (though elements of both exist in all, particularly the third). What is left? Women, children, nature, the universe ... So:

4. Green – Women, Children, Environment; Those Marginalized in 1, 2, 3

Challenges 1, 2 and 3, with their industrialized visions and neglect of those left on the outside or dominated from above, that is, women, children the environment, etc. Moves towards inclusion, either as part of a broader, more human 1, 2 and 3, or in cooperation to create a new vision.

Nevertheless, 1–4 originate in and come from the 'West', from the dominant cultures/countries/pathologies. Challenges 2–4 speak to the marginalized, not just those in the West, but on a broader scale. Like missionaries, NGOs, or peace workers whose aim is to bring salvation or to solve the problem, for others. What separate 2, 3 and 4 from 5–8 (see below) is that the former are the voices of the West speaking for the people of the non-West. What is needed? To listen to the people of the non-West speaking for themselves.

5. Buddhist

Like early Marx, focus on relations, interrelations; a network of all that is living and non-living, action and reaction, thought and contemplation, mutual causation and co-dependent origin. Much greater focus on *inner peace* and *peace by peaceful means*, rather than *peace through revolution* (possibly, though not necessarily, violent). Conflict is seen as a *relation*, requiring inner peace and harmony, righting of wrong action, and seeking to restore the universe/relation to its proper balance. Solution: *nirvana*. Everything grows together. Harmony with all that is living and non-living the means. Emphasizes the web, extending it far wider, beyond homocentric visions to nature, holistic-oriented, with responsibility distributed throughout the web, rather than borne by one individual. Time is not a beginning or end, but a flow, a relationship.

6. Daoist

Good within bad, bad within good, yin and yang (with yin in yang and yang in yin, etc.). Everything that is done has consequences, reactions, therefore, focus on doing only what can be undone, reversibility, learning from the good and bad, and recognizing the potential for both.

7. First Nations, Indigenous, Holistic, Nature-Oriented Societies

Planet as mother, universe, caretaker. Chaos a life-force, companion, generator of the world and order, or the world out of order, and needing to be restored. Humans existing in relation with all other creatures, with our spirits reflected in the natural world, in animals, plants, etc. The world within us and us within the world. Four sacred things: earth, air, fire, water. A fifth sacred thing: spirit, understanding, harmony. Small societies, everyone has a role, everyone is related to everyone else. *Sarvodaya*. Human beings as caretakers, caring for the world, for each other. Also as hunters, but only within the world, to survive as part of it, not on top of it, as dominators.

8. A Thousand Other Cultures, Voices, Dialogues

Always leaving room for more, plurality and complementarity rather than domination and exclusion. Where to look for them: in marginalized cultures within dominant ones, in marginalized cultures outside dominant ones. From individuals and communities, traditional and cultural networks, cosmologies, and approaches to conflict and to peace.

What To Do with Them All?

Again, both/and, rather than either/or. The individual and society, the knot and the web. Humans existing in and for themselves *and* in and for the world, embracing the particular within the whole and the whole within the particular. Conflict located within the web, within the structure, and the individual at the meta-, macro- and micro-levels, learning from all eight and always leaving room for more. Which is right? All of them, each with its own wisdom, with its own lessons. No one person/culture/cosmology has all the truth, therefore peace cannot come from only one person/culture/cosmology, but through all of them working together, cooperating, building. The challenge, to be able to take them all, and to create new ones, recognizing the limitations to any one approach and seeking to complement it and fill it out by drawing on others. Logic exists to be transcended, allowing for new logic, new visions. The road to travel: from the logic of war to the logic of peace. Our challenge is to embrace what is possible, that is, *peace*, and to make it a reality, through healing, working, building, dialogue and, above all, *peace praxis* (all of the above and more). Always reversible, always ready to recognize that even what is good can become bad, and what is bad can become good; therefore, movement away from absolutes and towards processes.

Where conflict the destroyer and violence are often founded on cultures which legitimize and reinforce violence, racism and hierarchy, conflict the creator is equally dependent on the development of mindsets and perspectives, and of cultures (not only at the superficial, light level, but at the deep, cosmological level), which open the way for creative and positive transformation of conflict. This means questioning previously held assumptions and beliefs and seeking to overcome/transform mindsets that promote dehumanization, the creation of enemy images, and feelings/beliefs (cultural, national, individual) at the expense of others (if one is to be superior, it is at the cost of another being inferior). A massive task, which needs to be met through cooperation and action if it is to be achieved.

A Story of Three Brothers

The story is of a Chinese doctor, some 2,000–3,000 years ago, renowned as a physician and for his skill and knowledge of medicines and his ability to heal even the most deadly diseases, he was asked why he was so much better than his two brothers, who were also doctors. His answer:

> My first brother heals sickness before it even develops, so his methods appear hidden, his science art and he is known only within our village. My second brother deals with illnesses while they are minor, preventing sickness from getting worse and returning the body to health. I deal with sicknesses when they have reached the level of disease and threaten to destroy the organism of to which they are a part. This requires numerous medicines, and skill and knowledge in their use. For this reason my name has become famous throughout the kingdom and I have been asked to be physician to the king. Yet it is my first brother who has the knowledge to deal with sicknesses before they arise and my second brother who is able to treat them at an early stage and prevent them getting worse. Though my fame has spread throughout the land, their knowledge is greater.

Drawing the analogy to conflict: The first brother is able to deal with conflicts before they arise. His knowledge is of the harmony of the world and relationships, and his art is in keeping that harmony in balance, recognizing patterns and structures that may lead to conflict, and transforming them, using the energy in conflict to create constructive and enriching relations which benefit the body and parties involved. His knowledge is knowledge of peace and of health, and his skill is in recognizing early on what might disturb the balance and harmony on which health is based.

The second brother is able to deal with conflicts while they are still small. To recognize them at an early stage, before they escalate, and to work to transform the conflict and return the parties and the body to health. He has knowledge of peace and conflict, though his energy is directed towards the sickness, not the health, of the body; towards alleviating pain, suffering, conflict, and strengthening the harmony and peace they have disturbed.

The third brother's knowledge is not of health of the body or the harmony of social relations. His knowledge is of disease. His skill lies in overcoming the disease and ending the affliction of the body, in dealing with large-scale conflicts, removing their causes and symptoms.

Each of the three has far more knowledge and wisdom than is generally applied by most modern mediators, and each deals with both the body and the sickness, though to varying degrees.

A fourth (or possibly fifth?) brother? The modern mediator or negotiator who has knowledge of neither the body nor the disease which afflicts it. His task (and he is almost always a he) is to 'bring the parties to the table' and to make sure that they come to an agreement. Often this does not deal with the underlying cause of the conflict, or the traumas and suffering it has given rise to. The focus here is not on healing, on restoring the body to harmony, but on bringing about a cease-fire (ending the symptoms without addressing the causes of the disease). He opens the space for healing, but does not do the healing himself. However, as he fails to cooperate with or even recognize the capacity of traditional and cultural approaches to conflict transformation, he treats the 'patient' as a victim rather than as an actor. The relationship is a hierarchical one – the doctor (expert)/patient (victim).

A new relationship (?) – doctor/patient / patient/doctor, where both are doctor and both are patient, both with the capacity to heal and something that needs healing. The myth of neutrality, of 'scientific objectivity', is overcome. Both are recognized as part of the relationship.

To be added, more, new relationships: listener, worker, healer, friend, partner in dialogue, builder, lover, etc. Yin/yang is good (always remembering that there is yin in yang and yang in yin), but 'yins' and 'yangs', thousands and thousands, are better. Not just black and white but thousands of colours, with different ones that can be used at different times, or in unison, but always coexisting, in relationship with one another. Beyond doctor/patient, opening up the door to the community, to local practices, wisdom and knowledge, complexifying the conflict, approaching it from many different perspectives and recognizing the many different roles and levels of activity necessary for transforming a relationship from conflict the destroyer to conflict the creator.

Knowledge, skills, tools, etc. can be introduced from abroad, but this must be done as a mutual learning process, a cooperative effort, rather than trying to enforce a foreign solution on parties to a conflict. Local knowledge of conflict and traditional and cultural approaches to conflict transformation are the most valuable resources to any peace-building process. A roof cannot simply be built in the air; it needs a structure. At the same time, the roof of the Empire State Building won't fit well on a tepee, or a bamboo house – or even a stone structure. Knowledge cannot be taken and

empowerment

imposed from the outside. Healing cannot be a purely prescriptive process. The structure and the roof must come from within the society itself, making it durable, sustainable. The body's ability to heal itself cannot be overlooked. Though outside medicines and traditional healing may be necessary, it is still the body itself that must return to health and keep itself healthy. A peace enforced *by force* from outside, or even from above, is not peace.

In Lieu of a Conclusion

The discussions and ideas developed in this chapter should not be taken as completed or final. They are part of an always continuing process, drawing in and learning from the experiences and work of people at thousands of different levels, with thousands of different approaches, all around the world. The central arguments, that mediation as practised by 'Western' practitioners is only one approach, and that in order to transform conflicts effectively it is necessary to involve a large number of actors at a variety of social levels and to address the underlying structures and causes of the conflict have been brought out time and again. What is necessary, however, is that the lessons to be learned from this remain not only on the level of theoretical discussion, but that we work to broaden and modify our approaches to practice and to welcome far greater involvement and participation in peace work than many previous methods have allowed for. Here, however, peace is understood not only as a static, lifeless noun, but as a dynamic, life-giving force – peace as a verb, with many peaces, not just one, and recognizing that what might be considered peace by one is not necessarily the same as what might be considered peace by another. Just as some cultures and ideologies focus on development and growth, while others seek to preserve harmony and sustainability, thousands of different understandings and interpretations of what peace is and how to work for it exist. What is important to recognize, however, is that they need not by exclusionary or opposed to one another. In fact, it may be that only by bringing them together and recognizing the many different contributions that can be made, can our efforts to develop creative and viable alternatives to war and violence – structurally, culturally and physically – be successful.

culture

11 September 2001: Diagnosis, Prognosis, Therapy

Johan Galtung

Diagnosis

Politics, like communication, is seen in terms of who does what to whom, how, when and where, and why. The what–how–when–where of the 11 September attack in New York and Washington is clear; the problems are who and why. But why is at least clear – up to a certain point. Like the presidential palace in Santiago, Chile, also bombed on 11 September (1973) somebody had something against what happened inside some buildings: the capitalism of the US world trade and the militarism of the US Pentagon for the year 2001;[1] the politics of the Unidad Popular for year 1973.

The text was written in building language, and as for all texts what is not written may be equally important: no museum, no cathedral, no parliament. The 19–20 hijackers hit what they wanted, just like the Chileah Air Force and its masters.

But there could also be a military motivation for these acts of criminal political violence[2] to incapacitate, put someone out of action, 'take them out'. That happened to Salvador Allende and later to more than 3,000 Chileans; and to 4,000–5,000 (or so) in New York and Washington. But democratic Chile recovered, although it took some time. US-led capitalism, today called 'globalization', was in decline for other reasons, but US-led militarism is as vigorous as ever. 11 September 2001 and 1973 were communicative and political rather than military.

Any thought/speech/action on these attacks has to reflect which symbols of America were targeted lest it becomes dogmatic, a priori. Someone had something against what emanated from those buildings. That gives us a cue to *why*. But *who* did it?

This is the dominant, mainstream, thriller question, not why.

The Dominant, Mainstream Discourse: 'Terrorism'

Answer: terrorism, more precisely Al Qaeda, even more precisely Osama bin Laden. To explore this discourse, 'terrorism' has to be defined, and there seem to be two different meanings.

First, *tactical*: 'Terrorism' is based on unpredictability in the who–whom–how–when–where, as opposed to a regular military campaign with predictable parties and most methods of killing and destruction. The where is known as the front-line, the when may move with the predictability of a Japanese *sakura*. There is the additional terrorist element of whom: civilians/innocents.

There are two subtypes: *non-state terrorism*, and *state terrorism*; from below ('have bombs, but no air force'), from above ('have both bombs and air force'). The 11 September 2001 kamikaze attack[3] – fascist, like all massive political violence – will enter military history for using airline carriers with fuel as bombs.

Terrorism from below is directed against governments or states as persons or institutions, and, of course, to bring about political change. Obviously, most governments, and the United Nations as a trade union of governments, are against terrorism from below because, like secession, it affects vital government interests, including being *causa sui*, game masters.

State terrorism as a military tactic also uses surprise and focuses on killing civilians to force capitulation. This is a major theme in modern warfare, one used by the US/UK air forces in their terror bombing of Germany and Japan 1940–45.[4]

In the campaign against Yugoslavia of March–June 1999 remarkably few military targets were destroyed, whereas the killing of civilians and destruction of Serbian infrastructure (factories, power, transportation/communication, schools and hospitals) was extensive. That brought about capitulation to avoid genocide.[5]

From the circumstance that terrorism is terrorism whether from below or from above, the conclusion is not that they are organized in the same way. 'Above' is almost by definition hierarchical with a vertical, well-protected chain of command. 'Below' has to use guerrilla tactics with a loosely connected horizontal organization of small cells with low vulnerability. The connecting cement, substituting for the vertical chain, would be a deeply internalized ideology. Theoretically, it is possible that 19–20 people organized the 11 September attack, got the money for tickets and flying training in a simulator, not the more difficult take-off and landing, and some box-openers. In that case there is no causal chain of command pointing to the single prime mover so dear to the US mind. There is nobody to search and punish or destroy if the cell was a closed system programmed to self-destruct like certain animals upon intercourse. All that is needed is perfect solidarity and single-mindedness.

The condition for this hypothesis to be valid is a context, an ocean of hatred with the capacity for spontaneous creation of such cells. Central to terrorism as a tactic is also the idea of provocation:

a terrorist attack leads to a massive state terrorist counter-attack which then, in turn, enlarges the ocean of hatred that not only produces terrorists but also feeds them; body, mind and spirit. The 'people' will rise, *levée en masse*. The German group *Rote Armee Fraktion* (RAF) had this theory; so did the Italian *Brigate Rosse*. But it did not work that way. Isolated people easily overestimate their social support.

However, to crush, pulverize, etc. an ocean – rather than a concrete hierarchy with orderly chains of command – of hatred and willingness to sacrifice, even one's own life, will not be easy. The BBC claimed that the US had 60 candidate target countries.[6]

Second, *ideological*. 'Terrorism' is seen as a state of mind, with fundamentalism as its cognitive perspective and hatred its emotional resource, an evil-doer whose only purpose is harm and hurt, violence for its own sake. The terrorist has no cause beyond this; and his tactic is chosen accordingly. He will hide in the dark, lurking, lurching, biding his time.

The metaphor for this within the Abrahamitic religions would be Satan himself, Lucifer, known as the leader of the angels who rebelled against God. That metaphor should be an important archetype in a country like the US, No. 1 in the world for believing in the reality of the devil[7] and with little difficulty seeing itself as the instrument of God's will (thus, Colin Powell himself once declared that 'America had been established by divine providence to lead the world',[8] George W. Bush that Jesus Christ is the political philosopher he most admires[9]). The metaphor fits bin Laden doubly as he once fought with the US the 'evil empire' at the time, the Soviet Union, but like Pol Pot, Saddam Hussein, Mohammed Aideed, Manuel Noriega and to some extent Slobodan Milosevic turned like Lucifer against the US, defying 'the enemy of my enemy is my friend' logic.

Fundamentalism as a cognitive outlook has three pillars:

1. *Dualism*, the world is divided in two; there are no neutrals.
2. *Manicheism*, who is not with the good, is with the evil.
3. *Armageddon*, evil yields to nothing but violence.

With George Bush's use of 'you are either with us or with the terrorists', and bin Laden's distinction between believers and infidels,[10] both justifying violence, they can be classified as fundamentalists. The 'war against terrorism' is between hard Christian (Baptist/Presbyterian?), and hard Islamic (Wahabbite?) fundamentalisms.[11] The reinforcing dialectic between the two is obvious, as is 'my terrorism is good, theirs is bad'.

The Alternative Discourse: 'Retaliation'

This discourse is found on the margin in the US, is frequent in the peoples of the West, and often even the dominant discourse in the Rest. 11 September was a retaliation, probably above all motivated by a combination of hatred, despair and 'violence is the only language they understand'; in other words, blocked communication. The second reason for major political violence – to incapacitate the enemy – presupposes a naïveté unlikely with attackers at that level of sophistication. But the third reason – to provoke political change – may have been on their mind, and the fourth – to provoke a retaliation for their retaliation big enough to provoke *big* retaliation against the US – possibly also.

This discourse constructs the 'other side', OS, so called because we do not know exactly who they are (could mean 'Osama Side') as at least partly rational, with causes, motives beyond just inflicting evil. Very important among these causes is OS retaliating for US violence. That would locate some of the cause for what happened to the US in the US itself, and more particularly in structural violence identified with the World Trade Center and the direct violence identified with the Pentagon.

But doesn't that justify the attack? No. Nothing can justify crimes against peace and humanity, whether by OS or US. But we can try to understand, explain. Hitler could partly be understood in terms of the highly violent, second Versailles Treaty (similar to the first in 1871). But that does not justify his atrocities. However massive the causal mass, there is always a residue of free will. Hitler, US and OS could have decided otherwise. Understanding is a necessary condition for removing causes, both in the causal and/or the motivational sense of that word, thereby making a repeat less likely.

The US track record of violence since the Second World War, to have a cut-off point relevant for the present generation, is overwhelming. But US violence was also caused by something; there were motives beyond inflicting the evil, the hurt and harm that is the essence of violence. Tactically very much of it, maybe most, can be characterized as state terrorism, but like terrorism from below motives may be neutral or valid even if the consequences for the victims and the bereaved are purely evil.

Immediately after 11 September, Zoltan Grossman made available a list of 'A Century of US Military Interventions from Wounded Knee to Afghanistan', based on *Congressional Records* and the Library of Congress Congressional Research Service. His list of 134 small and big, global and domestic, interventions covers the 111 years from 1890 to 2001, with an average of 1.15 interventions per year before the end of the Second World War, and an average of 1.29 after that; in other words, a small increase. If we focus on the period after the end of the Cold War, however, in eleven years there are 22 interventions, in other words an average of two a year. This is compatible with the hypothesis that as empire or hegemony expands more interventions are needed for protection.

William Blum, in his *Rogue State: A Guide to the World's Only Superpower*,[12] has much detail in 300 pages. Some of this can be debated. But our focus is on the victims, the bereaved, the displaced, the destruction of both man-made and natural environments, the damage done to social institutions and to culture by such an enormous propensity to violence.[13] There is no denial of some valid motives. But there is a denial that violence was the only recourse. For each single case an alternative course of action could be argued, but that is not our focus here.

Blum has a list of 67 'Global Interventions from 1945' (Grossman has only 56; but Blum includes nonmilitary interventions and much indirect, US-supported violence). In chronological order:

China 1945–51, France 1947, Marshall Islands 1946–58, Italy 1947–1970s, Greece 1947–49, Philippines 1945–53, Korea 1945–53, Albania 1949–53, Eastern Europe 1948–56, Germany 1950s, Iran 1953, Guatemala 1953–1990s, Costa Rica 1950s, 1970–71, Middle East 1956–58, Indonesia 1957–58, Haiti 1959, Western Europe 1950s–1960s, British Guiana 1953–64, Iraq 1958–63, Soviet Union 1940s–1960s, Vietnam 1945–73, Cambodia 1955–73, Laos 1957–73, Thailand 1965–73, Ecuador 1960–63, Congo-Zaire 1977–78, France-Algeria 1960s, Brazil 1961–63, Peru 1965, Dominican Republic 1963–65, Cuba 1959–, Indonesia 1965, Ghana 1966, Uruguay 1969–72, Chile 1964–73, Greece 1967–74, South Africa 1960s–1980s, Bolivia 1964–75, Australia 1972–75, Iraq 1972–75, Portugal 1974–76, East Timor 1975–99, Angola 1975–1980s, Jamaica 1976, Honduras 1980s, Nicaragua 1978–1990s, Philippines 1970s, Seychelles 1979–81, South Yemen 1979–84, South Korea 1980, Chad 1981–82, Grenada 1979–83, Suriname 1982–84, Libya 1981–89, Fiji 1987, Panama 1989, Afghanistan 1979–92, El Salvador 1981–92, Haiti 1987–94, Bulgaria 1990–91, Albania 1991–92, Somalia 1993, Iraq 1990s, Peru 1990s, Mexico 1990s, Colombia 1990s, Yugoslavia 1995–99.

The interventions took the form of bombings in 25 cases:

China 1945–46, Korea/China 1950–53, Guatemala 1954, Indonesia 1958, Cuba 1960–61, Guatemala 1960, Vietnam

1961–73, Congo 1964, Peru 1965, Laos 1964–73, Cambodia 1969–70, Guatemala 1967–69, Grenada 1983, Lebanon–Syria 1983–84, Libya 1986, El Salvador 1980s, Nicaragua 1980s, Iran 1987, Panama 1989, Iraq 1991–, Kuwait 1991, Somalia 1993, Sudan 1998, Afghanistan 1998, Yugoslavia 1999.

Assassinations, attempted or successful, of leaders, including heads of state, were attempted in 35 cases, and assistance in torture in eleven countries (Greece, Iran, Germany, Vietnam, Bolivia, Uruguay, Brazil, Guatemala, El Salvador, Honduras, Panama). Particularly vehement are actions against leaders who once worked with the US because they had an enemy in common: Pol Pot, Manuel Noriega, Saddam Hussein, Mohammed Aideed and Osama bin Laden. Blum also has a list of 23 countries where the US was 'Perverting Elections', interfering with a democratic process:

Italy 1948–1970s, Lebanon 1950s, Indonesia 1955, Vietnam 1955, Guayana 1953–64, Japan 1958–1970s, Nepal 1959, Laos 1960, Brazil 1962, Dominican Republic 1962, Guatemala 1963, Bolivia 1966, Chile 1964–70, Portugal 1974–75, Australia 1974–75, Jamaica 1976, Panama 1984, 1989, Nicaragua 1984, 1990, Haiti 1987–88, Bulgaria 1991–92, Russia 1996, Mongolia 1996, Bosnia 1998.

Critique the details, read the book. But much naïveté is needed to believe that this can pass without hatred and the thirst for revenge.

There is a spatial pattern in the sense that interventions have moved, with considerable overlaps, through four regions:

Spatial patterns of US interventions: Four post-Second World War regions

---

Region I	East Asia	Confucian-Buddhist
Region II	Eastern Europe	Orthodox Christian
Region III	Latin America	Catholic Christian
Region IV	West Asia	Islam

The first focus of US intervention was in East Asia (Korea, Vietnam, Indonesia; but also Iran), and extremely violent.

The second was on Eastern Europe (including the Soviet Union), the Cold War that fortunately did not become hot, at least not in Europe even though the Cold War continued in East Asia. The presence of a counter-superpower had much to do with that, and after that superpower disappeared US violence has been exercised on Orthodox territory, in Serbia and Macedonia.

The third was in Latin America, starting with and prompted by Cuba, then extending to the entire region, more or less. The violence was micro- and meso-, not the macro-violence of East Asia, not to mention the mega-violence feared for the European 'theatre'.

The fourth is in West Asia, starting with Palestine and Iran, then Libya and Lebanon/Syria, and in the 1990s Iraq, Saudi Arabia (for military bases) and Afghanistan.[14]

This change in focus over time may explain the delay in retaliation in the American homeland. The US sees itself as above other countries, under but near God.[15] US violence is not retaliation, but punishment from above; and hence is acceptable and accepted. But in Region I a war is a sign of bad *karma* to be improved by mutual efforts; hence neither capitulation, nor revenge. In Region II there was no violence. In Region III many Latin Americans share the US perspective. But Region IV? Never. Allah is never below God, no capitulation, revenge.

The US has taken on something they never experienced before.

Then there is the structural violence brought about by the rapid global expansion of the market system. A basic aspect of that system is monetization, that is, what is required for basic needs satisfaction is available only for money, and not labour, for instance. The basic needs for food, clothes, shelter and health care cannot be met on less than one dollar a day. As a result people die, probably at the rate of 100,000 per day, from under- or malnutrition, inadequate clothing and housing, and lack of health services, because these are also monetized and unsubsidized. At the same time, wealth accumulates at the top. Many people hate this.

As to the motives behind the enormity of direct violence: it is practically speaking all compatible with the hypothesis that US direct violence, overt or covert CIA, is directed against whatever can be seen as hostile to US business abroad.[16] That would include progressive countries and progressive people in any country, if by 'progressive' we understand policies that privilege distribution of economic assets downward in society and the satisfaction of basic needs for the most needy. If this is compatible with a favourable 'climate' for US business, then OK. But in less developed countries the political economy will pit these goals against each other, and the standard US reaction has been violent. We can talk of a military-industrial complex and of an international class struggle between and within countries.

A generation ago retaliation would refer to colonialism and to 200 British punishment expeditions by Rule Britannia. Today hatred centres on the US, overshadowing former colonial powers like France, Belgium and Portugal, and indeed Japan. Today that military-industrial complex is clearly symbolized by the Pentagon and World Trade Center.

Looking through the 35 (assassinations) + 11 (torture) + 25 (bombings) + 67 (global interventions) + 23 (perverting elections) = 161 cases of political violence, the conclusion is inevitable: practically speaking, all of them are compatible with the class conflict (between countries and within) hypothesis. No case is compatible with the 'clash of civilizations' hypothesis in the sense that civilizational symbols (like mosques, temples) or purely religious authorities were targeted. Nor is there any evidence for classical territorial expansion.

Of course, the justifying rhetoric has been different. For Regions I and II it has been 'containment of Soviet expansion', rightly pitting freedom–democracy–human rights against bondage–dictatorship, but silent about the bondage–dictatorship inherent in foreign policy, and the horrendous 'mistakes' in the theory and practice, revealed, for instance, by the former Secretary of Defense Robert McNamara in his *In Retrospect*,[17] now a classic.

For Region III the rhetoric centred on Marxism, with some containment of the Soviet Union (Cuba, Nicaragua), but more of students, peasants, workers and clerics (liberation theology). And for Region IV, the rhetoric has above all been about 'terrorism', possibly leading to 'containment of Islamic fundamentalism', which could then slide into clash of civilizations.

As conflict formation, today's global injustice succeeds slavery and colonialism and will probably end like them through change of consciousness and demoralization at the top. Today most Americans and many in the West are ignorant about this, even if they feel uncomfortable about it; like the Germans under Nazism. They prefer communism/terrorism rhetoric.

An anti-American analysis? Not at all. But anti-Washington hegemonical, exploitative foreign policy, certainly.

The Course of Action Flows from the Discourse

The choice of discourse matters. Discourse and the course of action influence each other, the discourse serving as action directive, and as rationalization of the actions taken.

The terrorism discourse leads to two possible reactions:

A: *Search and punish*, court-ordered police action; due process.
B: *Search and destroy*: uni- or multilateral military action.

The retaliation discourse also leads to two reactions:

C: *Retaliation*: hate-violence to hit back, an eye for an eye.
D: *Exit from the retaliation cycle*; US and OS change policies.

As the present author believes 10 per cent in the terrorism discourse (there are some very hard, evil people in the world) and 90 per cent in the retaliation discourse (sad, but, however unwise, retaliation is a human inclination fuelled by fundamentalism) reactions, or rather policies, A and D are preferred. US reaction so far is a mix of B (preferring military courts to due process[18]) and C; incapacitation of the presumed enemy and pure revenge; with some elements of A (UN legitimacy) and D (new Palestine policy).

There can be, and are, of course other US motives. No human being, no power, indeed no superpower is so single-minded as to act from only one motive. When the present author was mediator for Afghan groups, organized by the Afghan University in Peshawar, in February 2001[19] there was much talk of a US base to be built between Herat and the Iranian border to protect oil pipelines from Uzbekistan and Turkmenistan, and for control of Central Asia in general and Afghanistan in particular.[20]

Then come such traditional factors as reasserting world leadership, giving content to NATO's new role, and, indeed, to maintain the world class structure led by the centre of the Centre of the CENTRE: the elites in the United States.

What do people in general think on this issue? Fortunately, a poll was taken by Gallup International in 33 countries immediately after 11 September (between 14 and 18 September 2001). Unlike the US polls, people were given a choice: 'In your opinion, once the identity of the terrorists is known, should the American government launch a military attack on the country or countries where the terrorists are based or should the American government seek to extradite the terrorists to stand trial?' (Let us add: the latter is the Libya model.)

Only three countries were in favour of 'attack': Israel 77 per cent, India 72 per cent and the US 54 per cent. In Europe the highest in favour of 'attack' was France with 29 per cent. The 'stand trial' answer was in the overwhelming majority, around 80 per cent in the other 30 countries (UK 75 per cent, France 67 per cent; Latin America well above 80 per cent).

In other words, there is a solid basis for the Rule of Law rather than the Rule of Force in the world population on this issue, and also for a peace movement in the North–South. Governments, as mentioned, will react strongly against terrorism, maybe less to protect their people than to protect themselves and their class interests, the hard nucleus of a country. They are also afraid of US retribution if they are seen as turncoats, and they were in a state of shock after 11 September, probably since their intelligentsia had not warned them sufficiently about the obvious. This author has been expecting, with sadness, something like that to happen – like blowing up the bridges and blocking the tunnels to Manhattan – since 1988–91, when the US shot down a civilian Iranair plane over the Gulf, and started the massive destruction of Iraq, taking on key Muslim countries, non-Arab and Arab. The surprising thing is that some were surprised.

In short, there is a major people/government split on this. Of the four courses of action – A, B, C and D – the two chosen, B and C, are very costly[21] and can easily spill over from B to C when the collateral damage gets very high. But they are also fairly obvious; we have seen them before, for instance in the Gulf and Yugoslavia. The other two must be spelt out.

A police action differs from a military action by being court-ordered and legitimized, and by being precisely targeted on the suspects to apprehend them and arraign them in court for possible sentencing and punishment. The court in this case will have to be international since punishment is violence from above. The US (and some of its allies) may see the US as above all other countries, but most of the world stick to the equality of the UN member states. The exception is the UN Security Council, which takes on such roles but cannot do so in this case: of the five core, veto members, four are Christian (US Protestant, UK Anglican, France Catholic/secular, Russia Orthodox), one, China, is Confucian, and none represents the 56 countries of the world with a Muslim majority. The International Court of Justice (ICJ) would be better and so would the forthcoming International Criminal Court (ICC), but it is not yet there and the US will probably not ratify it anyway.[22] It is relevant that the list of accusations against Henry Kissinger, a former US Secretary of State,[23] is much longer than the list against bin Laden.

Nevertheless, there is the Libya model for the criminal violence against PanAm flight 103 over Lockerbie, Scotland; the process was slow and easily criticized, but it worked in the end. Countries that value the Rule of Law would support this and not military action that burns down forests and kills those who live there. The action in Afghanistan tries to combine these elements; but capture alive is unlikely.

How is it possible to exit from the cycle of retaliation? The question has to be directed not only to the US but also to OS, whoever that is – and the answer is probably changing as US violence develops. The point of departure would have to be reflections, not only reflexes, and that's not so easy:

For the US: What have we done that they hate us so much to do what they did on 11 September?
For the OS: Why do we respond so readily with violence?

The first question presupposes what the Swiss psychologist Jean Piaget calls 'reciprocity', the ability to see the action of the Other as something at least partly caused by the Self, by one's own ability to elicit good or evil in the Other. Obviously, the whole retaliation discourse is based on that perspective which comes earlier in girls than in boys, but should be fully developed by the end of childhood. The first period of childhood is marked and marred by 'absolutism', the idea that what comes from the Other whether good or evil is entirely caused by the Other, that Other is *causa sui*. The terrorism discourse fits well within that perspective: 'It has nothing to do with us, they would have done so regardless' – a reaction that is very prominent among boys of, say, four years old.

Self-reflection requires courage, and yet there has hardly been any period with so much reflection both in the US/West and in the Rest, particularly in Muslim countries, but 'only' at the people level, not among governments, for the reasons mentioned. In Islamic countries this may ultimately lead to some changes,[24] both towards more non-violent politics using democratic approaches and more Gandhian approaches, and in the sense of isolating both terrorists and repressive regimes. They are often motivated by the same hard branches of Islam.[25]

But how about the US/West? The formula 'some change in US foreign policy' should signal a willingness to change course in order to reduce direct and structural violence, and if at all possible, bring about reconciliation. Such signals would have to come now, and the problems are enormous. But the signals, if clear enough, could also have an immediate impact.

Here are seven signals indicative of an exit from retaliation: *Military-political, against direct violence*:

1. A willingness to recognize Palestine as a state: this has already happened, and the US should be commended for that.
2. Remove all US military presence from Arabia, recognizing that this is a sacred land for very many Muslims, opening the way towards democracy in that dictatorship.
3. Lifting the sanctions on Iraq, negotiating with the regime and apologizing for Secretary of State Albright's 'it was worth the price' remark. That's more difficult, and would require real statesmanship.
4. Accepting the invitation by President Khatami of Iran for an open, public, high-level dialogue on the relation between Iran/US, and West/Christianity vs. Islam in general. The US

fears that such a dialogue will be used for propaganda purposes, and some disagreeable things will probably be said about the US/CIA-supported coup against the elected prime minister, Mossadegh and in favour the non-elected shah. But after that critique, which any mature person should be able to stand, comes the constructive phase where one could only hope Iran is well prepared: 'OK, where to go from here?' is an excellent, standard American formulation.

5. Hands off Afghanistan. This is partly because any US presence will strengthen the argument about ulterior motives and may stimulate an anti-US coalition, partly as a sign of respect. A UN presence up to trusteeship level is a viable alternative.

Economic-political, against structural violence:

6. Globalization-free zones, in the regions where people die from globalization because they have insufficient money to buy their basic needs. The Kyoto Protocol already has the Third World as an exemption, so there is nothing new in the idea of differential approaches. The alternative would be a Marshall Plan for the poorest areas of the world – the Andes region, Black Africa and South Asia – strengthening the local, informal economy with a view to basic needs satisfaction for all.

7. Reconciliation: learn from the German approach to the 18 countries they conquered and the two nations they tried to exterminate, the Jews and the Sinta/Roma. Today, Germany has reasonable relations with all, and a key element went beyond apologies and compensation to including the rewriting of textbooks.

Together these could turn a page in history, and it would cost very little relative to the enormous expenses of courses B and C. The political gains would probably also be enormous. But the psychological costs are daunting.

To overcome them such processes would have to be initiated and strongly demanded by civil society. But will yielding to their demand[26] not stimulate terrorism?

It might stimulate some. But it would isolate most of them by no longer giving them the ocean of hatred in which they can swim and be stimulated whereas a policy of military attack will only deepen and widen that ocean. At the same time it would generate positive processes, virtuous cycles that would very soon overshadow the vicious cycles of retaliation, capture people's attention everywhere and, as the European Community did for Europe in the 1950s, constitute a quantum jump in world politics. This is indeed overdue. Now is the chance.

Prognosis

How is this going to end? The answer depends on the choice of 'this'. Do we mean the small picture embraced by Discourse A, the 'terrorism' of 11 September and the punitive action = military action + retaliation? Or the larger picture covered by Discourse B, a retaliation cycle embedded in a globalized class conflict?

For the former the answer may be a US 'victory' with bin Laden dead, Al Qaeda in Afghanistan 'crushed', and US oil and military interests in Central Asia secured.[27] But bin Laden may become a martyr, Al Qaeda may change name and regroup – both processes as global as US corporations and air force – with a multiplier stimulated by higher levels of hatred. Punitive force incapacitates, but does not remove the causes that produced terrorism. Terrorism has no central command that can capitulate. Afghans may also unite against the US, as proposed by some.[28]

A major problem is whether to declare victory. The punitive approach may produce more capacity for violence, making victory declarations self-defeating, inviting attacks the next day, as the Algerian government knows from bitter experience. But not declaring victory means a drawn-out, never-ending alert – very taxing for the US and the 'allies', government and people. The question, what is wrong with us since we have so many enemies? emerges. Alerts are stepped down unless adequately stimulated.

In a meeting in 1990 with some State Department people the end of terrorism was declared, based on downward turning curves. This was seen as due to the bombing of Libya in 1986. My warning then was that terrorists might have *longer time* perspectives, and hail from *a bigger region* than Libya. The US image tends to be a single-shot phenomenon that peaks and peters out; a better image is a wave-like phenomenon with ups and downs; depending on US policy.

We often hear 'the world will never be the same again'. For President Bush, the US lost its innocence (three buildings violated by jets being rammed into their wombs?). Clearly, US and, by implication, Western/Japanese vulnerability became public knowledge. That the destructive power of the US is bigger than any other side is a truism; $D(US) > D(OS)$. But the vulnerability is also bigger; $V(US) > V(OS)$. If Power = Destructive power – Vulnerability, then what sign do we put between $D(US) - V(US)$ and $D(OS) - V(OS)$?

But this all depends on how we conceive of vulnerability. Destruction is intended for incapacitation, and vulnerability serves as a multiplier of destructive power. 11 September witnessed three flying bombs, nothing relative to the number of US 'sorties'. But they had an impact on an economy already in trouble, and on the polity, peeling off one democratic layer after another, even if that polity was also on its way out following the November 2000 elections and the judicial *coup d'état*.

Vulnerability, both social and human, has many dimensions. One formula for the social and global vulnerability is *degree of connectedness*. The more vertical/centralized the society, the more trade-dependent, the more vulnerable.[29] This was probably a key factor in target selection on 11 September, and is replicable. Horizontal connectedness is less vulnerable, and no connectedness spells no vulnerability. If self-sufficient villages in Vietnam are 'taken out', exterminated, then the spillover effect on the rest of society is negligible. There is no doubt where nuclear arms would have more impact.

A part of human vulnerability is a short time perspective combined with a single-peaked time cosmology, easily leading to exaggerated optimism and exaggerated pessimism. A long time perspective and wave-like time philosophy inspire perseverance.

For the larger picture, embedded in the retaliation discourse and in the class conflict/American Empire perspective, the prognosis also becomes larger, drawn out in time. Which historical process could serve as a metaphor? A very useful one, because the US was so deeply involved, is *slavery*.

The system was despicable, the suffering indescribable, the level of self-righteousness unbearable. There was retaliation from below, terrorism we would have said today, like Nat Turner (a native American bondsman) and his slave revolt in 1831, with 70 or so rebels killing 59 whites. The whole dogma of white superiority was at stake, and the repression was swift, enormous and effective. Assembly of slaves was forbidden, as were education and movement. But something important had happened: the blacks had proved themselves capable of a revolt, at the same time as their violence from below served, in the minds of many slave-owners, to justify their own violence from above. The similarity, point for point, to the post-11 September situation is painfully clear. We can almost hear slave-owners explaining how the slaves were destroying themselves; like terrorists harming the poor by undermining economic growth.

The colonialism metaphor works in the same way. There were revolts and punitive expeditions galore, partly obscured by self-serving historiography. By and large, they were unsuccessful. But the abolition of the colonialism struggle opens up the role of Gandhi, and makes us ask an important question: What would have been the Gandhian alternative on 11 September?

We know how slavery and colonialism ended: with abolition, shortly after Turner, shortly after Gandhi. What therapy would give the same prognosis for massive exploitation, the essence of the global class conflict?

Therapy

We have already described seven policies as exits from the retaliation cycle. Had they been practised some months earlier, or even some months after ... But they were not, and the killing continues. What would be the concrete circumstances under which another course of action by one side could have produced a basic change in the other?

Let us this start time with OS, the other side, the Osama side. The Gandhian action on 11 September would have been to organize, with the same precision and synchronization, and on a global scale, massive demonstrations around all US/Western/Japanese embassies in the world, surrounding them by the thousands, totally non-violently, presenting the facts of global injustice, inviting dialogue. And not only the economic exploitation but all dimensions of class: the political monopolies and manipulation in Palestine and Afghanistan, the military violence in Iraq and elsewhere, the cultural domination through the media and other means, the sacrilege in Arabia.[30]

And there would have been a massive world boycott of the goods and products from the most objectionable, least socially and ecologically conscious, global corporations that same day, combined with promotion of concrete action for an economy privileging basic needs for the most needy; all of this far beyond Seattle, Gothenburg or Genoa. The demand would be for dialogue between people and government, assuming that they, democrats all, will never fear meeting the people.

Would this have an impact on the hard, corporate US/West backed by police and military power? In the longer run yes, and it would have saved thousands of lives in New York, Washington and throughout Afghanistan. Soon, maybe many, many more.

What are the steps on the road for that 'longer run'? We know them already thanks to two excellent and recent models: the end of the Vietnam War, and the end of the Cold War.

In both cases two factors were operating. There was heavy resistance to the ferocious fighting in Vietnam and the nuclear arms race in the Cold War, both processes going on unabatedly. *And* there was a strong, tenacious, ever-growing, world-wide movement against the war and against both the (nuclear) arms race and the repression in the post-Stalinist countries. Violent governmental action and non-violent civilian counteraction, in other words; with the latter gaining the upper hand, stopping the war and temporarily the arms race.

Will it be possible to mount a giant North–South peace movement, addressing both sides, like the giant West–East peace movement? Building on the old and new peace movements in the

North, the anti-globalization movement, and the movements critical of both terrorist and repressive tendencies in Muslim societies? Probably yes. And the second condition is already there: just as in the other two cases, the US has picked a struggle with no clear ending, very unlike the wars against Baghdad and Belgrade where the capitulation metaphor made sense.

And yet it is worth noting that there was a very important intermediate step in both cases: US 'allies' oscillating between the US and the peoples' movements, increasingly voicing, even publicly, some of the same concerns, increasingly reluctant to give the US a blank cheque to do whatever the US leadership deemed right.

That leads to an important point. Washington is sensitive to its own people, but works with and through governments abroad. But Washington is also sensitive to allied governments and always wants support and closed ranks. That's a major vulnerability.

When the chips are all down, like slavery and colonialism, massive global injustice is not a problem of force, counterforce and cycles of retaliation. Basically it is a moral problem. And here the underdog has the upper hand, it is low in status, but high on moral standing; and more so the more non-violently he conducts the struggle. The top dog may win the game of force, but not the moral issue – and when that dawns upon him and his allies, a change of consciousness sets in, and demoralization starts thawing the frozen heart. The game is over. And deep in their guts the better among those at the top already know this, having been brutally woken up by three planes raping three buildings: the 11 September alarm call.

But we also need some kind of mediation. At some points terrorists and state terrorists will have to meet and discuss what they have in common, not only oil, but also terrorism. A meeting on *Larry King Live* – a master of making people open up, the good, the bad and the ugly – between George W. Bush and bin Laden, or their seconds in command – is not very likely, today. But wise people could meet with both sides first, probe their goals, both those at the surface and the deeper goals, their world-views, their long-term philosophies, searching for overlaps, for ways of getting out of their vendetta like two Albanian families predestined to kill each other suddenly recognizing that the vendetta is the enemy, not the other family. Who could be better than three wise men like Jimmy Carter, Fredrik de Klerk and Nelson Mandela? Or the pope?

They are profoundly decent. And decent people would reject all forms of political violence and feel compassion for all victims, not a tribal compassion only for their own. The world needs all the decent, good, men and women – now.

Our War Culture's Defining Parameters: Their Essence; Their Ramifications (external; domestic; 'racism'; 'borders'; 'international law')

Carl G. Jacobsen and Kai Frithjof Brand-Jacobsen

Is Our 'War Culture' Immutable? Three Challenges

As noted in chapter 1.1, analysis of the massive 'Correlates of (post-Napoleonic) War' project compels the conclusion that the Western world's predominant security parameters throughout the nineteenth and twentieth centuries have been and remain those of a quintessential 'war culture'.[1] This is a culture whose realpolitik security prescriptions, though generally perceived as designed to deter threats, have in fact been conflict-stimulating and precipitating rather than conflict-avoiding or transcending. Three distinct yet complementary contrary dynamics have challenged this culture in recent years: post-1960s academic game theory; Mikhail Gorbachev's astounding inversion of past arms race and arms control truisms; and today's increasingly consensual acceptance that state-based and/or dictated conflict-resolution formulas rarely solve and often exacerbate underlying differences. At an even deeper level, Gandhi's *satyagraha* campaigns in South Africa and India, the emergence of peace research, the peace movement, and peace education from the 1950s on, the anti-colonial struggles and national liberation movements across the global South, the civil rights, women's, human rights and environmental movements, and the struggles for social justice arising again in the late 1990s and today to challenge the dominance of global capital and the erosion of democracy – all have embodied the counter-culture logic which seeks to transcend and go beyond the narrow confines and parameters of war culture-driven policies of exclusion and elite dominance/control. These dynamics or phenomenological challenges may or may not alone or together constitute or reflect an emergent 'peace culture'; but they do address core components of any such alternative.

Game theory's central message, encapsulated most dramatically by the 'Prisoners' Dilemma', demonstrated mathematically and conclusively, is that the cooperative-solidarity choice best protects the interests of both parties. While this was seen and taken as a revelation in academic circles and defence establishments, it had for centuries, if not millennia, been practised as the guiding principle of most of the world's communities, required for purposes of survival, social harmony and the well-being of all members of the community. Yet, while the logic and message are compelling, even players well versed in the theory will often choose betrayal as the surest route to temporal advantage, at least when the play is time- or turn-limited, as it perforce must be under most game conditions, and as it is all too often perceived in self-serving political calculations. Yet this factor is not present in historical time. (Therein, perhaps, is one reason why the same lessons always seem to have to be re-learned.) More sophisticated game theory, as developed by pioneers such as Anatol Rapoport, minimizes game/real-world differences.[2] Yet players' betrayal choices continue to defy the logic of the exercise. Clearly, game structure limitations do not suffice to explain the phenomenon. Might the answer be found in politicians' limited time horizons, compounded by our individual-focused competition-promoting culture? Western players' formative socialization years and memories (of sometimes extreme East–West hostility) as well as more current conflict response norms (as suggested by Afghanistan, the Gulf War and successor confrontations) have arguably ensconced them in 'war culture' assumptions – assumptions so pervasive that even those who recoil from their ramifications are subconsciously influenced by their terms of reference: competition is good, but only if it is *won*, for it is also a *threat*; state (and other?) interrelationships are *zero-sum*; a gain for one means a loss for the other. The acceptance of these terms of reference, as integral to the *realist* (read militarist) paradigm, by Ministries of Defence and Foreign Affairs and the Chancelleries of the world, is of course also why their officialdom found game theory irrelevant (or at least all but its original, narrow-focus genesis, developed to facilitate submarine warfare).

Yet the alternative vision or approach was percolating outward from its academic citadels and burgeoning peace movements, stirring interest in arms control associations, Pugwash (the East–West scientists' forum) and other NGOs, to surface finally in its first 'officially' approved incarnation, through the UN's Palme Commission, chaired by Sweden's former prime minister, with that Commission's adoption and embrace of the still state-centred concept of mutual security and the more transcendent vision of common security.[3] Not only was mutual and, indeed, common security possible, but their pursuit was conflict-avoiding and confidence-enhancing, in stark contrast to the realist zero-sum legacy.

Among those who sat on and testified to the Palme Commission were Russian specialists, who now gravitated towards Gorbachev's leadership challenge. With Gorbachev, to paraphrase Adlai Stevenson, 'something funny happened on the way to confrontation'. The Gorbachev team walked away from the postwar tug-of-war.[4]

Previous years' negotiations, East–West as well as Sino-Soviet, and their zero-sum paranoias, were characterized rather than caricatured by the decades-long, apparently never-ending Mutual and Balanced Force Reduction talks in Europe, in which even punctuation suggestions were assumed to camouflage fiendish advantage aspirations. Gorbachev cut the zero-sum Gordian knot. He embraced mutual and common security. Where previous Soviet leaders had sought to exclude and isolate the US and China from European and Asian security designs, Gorbachev included them as core and essential partners. Where previous Soviet leaders saw every US or Chinese security demand as necessarily and *ipso facto* against their interests (as they had also always viewed Soviet demands), Gorbachev sought to meet such demands when and wherever possible, in decisive rejection of zero-sum formulas.

In the Far East he stepped down the readiness status of many of the divisions stationed along the Sino-Soviet border (thus reducing their manpower) and withdrew others; those that remained were pulled back from the immediate border vicinity. Turning to the West, he announced a unilateral nuclear test moratorium, and followed this by declaring the withdrawal of 500,000 troops and significant tank and other weapon stocks from Eastern Europe. He paid the USSR's UN arrears, called for and declared a readiness to participate in a more cooperative, collective security regime, through the UN on the global arena, and through the OSCE (Organization for Security and Cooperation in Europe) in a 'Common European Home', stretching from the Azores to beyond-the-Urals Central Asia. In Washington and other NATO capitals, the 'Evil Empire' (the term in and of itself, of course, made negotiations and possible compromise positively sinful) suddenly appeared to be a prospective partner with whom 'one could do business', in the words of Prime Minister Thatcher.

With Gorbachev's political demise, however, more traditional, partisan approaches were reasserted. In the Far East, Sino-Soviet normalization and rapprochement survived the change, perhaps because the reality of a now far weaker Russia and a singularly triumphalist America made positive Russian–Chinese cooperation a precondition of securing a less than unipolar world. In the West, however, Washington effectively torpedoed the OSCE as the new

European security arbiter. NATO was not incorporated into that construct, nor was it retained as a fallback sub-organization, such as the West European Union (the WEU) within the European Union, as it might have been. Instead, it was not only reaffirmed as its existing members' ultimate security guarantee, but extended by members' directive (more precisely, Washington's fiat) to fill the Central/East European 'vacuum' left by the now defunct Warsaw Pact, and act as *the* primary UN peacekeeping-making enforcer in non-CIS ('Commonwealth of Independent States', the less-than-cohesive Soviet successor state umbrella) Europe, and perhaps beyond.

In the immediate post-Gorbachev period the Partnership for Peace programme, which NATO offered and extended to Russia and other post-Soviet states, might have served as a half-way house to ultimate membership of a truly pan-European successor incarnation. But the years that followed provided compelling evidence for the views of those who saw it from the outset as a minimalist sop designed to obfuscate the determination *not* to proceed to the pan-European 'common home'. NATO's declared intent to accept Central/East European membership applications, but to restrict these to non-post-Soviet states, promised a new line dividing the continent.

The line would, at least for the foreseeable future, be softer than the so-called Iron Curtain. Yet for Moscow, it constituted an historic rejection and became the principal reason for the 'Russia First' posture it now adopted, and for its renewed emphasis on ties with China and other non-Western actors. For some smaller post-Soviet states on the 'wrong' side of the new divide, it encouraged other paranoias. For, whether viewed from Moscow, Riga or other capitals, even the softest possible dividing line is inherently ominous because it bespeaks of exclusion and the return of zero-sum fears and mistrust, rather than the confidence-enhancing visions of mutual or common security and inclusion.

But the dramatic, consensual expansion in the 1990s of 'UN-mandated' peacekeeping and peacemaking agendas and aspirations – perhaps the single most notable novelty of the 'new world order' – soon appeared to burst the bounds of US means and will. The failures that ensued – most dramatically in the withdrawal from Somalia and non-interference in the Rwandan genocide, but also in the smouldering embers of 'post-settlement' Bosnia, the unravelling of the UN's Cambodia design, the carnage wrought in Kosovo/a, Sri Lanka, Afghanistan, Kashmir, Guatemala, Chiapas and all too many other unhappy locations and constellations – came to mock declarations of statecraft morality and purpose. If only in private, realpolitik advocates were increasingly compelled to acknowledge realpolitik limitations. The evident failures and shortcomings of state-based and dictated conflict resolution designs and the often counter-productive consequences of complementary NGO endeavours led to startlingly new state and UN interest in alternative theories and approaches. For the first time 'officialdom' at large appeared to accept that past truisms no longer sufficed. As the UN commissioned 'peace research' manuals with which to train putative 'peace workers' and develop conflict transcendence expertise, the accumulating legacy of game theory and Gorbachevian deviance appeared to acquire renewed life and purpose (see chapter 1.1).

Capitalism vs. Marxism: War Culture Internalized: The Search for Transcendence

Early and dominant evolving concepts of capitalism and Marxism and the "til death do us part' supposition of their irreconcilability mirrored and reinforced the 'war culture' that the Napoleonic era bequeathed, the war culture that spawned them. It was, as previously noted, a culture characterized by the zero-sum assumption that advantage to one equalled disadvantage to the other, and vice versa. Capitalism is quintessential war culture, in that it is power-focused and exclusive, seeing privilege as a preserve that can be secured only through ever-greater exploitation at the expense of non-privilege. For non-privilege alleviated is own-privilege curtailed, while non-privilege status quo is own-privilege threat – a threat containable only through buffers added to, ensconcing and protecting established power and privilege. As Marx asserted, capitalism's inherent logic is to exacerbate inequities in power and wealth distribution; it was and remains an economic system imbued by a structure of violence that seeks to perpetuate itself, aggrandizing the wealth and privilege of elites through greater impoverishment and marginalization of the social majority, and made worse under the extremes of neoliberal capital-driven 'globalization'.[5]

But Marx's counter-theology, and the variants offered by his followers and intellectual descendants, from Stalinist/neo-Stalinist authoritarians, whom he clearly would have abhorred, to today's social democrats, are equally reflective of war culture's tenets. Admittedly, Marx himself argued vigorously against all theology and ideology, seeing himself as engaged in a radical critique of the social processes and structures of the world around him, a critique that tackled root causes rather then just effects, yet Marxism's suppositions are equally zero-sum, equally power-centric. They assume the mirror-image need for confrontation, for victory is the only antidote to defeat; they are as exclusive (viz. the 'dictatorship of the proletariat' – though Marx allowed for democratic alternatives, and in fact posited the term only in juxtaposition to the 'dictatorship' of capital) and, when defined as such, equally perverse in their consequences – which in authoritarian and democratic variants alike tend towards *bureautocracy*, rules, bureaucracy and 'political correctness' aggrandizement, which may ultimately be as nefarious in their ramifications as capitalism's cruder inequities. The 'Marxist' perversion is arguably an inherent contradiction of every tenet of Marxism, though it evolved through asserted pedigree. It may be that the essence of the perversion of both capitalism and Soviet and other-type 'communism' is a corollary of the deeper permeating of the hierarchical, top-down, inherently elitist and authoritarian structures that inculcate our cultures, traditions and the very concept of the state itself. Perhaps unregulated 'capitalism' and 'Stalinism' should be seen as diversionary extremes. Perhaps the deeper qualities of 'statism' and elite control/domination (whether by the party, bureaucracy, or capitalists) of the means of economic, social, political and cultural (re-)production are the more fundamental phenomenon deserving attention.

Marx's early writings focus on man's need to transcend his alienation from nature, from himself, from his fellow man and from his labour. While capitalism is seen as a fundamental progenitor of this alienation, 'communism' must also address and transcend the deeper causes and structures of violence on which capitalism is based.[6] Yet it is no coincidence that both 'systems', as evolved and practised, have justified and condoned environmental degradation and non-sustainable development policies – expressing concerns in tandem with the vagaries of political correctness, but shying away from the hard consequences of corresponding policy decision(s). Both condone, indeed require, exploitation. Both proclaim recipes of exclusive progress, while asserting inclusive import. Both are industrially-centred, male-oriented, Western dominant world-focused, with deep elements of cultural imperialism.

Marx is indeed unjustly besmirched through association with those who have taken his name in vain, as are some of capitalism's more humanist exponents. (Some might argue the case for Maynard Keynes, and even Adam Smith.) The Communist Party as a revolutionary vanguard and wielder of monopoly power was a Leninist creation, though Lenin defined it not as the model for the future that it later became, but as a temporary necessity dictated, originally, by the omnipresence of the tsarist secret police and, later, by contingencies of civil war and foreign interventions. The command economy model was not Marx's, and to blame him for the Stalinist perversion is indeed akin to blaming Christ for the Spanish Inquisition.

Although obviously a child of his male- and state-centric era, the logic of Marx's writings indict imposed inequities; they demand equal opportunity, which must perforce rest on equal social control (the ultimate empowerment), for all – in education, employment, health and all realms of social life and intercourse; they are non-discriminatory in terms of sex, race, faith or other ground(s); they are quintessentially inclusive – not exclusive, as too often interpreted or presented.[7] The early twentieth-century prominence of feminist revolutionary pioneers such as Rosa Luxemburg, Alexandra Kollontai, N.K. Krupskaya and Emma Goldman, and the transcendent internationalism of Lenin, Martov and Trotsky, speak to this core content.

Therein lies the abject failure of Marx's dominant Stalin era and later heirs. Reflecting, perhaps, the dominance of cultural over Marxist roots, chauvinism towards both women and minorities would be an abiding characteristic. As in the dictatorship of capital, they also perpetuated exclusive privilege, embedding the disadvantages of the excluded, while forsaking long-term sustainability and the environment; their Marxism was effectively transmuted into state/monopoly capitalism. Thus 'dictatorship of the proletariat' became instead dictatorship by the party–military–bureaucratic elite, as the proletariat and people were transformed again (as under tsarism and capitalism) into *objects* to be ruled over and directed rather than *subjects* forming their own course and history. *Radical democracy*, based upon direct rule and participation by people's *soviets* (councils) and referendums with government by the people, for the people and with the people, was seen as too threatening, and was crushed, if not stillborn, as the tyranny of *elite control/power over people*, rooted in deep-seeded structures and cultures of violence and enforced with the direct violence of the military and *gulags* took hold.

Therein, in turn, the progenitor of the quintessentially humanist (neo- or post-Marxian) vision propounded by TRANSCEND, ICL/Praxis for Peace and others: promoting complementarity and diversity, and fora for the voices of all – peoples and cultures – in a constant transformative process. Their vision is that of a *permanent revolution* based on dialogue, communication, *conscientization, organization, mobilization* and *empowerment* (COME) – a revolution of means and ends, as embodied in the slogan 'Peace by Peaceful Means' and its concomitant concepts 'Peace Praxis' and 'Peace Actor Empowerment', transcending violence, and the structures, actions and cultures that are themselves violence-dominated and perpetuating. Gandhian beliefs in people's power, as groups, communities and individuals, to find creative and viable alternatives to violence and thus to transform the world, resonate.

One does not have to be a Marxist to agree that today's obscenity of three men controlling wealth equal to the gross national product of some 50 states is just that – an obscenity.[8] Or that the massive debt-burden and restructuring being used to enslave countries and populations of the South – preventing any meaningful social/economic development, democracy and/or independence – to the interests and gain of global economic and financial centres (TNCs) almost entirely located in the North (often with the complicity of elites in both the North and the South), is a more devastating and refined form of colonial and imperial control.[9] But the essential issue is not zero-sum and should not be seen as such. In the security realm militarist zero-sum dogmas have been transcended, at least intellectually: first, as noted above, by the still state-centric concept of mutual security, which, extrapolating from conflict and peace research studies, posits the greater benefice of mutual advantage strivings; later, by the more catholic (global) civil society aspirations of common security and 'human security' – crystallizing the ultimate logic of the most recent conflict/peace research findings. When focused on domestic socio-political and socio-economic ramifications, as on external or internal security precepts, they prescribe a non-conflictual or, more realistically, a conflict-transcending approach. It is not conflict itself that is negative. It is how we handle conflict that produces positive or negative, creative or destructive consequences. Thus the aim of this book: to broaden our repertoire of skills and knowledge in approaching conflicts, and to help establish conflict transformation as a viable and necessary alternative to the violence-enhancing and violence-promoting essence of traditional outside-state interventions.

The thwarting of developmental prospects and worsening impoverishment and exploitation, which are integral consequences of today's systemic failures, are clearly today's primary violence generators, both intra-state and internationally. Its components – most glaringly: developmental states' debt interest payments and terms-of-trade penalties both outstrip total aid figures; the number of absolute poor (earning less than one dollar a day) has increased eight-fold in just two decades; over 4,000 children die each day from drinking contaminated water; women's education, the single most effective development tool and guarantor, remains disastrously under-prioritized and underfunded – all are untenable in a world in which knowledge and the possession of weapons of mass destruction is rapidly proliferating. In such a world zero-sum mindsets prescribe catastrophe.

As with Samuel Huntington's 'clash of civilization', such mindsets and the policies they prescribe provide ideological justification for actions which themselves often result in the very ends they were meant to prevent (as in NATO's war to 'prevent catastrophe' in Kosovo/a).

Yet there is a sustainable, transcending option. It is compelling, and its time has come. It is the Tobin Tax (or Currency Transaction Tax), named after a Yale professor, James Tobin, who first proposed the idea in the late 1970s, when the fact of a dramatically increasing, purely speculative component and share of international financial transactions first became evident. Its essential advocacy – to institute common good, global development-financing, minimal taxation regimes for hitherto untaxed profit spheres and activities – was incorporated and dramatically extended by Morris Miller's seminal 1986 (and later) work, which calls for commercial rent for any commercial or for-profit utilization of the 'global commons', deep oceans and outer space (satellite and other usage).[10] It has been brought back onto the global stage and the agenda of many citizens' movements today through the committed work of organizations such as ATTAC (Association for the Taxation of Financial Transactions for the Aid of Citizens) and the Halifax Initiative.[11]

Even a farcically and, to some, obscenely minimal Tobin (or Miller) tax would suffice to finance the developmental prerequisites of debt relief, health and education, environmental restoration and rehabilitation, and resource sustainability and/or substitution, elaborated and costed by UN and other agencies. The *tsunami* of now US$3 trillion a day of purely speculative transborder financial transactions, surging upwards at a compounded rate of 32 per cent annually, is a flood that engulfs more immediately productive trade and investment funds; it emasculates chancelleries' and central banks' (whose total world reserves are a mere US$640 billion in comparison) fiscal and monetary control prospects, and is today wondrously untaxed – as is the potentially even richer domain of the larger 'global commons'.[12] Using recent figures, a mere 0.025 per cent tax on speculative flows alone would suffice to fund the most ambitiously calculated global development programmes.[13]

There are, of course, alternative revenue sources, such as increased general (or higher-rate) taxation and/or diversion of funds from militaries or military industries ('conversion'), but these would clearly entail significantly higher political, and perhaps economic, cost. The Tobin/Miller proposals would be minimally disruptive. They would transcend the unpalatable alternative of increased individual taxation in either the developed or the still-to-develop world; they would transcend pressure to divert funds from military-industrial complexes and other establishment icons (though the decreasing threat plausibilities of more equitably developing civil societies would presumably impact on their legitimizing premises);

and, while they would not guarantee a just world, they would transcend the immediacy of its non-sustainability.

Capitalism and Marxism/socialism are both arguably responses to perceptions of a security threat, to individuals and hope. In this sense, maybe *Peace is the Revolution*[14] – assuming the definitional premise that peace imposed is the ultimate conundrum – following the Gandhian tradition, with peace both the means/process (*satyagraha*, peace praxis) and ends. There are, of course, innumerable prescriptions for its translation into practice, ranging from Gandhi's concepts of *swaraj*, *sarvodaya* and *antodaya*, through Marxist-derived visions of workers' self-management and Noam Chomsky's anarcho-syndicalism, India's *Living Democracy* and Chile's *Sustainable Chile*, to Metta Spencer's and *The Economist*'s arguments for citizen-empowering referendums and, perhaps, vote flexibility and maximizing allowances (assigning, say, ten votes for ten referendums, but permitting multiple votes on issues of greater concern, with corresponding non-participation on issues of lesser concern), to Kai Frithjof Brand-Jacobsen's advocacy for the empowerment of multiple human and community networks linking people at every level of society, transcending state limitations, to develop always active, self-sustainable but also interconnected intra- and inter-state peace worker capacities – *satyagrahis*.[15] But the ideals, though their propagators span the ideological spectrum, are all those of more genuine democracy, and, as such, complementary and inclusive, not exclusive. Perhaps the last word should go to Alec Nove, founding director of Glasgow University's Institute of Soviet and East European Studies, and doyen of Western expertise on Soviet economic history and policy (and one whose Menshevik roots in many ways epitomize the search for transcendent values): at the national meeting of the British Association of Soviet and East European Studies in 1968, as Soviet and Warsaw Pact tanks put an end to the Prague Spring, he noted that 'Communism with a Human Face' might be equated with 'Capitalism with a Human Face' – both effectively translating into social democracy. Indeed, as noted by this author, perhaps our ideals are not as incompatible as we have been taught to believe, though social democracy is also state and control rather than people and freedom-centred, and must itself ultimately be transcended.

War Culture/Realpolitik: Racism as Catalyst?

The exclusive rights-seeking secessionist demands of alienated religious and/or ethnicity-defined belief collectives ignited and drove many of the conflicts of the 1990s, from Croatia to Tajikistan, Afghanistan, Sri Lanka, Rwanda and Kosovo/a. Yet the phenomenon was arguably not as new as some have postulated. Arguably, they appeared new only when juxtaposed against the aberrational preceding half-century of superpower dominance and suppression. The Cold War's end lifted the lid, so releasing the pressure.

The phenomenon of exclusive rather than inclusive agendas was remarkably consonant with the defining characteristics of the post-Napoleonic war culture, which defined Indo-European and Indo-European-influenced security postures through the nineteenth and twentieth centuries – and the underlying dictates of realpolitik. They are informed by and imbued with the same self-serving partisanship of proffered options, whether in the political, economic, legal, social or strategic realms. Their policy prisms are mired in self-interest, zero-sum assumptions and fears, seeing self-advantage as the only route through which self-interest can be guaranteed, protected, perpetuated and ensconced.

Their theologies mirror the tenet espoused by Israel's Jewish establishment of a 'Chosen People' – which by definition imputes that others are not chosen, and are therefore of lesser value. Among (subscribing) Jews this manifests itself in the refusal to acknowledge or see similar traumas in others' genocides, others' holocausts. And it manifests itself in the refusal or inability to equate Palestinian (or others') rights with theirs. Its essential tenet of moral exclusivity, and the policy options that derive therefrom, are, of course, quintessentially racist.

But while there are Greek tragedy dimensions to a horribly victimized, essentially émigré Jewish consensus embracing and pursuing the very security dogmas and group protection theologies that once decimated their Central and East European communities – as there is to the perverse psychological compulsion that drives so many abuse victims in turn to inflict abuse on their spouses, their children and others – there is also commonality, grotesque, but real.

Japan's pre-war, wartime and postwar nationalist propaganda – still vibrant, as evidenced in her establishment's continuing refusal to see shame in horrors inflicted on 'lesser' races – is surely as exclusive in its moral parameters, and thus equally racist. The point is equally applicable to China's traditional self-image as the Middle Kingdom, the very definition of civilization, with all living beyond its borders designated 'barbarians', distinguished only by their geographical locations.

And it is no less applicable to the tsars (whose civilizing superiority and mission was ordained directly by God – as were those of China's emperors and Israel's orthodoxy). And 'Great Britain', France, Holland, Germany and others, while usually not ascribing the same mandate from God (as to God's pleasure or otherwise, there were some who ascribed Britain's attainment of an Empire on which the sun never set to the fact that God didn't trust the English in the dark), they were no less certain of the superiority of their cultures and destinies, and the lesser moral authority – and therefore rights – of others. Racist arrogance was reflected in contemptuous epithets – Frogs, Krauts and 'Perfidious Albion' – or in outright exclusion from human consideration: 'savages'.

The United States' Manifest Destiny, Joint Chiefs of Staff (JCS) 570/2, the Kennan/Schelling Doctrines, and the 1992 Pentagon Papers are but the latest dominant manifestations of this phenomenon.[16] Their contempt for others is epitomized by school curricula and media that ignore, disdain and twist other histories and cultures; there is 'America' (itself a term of extraordinary arrogance, bereft of both historical and geographic justification), and there are the non-chosen, the lesser. Nazi Germany designated particular groups to be victimized and blamed – Jews, Gypsies and Slavs (especially Serbs and Russians) – as *Untermenschen*, 'subhuman', and thus not deserving of human consideration. The US did the same in Vietnam, where their opponents were dehumanized as Viet Cong (thus the description of My Lai massacre victims, and hence, presumably, the rationale for Lieutenant Calley's perfunctory slap-on-the-wrist sentence at the ensuing trial), as have other powers in other contexts.

But if all others are excluded from the community of virtue, as they essentially are in American, Israeli and other theologies, is this not to decree that they are all *Untermenschen*, the ultimate racial epithet?

Racism is an inadequate term. Yes, all groups that define themselves as distinct from others, be it on religious, ethnic or other grounds, and who seek to take pride in and from such exclusivity, are to a degree racist. And certainly, racism is not the preserve of particular theocracies, ethnicities or states. It is as evident in the mutual disregard jarring relationships between ethnicities in 'Arab' and 'Black' Africa, and among 'First Nations' in the Americas, as it is in WASP, Jewish, Mandarin and other establishment clubs.

But as arrogance in an individual may mask innate insecurity, so group racism and self-exclusion may reflect real, imagined or manipulated fears. Such fears may be multifaceted, complex and varied. They may reflect or respond to grievances caused or conjured by analogous biases propounded by others. Or, when inculcated and manipulated by community leaders (as they often are), they may mask considerations of power, the desire to retain power or fear of losing power.

In a humane world the power-hungry's fear of losing power elicits scant sympathy, though in all too many places it remains a real barrier to prospects for democracy and equitable (or any) development.

The crux clearly is the insecurity of individuals, the real or perceived insecurity that defines their personal or economic reality or attends their beliefs and proclivities. It is this that needs to be addressed. Democracy defined as majority rights can too easily mask majority tyranny. 'Political correctness' protecting majority sensibilities may justify minority discrimination and oppression. 'Human rights' are defined by their extension to minority rights, even, and perhaps particularly, when these appear 'deviant' – though, of course, and by definition, not when these are such as to infringe on or circumscribe those of others (with the all-important caveat that intellectual or belief discomfort alone does not justify proscription). Self-proclaimed democracies, particularly those that give their citizens only the rarest of opportunities to indicate preferences – be it once in four, five or even six years – also often contain stark social and economic disparities, making political and civil rights and freedoms a luxury which, while theoretically available to all, can only be fully enjoyed and practised by a small minority. Given widening extremes of inequality, marginalization and disempowerment in many of these communities and the absence of any meaningful form of *demos kratia*, *people's power*, it is doubtful whether the states of Western Europe and North America, or any other in the world today, are truly deserving of the label 'democracy'. More appropriate may be another word given to us by the ancient Greeks: *demagogy* (*demagogia*: *agogos* from *agein*, to lead to drive); one who gains popular support (= power) by promising to do things for the people or to represent them.[17] Democracy, then, may be seen more as a goal, something to strive, and to struggle for, rather than as an actually existing reality in the world today. Dynamics of the last ten years and today have done more to erode the promise and potential of democracy than to bring us closer to its realization.

There will perhaps, and tragically, always be those who fear and seek to blame, or can be persuaded to blame. But clearly, if the dominant pathology of racism and its potency as violence instigator and propellant, is to be combated, it can only be through more compassionate and inclusive education, through political and electoral reforms that propagate and confirm minority and individual rights, and through dialogues between peoples and communities that seek to break down stereotype concepts of the 'enemy' (whether based on ethnicity, colour or other prejudice), and 'good' vs. 'evil'.

Recipes for truer democracy range from calls for more frequent referenda, perhaps with weighted voting options, to proportional representation variants which might compel increased cross-

communal cooperation, to those that insist not only that
meaningful democracy must involve far more frequent and effective
input from its citizens than allowed by current norms, but that the
citizenry's final authority must be extended also to other realms –
as in the decision to go to war. Particulars compel debate,
discussion and dialogue; the principle should not.

Borders – Conflict-provoking and Rights-protecting: Oxymoron, Fixed-relation Antipodes or Opportunity for New Thinking?

Nation-state borders, as also other borders and (other) borders of
the mind, are often thought to be 'natural' and inviolable. Yet in
light of Johan Galtung and Haakan Wiberg's observation that there
are 2,000 'nations' (ethnicities/groups with deep attachment to
'their' lands and, usually, with distinct cultures and language) in
the world, but only 200 states and no more than 20 true nation-
states (whose borders may be said to be congruent with the
essential living space of just one nation), such concepts appear
questionable, if not downright ludicrous. They are also dangerous,
and more often conflict-stimulating than conflict-calming.

State borders always reflect (past) state power reach – as borders
of the mind may be said to reflect belief systems' reach and limits.
This characteristic has always been conflict-inducing if or when
the power that is attained later either grows or shrinks (or
anticipates the probability that it will shrink) disproportionately to
its neighbours. It may also be conflict-perpetuating even if the
power neither grows nor shrinks substantially, if the power reach
served to incorporate others alienated from or otherwise non-
absorbable by the dominant nation-authority. A variant of this
constellation proliferated in the early 1990s, with the recognition
of new-state borders of Yugoslav and Soviet administrative
divisions that lumped smaller 'nations' or nation components with
majority nations from which they were alienated by reason of
perceived history or accepted culture, administrative borders
decreed by authoritarian governments' fiat and in pursuit of
agendas that never included 'independence'. One or other of these
permutations constituted the defining feature of all the wars of the
early post-Cold War era.

But there is another phenomenon that may prove even more
weighty, though its ramifications are in some ways the hardest to
predict. The power whose reach defined and defines today's
borders, was and is state power, which increasingly appears to be
the power of the past rather than the power of the future. Through
most of the confrontational post-world war era, state power was

supreme within its recognized domain, circumscribed only by the directional framework imposed by the hegemonic state power – and the compromises demanded by domestic socioeconomic and political dynamics.

The last two decades of the twentieth century, however, witnessed a revolutionary transfer of power from state structures and organs to multilateral corporations and international financial institutions – 'the global economy'. The decline in state relevance, authority and scope for intervention was perhaps most dramatically manifested in international financial transactions, wherein the proportion accounted for by trade and investment, areas of traditional state involvement and relevance, shrank from over 90 per cent to less than 10–15 per cent. As noted: by the year 2000 the purely speculative and non-government-controlled 80+ per cent reached US$3 trillion a day, rising at 32 per cent compounded per year – while an ever-larger proportion of the trade and investment residue signified inner-conglomerate transfers and advantage calculations unaffected by state chancelleries. A mere 0.001 per cent tax on this speculative investment flow would have sufficed to pay for all the UN's activities; 0.025 per cent could have funded long-term sustainable development programmes designed to provide debt relief, education and health care, stabilize the world population, preserve natural resources and regenerate the environment (including cropland preservation and reforestation) and stopped CFC production.

Alternatively, if international speculative finance is now sufficiently dominant to resist even minimal government encroachment, as the record would appear to indicate, there are other 'painless' revenue sources that could be equally gargantuan in their import – viz. the Miller proposal to collect economic rent on profits extracted from 'the global commons'. The 'opportunity benefits' were and are dramatic.[18]

The inability to impose such a tax testified to an apparently extraordinary immunity from traditional authority, as did the scythe-like slashing of tariffs and trade restricting regulations ordained by regional and global free and freer trade regimes, by the International Monetary Fund (IMF) and World Bank lending and aid stipulations, and by the World Trade Organization (WTO).[19] The elite wealth enhancement this generated was ever-less leavened by redistributory taxation or delivery. But in thus perpetuating and indeed exacerbating the despair of the less advantaged (developed nations' own widening social divides were illustrated by Canada's 58 per cent increase in child poverty within five years of signing the North American Free Trade Association), it also threatened to destroy the societal compacts on which rested the essential stability of the nation-state system. From Mexico to

Russia, China to Indonesia, ever-sharper juxtapositions of extreme wealth and spreading impoverishment mirrored the societal backdrop of past revolutions.

While the 'global economy' may have largely superseded the nation-state, it appeared unable to replace its societal adjudicatory role. It could and did employ mercenary armed force and security personnel in local and less developed contexts, but these could not rival larger nation-state potentials. International conglomerates were arguably less anarchic in their interaction and inter-regulation than nation-states, but they were quintessentially non-representative, that is non-democratic, and conversely could themselves claim no independent social mandate.

The borders that marked power's reach were power protective, and protective also of the social mandate and compact on which that power ultimately depended. Traditionally, a core component of that compact was the readiness to erect tariffs to protect industries unable to compete on even terms. Thus was the United States developed; thus were all now-developed nations developed, save England – against whose efficiencies none initially could compete. If today's non-protective injunctions had then been in force, the sun would still not have set on the Empire, while US industries would jostle with those of (other) less developed nations. The ubiquitous intrusiveness of the 'global economy' threatened a dependence deeper and more immutable than that associated with postcolonial neocolonialism, whose defining characteristic of dependence on imposed, inequitable terms of trade nevertheless allowed room for developmental optimism, illusion or delusion.

Development-protective tariffs, of course, are not a panacea. In the USSR their combination with enterprise gigantomania eviscerated the remaining, competitive dynamics in the civilian industrial sector, and led, ultimately, to stagnation and self-perpetuating obsolescence. The same problem occurred in the US military sector, wherein the post-1970 trend away from contested procurement bids also brought increased and increasing inefficiencies – finally propelling the US administration's move in March 1998 to thwart the proposed merger between its largest defence contractors, Lockheed Martin and Northrop Grumman. The collapse of Russia's economy brought a graphic reminder that unfettered robber-baron capitalism could be as competition-denying and, in the absence of state leverage, *diktat* and/or enforcement prospects even more calamitously unable to generate or sustain developmental growth. In the US, a century earlier, robber barony, though arguably never eviscerated, was transformed through the barons' need to de-fang the burgeoning revolutionary antithesis, and their consequent embrace of regulatory norms and a state alliance structure that promised greater and more sustainable (though only marginally more equitable) growth. But they enjoyed the luxury of more time than do their Russian emulators.

The late twentieth- and early twenty-first-century fact of ever-more rapid technological change may fatally undermine the development-protective potential of tariffs. Some have also argued that the international conglomerates' remove from national *diktat* or influence, their fundamental contradistinction from yesteryear's and still surviving 'national' firms (whether nationalized or merely state-aligned or state-favoured), makes investments into low-wage regions more compelling, and hence probable. With national authorities sidelined, logic dictates that immiserization and poverty-line wages will attract investment. The argument would appear compelling, except that with immiserization, minimal wages are usually accompanied by absolute or relative illiteracy, which eliminates their allure for all but minimal technology and (thus) dependence-perpetuating investments.

In this context it might be worth noting one unanimous conclusion to all development studies, namely that education is crucial to development, and that education for women is the single most potent development guarantor and multiplier. Furthermore, while state planning and developmental direction (whether Soviet, Japanese or Western bureaucratic-type) cannot compensate for market-derived competition, markets *per se* do not and should not equate with non-trammelled markets. The need for competition does not require, and may ultimately be incompatible with, unregulated competition and near-monopoly competition-denying control by TNCs.[20] Competition and free trade between unequal partners, whether inter- or intra-state, promotes inequalities and increased disparities. But while neither competition as such nor its market progenitor preclude regulation (indeed, equitable competition requires it), both may be negated by over-regulation, however contentiously defined.

The late 1990s US anti-trust actions against Lockheed-Northrop and Microsoft, and the EU's and, subsequently, other governments' decision not to sign the Multilateral Agreement on Investment (MAI), with its lifting of restrictions on international investment and profit extracting, signalled governments' residual legitimacy and potential import.[21] The spreading government assertiveness, or caution, in turn reflected growing, dissenting citizens' movements, movements that sought and nurtured increasing and therefore increasingly potent, coordinating, transnational ties and alliances – cooperative, internally democratic citizens' movements that could be said to possess 'natural' legitimacy.[22] In this they transcended NGO networks, if only because of the degree to which NGOs remained far more dependent on governments and their agencies for funding.

The citizens' movements – a still too multifaceted and still-to-be fully defined amoeba on the world stage – as yet represented only a putative challenge to the power and reach of 'the global economy'. But the force of their moral credentials and their burgeoning ability to exert an impact on governments in need of a democratic mandate, both reinforced by the fact of these governments' diminished sovereignty, also served to provide new reason and potency to government collectivities seeing the need and seeking the means to curb at least the more brutalizing excesses of international, non-regulated finance and business. They thus served to strengthen governments' residual legitimacy, while at the same time confirming their increasingly archaic limitations.

The logic of the latter function and impact in turn promised at least somewhat increased future scope for the consideration of less restrictively defined border interpretations. Whereas traditional, restrictive, defensively self-protective nation-state border definitions generally precluded jointly managed 'peace' or free economic zone territorial regimes – a core component of some conflict amelioration designs – the emergent logic provided reason and latitude for different calculations.

There are historic precedents for joint territorial management arrangements, and for referendums or plebiscites informing border determinations (notably in the finalizing of the German/Danish border). In nation-state-focused times and paradigms these tended to be seen as or suggestive of something less than politically correct, and were therefore most often ignored by analysts and political commentators. In the nation-state eroding, complexly fluid context of today's inter/intra-state and global dynamics, however, their addition to the respectable options menu – together with more novel concepts such as fora uniting state and intra- and trans-state sub-state assemblies or representational groupings (such as the Nordic Council and confederations of autonomous communities/municipalities) – may provide important tools or venues for purposes of conflict mitigation and resolution.

International Law: the Mirage that Beckons – and Recedes

International law is of course a misnomer, if not an oxymoron. There is no international government or legislature with the authority to promulgate international law. There is no court with a universal judicial mandate. There is no global enforcement agency. The international system is essentially anarchic: law-avoiding rather than law-friendly.

What is misleadingly termed international law are essentially conventions of mutual advantage, signed by those who so judge them, and upheld by those who continue to so judge them. Their membership may declare them universal once signed by an arbitrary number, but non-signatories deem themselves exempt. In fact, signatories will themselves defect from the declared regime if and when its provisions are judged no longer to be of advantage, or, at least, when the advantage of defection is thought to outweigh the sanctions or penalties that may be levied or imposed by remaining members. Depending on the regime in question, these may take the form of withdrawn trade privileges or, in more serious realms, military action – which may in turn range from such limited engagements as Britain's naval protection for its fishermen when defying Iceland's then unilateral extension of its territorial waters, to Washington's more devastating strikes against Iraq's non-discovered 'weapons of mass destruction', and NATO's 'murderous bombing' of Yugoslavia. Yet, while some defections have been and are deterred by threat or action, more determined defectors (such as Iceland, Iraq and Serbia/Yugoslavia) will often not be dissuaded.

Signatories to regimes or conventions will in fact often issue written or verbal caveats, giving themselves the right to withdraw when or if ever they consider membership a detriment to 'national security' or other vital interest – arrogating to themselves the sole right to make that judgement. Other caveats are designed to exempt members from particular treaty provisions or possible treaty ramifications. Thus, when the World Court in the Hague agreed to hear and later found in favour of Nicaragua's charge that the US was conducting an illegal war (the so-called Contra War) against it, Washington found cause to declare the issue and itself beyond the Court's jurisdiction, and to ignore the reparations it ordained.

Through the Cold War(s), as in earlier eras, sometimes competing notions of international law were promulgated and enforced by or with the authority of the hegemonic power(s). The corollary to this characteristic of 'international law' is the fact that dominant powers can, will and do transgress and flout 'laws' with impunity when they deem, in their sole judgement, that such transgression or flouting is 'necessary', while lesser powers may do so only when this is deemed non- or insufficiently threatening by the greater power(s). Great powers may ignore or declare superseded established notions of international law, as in the Helms–Burton Act's 'extra-territorial' declaration that US anti-Cuban legislation and investment-deterring penalties would be universally applied;

and they may also, as in this case, ignore the hypocrisy of disregarding the implications of reverse applicability.[23] (The same principles applied to 'nationalizations' and forfeitures following the American revolution would see the return of Florida to the Duke of Westminster and reparations to Canada sufficient to eliminate its debt and pay for its national health programme.)

Thus the single most important aspiration for and yardstick of the new world order proclaimed by President Bush Sr. during the build-up to the Gulf War may be the concept of generic international law: international law not as a manipulable tool of great power interest, but as civilizing ground rules applicable to all. The occasion of Bush's proclamation did not augur well. The opportunity to extend international law and confirm its universality was not taken. Iraq's occupation of Kuwait was condemned and declared to legitimize countering military action. But others' occupations, some similarly condemned by UN resolution – but exempted from military response – such as Israel's occupations of Gaza, the West Bank and the Golan Heights, or Syria's occupation of Lebanon's Bekaa valley, remained exempt from retribution; so did China's occupation of Tibet, and all too many other cases of gun-adjudicated power and privilege (including earlier occupations such as Russia's of the north Caucasus and the United States' of Texas).

Partisan and selective application of 'international law' remained a dominant feature of international relations through the 1990s. Thus, as previously noted, the international community acceded to Germany's demand to recognize Croatia's secession from Yugoslavia, without extending the same right to Serb and other communities to secede from the new entity, even though this contravened the only relevant 'international law' statute (the Helsinki Final Act provision which sanctified postwar European boundaries) as well as international 'common law' (the US, and others, had previously always opposed secessionist aspirations, such as Biafra's and Katanga's, even when they clearly enjoyed popular support) and the recognizing nations' own laws or statutes detailing the conditions for new-state recognition. The refusal to extend analogous rights to Serb communities was the single (non-) act most responsible for unleashing the subsequent wars.

It also underlined the absence of law's defining principle, that it must be generic and apply equally to all – at least in principle, if not always in applicability. The same selective, purely partisan application of 'law' was later evident in the non-prosecution of Croat and Muslim rapists juxtaposed to prosecution of Serbs, non-excavation of Croat and Muslim 'mass grave' sites and only the most cursory investigation of Croat and Muslim prisoner (sometimes disappearance and always rights-depriving) camps versus the rigorous excavation and investigation of Serb shame.

Shortly thereafter international law was again inverted. Now it was the Parti Quebecois in Quebec that wished to break away, insisting, like Croatia's separatists, that *their* right did not extend to non-French ethnicities within their borders – though Quebec, like Croatia, had been given lands with other-ethnicity majorities by federal authorities, for federal purpose, and the Cree and Inuit of the north, like the Serbs of Krajina, voted overwhelmingly not to be part of a separate entity. Now the Canadian government declared that international law granted rights of self-determination to colonized peoples only; if grace and goodwill nevertheless led Ottawa to accept and comply with a hypothetical future (French) Quebecois majority vote to secede, then, certainly, the same right must and would also be granted to other ethnicities' majority vote(s). The US, and indeed all who had denied that right to Croatia's Serbs, now declared support for the Canadian position.[24]

Within a few years 'international law' would be inverted again, when NATO decreed Kosovar rights to autonomy/self-rule not extended to Kosovo/a's Serb and other minorities (and rights of return not extended to Serbs cleansed from there or elsewhere).

The problem with international law's 'Croatia variant' (which was also applied to seceding formerly Soviet entities whose previously purely administrative borders also encompassed competing ethnicities, sparking similar descents to civil war hell) lay not just in the blatant selectivity of its blessings. Nor did it derive solely from thereby unleashed and thus legitimized conflict dynamics. It was, rather, that its definition derived not from legal principle, not from moral suasion, but from calculations of economic or other advantage or consequence – often in regions or domains far removed from the immediate, apparent concern. It was, to paraphrase Clausewitz's famous dictum on war, the fact of international law as an extension of (great power) politics.

All 'international law' is not great power-derived. The 1997 treaty to ban land mines, a consequence of Canadian, Norwegian and others' initiatives, is illustrative. But while embodying the ideals of moral and judicial foundation and generic applicability, it also illustrates their limitations. Its perceived moral imperative secured expressions of great power empathy, declarations of non-production and mine-clearing aid, and declarations of ultimate intent to join. But the 'great powers' did not join the treaty club; nor did other state and sub-state actors with major arsenals and/or strategic or tactical dependence on land mines. Thus, while the treaty clearly reflected and reinforced a widely shared moral demand, its successful championing and signing was arguably due to the fact that it was essentially non-threatening for and irrelevant to great power interests.

The prominent role played by NGOs' and citizens' organizations in the drive for the land mine ban, the growing movement for indigenous and non-recognized peoples to be given voice and status, the impressively attended and ambitious 1999 Hague Appeal for Peace (reminiscent of the halcyon days of the 1950s Campaign for Nuclear Disarmament) and the multiple follow-up initiatives that derived therefrom, all appeared testimony to the growing power and activism of an increasingly global civil society. The burgeoning global movement for social justice which came onto the world stage in Seattle, Bangkok, Okinawa, Prague, Melbourne, Washington, Quebec City, Göteborg, Ottawa, or, even earlier, in Chiapas, the Philippines and Indonesia, and, perhaps most importantly of all, Porto Alegre with the World Social Forum (first held in 2001), also provided further evidence of increasing participation and activism on the part of citizens around the world working for the strengthening/building of democracy and the transformation/transcending of direct, structural and cultural violence.[25] Yet the CND analogy interjects a cautionary note. As does the dominance of 'Western' NGOs, which some Hague Appeal participants found as threatening, damaging and 'colonialist' as the state-centred governance and dialogue they seek to enrich/supplement/transcend. True global civil society must perforce involve and represent also the unlistened to and unrepresented – perhaps 80 per cent of the world's population – building real alliances and true solidarity between people's movements and citizens' organizations in the North and the South. Linking the movements for social justice with the peace movement in the struggle for *peace by peaceful means* will be a crucial part of this. While *'basta!'*, *'enough'* is perhaps the most revolutionary cry uniting those opposed to the growing injustices of global inequality and exclusion in the world today, the building of *positive programmes* and *constructive action* for *direct*, *structural*, and *cultural peace*, is perhaps the greatest challenge.

Meanwhile, great power foci remained selective and self-serving. In early 1998, for example, when an Anglo-American build-up again threatened major strikes against feared or purported Iraqi sites of 'weapons of mass destruction' deployment or development, and later that year, when they unleashed a three-day missile barrage against 'targets' not found by UNSCOM's US and Israeli intelligence-coordinated inspection regime, and absent UN sanction, there was no suggestion that Israel's very considerable nuclear arsenal might deserve similar attention – though it was, *sui generis*, the fuel and legitimator of Iraq's efforts. It was the same double standard that underlay great power reluctance to comply with the disarming provisions that were their *quid pro quo* reciprocal obligation under the terms of the (nuclear) non-proliferation treaty. Such double standards are not new. They are the historic norm. So also with the possibility that Britain's 1998 posture reflected calculations of US trade and investment-affecting regulatory consequence; much as her embrace of Germany's Croatia policy had reflected German concessions in Maastricht Treaty negotiations. (Corresponding bribes were given to other EU members.) Policy determinants are not necessarily action-specific; they are however never interest-blind.

Yet such 'permanently operating factors' offend the very notion of international law. International law, if it is to be of substance, must be generic and impartial, and based on neither calculations of temporal advantage or benefit, nor whim, personal need or spite.

The world needs a non-beholden, non-circumscribed World Court; it needs a War Crimes Tribunal with global reach and a mandate that embraces great power actions as well as the actions of arbitrarily designated rogue states; it needs uniform enforcement principles and effective, generically-derived and applied and responsible means. The latter, in particular, may be an unrealizable concept for the foreseeable future. But it is a precondition for the vision – which presupposes authority that is blind to gender and inclination, race and faith, at least in terms of its constitutional and operational mandate.

The world also needs a regime through which to address the underlying structures and causes of the rising number of inter- and intra-state conflicts. The hegemonic impulse that seeks to cement over unresolved conflicts through *diktat* and KFOR-style missions, prescribes a peace that is at best ephemeral. That fact, of course, in turn highlights the need for a more effective forum to address underlying structures and cultures of violence, and the need for new language, dialogue and perspectives such as might offer more creative and viable alternatives for the twenty-first century.

CHAPTER 1.5

The State/Nation Dialectic: Some Tentative Conclusions

Johan Galtung

Thirty+ TRANSCEND Experiences with State, Nation and Territory

1. The dialectic between national identity and state integrity, and the right to self-determination

With about 200 states, 2,000 nations with claims on sacred space and with memories of sacred time, and about 20 nation-states, there is a world potential for 1,980 independence wars, pitting status quo-oriented states against change-oriented nations. The 'sacred space–sacred time' combination, probably best understood as a secular sequel to the religious tradition of endowing space and time points with sacredness, is then used to define 'nation' as distinct from 'culture', defined in terms of symbols, like language, religion, myths. A nation is or has a culture, but a culture is not necessarily a nation. Cultures do not have claims on points, even regions, in space and time; space being the most important, since that is where territorial conflict arises. Territory is tied to the sovereignty of states and states to the monopoly of power. States come and go, but nations remain – a major source of human identity, often crazy, often violent, because of the psychological energies generated.

About 180 states are multinational, almost all dominated by one nation, often the result of historical patterns of conquest. Expansionist nations, many of them European-Christian or Arab-Muslim, have come to dominate others with similar patterns among themselves before the uninvited arrival of the Abrahamitic Occident in Asia, Africa, the Americas. It is difficult anywhere in the world to identify more than one state, or country, that is both multinational and symmetric. The name of that country is, of course, Switzerland, possibly because of the high level of autonomy given to the non-Germans, and the low level of conquest.

The word 'sacred' is used to inform us that nationhood is serious, and not a matter to be psychologized away as prejudicial and discriminatory only, even if these two patterns of attitude and behaviour play important roles. If two or more nations lay claim to the same points in space, then we have a genuine incompatibility/contradiction/problem, or whatever we choose to call it, even if their relationship is symmetric and egalitarian. They may simply not like to live too close to each other; there are signs of that in Switzerland. The problem is unlikely to go away by preaching 'tolerance', by which is meant tolerating the close presence of the Other. Even equality may not help, or help only in the longer run. Individuals have their private sphere; nations may do the same and yet be hospitable to guests that do not overstay their welcome.

Correspondingly, a nation divided among two or more states may long to unite. Their separation by the structural violence (often supported by direct violence) of forcing apart those who want to live together is similar to the structural violence (also supported by direct violence) of forcing together those who want to live apart. We may regret that people, like the Koreans and the inhabitants of Bosnia, do not like to be forced apart, or forced together, but we may come closer to a solution by regretting that structural violence (and the direct violence behind it) and trying to do something about it.

To develop patterns of conflict transformation by peaceful means for this ubiquitous conflict, the state/nation interface, is a top global priority to avoid war. Obviously, conflict arenas like the former Soviet Union, ex-Yugoslavia, Northern Ireland, the Basque Country inform us that we have not been good at it. There has been too much violence, too much oppression, too much suffering.

As we know only too well today, in early 2002, many of these nationalisms erupted when the Pandora's box of the Cold War was prised open. Those uninformed by history tried to believe that they were created by that event. They were not. They are mainly age-old, but had been suppressed by a socialism convinced that under a unified working class, with the means of production socialized, national struggle would disappear as a major social force, surviving only as a relic kept alive artificially by other feudal relics: clerics, nobility and the bourgeoisie. They were wrong, and stimulated nationalism by imposing taboos on any manifestation beyond the arts and language. When they then went about reconstructing their societies after the Cold War they made the mirror image mistake, guided by a liberalism convinced that under a unified nation, with power democratized and the market privatized, the class struggle would disappear as major social force and survive only as a relic kept alive artificially by relics like old communists and nostalgic people. They are also wrong.

The question then is, whether, under what circumstance and to what extent, the right to self-determination can serve as a mechanism for conflict resolution, or at least transformation. Ideally, it might run like this: any nation living on the territory of a state it views, rightly or wrongly, as a prison of nations organizes a plebiscite for its nationals, invites observers from the 'international community' to supervise the plebiscite and, if the majority exceeds some (fairly high) floor (say, two-thirds, or three-quarters or four-fifths), declares that the national self has determined – precisely what? The right to their own state, meaning to their own territory protected by their own power monopoly? In other words, that a new state has been born?

What guidance do we get from the International Bill of Human Rights? Article 1 of the 16 December 1966 International Covenants on Civil and Political Rights, and on Economic, Social and Cultural Rights, reads (also see UN Charter, 1(2), 73):

1) All peoples have a right to self-determination. By virtue of that right they freely determine their political status and freely pursue their economic, social and cultural development.
2) All peoples may, for their own ends, freely dispose of their natural wealth and resources without prejudice to any obligations arising out of international economic co-operation, based upon the principle of mutual benefit, and international law. In no case may a people be deprived of its own means of subsistence.

However, independence is not mentioned. Moreover, this collective human right is not treated like individual rights. Whereas the right of assembly, or free speech, can be practised immediately, the right of self-determination is conditional on the right being recognized. But by whom? By the state having that nation in its midst? Like a slave-owner recognizing the right of a slave to freedom? Or, by certain big powers such as the US/UK, with a strong international law tradition and a keen sense of the precedents that might arise from any recognition of the right to self-determination? Or, by the International Court of Justice, as in the Western Sahara case (1975 ICJ Rep 12), making self-determination the overriding principle, as opposed to the Eastern Greenland case, 1933, viewing the case as a conflict between two colonizing countries (Denmark and Norway)? Is this really an intrinsic right, or is it contingent, like the 'right' to conscientious objection? If so, are we talking only about some convenient, Wilsonian, post-First World War rhetoric for dismantling the defeated and dying Habsburg and Ottoman Empires; or post-Second World War rhetoric for the administration of ending a colonization that should never have existed?

Some of the reasons for this may lie in Article 1(2): 'freely dispose of their natural wealth and resources' and 'a people may [not] be deprived of its own means of subsistence'. These are laudable but also very strong words, pitting the basic needs of the people against the power of the sovereign state and the corporation operating in that territory. There is at least an economic basis for the conditionality. Like the status as conscientious objector, there is a clear and present danger to the state and state logic if self-determination is recognized.

But how about people logic? It can exercise the strength of freezing water in the crevice of a mountain or of budding seeds under asphalt: it is difficult to contain in the longer run as evidenced by, say, the American Revolution/War of Independence, 1776–1812. That force goes beyond the 'right to dispose of their natural wealth and resources' for the satisfaction of material needs. There is a solid non-material need at stake, which is not sufficiently clearly written into democratic theory: not only the right to invite, and then to disinvite, the rulers to rule them, but also the right to be ruled by one's own kind.

Sovereignty over a territory is neither a necessary nor a sufficient condition for this right to be met. If that sovereignty is not a part of the package, then we are talking about autonomy, not about statehood. (Sooner or later statehood may follow, 'trusteeship' being one example of a transition formula.) Autonomy, then, becomes the lower-level outcome of self-determination; independence, the newborn state, being the higher level. Autonomy carries some sovereignty but not ultimate sovereignty, as the state in command still possesses the *ultima ratio regis*, the king's last argument: the heavy guns.

So the right of self-determination is not only conditional; it can also be eroded by offering a lower-level outcome, which may or may not be acceptable to the nation exercising its right to self-determination. On the other hand, a situation whereby any group declares itself a 'people' and makes off with 'their natural wealth and resources' is also unacceptable. The UNESCO Expert definition of 'a people' is in terms of racial or ethnic identity, linguistic unity, religious or ideological affinity and territorial connection. There are many of those. The definition can also apply to people of power and privilege, often living in separate niches within a country. In the age of globalization they may declare themselves 'a people' and convert their territorial niche into a global finance economy node.

The UNESCO definition is helpful, but is the broad term 'a people' helpful? 'Territorial connection' is also too soft to cover 'nation', as defined here. We are dealing not only with 'connection', but with 'attachment', to the point of cultural sacredness and territorial claims juridically.

The problem does not lie in definitions, however, but in what happens when two or more groups/peoples/nations have 'attachments' to, even claims on, the same territory. The relation is usually asymmetric, between the powerful and powerless. We may sympathize with powerless, suppressed and stateless Jews, Roma and Palestinians and their right to possess territory and a state, like the individual right to possess property. But the powerful may have lived there for generations, be not only 'connected' but 'attached', and voice their claims eloquently. There is a complex dialectic not only of power, but of rights. There may be good arguments on both sides of that dialectic.

Can we cut that Gordian knot by a simple decision-making mechanism? There are three nations in a country and a referendum in one of them, N, establishes its will to secede. The other two vote against that secession. They use their majority status to impose a referendum on the whole population, proving that only a minority vote in favour of independence.

Of course, this argument only restates that N has been denied the right to be ruled by its own kind. The three separate votes define the parties, the actors. But the combined vote of three nations tossed together in a country may only be a signal from an entity about to disappear. Self-determination is a right of the Self, not of the Other to exercise Other-determination.

Could we recognize the recognition institute and the two-step process:

1. recognition of the right to self-determination for N;
2. the exercise of self-determination by N.

The problem is the step from recognizing the recognition to recognizing a recognizer. Neither big powers, nor their lawyers, nor the UN General Assembly, a trade union of states, nor, for that matter, a trade union of nations will do: their conclusion is too linked to their own interests and all too predictable. Their opinion should be known, but not obeyed. The search for disinterested parties, possibly the International Court of Justice, is ongoing; but the outcome is by no means clear. And the reason may be that we are talking about absolutes, even with sacred connotations. We have indicated above that decisions in this matter cannot be made by voting; votes against sovereignty will not necessarily be respected. Can problems of national will be subject to law at all? The details, yes; but the 'law of the land' has not been able to silence the struggle for freedom.

Moreover, self-determination works like a set of Chinese boxes. A state may be 'a prison of nations' and cause violent conflict, often called 'internal war', even if no such thing exists in the age of intervention. But this also applies to states emerging from such conflict, giving rise to the problem of recognizing nations, within nations, within nations, etc. The principle of *uti possidetis*, respecting existing borders within (colonial) empires and federations like the Soviet Union and Yugoslavia (used by the International Court of Justice in the Frontiers Dispute case, 1986, between Burkina Faso and Mali), gives too much weight to past administrative decisions. Rights to self-determination for Slovenia, Croatia and Bosnia-Herzegovina were recognized, but not for Serbs in Krajina/Slavonia, Serbs and Croats in Bosnia-Herzegovina and Albanians in Kosova. The result was war and immense suffering, which might have been avoided had 'lower-level' equal right to self-determination been recognized.

The conclusion so far can only be that the right to self-determination is an important collective human right. But it should not be interpreted as an automatic right to secession, independence and recognition by the inter-state community as a state, or even to a high level of autonomy within a state. The right to self-determination is the right of a people itself to determine its status within a state, and by implication in the world, including the option of independence and the option of status quo. But, regardless of the decision, a right to autonomy at a low or high level is not a right to be autistic, disregarding others completely, just as the right to free speech does not imply the right to disregard the consequences of exercising that right. There is an overriding principle of responsibility.

2. The dialectic between national identity and state integrity, and the duty to conflict transformation

Our conclusion so far has been that the right to self-determination is a necessary but not sufficient basis for guiding the national identity vs. state integrity dialectic to outcomes that satisfy the conditions for conflict resolution: acceptability by the parties concerned, and sustainability (the outcome does not have to be propped up). There are many disciplines dealing with this; law is only one. A vast spectrum of alternative dispute resolution formulas has opened up, all of them, or so it seems, based more on dialogue between or with the parties, and less on codified law. Whether this is a process of *de lege ferenda*, law in the making, or not, remains to be seen. History usually moves in cycles from the code to the search, from the cooked to the raw, *le cuit et le cru*, and back again.

The following will be based on the experience most familiar to the present author, the TRANSCEND method, and on conflict practice with 33 cases involving states, nations and territory. Of

course, this is only one kind of experience out of very many around
the world, but maybe it speaks to the conditions of some people
and peoples. The perspectives on the conflicts have all been derived
from long in-the-field dialogues with many conflict parties and
participants; they are not textbook exercises.

The pattern to be explored below was not at all clear from the
beginning 30–40 years ago, not even the simple typology below. It
takes time and experience before patterns emerge. And there is
certainly no assumption to the effect that what follows is the final
word; nothing ever is. But there is some advantage to numbers
when patterns are in demand, and 33 is a good number, not very
high, but high enough for some pattern to emerge.

We imagine a piece of territory, and on that territory:
'one state', or 'two or more states'; and inside them:
'one nation', or 'two or more nations' and four combinations:

Table 1: Number of States/Territories × Number of Nations

No. of States No. of Nations	One State/Territory	Two or More States/Territories
One Nation	A. 20 Nation-States: (Almost) Homogeneous (Almost) No Diaspora Ideal Not Real Reality	B. Korea The Kurds The Mayas The Samis
Two or More Nations	C. Israel/Palestine Rhodesia-Zimbabwe Hawai'i Hindu-Muslim Somalia China Lebanon Japan-Russia Ecuador-Peru	D. Cyprus Northern Ireland Kashmir Pax Pacifica Yugoslavia A Yugoslavia B Sri Lanka Caucasus Okinawa The Great Lakes Euskadi Gibraltar/Ceuta- Melilla Afghanistan East-West A East-West B Gulf A Gulf B Christian-Muslim Tripartite Europe Christian-Heathen

The reader will find the 33 conflict arenas, as indicated by national and/or geographical terms. The conflicts are over control of territory and involve nations, which is to say, geopolitics. For brief diagnosis-prognosis-therapy characterizations of the 33 conflicts, see Part 2 below; for more see <www.transcend.org>.

The reader will notice that there are only four 'one nation–two or more states' cases and nine of the 'two or more nations–one state'; the bulk, 20, being in the most complex category D. The classification depends on the number of states and nations in the conflict arena, and that makes for some ambiguity in the classification, but of no great consequence.

Let us now make use of the same basic typology, but this time not focus on the classification of concrete cases, but on what can be done, the possible remedies/therapies:

Table 2: The State/Nation/Territory Dialectic: Therapies

No. of States No. of Nations	One State/Territory	Two or More States/Territories
One Nation	The classical case, now challenged by globalization and migration, and then 1. B, C, or D or 2. nation-absorption into super-nations; withering away of nations 3. state-absorption into super-states; withering away of states into regions	1. unitary solution, integration with • equality, symmetry • human rights • tolerance within states 2. autonomy, within all states 3. confederation, of autonomies or states 4. federation, of autonomies or states 5. new unitary state
Two or More Nations	Increasing functional sovereignty: 1. unitary solution, integration with • equality, symmetry • human rights • tolerance 2. autonomy 3. federation • territorial • non-territorial 4. confederation • territorial • non-territorial 5. independence 6. condominium	Creating a context with increasing regionalization: 1. associative system of states 2. confederal community of states 3. federal union of states 4. new unitary state

Table 2 shows many options; no doubt there are more. The general point of departure is a simple assumption: The higher the number of alternatives to the awesome dichotomy status quo in a unitary state vs. secession-independence, the lower, *ceteris paribus*, the probability of violence. Since the (understandable) recognition institute often blocks the road from self-determination to independence, the nation in search of statehood may see violence as the only alternative.

Should this not imply that self-determination as a human right is given up? But the right to self-determination must be linked to a duty to conflict transformation. To secede, doing nothing to clean up the mess, is like a spouse walking out of his/her marriage with no regard for the other party and third parties (children, in-laws, friends, neighbours), whether the person walking out is a battered, exploited wife or an egoistic, tyrannical husband (or any other combination).

After violence there is more mess and less inclination to clean it up, so the conclusion can only be to engage in conflict transformation before, not after, any violence, hopefully preventing that violence. Even if self-determination is a right, like women's right to parity, its exercise may lead to conflict. That conflict has to be transformed within the context of the human right. The conflict does not invalidate the right. But neither is that right the only consideration in the conflict.

Before we proceed, let us dispense with one argument: that secession may lead to small and unviable states. Europe has a number of small and viable states, both economically (wealth well distributed) and politically (democracies), like the mini-states of Liechtenstein and Andorra, and the small states of Iceland and Luxembourg. The world also has very large states whose viability economically and politically can be disputed, among other reasons because they are 'prisons of nations'. Their worry about small states is a vicarious argument. The history of city-states should be indicative; they were highly viable until they were absorbed by some of today's 'nation-states'. More problematic would be a UN with 2,000 members, but then confederations might be encouraged (like the Nordic Community) with joint delegations.

Let us combine Tables 1 and 2, applying perspectives and approaches from Table 2 to the conflict cases in Table 1.

A: One nation–one state/territory. We cannot blame Herder and Fichte: whatever they said seems to have fallen on fertile soil as spelt out in the first section. However, these are not eternal, essentialist truths. Other fault-lines, such as gender and class, are or could be more salient, as feminists and Marxists argue. Or fault-lines may recede into the background in favour of an unstructured, amorphous mass of individuals, as postmodernists seem to think. But today nation matters, and will continue to do so for some time; states probably less so.

We have indicated that however that may be, open borders and a globalizing world carry migration in its wake, by push and pull. Each migrant carries a foreign culture, with claims not on niches in geographical space, land (migrants are not nations when abroad, or only after several generations like the Northern Ireland Protestants), but on niches in cultural space. Over time this may lead to B-, C- or D-type problems. But then something else may happen, also involving countries of origin:

- Nation-absorption; they all over time join a super-nation, as has been happening for some time in the Nordic countries linked to heavy intra-Nordic migration, and to the EU countries. It may take generations, even centuries, before 'I am Nordic', 'I am European' stick. The experience with '*jesam jugoslav*' and '*sovjetskij tchelovjek*' indicates that it cannot be enforced.
- State-absorption; this process is (European Union), or is not (Nordic Community), accompanied by the creation of a super-state. Is the problem solved? No, super-nations/states are similar to nations/states; super-levels also leading super-conflicts/wars.

B: One nation–two or more states/territories. Four cases, similar and different, of divided nations: the Koreans divided between North, South and Japan; the Kurds divided between five countries, Turkey, Iraq, Iran and (less) Syria and Armenia; the Mayas divided between Mexico (Chiapas), Guatemala (as majority) and Honduras; and the Samis between Norway, Sweden, Denmark and Russia. A difference: the Koreans are alone in divided Korea.

Table 2 offers five outcomes or stages. What is acceptable and sustainable depends, as usual, on the circumstances:

First, human rights wherever they live, are certainly not realized for the Kurds and the Mayas, more so for the Samis, more for the Koreans in the South than in Japan and less in North Korea.

Second, autonomy within the states, meaning not only human rights but the right to be ruled by one's own kind based on the 'territorial attachment'. This is not a problem for Koreans in Korea, but probably not viable for Koreans in Japan, and highly meaningful for Kurds, Mayans and Samis where they are numerous.

Third, linking the autonomies in a confederation, possibly with its own parliament which may have to meet in some other country, and its own representations abroad, taking on the functions of a state without being one. This is highly relevant in all four cases.

Fourth, linking the autonomies in a federation, i.e. statehood with some autonomy for the constituent parts, like creating the United States between 1776 and 1865. Again, highly relevant in all four cases.

Fifth, a unitary state solution, taken by the two Germanies in 1990 (the federal aspects are along other lines). Like the fourth step (and maybe also the third) it is likely to be heavily resisted by the states. Most relevant for the Koreas; in fact, President Kim Dae-Jung has a three-stage formula (3)–(4)–(5).

C: Two or more nations–one state/territory, the state-territory being a 'prison of nations'. Five outcomes are offered; what is acceptable and sustainable depends on the circumstances. They can also be seen as five stages, this time reflecting state disintegration more than integration:

First, a unitary state solution, meaning that all irredentist, recalcitrant nations are given most favoured citizen status, enjoying equality/symmetry, human rights and tolerance. If this is acceptable/sustainable, so far so good. This turned Rhodesia into Zimbabwe, and has been the formula for Muslims in India, demanding symmetric approaches to the Ayodhya conflict.

Second, autonomy within the state, 'sovereignty', is what has been offered to the Palestinians and what may emerge in Hawai'i for Hawaiians. Being asymmetric it may not be viable in the short or long run, calling for independence and possibly confederation for Israel-Palestine, federation being too close for comfort.

Third, the federal state, based on territorial attachment or cultural identity, territorial or non-territorial with joint finance, foreign and security policies, like Switzerland. The formula has the advantage of symmetry, and a non-territorial version based on clans is interesting for Somalia. This, or (4), may solve Beijing's troubled relations with Taiwan, Hong Kong, Tibet, Xinjiang and Inner Mongolia. Could it work in Lebanon?

Fourth, making the state a confederation, with *de facto* independence for the constituent parts to have their own finance, foreign and security policies. Possible for India?

Fifth, secession and independence, one (or more) new states are born both *de facto* and *de jure*. Indispensable for Palestine, and possibly a solution for an Okinawa lorded over by US/Japan.

Guiding the choice of alternatives is how much sovereignty an 'imprisoned' nation actually wants. To find out, ask questions like 'How about separate postage stamps?', 'How about your own Olympic teams?', 'How about a separate currency?', 'How about a seat at the UN?', 'How about your own army?', etc. Classical nineteenth-century independence with a resounding yes! to such questions is on the way out. Other options have entered the discourse; statesmen, diplomats, journalists at least should learn, even if they cannot create these options. People may in fact be much less dualist than the stark 'prison'/independence formula indicates, and not reject the formula out of hand. Sovereignty is a question of degree, of what is functional.

What remains are Ecuador–Peru over *la zona inejecutable*, the disputed territory in the Andes mountains, and Japan–Russia over the Northern Territories/South Kuriles, the disputed territory off Hokkaido. The cases are somewhat different from the cases above. There are certainly two nations (Ecuadorians and Peruvians in the first case; Japanese and Russians in the second), and there is a territory, but not with an 'imprisoned' population of any magnitude. It is difficult to conceive of independence or steps in that direction, which is essentially what (1)–(5) in Table 2 are about. So (6) has been added for this case: owning it together, making it bi-national, a condominium, with shared/joint sovereignty, which may also be possible in Northern Ireland and Basque Country and the Demilitarized Zone (DMZ) between the Koreas. As a zone of peace there would be a number of non-threatening, cooperative measures such as natural parks, joint economic zones, camping grounds, conflict centres, etc., gradually attaining a model character.

D: Two or more nations–two or more states/territories. We then turn to the most complex, and most frequent combination, typical of today's world, combining B and C. Generally speaking we are dealing with a messy combination of nations and states, as in the Caucasus which has three states, 28 nations within them and each other, and four states intervening from the outside; something for those who think the Basque Country, Northern Ireland and Yugoslavia/Balkans are complex to consider. They can be, but are not always, found in mountainous areas; the Caucasus, Pyrenees, Yugoslavia, Himalayas, Hindu Kush, where groups can be nesting in a valley for centuries only to be 'discovered' and claimed by the centre on the plains (Moscow, Paris/Madrid, Belgrade/Zagreb, Beijing, UK/US). For the Alps: the Swiss/Austrian models.

The general formula is obviously to combine the approaches in B and C. The intellectual task of finding comprehensive and comprehensible formulas should not be underestimated. But there is another guiding formula: creating a context. In principle all these problems should be more tractable in a context of increasing regionalization and globalization, based on inter-state, inter-corporate and/or inter-civil society cooperation.

A new territorial border becomes less dramatic if it is osmotic, with those three types of cooperation seeping through at many points. Wherever there is a conflict because more than one nation has claims to the same territory, IGOs, TNCs and NGOs should be encouraged to be rooted in all nations concerned, providing closeness across borders. The intergovernmental umbrella may be needed, whether in the form of an associative system, a confederal community, a federal union or even a unitary state; in this case the regional super-state.

More concretely, here is a list of inter-state contexts that either exists, could be strengthened or could be created (organizations that will have to be created are in square brackets):

United Nations (UN, N = 189) (inadequate, but the only one)

- for East–West b, the NATO–Russia/China/India–AMPO triangle
- for Europe; the Catholic/Protestant–Orthodox–Muslim triangle
- for the Christianity/Islam, Christianity/'heathens' formation

Organization for Cooperation and Security in Europe (OSCE, N = 55)

- for East–West a, the NATO–WTO/Nonaligned/Neutrals triangle

European Union (EU, N = 15)

- for Cyprus, with both parts as members, with Greece and Turkey
- for Northern Ireland, with separate status as 'entity' (and, in addition, a [Confederation for the British Isles])
- for the Basque Country, giving it separate status as 'entity'

South Asian Association for Regional Cooperation (SAARC, N = 7)

- for tripartite Kashmir (Azad Kashmir, Valley, Jammu–Ladakh)
- for tripartite Sri Lanka (Sinhalas, Tamils, Muslims)

[Pacific Hemisphere Forum]

- for Pacific Islands, Australia/New Zealand and Pacific Rims
- for Japan–Russia
- for Hawai'i (with sovereign Hawai'i as a possible centre?)

[Organization for Security and Cooperation in the Middle East]

- for Gulf a over Iraq's relation to neighbours
- for Gulf b over monitoring Iraq
- for Kurdistan
- for Israel/Palestine

[Organization for Security and Cooperation in Southeast Europe]

- for Yugoslavia a over Serbia–Croatia–Bosnia-Herzegovina +
- for Yugoslavia b over Serbia–Albania–Macedonia +

[Organization for Security and Cooperation in the Caucasus]

- for the Caucasus

[Central Asian Association for Regional Cooperation]

- for Afghanistan and neighbours

[Community of Central African States] (Indian Ocean to Atlantic)

- for The Great Lakes

[Organization for Security and Cooperation in the Mediterranean]

- for Gibraltar/Ceuta-Melilla
- for Israel/Palestine

[East Asian Community]

- for China/Korea/Taiwan/Okinawa/Japan/NT

[Organization for Security and Cooperation in Asia/Pacific]

- for the whole region

All of them are useful – and dangerous if they become super-states.

3. Conclusion: There is work to be done

Apart from inter-state regional organizations, five modelled upon the OSCE, there are some new ideas in need of exploration:

- non-territorial (con)federations, functional sovereignty, and
- condominium/joint sovereignty. Below are some remarks on each.

Non-territoriality is an answer to mobility that lowers the correlation between the culture and the territory of 'a people'. Thus, a Norwegian Sami registers as a Sami, not defined by the territorial connection (address), but by territorial attachment (nation). A country with nations living around each other could have one parliament for each and a super-parliament for federal matters. That arrangement could take much of the heat out of a mixture that becomes even more volatile and dangerous the less the nations are territorially separated (Yugoslavia, Rwanda).

Functional sovereignty softens the status quo/independence dichotomy, introducing degrees of sovereignty, i.e. control. The point of departure would be a list of functions attributed to countries in general, and states in particular; asking independence people what they really want, and status quo people what they could concede. The process defines areas that can be negotiated, subject to review after X (to be negotiated) years.

Condominium/joint sovereignty challenges the idea that each piece of land belongs to one and only one state and that *res communis* = *res nullius*, what is owned in common is owned by nobody. Condominium brings modern marriage into geopolitics, so far it has been used only in colonial regions (New Hebrides, the Cameroons), and the Antarctic. The idea carries great conflict-solving potential, but also leads to problems about the legal status of people living (not to mention born) in the area.

That concludes this exploration of the dialectics between national identity and state integrity. Neither is absolute. If a state fails to meet individual human rights, civil-political and economic-social-cultural, it forfeits its claims on citizens to honour that state, pay taxes and lay down their lives for the state. The right to self-determination is the right of a nation to secede from such a state and to be ruled by their own kind, or else to demand major reorganization short of independence, in line with Article 28 of the Universal Declaration:

Everyone is entitled to a social and international order in which the rights and freedoms set forth in this Declaration can be fully realized.

No nation can opt out of one state to set up another and then deny the same rights to peoples now under their control. There are limits to national identity, as there are to state integrity, regardless of how much the nation considers itself a chosen people, with the glories of the past lining the future, compensating for the unspeakable traumas suffered and inflicted.

States and nations should be demystified. But so also should discourses about majority vs. minority (a historical right is not numerical, it remains even if there is a majority to be concerned about), about multicultural societies (cultures as such have no territorial claims), about internal vs. external suppression (suppression is suppression), salt water colonialism (salinity is immaterial). No nation should be forced to choose between the status quo and total independence because alternatives are not offered, and no nation should be forced to choose between acquiescence and violence because their right is not recognized. Adequate conflict transformation becomes a right, not only a duty. And it becomes a major task of the international community.

Beyond Security: New Approaches, New Perspectives, New Actors

Kai Frithjof Brand-Jacobsen with Carl G. Jacobsen

Setting the Stage: Understanding Security

Recent events in South Eastern Europe, Afghanistan, Colombia, East Timor, Southern Africa, New York, Washington and elsewhere have shown the failure of traditional approaches to security and security guarantees. Conventional conceptions of security, focusing on the security of the 'state' and freedom from the threat or use of force, have proved inadequate to address the diverse range of challenges faced by the world community at the dawn of the twenty-first century.

From environmental devastation – resulting in widespread flooding, deforestation and depletion of the ozone layer – to limitations on the human rights and freedom of individuals and communities, acts of individual and state-sponsored terrorism, and the rising number of intra-state wars, new security issues are constantly arising. Although what is actually considered a 'security' issue varies widely according to the approach and perspective taken, the fact that the concept of security used during the era of the Cold War is no longer sufficient for the world of today cannot reasonably be denied. While many of the factors relevant during the 57 years since the end of the Second World War remain, a number of other issues have arisen, which now demand our attention. Concepts of security (and the instruments created to serve as security 'guarantees') cannot be successful unless they are able to address the challenges posed by the increasing number of issues affecting not only the security of the state, but also the security of the community, the individual and the environment. Group security, human security, environmental security and security from fear and want are only a few of the concepts and approaches (some of which have a long history) necessary to broaden our understanding of the meaning of the word. What is worth emphasizing, however, is that multiple and diverse understandings of 'security' should not necessarily be seen as mutually exclusive or contradictory. Perhaps one of the failures of security in the past has been the attempt to conceive of the world in terms of either/or – security or insecurity, strong or weak, 'good' or 'evil'.

One of the tasks facing those seeking to redefine our under-standing of security and to meet the challenges facing the world today is to go beyond conceptions of 'either/or', towards under-standings based on 'both/and', and the recognition that security for oneself that does not allow for the security of others can often provoke insecurity. At the same time – something recognized more and more frequently in recent years – challenges to security can no longer be seen as limited to the purely military, as has often been done in the past, but must be extended to include economic, political, social, cultural and ecological factors as well.

The need for new thinking and new approaches to the concept of security, and for the development of creative and viable alter-natives capable of meeting the security needs of a wide range of actors, is paramount. Unless the world community, as groups, states and individuals, is able to come up with new ways of addressing security concerns and to transcend the limitations inherent in traditional conceptions of security and inter- and intra-state relations, the tragedies which so recently took place in New York, Washington, Afghanistan, Yugoslavia (Kosovo/a), East Timor and Rwanda will not be the last. In order to realize the aspirations of the founders of the United Nations and the lofty goal of 'saving future generations from the scourge of war', new resources, new approaches, new commitment and new strategies for dealing with the rising number of challenges facing the world must be found. At the same time, and as this book has shown, it must be recognized that other 'scourges', not just that of war, exist, as direct, structural and cultural violence, threatening security on a number of levels.

Security: A Changing Phenomenon – New Actors, New Perspectives

While the need to recognize the changing nature of the challenges posed to 'security' is of great importance, the parallel search for and recognition of the roles and potential of a number of different actors, *not* just the state, to play a role in meeting those challenges, should be addressed. Thus, three questions originating from the discussion above, all deserving a multitude of answers, can immediately be identified:

1. Security from whom/what?
2. Security by whom/what?
3. Security for whom/what?

Depending on one's position in any given society and the world, or one's perspective on what 'security' actually means, a number of answers to these questions are possible. For a child dying from malaria, a single mother caring for her family, a Wall Street banker or a local gang leader or warlord, perceptions of what 'security' is may be dramatically different. To choose a conception based on a world-view that recognizes the 'state' and inter-state relations as the dominant (or only) factors defining security and the world is to attempt to impose one particular perspective to the neglect of others; much as the term 'development' is often taken to mean development towards a 'Western' capitalist market and consumption-based economy, neglecting and ignoring the tens of thousands of alternative forms of human community which may have different conceptions of development, or which may not even have a conception of 'development' at all![1] Thus, rather than speaking of 'security' and 'development', it is necessary to recognize that there are many different *securities* and *developments*. What may be secure for one, could be the complete opposite for another. Or what may be taken to be 'security' in one day and age, could be seen as promoting insecurity in another. To seek to impose one view or one understanding on those who do not support or share that view may in itself be conflict-provoking and engendering, promoting insecurity and destabilization rather than security. In the same way, enforcing one culture's ideals and standards of 'security' and 'development' on the rest of the world may serve to promote conflicts and threaten security on a global level.

International relations and security studies throughout much of the last 50 years, at universities and institutions around the world, have focused on the threat or use of direct physical violence in the form of aggression or threat of aggression by one (or more) states against another (or others). At the same time, other forms of violence and threats to security – such as the structural violence exhibited when large sections of the human population are prevented from fulfilling their potential due to economic and social structures based on inequality and exploitation, or cultures of violence which legitimize and reinforce the role of violence as an 'acceptable' means of responding to conflict – have often been only insufficiently addressed. From this perspective, many of the 'security' institutions which have existed in the past (some of which continue to this day), such as NATO and the Warsaw Pact, can themselves be seen as having been (and continue to be) direct threats to security. In so far as they served to divide the world between opposing 'blocs', to promote confrontation based on black/white, good vs. evil, win/lose, zero-sum thinking, and to militarize their societies (and the world) to the point where mutual annihilation became an all too real possibility, they served, contrary to their own self-justifications, not to increase security, but to promote *in*security. In the same manner, states that promote massive military expenditures and militarization of their societies at the expense of social spending, health care and education may themselves be seen as threats to the security of a population.

Perhaps one of the greatest threats to security today, however, is the fact that, long after the implosion of the Soviet Union and collapse of the Cold War, the mindsets and mentality which dominated the world during 45 years of 'superpower' struggle remain dominant. Zero-sum, win/lose, competitive and conflict-provoking thinking remains prominent.

However, as the experiences of NATO's war against Yugoslavia and the 50 years before have shown, attempts to enforce conflict 'resolution' or 'security' through *diktat* backed by military force may in fact worsen the dynamics of conflict and fuel even larger-scale violence, while sowing the seeds for further violence in the future.

The security *industry* itself can, in many ways, be seen to be a leading contributor to insecurity. By conceiving of security solely in military terms – based on relations of 'force' and one's ability to coerce others to achieve certain goals or to prevent the ability of others to coerce – strategists and planners have long been able to justify the search for ever greater armaments, smart bombs, military alliances and control by elites over the decision-making powers of entire countries and nations.

The fact that something is defined as a 'security' issue is often taken to mean that it is an issue deserving of *extra*ordinary attention and measures, requiring the expertise and knowledge of 'specialists' and those in the position to 'know'. The fact that it is often these very people who have, through their choices and decisions, exacerbated insecurity and brought countries and entire continents to the brink of war, is often neglected. By empowering elites to define the parameters of discussion for what is a security 'issue' and then to take the steps 'necessary' to deal with that issue, is to promote the disempowerment of large numbers of the human population (an inherently undemocratic and authoritarian process).

At the same time, by promoting security on one level, one can often promote insecurity on another. Just as one country increasing its ability to 'defend' itself may lead another country to feel threatened and believe that it too must increase its efforts to 'defend' itself, so leading to an arms race and an ever-escalating spiral of insecurity, so promoting security of *self* without recognizing the need for security of the *other*, is itself a source of conflict and insecurity between the two. (This was seen clearly during the years of 'super'power confrontation and, today, in the rivalry and con-frontation between India and Pakistan, and in Israeli–Palestinian and so many other relationships.) Thus also the worker in an armaments factory who faces redundancy because of reductions in military spending may face a high degree of personal insecurity while the security of the country as a whole may rise through reduction of its dependence on military force, allowing for increasing spending in other areas.

A more extreme example of insecurity for one at the expense of 'security' for another can be found in societies in which minority questions or conflicts with neighbouring countries and peoples are 'resolved' through the annihilation and eradication of the 'Other' – an attempt to achieve the ultimate 'security' by removing even the possibility of threat from one's opponent (or perceived opponent).

A similar process can be seen in the ever-expanding world of the 'free' market in its attempts to make countries 'safe' for investment. The increasing alienation and impoverishment of large portions of the human population, together with the culturocide by which differences are eliminated as the world is transformed into a homogeneous commodity exchange, are the reverse side of this safety.

The logic that founds security on the elimination of threat by force can often give birth to far weightier dynamics, which may, in turn, consume the very society they were meant to protect. Just as a conflict cannot be said to be 'resolved' if it is based on the annihilation of the Other, so can 'security' based on destruction (either real or threatened), be no more than a mirage – a mirage that may often be more dangerous than what it seeks to protect against.

However, human beings and societies exist not only in interlinking relationships with one another, but in their relationship to the world at large, and the environment that they inhabit and which surrounds them. For thousands of years, human beings lived in a precarious balance with the natural world. With the birth of industrialization (a process multiplied a thousand-fold by the subsequent rise of 'technologization'), one aspect of security was conceived of as security over and above the natural world.

Nature became conceived of as a threat, a resource and a sink – a frontier to be constantly conquered and pushed back, a source of materials fuelling the expansion of industrialized society, and a dumping ground for our waste. Our ability to dominate nature, to extract from it the resources we needed to survive and to fuel our mode of economic production, became the centre point of 'man's' (humanity's) relationship to the natural world in all societies ('communist' and 'capitalist'), which based themselves on economic processes founded on industrialization and ever-increasing and expanding rates of production and consumption.

The linking of indigenous peoples and cultures with states of 'backwardness' and 'savagery' which needed to be 'tamed' and 'civilized' through the process of colonization is extremely interesting in this respect. By identifying peoples and cultures with a state of 'savage nature', colonial rulers justified their attempts to take *control* of an area through forcing its 'natives' and its environment to obey the civilizing whip of the white man. Thus, the aim of colonization became not only to conquer territories, but to conquer peoples and nature, and to subjugate that which was 'wild' and 'untamed', through a combination of railways (domination over nature), and courts, prisons and schools (domination over the minds and bodies of the ruled).

Security of the 'mother' country, was guaranteed through the exploitation (= extreme threat to security) of the colonized. Later, as colonization became more developed, it was recognized that internalizing the chains of slavery by educating and inculcating the 'colonized' in the ways of thinking and living of 'civilized', 'Christian' Europe and North America, was a more effective way to guarantee the stability and permanence of colonial rule. Thus, even after formal independence, many colonized countries found themselves applying for help to their former colonial masters in order to follow in the steps of development *pioneered by their colonizers*.

The entire history of colonization – a history which, in many ways, continues to this day – can, to a very great extent, be seen as a process of securing the resources (and later markets) necessary for the growth of capitalism in the countries of Western Europe and North America. The fact that this process could not have taken place without the legacy of colonialism is one of the key factors holding back the 'rapid development' of many formerly colonized countries.

'Western' man's (as industrialized societies – both then and now – have most often been dominated by men) relationship to the natural world paralleled his relationship to the colonies. Nature existed to be colonized, that is, to be transformed into raw materials and commodities to guarantee constant improvements in the standards of living of those able to 'control' it.

Only in the 1970s and 1980s did concern over the environment and our relationship to it become a major issue, arising for the first time in nearly 300 years as a threat to the security of the industrialized way of life. From this point on, and culminating in the Brundtland Report, security with regard to the environment became conceived of as a managed state in which limitations of natural resources and damage to the environment by industrial waste be controlled so as not to damage the life-style and mode of production of industrialized societies. (Non-industrialized or industrializing societies would have to remain content with the level of industrialization they could reach without becoming a threat to the dominance and way of life of the 'West'.) Security, therefore, became security for the mode of production of industrialization from the threat of natural limitations and enforced destruction of the environment, a way of thinking rooted in a homocentric conception of the world – one that took account of the environment, not for what it was, but for what it was to 'man'.

Thus, as opposed to other societies such as the indigenous peoples in North and South America and many other parts of the world, whose world-view is based on their interrelationship with nature, where human beings are considered as one part of the whole in relationship with all other parts, the view adopted by proponents of 'environmental security' was most often that of a world in which nature still existed to be exploited by man, but in which that exploitation must be managed in order to ensure that it be 'sustainable'.

The contrast between these two views is startling and worth taking note of, for it bears relevance to our conception of security as a whole, whether with regard to nature and the environment, or to the social, political, cultural, economical and other aspects of security. For many of the indigenous peoples of North and South America, security came through living in harmony with the natural world. It was based on respect for the world around them, and recognition of the importance and sacredness of all living and non-living things. Human beings were one among many, although special to the extent that they conceived of themselves as caretakers, whose role it was to ensure the balance of nature and to protect against disturbances.

Security in the 'traditional' sense – how it is most often perceived by military and strategic planners and in institutes and universities around the world – is viewed as security against or security from. Our relationship with the other is seen as being one, not of harmony, but of confrontation, that is, in fulfilment of the Hobbesian conception of the world as one of 'bellum omnium ad omnes'. Security is guaranteed by making oneself secure, often through weakening the security of others. While major steps were taken to go beyond this conception of security, in the work of the UN Palme Commission and its embrace of concepts such as mutual and common security, and in Gorbachevian policies of unilateral disarmament and troop reductions, the road to travel, from egocentric conceptions of security to more holistic approaches, remains a long one.

Security is still commonly seen as the need to protect against threats from others – other states, peoples, cultures, societies, nature, etc. The attempt to *go beyond* or *transcend* 'threats' by addressing the underlying structures and causes that give rise to them remains virtually unheard of.

One of the reasons for this is that security itself, and the world-view it endorses, is one of the key dynamics and causes which must be transcended in order for any real 'security' to exist. Perhaps here, however, security is no longer the right word, for, as discussed above, security is most often conceived of as security over and against, rather than for and together. Though mutual and common security may seem to go beyond this, they still remain within the dominant structures and parameters of the security paradigm and the world-view it both enforces and rests on.

What is suggested here is the need to question those very structures and parameters, to go beyond the concept of security and recognize that alternatives exist, which may be more constructive and fruitful. Thus, one concept which comes to mind is that of 'cooperation', of peace by peaceful means, and the positive transformation of the underlying structures and causes which give rise to '*in*security' and 'threat'.

Here, however, it becomes necessary to replace the concept of threat with that of challenge, not along the lines in which 'challenge' has often been conceived, but as a challenge to our imagination and creativity to be able to come up with new approaches and new ideas when we find ourselves presented with a situation which appears conflictual or insurmountable. Whereas, according to Jean-Jacques Rousseau's dictum, 'wars occur because there is nothing to prevent them', according to this way of thinking, wars and 'security threats' occur because we lack the creativity and imagination to think of alternatives, and the understanding and wisdom to transform the underlying structures of conflict through a creative and constructive process.

Thus, whereas security most often embraces the concept of conflict the destroyer and prepares for ever greater levels of destruction in order to protect against the possible outcomes of conflict, cooperation and peaceful conflict transformation base themselves on the concept of conflict the creator, recognizing the positive and constructive opportunities which conflict makes available to transcend the existing status quo, and to go beyond compromise (at the heart of theories of détente and mutual security), towards an area in which the needs and interests of all parties can be met (what is often referred to by some practitioners and theoreticians as the TRANSCEND method).

While state-centred, international relations approaches both accept and enforce the dominance of elites and their control of information and decision-making powers, a broader conception, which recognizes cooperation as fundamental to guaranteeing 'security' *for* (rather than against) all people *and* the environment (living and non-living), would embrace more horizontal or web-like and holistic conceptions of society. Domination above and against would be replaced by cooperation for and with.

This does not mean that the state would not have a role to play, but that the nature and position of the state itself would be left open to question, that rather than enforcing this model of human community on all the peoples and accepting a state-based system as the only and natural structure of the world, other approaches and other forms of human community would be identified. This would demand creativity and imagination, and the ability to transcend traditional conceptions of society and security as enforced through the state-centred model.

In carrying out this task it is also necessary to go beyond the recent trend in Western Europe and North America (repeated in many areas throughout the world) to recognize everything that is not part of government as 'non-governmental'. Would it not be better to recognize citizens' organizations and associations of people outside the structure of the state as people's organizations, thereby making states 'non-people's organizations'? These ideas are not meant to be radical (though if radical is taken in its original meaning, 'going to the root', then that is exactly what we must be), but emphasize the need to approach our understanding of concepts such as the 'state', 'security', the 'environment' and 'development' from a variety of perspectives and approaches, and not to limit ourselves to the dominant discourses and structuring of thought and the patterns they enforce.

Just as it was necessary for Gorbachev to break free of the logic (or rather, psycho-logic) of the Cold War in order to provide for at least a minimum of the security sought by all sides to the conflict, so it is necessary to go beyond the concept of security in order to transcend the limitations of compromise and antagonism and move towards the possibilities of holistic, transformative cooperation and creativity.

Crafting Peace: On the Psychology of the TRANSCEND Approach

Johan Galtung and Finn Tschudi

Introduction: Some Basic Assumptions

Conflict is ubiquitous, violence is not. Hence the big question: how can we approach conflict in a non-violent way? Here is one trend of thought, a trail of ideas, suggesting an answer:

1. Conflict is about *incompatible goals* that may not be that incompatible, within an actor (dilemmas), among actors (disputes) or (usually) both. Other terms: contradiction, clash, issue, bone of contention.
2. The conflict appears to the parties as a bloc: something stands in the way of attaining goals; their other goals and/or the goals of other parties. Other term: knot.
3. Blocked goal-attainment is also known as frustration, but the range of reactions goes beyond aggression,[1] and includes:

   A. attitudes, cognitive and emotive; ranging from glowering hatred of self or other to denial, from inner boiling to inner freezing;
   B. behaviour, physical and verbal; ranging from deliberate efforts to hurt and harm the Self or Other to withdrawal, ranging from outer boiling to outer freezing, via wait-and-see, and constructive attempts to overcome the bloc.

4. What actually happens depends on personal, structural and cultural parameters. The person may have a settled conflict repertory. If another actor is seen as blocking the goal, direct aggression presupposes an opportunity to prevail, which depends on the relative power in the structure. There may be blind aggression, and the culture may prescribe or prohibit self-assertiveness.
5. The inner and outer reactions are not necessarily at the same temperature (murder in cold blood, 'boiling inside').

6. We then add:

    C. contradiction, the root incompatibility of goals, and arrive
    at the *conflict triangle*: **a**ttitudes, **b**ehaviour and **c**ontradic-
    tion. Causal flows can start anywhere, but most often start
    in C, contradiction.

7. However, conflict attitudes and behaviour are projected on
   others with whom there is little or no goal incompatibility.
   But there will be blocked goals somewhere, if we look closely.

8. A contradiction left unresolved leads to an accumulation of
   negative energies at A and B: to violence ('war' for collective
   actors) sustained by genuine hatred; to mutual isolation
   sustained by apathy; to the self-hatred of nations that have
   suffered major trauma, including being defeated: the Jews,
   Germans, Japanese after the Second World War (Serbs?
   Iraqis?).

9. From the root conflict the conflict has now spread to A and
   B as people react to having their needs insulted by hatred and
   violence. Parties and the media will focus on the *meta-conflicts*
   built around being hated and/or hurt and harmed; they are
   much more dramatic, newsworthy. Thus, in an unpublished
   study for his master's thesis, Dylan Scudder reports that the
   International Herald Tribune in July 1998 had 44 reports on
   violence in Kosovo and two on possible solutions to it. This
   also plays into a tendency to psychologize the conflict, focusing
   on A, cognitions/emotions of the actors, and not on C.[2]

10. A focus on violence, 'troubles', is often accompanied by an
    inability to explore, let alone talk about, root problems veiled
    in taboos. Efforts to break the taboos are strongly resented.
    The discourse permitted is inadequate to dissolve the problem
    by dialogue (*dia* = via, *logos* = word). Violence, with its simple
    winner/loser logic, is promoted by focusing on violence.

11. One basic assumption at this point would be that *people are
    better able to discuss a root problem when they sense there is a
    solution to it.* A glimmer of light at the end of the tunnel makes
    it considerably easier to admit that we are in a tunnel. If there
    is no light, then it's better not to mention the tunnel in the
    first place: the truth becomes unbearable. The all-too-human
    fact that at the end of the tunnel lies another tunnel does not
    make the truth easier to bear, unless there are some shafts of
    light.

12. The second basic assumption is that if we manage to develop
    a perspective on a *transformation of the root conflict, then that
    opening at C may drain negative energies at A and B, so
    normalizing inner and outer relations.*

13. Our argument is in favour of recovering the primacy of the root conflict, the contradiction, the incompatibility itself. To soothe hurt egos and teach non-aggressive behaviour is good, but hard, root issues have to be approached, for they are couched in deep emotions, the basic one being hatred of the other side for not 'seeing the light', that is, yielding, and for being violent.

14. Three basic, and frequent, mistakes in conflict practice follow from the failure to take into account the whole triangle:

The **A mistake**, the liberal fallacy, focusing on attitudes only, making people more loving (religious), aware of their own mental baggage (psychological). No contradiction is unravelled.

The **B mistake**, the conservative fallacy, modifying behaviour only by putting a lid on aggressive action. The bloc doesn't disappear.

The **C mistake**, the Marxist fallacy, focusing only on the contradiction between labour and capital, regardless of costs to mind and body. We know what happened: the negative energies in A and B caught up with Soviet achievements and destroyed them.

The TRANSCEND Dialogue Method for Conflict Transformation

The method[3] is based on trained conflict workers meeting the parties in a conflict, singly, not together, one to one, typically in a conversation-style setting. One experience[4] is that high-level conflict parties are usually intelligent, articulate, charming people, with a high capacity for leadership. There is little doubt that they believe what they say, they are not posturing – at least not after some quiet dialogue disarms their defences. Nor are they necessarily longing to use violence regardless of the situation. Readiness is something else. They are wedded to their positions, but are not necessarily inflexible – a characteristic they tend to attribute to the other. They should not be pathologized or criminalized; they are not sicker or more criminal than most.

The basic point is that they see no way out, are blocked, tied up in knots partly of their own making. They are often irritable, inflexible and secretive, bordering on inarticulate. The TRANSCEND method, based on dialogues with all parties to a conflict one at a time, is an effort to expand their spectrum of acceptable outcomes. The method is not based on arguing positions closer to the other parties, that is, compromise. That they can do themselves in a process known as negotiation. Experience shows that direct contact may exacerbate conflicts for a number of reasons: because of the verbal violence often used in face-to-face encounters, because compromise means accepting some of the Other, and because of the absence of creativity when the Other is present. In one-to-one conversation-style dialogues the task is to stimulate creativity, so developing new perspectives. The task is to make the conflict parties 'ready for the table'.

The First Round

There are five processes.

The first is to probe the negative goals (fears) and positive goals (hopes), exploring beyond public posturing. Thus, in Northern Ireland, Protestant fears may be less to do with religion and more about 'being absorbed in lachrymose Irish sentimentality and emotionalism'; Catholic fears are to do with 'cold, English, so-called rationality'; not to mention the fears of unemployment (Catholic) and of being killed (both). The positive goal is to be surrounded (and confirmed!) by one's own kind, in a setting of economic and physical security.

The second is not to try to dissuade the party from their goals, but probe more deeply into the nature of the goals. Goals are multi-dimensional. Thus, the 'Korean conflict' is not only about political-military issues, but also cultural-economic ones. The broader the goal, the more likely that a perspective can be developed, *ceteris paribus*.

The third process, the kernel, will open cognitive space to new outcomes not envisaged by the parties. These outcomes will relate to the range of goals the parties can see, allaying the fears, satisfying the hopes, but from another angle. At this stage much creativity is needed. For example, in the conflict in and over Korea (including the United States and neighbours) it may be useful to put the complex and incompatible political-military goals to one side and proceed from a cultural-economic angle. There is the rich, shared Korean culture and history. Opening rail and road links would unleash enormous economic potential, connecting North Korea/China/Vietnam to South Korea/Japan/Taiwan. Military-political issues can come later; or even better: wither away.

In Northern Ireland, there is a possible Ulster identity built on the richness of both cultures, being an enclave of high technology, owned by neither one nor the other, relating positively to both Ireland and England, to Wales and Scotland, in a process of devolution that ultimately may lead to a Confederation of the British Isles. Again, the point is not so much to be for or against any formula as to know that there are formulas further down the road, not uncharted wilderness.

The fourth process has conflict party and conflict worker construct a new cognitive space together, seeing the old goals as sub-optimal and formulating broader goals. 'Don't be so modest; go for something better than what you used to demand!'

The fifth process explores whether all parties embrace the same points in the new cognitive space. If they do in Korea, conflicts will remain. NAFTA/EU will fear East Asian markets with free flow of goods and services. The Koreas will fear the free flow of people and ideas. There will be quarrels over costs and benefits. But all of this can be handled without violence.

The dialogue between conflict party and conflict worker ends when they have successfully completed the last two processes: discourse/Gestalt enrichment, *complexification*; and a change in cathexis towards new points in the cognitive space.

The conflict worker goes on to the next conflict party, or shares the findings with team members who have been in dialogue with other parties. The latter may be preferable if conflict party No. 2 sees the conflict worker as an envoy of conflict party No. 1. In either case the process with No. 2 has to start from the beginning, not from the outcome from No. 1. The process is new for No. 2 even if it is not for the conflict worker.

At the end of this first round the dialogue processes have to be compared. This is simpler if there is only one conflict worker. Not only the outcomes, but also the processes leading to those outcomes have to be 'processed' to arrive at new and shared perspectives.

The Second Round

The new cognitive space is handed back to the parties. The space should be complex, with more than one point, but the points should not be spelt out in too much detail. The second round should not be a copy of what conflict parties often do: this is the position, take it or leave it.

If the first round has been done well, *mutual acceptability* has been built into the new cognitive space by taking into account all kinds of objections. The task of the second round is to probe for *sustainability*. What would make outcomes of these types stick? What are the vulnerabilities, the weak points? The five processes will be more or less the same as those employed in the first round.

The Third Round

The parties now meet to negotiate the details of a transcending outcome, not a compromise. They should now be 'ready for the table', equipped with expanded cognitive spaces. Even better, one of them will make an opening move and the other will follow. For this process they may not even have to meet; the conflict may simply have 'evaporated'. This is what happened to the Cold War with its countless dialogues.

To open the cognitive space forgotten parties and goals may have to be included in order to have more cognitive complexity to work with. A common goal can then be identified – transcending, going beyond, the original goals – expressed in short, evocative formulations, preferably of 1–4 words, which are difficult to reject.[5] Concrete steps will then have to be identified for all parties. Obviously, this work is difficult. It requires experience, intelligence, the capacity to internalize vast amounts of emotional/cognitive material and make a quantum leap to a new image/perspective with sufficient clarity, combined with the wordsmith's ability to find the right words.

A crucial requirement for the dialogue is that the conflict worker has no conflicts with the parties, often phrased in terms of 'objectivity/neutrality' (meaningless in conflicts over, say, the abolition of slavery or decolonization). The inter-state system is filled with conflicts and alliances, so it is highly unlikely that countries/people with strong allegiances in that system can function as conflict workers (an example is the absurd assumption that the United States is an 'honest broker' in the Middle East 'peace process'). A former president, say Jimmy Carter, might function well, having some authority, though at peace with the parties.

A comment on the setting: Generally those who are in the room call the tune. The TRANSCEND method is based on stripping that room: one conflict worker, one conflict party, two chairs, a table for drinks and snacks. The conflict worker is non-threatening, non-punitive and non-rewarding, having neither sticks nor carrots, only knowledge and skills. She or he may become a significant Other, even a generalized Other.

Evict the conflict worker, introduce the antagonist, the mediator and the public, and the negotiation easily degenerates into a shouting match or verbal duel, with the mediator and public as umpire. In this situation, it is highly unlikely that creativity or quantum leaps will emerge. This is often blamed on 'lack of trust', but 'lack of creativity' would be more accurate description. The parties are not 'ready for the table'. The TRANSCEND method is designed to make them ready.

Psychological Processes in the TRANSCEND Approach

There seem to be two psychological processes involved, one cognitive – *cognitive expansion and reframing*; the other emotive – *a shift in cathexis towards new goal-states*.

Cognitive expansion and reframing

Cognitive expansion and reframing occur when a simple two-points discourse (status quo vs. independence, for example) with totally incompatible goals yields to a more complex discourse with goals at the time held by nobody, like giving the disputed object away (*res nullius*) or sharing it (*res communis*). The original positions are still on the map, but in a context of new positions that at a first glance may look strange, but worth exploring. As cognitive reframing emerges, a simple Gestalt, providing building blocks for another and more complex Gestalt, emotive suffering and cognitive pain may be high. A shift in perspective on the conflict is a part of the process known as reframing in psychotherapy.[6] The terms disembedding and re-embedding are more evocative, however. The conflict, and the accompanying discourse, have come to rest, have been 'embedded', usually in a dualistic framework. One way of disembedding introduces more goal dimensions with or without clashes, more actors, more concerns. Sexual infidelity looks different when four other ways of being unfaithful are also considered: of the mind (the secret love), the spirit (no concern for the partner's life project), socially (no social support), economically (having a secret bank account, 'just in case'). Options like separation or divorce look different when children, grandparents, friends and neighbours enter the cognitive space, rather than just the couple defining themselves as the centre of the universe, wrapped up in their fight over sexual monopoly.

The word Gestalt invites the use of drawings in the dialogue.

Level I. Draw two boxes next to each other. Write the word 'status quo' in the box on the right and the word 'independence' in the box on the left. The Gestalt is 'boxed', opening for no possibilities whatsoever. It is closed, inviting no creativity.

Level II. Now draw a line, the political 'spectrum' people are used to, from left to right. On the extreme right, circle a point, labelled 'status quo'; on the extreme left, circle a point, or counter-point, labelled 'independence'. Now intermediate positions – compromises like 'independence, but not immediately' – can be accommodated. This Gestalt invites some creativity, crying for those with good hearing, eyesight, imagination.

Level III. Draw two lines, one perpendicular to the other, that old intellectual tool known as a Cartesian space. Put Party A on one and Party B on the other. Put 'status quo' at one extreme ('all to A, nothing to B') and 'independence' on the other ('all to B, nothing to A'.). With two dimensions to play with there is little constraint on creativity. Three points can easily be added to the two already given: 'nothing to A, nothing to B' (the territory reverts to the indigenous or becomes League or UN trust territory); 'something to A, something to B' (the compromises mentioned) and then transcendence, 'going beyond': 'all to A, *and* all to B' (the territory becomes a condominium, bi-national). These were the options missing when an International Court of Justice adjudicated the Eastern Greenland case in 1933 with a legalistic cognitive space at Level I only.

Level IV. No reason to stop here. However, going beyond two dimensions, introducing more actors and/or more goals, makes the Gestalts less compelling, given limited spatial imagination.

The basic point is the low level of awareness of one's own conflict philosophy. Thus, most lawyers tend not to reflect on the sad circumstance that they operate at Level I, the most primitive, in both criminal (the state vs. X) and civil cases (A vs. B). Justice tends to be delivered to one or the other; moreover, the parties themselves define to whom. Justice cannot be meted out in percentages, 50:50 or 25:75; that would relativize justice. X is found guilty and sentenced, or found innocent and acquitted. True, there is the third possibility of dismissing the case, for instance because the case does not fit the Level I formula. As a special case, A and B, and S and X, may have reached a settlement 'out of court', a formula that is no compliment to the court system.

Violence or war and the courts share the same Level I logic: 'either you or me', 'win or be defeated'. In rare cases wars are undecided. There is no *experimentum crucis*, that final battle determining the victor. Put in other terms: the war as a conflict decision mechanism 'dismisses the case', which may then open for a settlement (as in the Treaty of Westphalia 1648).

Cognitive expansion to Level II introduces compromises; and Level III adds two more possible classes of outcome.[7] We need Piaget-type studies relating cognitive complexity in conflict outcomes to age, gender and other factors. One hypothesis may be that girls enter Level II earlier than boys, who stay at Level I, reinforced by competitive sports modelled on the same military/legal dualism model. But if boys do graduate from Level I, they may make the jump to Level III more easily than girls, who feel comfortable with the Level II idea of being reasonable, accommodating.

Creating cognitive dissonances and new consonances

The point of departure is usually a two-point, dualism discourse reflecting a polarized conflict formation. There is cognitive consonance: the Other and his/her position are both viewed negatively, self and own position are glorified, the positive identification of each party with their positions is highlighted. To move from this ultra-stable position, dissonances have to be introduced.

One approach is to move the dialogue from a concern with the present (diagnosis) to the future (prognosis). Ask what the positions taken will lead to. The answer 'only by being firm can we find a solution' can be followed up by the question: 'what if Other thinks he has to be firm?' Silence may indicate a recognition of the possibility of endless cycles of revenge that may spell disaster to Self. The assumption would be that 'peace by peaceful means' has some attraction. And that is where the expanded cognitive space and the new angles can come in: 'What would happen if we proceeded along the following lines?' 'What would life be like for your children and grandchildren?'

This process is not a Socratic 'dialogue' in which the conflict worker knows in advance what she or he wants as a conclusion. The process is mutual, taking place inside the conflict worker too. For her or him the negative goal, fear, is violence and the positive goal, hope, some constructive outcome for all parties, that history moves on. If the conflict worker is inflexible, refusing to budge, closed to new facts, theories and values, she or he may have to yield that position to somebody else. The task is to elicit, suggest, propose, not to impose. Sentences end with the question mark typical of a dialogue, not with the exclamation mark typical of a debate.[8]

A dialogue should be between equals. They meet away from the power paraphernalia of the conflict party (seals, titles, flags) or of the conflict worker (books, titles, awards). The conflict worker knows more about general conflict theory; the conflict party more about this specific conflict. The conflict worker should not be too well prepared on the specific conflict lest she becomes over-whelming, looming well above the conflict party, both on generalities and specifics. Exchanging general and specific knowledge is not a bad basis for equality.

But there is another inequality. Conflict party and conflict worker are both exploring new outcome spaces for exits. The conflict worker is bound to the principle of hope: there must be an exit somewhere. The conflict party may share that hope but also be convinced, in the head or at gut level, that there is no such point, thereby vindicating the position adopted. Violence is legitimated negatively: there is no alternative! The hope of confirmation makes for blindness to transcendence.

A way out is to use the diagnosis/prognosis/therapy formula creatively. Each defines a dialogue mode, a discourse. Diagnosis and prognosis are both descriptive, of past and future respectively (past because facts that have become data reflect the past). Therapy is prescriptive, of the future. That map reveals an unexplored spot: *the therapy of the past.*

The question, 'what went wrong, when, where, and what could have been done at the time?' is designed to make the party reflect on the past to the point of owning it, coming on top of history rather than allowing history to come on top of Self; giving in to fate, to destiny. Counterfactual history, in the subjunctive rather than the indicative, has to be elicited.

In our experience, after some reluctance, conflict parties are willing to engage in history 'as if'. History is distant, or they can make it distant, pointing to events that occurred a long time ago, far beyond their current responsibility horizons. Suggestions usually emerge, creating a discourse that is more creative, less filled with terrible 'facts' that lead us nowhere. 'Maybe at that point in history we should have ...'

The conflict worker will elicit maximum creativity, and then move across both dimensions, from past to future, and from the prescriptive to the descriptive: 'What do you think is going to happen now?' Obviously, it is an effort to provide a positive anchorage in some hope, some perspective emerging from the 'therapy of the past' (with the great advantage that it cannot be subjected to the test of reality), and a negative anchorage in the fear, of a dark prognosis coming true. But what if they say, 'we want only one thing: to win'? Extend the time horizon by asking: 'What if they take their revenge, in twenty years' time'?

Let us try a cognitive consonance/dissonance model of what may happen. The point of departure is Self, Other and their positions P, P(Self) and P(Other), and the well-known polarized, balanced, dualism configuration:

$$\text{Self} \text{-----} \text{Other}$$
$$| \qquad\qquad |$$
$$\text{P(Self)} \text{----} \text{P(Other)}$$

The Gestalt is symmetric, with aesthetic beauty even if it leads to death, with both killing for their position to prevail. They are both strongly committed to their positions; they hate each other and what the other stands for. How would positive and negative anchoring break down this cognitive/emotive prison?

The positive anchor, **Pos(Anchor)**, would be a position acceptable to both by including the positions to which they are committed as special cases. In other words, that transcending outcome would relate positively to all four points in the diagram. For example, Kosovo/a as a 'Third Republic' in the Yugoslav Federation, in addition to Serbia and Montenegro, would give a high level of independence to the Albanians, and a high level of status quo to the Serbs. Both parties might be sceptical of the long-term sustainability of any such formula. But even given that ambivalence, the overall relation of the positive anchor to all four points in the figure above could be positive.

The negative anchor, **Neg(Anchor)**, is a dark prognosis which relates positively to P(Self) and to P(Other), flowing from the enactment of the positions taken (we then presuppose symmetry, that Self and Other in the dialogues have developed the same images of the configurations). Neg(Anchor) would also spell something negative for Self and Other, the dark consequences.

The anchors have now been added, with lines to the four original points for each, and one line between the anchors. How do Self and Other react to this more complex configuration?

By simplifying it. The cognitive overload of six elements with 15 relations is considerable; in addition, there are the numerous imbalances. In other words, two approaches are postulated, based on the assumption that human beings, including diplomats, statesmen and conflict workers, will try to organize their cognitive fields so as to minimize both overload and dissonances. Work will continue until a comfortable equilibrium is obtained that is simple and balanced. In the meantime there will be inner pain, even with aggressive manifestations.

The first approach will be to return to the original configuration of two hostile camps pitted against each other:

1. by denying acceptability/sustainability of positive anchor;
2. by denying the dark prognosis of the negative anchor.

With both anchors eliminated, or surviving as detached memories only, the old configuration is restored. One denial alone would probably be sufficient to make the original configuration prevail, resurrected, even strengthened by the attack.

The second approach leaves the original dualism structure. There is no longer any call for a decision, by war or by law, producing a victor and a vanquished. A new configuration emerges, and one triangle, Self–Other–Pos(Anchor), has positive lines only. Not only do both parties embrace the positive anchor, they even embrace each other, as in the early days of the Oslo Israel/PLO accords (before suicide bombs and the assassination of a prime minister made it clear that major parties had been excluded from the process). The positive triangle is a long jump. How would we arrive at such a positive configuration?

By the logic of cognitive triangles: if there are two positive lines and one negative line, then there is cognitive dissonance. Consonance can then be obtained by changing the negative line to a positive one, or by changing one of the positive lines to a negative. Let us look at it from Self's angle.

Self dislikes the consequences of the prognosis and likes Self's position; the problem being that the prognosis follows from that position, when enacted. Now there are three choices:

1. deny that the prognosis follows from that position;
2. welcome the dark prognosis, wanting a trauma; or
3. give up the position.

The second position is important in explaining Iraq/Saddam Hussein, and Yugoslavia/Slobodan Milosevic, in terms of their political behaviour. Glory is the best, but trauma is a good second best, deposited in the world trauma bank at a high interest rate and drawn upon: 'Think of how I have suffered!' The worst is the grey zone in-between.

What would influence the choice of 1, 2 or 3? Above all the positive anchorage, the overarching, transcending goal, seeing one's own position as compatible, even if far from identical with it. If cathexis is transferred to the positive anchor, then the link to the original position weakens. An ambivalence emerges: the positive anchor is compatible with old positions, but then there is something new. This ambivalence has made the transfer of cathexis to the new position possible; that transfer now being on track, time has come to loosen, even cut the link to the original position. This is alternative 3, not the non-starters 1 and 2. A very good beginning, as when Ecuador and Peru embraced the idea of a bi-national, natural park in October 1998 as a solution to a border conflict.

But the real test is what now happens in the Self–Other–Pos(Anchor) triangle. Imagine Self and Other have both come to accept Pos(Anchor) in favour of their old positions. Will they also come to accept each other? President Clinton's stance as a father-figure behind the old antagonists Yitzak Rabin and Yasser Arafat, in the White House garden on 13 September 1993, was not so much to tie them together as to prevent Arafat from embracing Rabin. The counterexample would be Reagan and Gorbachev when the former understood that real change had taken place in the Soviet Cold War position, on Eastern Europe, arms and basic ideology. There was a shared anchor, and a changed relationship.

The key may be in the negative anchor, the dark prognosis. It was and is bad enough for Israel and Palestine: incessant fighting, insecure positions with high population pressure on a limited territory, Palestine in addition without the protection of a state. For the Cold War parties, mutual nuclear holocaust.

The acceptance by both parties of a positive anchor, using the instrument of a joint declaration, would have an integrative impact; or, at a very minimum, it could change the relation from negative to neutral, that is, a non-relation. However, if we now introduce the negative anchor, so negative to both of them, then there is more raw material for a positive Self–Other relationship. The enemy is no longer the Other, but the joint fear of a highly undesirable state of affairs: a devastating war. A common enemy.

In other words, the stable, balanced, non-polarized and at the same time simple configuration to aim for as a goal is:

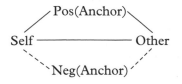

In the configuration the positive triangle wanted as an outcome is solidified by shared negative relations to a negative anchor.

This assumes a universal tendency to prefer and strive for cognitive balance/consonance; in other words, a high level of intolerance of ambiguity/contradiction. Given the importance of Aristotelian/Cartesian logic in the West as opposed to yin/yang logic (much) further East this may be limited to the West (and perhaps to men more than to women?). Empirical studies of the relation between deep culture (and other factors) and the validity of the cognitive balance hypothesis might clarify to what extent this tendency holds across human divides.

To repeat, the conflict worker has two major tasks:

1. The positive task is, through dialogue, to elicit a new conflict perspective and a positive anchor, learning from the parties, contributing own ideas, until something creative and solid emerges. The general method is to expand the cognitive space so that the old conflict positions are still identifiable, yet a new transcending position has emerged. The conflict is disembedded, and re-embedded elsewhere.
2. The negative task is to open the full spectrum of invisible consequences of violence, the 'externalities'.[9] Just as the 'science' of economics keeps major effects invisible as 'side-effects' or 'externalities' and so makes it easier to engage in exploitative economic practices, so the military HQ approach in terms of numbers killed, wounded and material damage only, without reference to such side-effects such as structural and cultural damage, glorification of violence and the urge for revenge, makes it easier to engage in violent conflict practices.

An important question is where this approach places the conflict worker on the dialogue/debate axis. Conflict workers have a double goal, and an agenda to arrive at the positive and negative anchors:

starting with the therapy of the past, moving to the prognosis, risking a joint exploration to arrive at a diagnosis, then making an effort to identify therapies of the future. And then, the same process again ... and again, until something fruitful emerges; if necessary by replacing both the conflict parties and the conflict workers.

But having an agenda does not define the content of the two anchors in advance, and there may be substantial surprises down the road even for the most seasoned conflict worker.

The process is meaningful only if the dialogue is a genuinely mutual brainstorming process, something like a cross between a good conversation and a lively university seminar. If the conflict worker is pushing a specific position, then she/he is ripe for replacement.

It should be noted that the peace-building function of the positive anchor is not limited to the case where it leads to a joint declaration of principles, or agreement. The existence of a conflict perspective that looks reasonable to reasonable men and women everywhere may already serve as a war-blocker. But that existence has to be known in public space, well publicized so that a sufficient number of elites and people in general will say, not only think: 'But why this talk about war? A reasonable perspective is already before us; all we need is a process turning that perspective into an agreement. Hurry up!'

The crisis over UNSCOM's inspection in Iraq in February 1998 may serve as an example. That the US and UK wanted to bomb Iraq 'to the table', or punish Iraq for non-compliance, was clear. But Kofi Annan, the UN Secretary-General, went to Baghdad and came back with a perspective that looked 'reasonable to reasonable men and women'. The basic idea was to attach a diplomat to every team so that verbal encounters could be engaged more in accordance with diplomatic protocol. An important point was the difference between plain, colloquial American-English and an Arabic richly endowed with honorifics; a literal translation would sound even more insulting and 'undiplomatic' to Arabs. The perspective became a shared point of reference and built a consensus which in the end was joined by the US and UK. The positive anchor had prevailed for some time, the final outcome being hidden in the future.

But why not leave the processes to the parties themselves in a face-to-face encounter? All well and good, if they can manage it. But experience shows that in a hard conflict they do not. They are emotionally overwhelmed by their hatred for each other and fear what may happen if they are seen to be yielding on some point. Furthermore, they are cognitively blinded by their efforts to defend untenable positions rather than searching for something new. Creativity is at a minimum. Having the 'enemy' a metre away does not serve to open up cognitive spaces or let dissonances in, let alone permit them to start dismantling their entrenched configurations.

Anger may well be a dominant emotion if the conflicting parties are brought together too early. No emotion is likely to be more contagious. Trying to create a dialogue when anger prevails is like trying to erect a tent in a tornado.[10] The storm has to abate before the tent will stay up. That is where the conflict worker, or 'specialist' if 'worker' sounds too humble, enters: calming them down by talking with them one at a time. There may be no time to lose before violence erupts.

With only negative emotions towards each other the parties are likely to stick to their positions, and real listening will be minimal. What they hear will sound like familiar tape-recordings and serve only to elicit defences of their own position. At best it leads to debates that quickly degenerate into quarrels, but not to real dialogue. Real dialogue requires empathic listening, not so much concern for the other as concern for the total, inclusive 'system' (like 'Europe' in a broad sense during the Cold War, 'the subcontinent' in any Indo-Pakistani encounter), and a willingness to take a fresh look instead of running up and down fixed grooves of thought.

Access to prominent niches in public space is essential. That access will probably be controlled, or control of it will be attempted by state (censorship) or capital (corporate media) lest a perspective should serve as a war-blocker when that war is wanted for some reason. The more a war seems imminent, and the higher the status of the country in the international community, the more closed are the major mass media to perspectives on conflict transformation by peaceful means. Breaking this invariance is a major task. The Internet does not solve the problem: it is publicly accessible, but it is not public knowledge that possesses that public knowledge. Big powers prefer perspectives developed behind closed doors, producing a heavy pluralistic ignorance (ignorance about where the plurality stands) and a wait-and-see attitude in the public.

A meta-script seems to be at work here, driving not only the media but diplomats too. A good story starts softly, builds to a dramatic peak, winds down and flattens out, to silence: the End. Admit early violence, let it escalate, let it peak; then the time is ripe/mature. People are begging for 'peace', handed down to victims and bad (violent) boys, by the intervention of big (powerful) boys, putting an end to conflict.

The idea of an ending already spells disaster. Violence may end, but a conflict always leaves its residues. Violence will be reproduced if they fester and the causes are not sufficiently rooted out. Was the agreement really accepted by all parties? Is it self-sustainable or does it have to be propped up from the outside? In which case, for

how long? Has there been any reconciliation? Any professional
knows this. Inter-state and inter-nation conflicts are not handled
with much professionalism.

A Note on the Deeper Psychology of the TRANSCEND Approach

What has been said above is heavily biased in favour of conscious
and cognitive processes. If we divide psychology, individual as well
as collective, into four fields, then so far we have favoured the
northwestern corner:

A division of the field of psychology

	Cognitive processes	*Emotive processes*
Conscious	Ideology	Love/Hate
Processes	True vs. False	Good/Right vs. Bad/Wrong
Subconscious	Cosmology	Glory/Trauma
Processes	Deep cognitions	Deep emotions

At the conscious level there is awareness or easy retrieval, a test
being the ability to verbalize. At the subconscious level there is no
awareness, retrieval is difficult, even painful, and not possible under
normal circumstances. Professional help may be needed to
construct a map of the subconscious from manifest indicators.
Psychoanalysis in the Freudian tradition has had a tendency to
focus on the *individual*, the *subconscious*, the *emotive* and the
traumatic; a necessary, but also narrow approach.

The southeast corner is needed to correct the northwest corner
bias. Dialogues have been explored in order to rearrange cognitive
structures, using emotionally positive and negative anchors. But
that is only part of the story. We may enter the deep personality of
conflict parties and conflict workers, but it should be noted that in
political and particularly geopolitical conflicts the conflict party is
a representative, a diplomat. Consequently, the table above has to
be read as reflecting collective, that is shared, psychological
processes.

The terms in the table are already adjusted to fit the collective
level of analysis.[11] The two subconscious categories add up to the
deep culture of that collectivity, which could be a collectivity shared
by the representatives/diplomats.

Corresponding to *glory/trauma* at the collective level is
pride/shame. These deep emotions, especially shame, have been
neglected in the literature. An exception is Tomkins:[12] 'While

terror and distress hurt, they are wounds inflicted from outside, but shame is felt as an inner torment, a sickness of the soul. The humiliated one who has been shamed feels naked, defeated, lacking in dignity and worth.'

No wonder that shame, perhaps more than sexual and aggressive feelings, has been ignored in both everyday life and in the literature. The more a society is based on exploitation and oppression, the more intolerable shame will be for the oppressor. Shame and fear are instilled in the oppressed, while anger and contempt dominate for the oppressor.

Scheff[13] has drawn attention to how unacknowledged shame may lead to anger, and how spirals of shame/anger figure prominently, not only in quarrels but also in international relations, and how war may be a way to ease chronic shame. Nathanson has a broader perspective on shame, and one powerful strategy to evade the experience of shame is to 'attack others'.

Healthy pride, enjoying one's own accomplishments, is a joy to see in children. But the dangers of extracting undue glory from deeds vicariously earned as in celebrating yesterday's battle victories or 'our' team in sports, are ubiquitous. Hubris is a well-known human affliction. We hypothesize that the stronger the pride, the more vulnerability to shame, and shame in turn will lead to escalating anger. As a shared sentiment this cycle may become dangerous.

Insight into the collective deep culture would seem to be essential for the conflict worker; insight into the deeper layers of the personality of the specific conflict party perhaps less so. Representatives come and go; the deep culture stays about the same, even for Braudel's *longue durée*, the longer run.

To take an example: imagine a conflict party, a major country, and a representative, a major person. There is a dialogue with the conflict worker, and a high level of verbal agreement about both the positive and the negative anchors is achieved. Yet there is no acceptability in the sense of acting upon that consensus; there is unarticulated resistance.

Imagine now that in the collective subconscious of that country, in the deeper recesses of that collective mind, two ideas are lurking:

1. no perspective on a conflict is valid unless it can be seen as originating with us (written US?), the centre of geopolitics; and
2. no transformation of a conflict is valid unless military power has played a major role.

Whether those beliefs are consciously present and the conflict party prefers not to articulate it, or absent from consciousness and unarticulated, may be less important. The conflict worker has an array of choices: bringing such tacit assumptions out in the open as a dialogue theme; taking the assumptions into account without explicitly saying so. The first course of action is preferable, but perhaps in a roundabout way: 'Sometimes there are countries that have a tradition of feeling that ... What do you think?' To ask that question, however, the conflict worker must have the ability to hear the inaudible, that which has not been said, and to see the invisible, the (too) well-controlled body language.

This model becomes more complicated if we think in terms of two persons aiming at conflict transformation. There are three cases:

> two conflict parties, known as *negotiation*;
> one conflict party and one conflict worker, known as *dialogue*;
> two conflict workers, known as a *seminar*.

However, whenever two psyches meet, four layers interact:

> the collective conscious, meaning *role behaviour*;
> the personal conscious, meaning *personal outlook*;
> the personal subconscious, meaning *personal baggage*;
> the collective subconscious, meaning *deep culture*.

To start with the conflict worker: no doubt s/he should know more than the role repertory, as spelt out in manuals. Drawing on experience she or he should develop the personal touch, adding and subtracting from the prescribed repertory, like any psychotherapist, social worker, mediator, diplomat would do. She or he should also have some insight into the deeper forces at work at the personal and collective levels, rather than pretending to be a *tabula rasa*. Any conflict worker, like any other human being, has a biography. Like a psychoanalyst undergoing psychoanalysis as part of her training, the conflict worker may have conflict transformation at the personal level as hers.

This knowledge cannot be demanded of any conflict party. The only thing that should be demanded is conflict worker awareness of such factors, as indicated in the example above.

But the conflict worker might also do well to consider her or his own personality, especially at the subconscious level of deep emotions. Could there be some shame, some false pride? How about compatibility with the conflict party, with regard to the taste for anecdotes, humour, knowledge display, etc.?

How do two conflict parties participate in a negotiation? Their verbal exchange is a debate, not a dialogue; a verbal duel. There is a winner and a loser, according to whose position best survives the battle. There is mobilization of conscious and subconscious energies to fulfil the collective programme, delivering the cultural script intact into the final document.

A critical and very often neglected point is the role of the collective subconscious in this connection. Consider the four possible outcomes in the following table.

	Identical collective subconscious	Different collective subconscious
Verbal agreement	A	B
Verbal disagreement	C	D

In **Case A** the agreement is unsurprising, assuming that the collective subconscious dictates 90 per cent of the positions, making the agreement pre-programmed. The European Union Treaties?

In **Case B** the agreement is more interesting, bridging gaps in underlying assumptions. Sustainability of the agreement may be questioned, however. The US–Japan Security Treaties?

In **Case C** the disagreement is interesting, reflecting genuine ideological disagreement, questioning the sustainability of the dis-agreement under pressure. France and NATO in 1965/66?

In **Case D** the disagreement is unsurprising if we assume that the collective subconscious dictates 90 per cent of the positions taken, making disagreements pre-programmed. US–China relations?

An agreement may be little more than a celebration of the collective subconscious, not backed by real dialogue. 'Good chemistry' between individuals may bridge the gaps. But be sceptical: such agreements may be based on false assumptions.

Conclusion: Towards a Conflict Transformation Culture

Conflict releases and builds human and social, individual and collective, energy; the problem is how to channel that energy in constructive rather than destructive directions. Look at the faces, at people's eyes when in conflict: some look dull and apathetic; others' eyes are shining, ready for action. The question is, for what? – the battlefield or to scale peaks of human creativity?

We have not tapped the psychology of creativity,[14] focusing on the (often lonely) creative individual and how insight comes as a flash, through analogic rather than logic. An exception is provided by Edward de Bono[15] and his 'lateral thinking' to arrive at fresh perspectives. We are, however, looking for how people can be creative together, as in the Somalian *shir*.[16]

> a traditional conflict resolution structure that brings together all the mature men in the clans involved in a conflict. Women, children and young hot-blooded warriors are excluded. Men lounge under the thorn trees during the hot, dry day. They chat and drink tea. They also spend long hours chewing qat, the mildly euphoric drug grown in the Horn of Africa, smoking, greeting each other, delighting in the pleasure of meeting old friends – or old foes. At some point, things will gel. The various pieces that make up the main issue for which the *shir* was called will fall into place because a social climate conducive to a solution will have slowly emerged. The result will be proper peace – a peace felt from the inside – a peace that will have nothing in common with the quick-fix conferences in air-conditioned hotels in Addis Ababa organized by the UN –

In short, a conflict market filled to the brim with dialogues!

There is no assumption that the model described in this chapter is easy.[17] We would like to emphasize the intellectual effort involved in developing fruitful conflict perspectives. No attention to the emotive and the subconscious, however warranted, should detract from this intellectual aspect, and whether conflicts mobilize sufficient numbers of people with the talents needed. The verdict of the twentieth century is a resounding no. We have much to learn, and to do, to handle conflicts better.

PART 2

The TRANSCEND Experience:
Diagnosis, Prognosis, Therapy

TRANSCEND: 45 Years, 45 Conflicts

Johan Galtung

The 45 Years

When peace research was launched as an academic field of research, later as a discipline, in Oslo, in early 1959, the idea from the beginning was that this should be an applied social science with a value commitment: *peace by peaceful means.* Parallels were drawn with social work and medical science. And when the *Journal of Peace Research* was launched in 1964, contributors were asked to add 'some policy implications'. The demand met resistance given the prevailing trend in social sciences at the time: don't mix science and politics. Moreover, the task was not easy. Needless to say, mainstream politics and science had been mixing for a long time in the field of 'security studies', delivering premises and conclusions for the military option. All we wanted was to do the same for the peaceful option.

Politics and science had been mixed for some time in an effort to build an intellectually coherent basis for 'peace by peaceful means'. Politically, this was expressed as a demand for a peace service for conscientious objectors (COs), backed up by a strike, which resulted in my receiving a six months' jail sentence in 1954–55. When launching the idea of a Norwegian peace corps in early 1960, later heading a semi-official committee, the potential of a peace corps beyond a development assistance corps was explored – conflict workers proving themselves useful to local people. Moreover, to become meaningful as a peace corps that could be useful in conflict, development assistance had to be reciprocal, not only 'we helping them', but also 'they helping us', with advice and concrete work, such as teaching, and in the social sector. At the time only the development assistance corps was accepted, not peace/conflict work or reciprocity.

I had become a conscientious objector in 1951. In 1952 I started 18 months' civilian service (six months more than military service), did 12 months, and then refused to do the remaining six, arguing that the whole service, organized by the Ministry of Justice, was a waste of time for young men dedicated and willing to work non-violently, for the cause of peace. Moreover, if these six months were to be served as a punishment, so be it. The court agreed: I served six months' solitary confinement in Oslo's main prison. I was not the first, nor the last. Other pacifists have done the same in despair and protest against the civilian service. Standard criteria for non-violence were satisfied: the grievance was clear, the alternative was clear, the protest was non-violent. There was a price to be paid: solitary confinement.

About ten years passed, and it looked as if we had been tilting at windmills. But then, one day, when I was director of the Peace Research Institute in Oslo (PRIO), I received a telephone call from the Minister of Justice, a conservative, who wanted to know whether COs were still wanted for peace work, by which she meant peace research work, and if so how many, where and when, and what kind of work. We very quickly agreed on numbers and tasks, and that was it.

Non-violence for the COs had worked ('If he is willing to sacrifice that much he is either mad, or there is something to it, or both'). The pattern spread throughout Europe and beyond, and still by and large exists. (But it turns on the fact that the minister's mother and mine, members of the same social class in Oslo, played bridge together regularly. Non-violence needs a network.)

In 1964 I published a booklet, *Norske Fredsinitiativ: 20 Forslag* (Oslo: PAX, 1964; 'Norwegian Peace Initiatives: 20 Proposals'). The 20 proposals (with 65 concrete sub-proposals, and 15 sub-sub-proposals) cover development assistance (the first is about reciprocity), East–West cooperation (including development assistance), arms control and disarmament, extended defence concepts, globalization of peace politics (with UN embassies in all countries) and peace planning (with a directorate, or ministry, for peace). Some of these proposals suggested close cooperation between Norway and Poland. In 1965 I was invited by the Polish Foreign Ministry to attend detailed discussions, with a brief to report back to the Norwegian Ministry.

However, by far the most important background experience shaping TRANSCEND occurred in Charlottesville, Virginia, in 1958. I was an assistant professor at Columbia University, and with graduate students made an empirical community conflict study, with a population sample and a panel study of leaders of three groups: white segregationists, white desegregationists and the blacks. About 2,000 interviews were carried out.

Everything looked promising: a book was in the making about a community steeped in a conflict that was incompatible with their self-image not only as peaceful, but as a centre of Jeffersonian humanism. But that book was never written in spite of the excellent data. Something more important than one more item on the list of publications came up: the politics of conflict work. At that time the identity of a case-study community was supposed to be concealed (cf. *Middletown*, by the Lynds). As news about the conflict work reached the national press, the conflict *study* had to be sacrificed for the conflict *work* (but the data do exist).

In a sense the choice was easy. We had obtained more information than was available to the mayor or the sheriff about the basic concern of all: would there be violence, here, in Thomas Jefferson's home town, an icon for the whole country? The three groups knew very little about each other due to the dual polarization of race and ideology. We decided to try to facilitate dialogue by making the groups more transparent to each other, breaking down 'pluralistic ignorance' about violence (there was actually no real threat), showing that exits could be identified that would leave most people reasonably satisfied, and that there were still more exits to be identified down the road.

It worked, through patient explanation of their own processes, the processes working in them and on them, from a general social science point of view, demystifying the conflict. The reward came in the end: we received a letter saying they had desegregated peacefully, thanks partly to that conflict work.

At the same time, obviously, a role was taking shape, the role of the conflict worker, with many facets such as demystifying conflict processes, explaining the life cycles of conflicts, identifying points of intervention, engaging in dialogue with parties on all sides. After that my life ran on two tracks: as a peace/conflict researcher and as a peace/conflict worker. The tracks ran in parallel and still do.

That was in 1958. In 1998, 40 years after Charlottesville, the number of conflicts taken on was also 40 (for Nos. 1–40, in the order in which they were taken on, see pp. 183–8 below). The reader will identify Nos. 1 and 3 (Peace Service and Community Race Relations) as the conflicts mentioned above.

During those 40 years much has been added, and in 1993 it became clear that the work had had some significant effects. At the time of Conflict No. 20 the decision, very much inspired by my wife, Fumiko Nishimura, was made to create an organization, TRANSCEND, for 'conflict resolution by peaceful means'. The idea was to experiment, research and be pragmatic, for about five years. People with the skills needed as 'scholar-practitioners' were invited to join; almost all did.

By 1998 TRANSCEND had to some extent taken shape. But before a short account of that, let us continue the narrative of early experiences. Conflict work takes time. Seeds are sown, the time needed for fruition is unknown, maybe even unknowable: harbour no illusions about the 'quick fix'. So let us return to those early years; maybe some patterns can be identified, and also, at a very minimum, some experiences that shaped the work of TRANSCEND.

Our generation was shaped by the Cold War. Three weeks in the Soviet Union (as a member of a student delegation) at the time of Stalin's death in March 1953 led to a conclusion: Stalinism is as terrible as they say, *but these people do not want war.* During over 35 years of conflict participation in the East–West conflict many things happened: being arrested in the Soviet Union twice, handing out pamphlets about nonmilitary defence in Prague immediately after the Warsaw Pact invasion, being forced from a rostrum in East Germany and into a black car headed for the airport.[1] But most important in shaping TRANSCEND was the project for the Council of Europe, in 1967, to explore how countries in Europe – North, South, East and West – saw the future, from Moscow to Washington, DC, from Oslo to Athens.

Long and deep dialogues with 19 directors of political sections of the Foreign Ministries brought out how much more know-ledgeable, charming and creative they were face-to-face than in their public guises, particularly when 'the other side' was present. No doubt this shaped the preference for dialogue with the parties rather than negotiation among the parties.

From those discussions an idea emerged that looks trivial today: the parties to the East–West conflict could meet in a UN Security Commission for Europe, similar to the UN Economic Commission for Europe, with all parties discussing all issues and not only one issue at a time (like arms control), instead of targeting means of nuclear mass extermination at each other.

In autumn 1967 this idea was presented throughout Europe,[2] usually at meetings organized by institutes of foreign affairs. The general reception was positive, particularly in an Eastern Europe that sounded more independent of Moscow than Western Europe did of Washington. Nevertheless, the verdict of the Czech Foreign Minister was that 'the time is not ripe'.

However, at the back of that room in Prague a young man was listening. As a dissident he was sent to the countryside after the Soviet invasion in August 1968, and became No. 2 in the Foreign Office after communism imploded. They wanted the Soviet Army out. The formula suggested was 'the Galtung plan'; the time now being 'ripe'.[3] Edvard Shevardnadze[4] reacted positively. Even if he wanted the Warsaw Pact[5] to be modernized, he needed a successor to the Cold War system. A more permanent CSCE was one such formula.[6] So he not only supported withdrawing the army, but wanted that organization as the basic pillar in the framework for peace in Europe, the Paris Treaty in autumn 1990. And that is what happened.

Maybe there are three things to learn from this case.

Sow seeds. Do not be deterred by those who say ideas are too idealistic, or not realistic enough. If they had been 'realistic' they would have been available in mainstream discourse among elites. Elites are not stupid; such ideas would have been taken up. When the conflict does not die down, it is because 'realistic' ideas often are not realistic. From this it does not follow that all elite ideas are silly and all good ideas are counter to the trend. But for elites to rise above the status quo is not easy. In the climate of the late 1960s, following the brutal invasion of Czechoslovakia, to suggest that East and West should sit down together as equals with shared concerns was utopian.

The ways of the Lord are inscrutable. Sow seeds, but where they sprout may not be easy to predict. In 1981–85 I gave about 500 talks across Europe, with that idea and many others (defensive, non-provocative defence as military doctrine; non-violence in Eastern Europe against (post-)Stalinism; people's diplomacy; unilateral disarmament, like Charles Osgood's fine Gradual Reciprocated Initiatives in Tension-reduction, GRIT). Likely recipients were supposed to be small, democratic, even social democratic, NATO countries in northwestern Europe. But this proved not to be the case; they took no initiatives for they were both US clients and status quo countries, unlike insecure Eastern European countries seeking some Western recognition.

Perseverance takes time. A seed was sown in 1967. An assistant who became Deputy Foreign Minister carried the seed, it sprouted in early 1990, which he told me about at a conference in Luxembourg in February 1993, 25 years after it had been sown. Many will hear nothing, nor should it matter. But it felt good!

However, as mentioned, this did not exhaust what many of us in various parts of the peace movement tried to advocate during the Cold War. In a sense it is typical that institutional suggestions are what tend to be picked up by the state system.

The concerns, and not only ours, could be expressed under two headings:

1. *Stalinism*, meaning repression and general infraction of civil and political human rights; and
2. *nuclearism*, meaning a realistic threat of nuclear war, combined with police state secrecy.

The East in general, and the Soviet Union in particular, were plagued by both pathologies; the West in general and the United States in particular by the latter; and the NN (neutral-nonaligned) by neither.

The response advocated to repression was *non-violent struggle* in the East. Much time was spent disseminating information about forms of civil disobedience/non-cooperation/constructive action in Eastern Europe, particularly Poland, East Germany and Czechoslovakia. Others were doing the same, with some impact in all three countries.[7] To preach human rights and democracy was not enough.

The response advocated to nuclearism was *alternative defence*: a mix of defensive military defence, militia and nonmilitary defence.[8] Others were working along the same lines, and possibly had some impact on Gorbachev's thinking on sufficient defence.[9] Promulgating disarmament was insufficient.

Bridge-building between people in East and West through people's diplomacy was very important, bridge-building between a dissident movement less concerned with nuclear war and a peace movement less concerned with repression. As the 1980s unfolded the movements became fairly well unified.

Proposals and concrete action have been emphasized. But, coming back to the Charlottesville experience, the role of communicating social science, provided the focus is peace by peaceful means, should not be underestimated. A short story on communication during the Cold War, as a little drama in three acts, will illustrate this point.

Act I: From the start of what later became the International Peace Research Institute in Oslo (PRIO), and then from the Chair in Conflict and Peace Research at the University of Oslo, research papers outlining peace policies by peaceful means were distributed all over the world, including to IMEMO in Moscow, a major think tank for Soviet policy. There was no reaction at all, no answer, no comment, no reciprocation. We jokingly referred to IMEMO as the 'black hole in the universe'.

Act II: Then, in 1982, a conference was held at IMEMO, where I presented the manuscript of a forthcoming book.[10] After lunch the librarian organized a visit to the innermost sanctum of the library. And there they were, all the publications we had sent, a better collection than we had, underlined, marked, scribbled on! The 'black hole in the universe' had been located. It did attract matter, energy, information, receiving, not emitting. The librarian gave us a huge smile and a bear hug.

Act III: In 1991, at a meeting in Oslo, the Soviet Deputy Foreign Minister[11] reported how a study group of young assistants had used those papers, and others, as a basis for what later became known as Gorbachev's 'New Thinking'. He was very generous in his praise of people who continued to communicate in spite of no response, and all the Western 'boycott the Soviet Union' doctrines. One more bear hug.

Another story, this time a more recent one, which I experienced; with the passage of time it may come to look quite different.

Ecuador and Peru (Conflict No. 28) had suffered a succession of wars since 1941. A zone between the two, *'la zona inejecutable'*, because they were unable to demarcate a border given certain geographical circumstances, was a major bone of contention. There was one more war in 1995. At a meeting with the ex-president of Ecuador in Guatemala City, when asked to make a proposal, I extrapolated from my experience of Latin America in general and some ideas (from 1965) in connection with the Chile–Bolivia–Peru triangle, and suggested 'a bi-national zone with a natural park'. The ex-president was very positive but said that the idea was so novel that just to get used to it would take at least 30 years and the matter was urgent.

The idea was used in TRANSCEND exercises in conflict transformation for UN diplomats in Geneva. The Ecuadorian ambassador found the 'exercise' most interesting, and suggested a trip to Quito. A talk was given at the Military Academy in Quito on 5 June 1998, with much detail and informed discussion.

This angle on the story ends with a report in *Japan Times* (October 1998) that Ecuador had suggested 'a bi-national zone with a natural park' with the whole border issue to be negotiated. Peru agreed, but none the less wanted a fixed border. Apparently this solved the issue and the treaty was signed immediately afterwards. The matter took three years, not 30; and a little bit of good luck and a happy coincidence in Guatemala City, brokered by another ambassador.

Again the same point: parties in a conflict easily get stuck, and may reinforce each other in looking at the conflict in the same, unproductive way, blocking new ideas. Outsiders can/may introduce other/new angles.

The 45 Conflicts

What do we mean by 'conflict', how do we classify them, and what do we mean by 'studying conflicts' and by 'conflict work'?

Conflict is a synonym for violence. Conflict arises when there are incompatible goals, 'issues', contradictions; as human as life itself. If the conflict is sufficiently deep and not resolved or transformed, then it may enter a violent phase. *Conflicts cannot be prevented; but violence can.* Conflict energy can be channelled in positive, non-violent, constructive, transforming directions. That is our task.

TRANSCEND Programme I:

Conflict Transformation Experiences

Meso-level: Inter-Gender Conflicts
[30]   'Comfort Women'

Meso-level: Inter-Generation Conflicts
[40]   Inter-generation Conflict and Sustainability

Meso-level: Inter-Class Conflicts
[33]   Hostage Crises
[34]   Albania
[38]   Colombia
[39]   Inter-class Conflict and Globalization

Meso-level: Inter-Race/Intra-Community Conflicts
[3]   Community Race Relations

Meso-level: Intra-State Conflicts
[1]   Peace Service
[20]   Anomie/Atomie and 'Sects'
[24]   Reconciliation Conflicts
[42]   Angola Civil War

Meso-level: Two or More Nations/One State Conflicts
[6]   Israel–Palestine
[8]   Rhodesia–Zimbabwe
[13]   Hawai'i
[19]   Hindu–Muslim Relations
[22]   Somalia
[25]   China
[35]   Lebanon

Macro-level: One Nation/Two or More States Conflicts
[11]   Korea
[15]   The Kurds
[23]   The Mayas
[43]   The Samis

Macro-level: Two or More Nations/Two or More States Conflicts
[7]   Cyprus
[9]   Northern Ireland
[10]   Kashmir
[12]   Pax Pacifica
[18a] The Yugoslavia Conflict I
[18b] The Yugoslavia Conflict II
[21]   Sri Lanka

[29]   Caucasus
[31]   Okinawa
[32]   The Great Lakes Region
[36]   Euskal Herria
[37]   Gibraltar/Ceuta-Melilla
[41]   Afghanistan

Macro-level: Inter-State Conflicts
[4]   Cuba
[14a] The Gulf Conflict I
[14b] The Gulf Conflict II
[16]   Japan–US
[17]   Japan–Russia
[28]   Ecuador–Peru

Mega-level: Inter-Region Conflict
[2a]   East–West Conflict, Cold War I
[2b]   East–West Conflict, Cold War II
[5]   North–South Conflict, Development Crisis
[27]   Tripartite Europe
[45]   The US, the West and the Rest

Mega level: Inter-Civilization Conflict
[26]   The Christians and the Muslims
[44]   The Christians and the Heathens

The reader will identify many missing conflicts. We make no claims to comprehensiveness, but claim that a variety of experiences has been made, going deeply into diverse conflicts using dialogues with the parties, searching, probing for ways out, for outcomes, and processes leading to outcomes.

For each one of the 45 (48) conflicts the next section offers a densely worded perspective, a way of looking, usually with diagnosis, prognosis and therapy. Most perspectives are limited to one and a half pages; some are over two. Obviously, much more can be said about anything as complex as a conflict. But this has been compiled for people searching for quick overviews, and for some ideas about how to proceed with that conflict. Some people prefer reading in DPT order, starting with the diagnosis; others prefer TPD, starting with therapy, then continuing upwards if they find anything interesting (for them).

For an even quicker overview of the 45 (48) conflicts, see pp. 183–8: the conflicts in chronological order as they were taken on, with one-liners for all the D, P and T. For more information, there are short background papers on some of the conflicts, with some of the reasoning underlying the perspective, and more extensive papers on the conflict in and over Yugoslavia available on the web-site <www.transcend.org>.

Of the 45 conflicts, 32 are over territory one way or the other, most of them (24) dealing with the nation/state dialectic. Since this is the bulk of the experiences, the reader will find a special analysis of the nation/state dialectic after the perspectives. And after that an analysis of the underlying approach, the TRANSCEND method, with some pointers to the future. But now, back to the TRANSCEND story.

A recent publication, *Prevention and Management of Violent Conflicts* (Utrecht: European Platform for Conflict Prevention and Transformation, 1998 edition) presents 'profiles of 475 leading organizations and institutions in the field'. Almost all of them can be said to work for 'peace by peaceful means'. There are thousands involved, mostly nongovernmental, some governmental, almost nobody related to the corporate world. Together they produce a wealth of ideas and engage in peace-building, across complex conflict borders. Most of them were started in the 1990s, many with roots in the peace movements of the 1980s. It is inconceivable that they are not having an impact on the way we think and act about peace.

TRANSCEND is one of them. Did TRANSCEND have an impact? Did we achieve anything? The case can be made for No. 1 and No. 2, the use of a Security Commission for Europe; for No. 3 and for No. 28 (Ecuador–Peru, the idea of a bi-national zone). They grew out of many dialogues. No doubt, if TRANSCEND had not suggested it somebody else would have done so; no doubt somebody else did. Causal chains in such matters are complex; and it is the epitome of megalomania to see one person as the cause and 'peace' as the effect. What we can hope for is to be a little tributary to the river of peaceful approaches, of cultures and structures of peace, for a culture of peace. Schopenhauer's words are wise:

All truth passes through three stages:
First it is ridiculed,
Second it is violently opposed,
Third it is accepted as being self-evident.

Perhaps he overlooked stage zero: The Big Silence. But Schopenhauer here is talking about truth, not about organizations and individuals. Our task is exactly to make the truths about conflict transformation by peaceful means self-evident.

45 Years, 45 Conflict Perspectives, 1956–2001

D, P, T: Diagnosis, Prognosis, Therapy: maxi-brief formulations

[1] Peace Service, 1953–64
D: Wasting time for a growing fraction of peace-oriented youth
P: Increasing polarization and marginalization from government
T: Alternative, non-violent service for peace as a human right

[2a] East–West Conflict, Cold War I, 1953–89
D: Reductionism to [2, 1] conflict; Stalinism, nuclearism
P: Protraction–Third World warfare–nuclear war/mutual genocide
T: CSCE, GRIT/defensive defence, people diplomacy, non-violence

[2b] East–West Conflict, Cold War II, 1996–
D: Expansion of NATO and AMPO puts Russia–China in a squeeze
P: Russian–Chinese cooperation, possibly with India–Pakistan
T: Drop plans or make them totally defensive, privilege UN/OSCE

[3] Community Race Relations (Charlottesville, VA), 1958–60
D: Lack of transparency among the three conflict parties
P: Exaggerated perceptions could lead to violence
T: Sociological findings communicated to all, de-escalation

[4] Cuba, 1960–
D: Manifest Destiny in the Americas at stake; Cold War concerns
P: Endless efforts to destabilize, including war
T: Cuban self-reliance, political pluralism US model

[5] North–South Conflict, Development Crisis, 1962–
D: Imperialism, economism, asymmetric externalities
P: Massive misery/violence/migration South; unemployment North
T: Alternative economics, self-reliance I, self-reliance II

[6] Israel–Palestine, 1964–
D: Settler colonialism, traumatized chosen people vs. indigenous
P: Protracted structural and direct violence, escalation
T: Non-violence (*Intifada*), autonomy–two states–confederation

[7] **Cyprus, 1964–**
D: Two nations on a small island, the mother-states old enemies
P: Intermittent violence, as part of Orthodox/Muslim fault-line
T: Turkish part recognized, Cyprus joins EU as (con)federation

[8] **Independence Struggles (Rhodesia–Zimbabwe), 1965–70**
D: Settler colonialism, *mission civilisatrice* complex
P: *Economic sanctions will not work to unsettle the regime*
T: Independence through massive non-violence

[9] **Northern Ireland, 1970–**
D: Institutionalization of 300+ years of historical conquest
P: Mutual alienation, polarization, protracted violence
T: Anglo-Irish condominium, high Ulster autonomy/independence

[10] **Kashmir, 1971–**
D: Many people live in Kashmir/India against their will
P: Protracted terrorism/torturism; occasional Indo-Pakistan wars
T: Tri-partition according to monitored local plebiscites

[11] **Korea, 1972–**
D: Separation of a nation, division of a state, by outsiders
P: Korean War 1950–53 repeated with some modifications
T: Korean insertion in East Asian Community, opening rail and road

[12] **Pax Pacifica, 1988–**
D: Vulnerability of small island states to all kinds of violence
P: Structural, cultural and nature invasion/inundation
T: Associations, confederations, upgrading of zones of peace

[13] **Hawai'i, 1989–**
D: Settler/migrant worker colonialism, destructure/culturation
P: Protraction of indigenous as second-class citizens, violence
T: Bicameral legislature in an ever more independent Hawai'i

[14a] **The Gulf Conflict I (The War), 1990–91**
D: Reductionism to [2, 1], God vs. Satan, Armageddon; CGT/DMA
P: Massive genocide, also through economic sanctions
T: Historical/cultural complexification, negotiations; CSCME (Conference on Security and Cooperation in the Middle East)

[14b] **The Gulf Conflict II (Inspection), 1998**
D: State (US/UK), and Bedouin, warrior logics at work; c'mon!
P: Once again, double celebration of victory and deadlock
T: Take the issues as they come, clear timetable; CSCME

[15] **The Kurds, 1990–**
D: Five countries separating one nation
P: Protracted, endless violence, terrorism and torture
T: Human rights–autonomy–Kurdish confederation; by non-violence

[16] **Japan–US, 1990–**
D: Rank incongruence: Japan top economically, US politically
P: Second opening–imitation–conflict–war cycle; tension, war
T: Less trade, end to AMPO, recoupling with equity, equality

[17] **Japan–Russia, 1991–**
D: Ownership over South Kurile islands/Northern Territories
P: The issue continues poisoning relations between neighbours
T: Sacred territory, Japanese ownership, managing together

[18a] **The Yugoslavia Conflict I (Northwest), 1991/93–**
D: Reductionism [2, 1] formula, God vs. Satan, Armageddon; CGT
P: Massive genocide, also through sanctions, major escalation
T: Equal right to self-determination, confederation; CSCSEE

[18b] **The Yugoslavia Conflict II (Southeast), 1998**
D: Albanian independence movement on Serb sacred and rich land
P: Occupation and third party governance; like Bosnia-Herzegovina
T: Kosovo Third FRY Republic, South Balkan confederation

[19] **Hindu–Muslim Relations (Ayodhya), 1992**
D: Limits to tolerance; insufficient respect for Mother India
P: Sporadic violence, separation of communities
T: Hindu–Muslim dialogue, and concrete local cooperation

[20] **Anomie/Atomie and 'Sects', 1993–**
D: Sects/nationalism as reactions to postmodern anomie/atomie
P: New group formation within and across societies; violence
T: Contracts protecting group-formation and individual exit

[21] **Sri Lanka, 1993–**
D: Imposition of a unitary state on a multinational people

P: Protraction with institutionalization of violence
T: Non-territorial federalism, separate legislative autonomies

[22] **Somalia, 1993–**
D: Civil strife along clan lines following hunger and war
P: Foreign intervention defining Somalia as nation-state fails
T: Dual federal structure, territorially and based on clans

[23] **The Mayas, 1994–**
D: Conquest of America 1492–, marginalization, liberation fight
P: Endless revolution–repression cycles
T: Human rights–autonomy–Maya confederation; by non-violence

[24] **Reconciliation Conflicts (Argentina), 1995–**
D: Ambivalence favours, Christianity and legalism impede, reconciliation
P: No deep reconciliation will take place
T: Bring the issues out in open dialogue

[25] **China, 1995–**
D: Major autonomy movements in world's oldest unitary state
P: Destruction of Tibet, alienation, protracted violence
T: China as confederation with five parts (+ Inner Mongolia?)

[26] **Christian–Muslim Relations, 1995–**
D: 1095 declaration of holy war with no peace declaration
P: Protracted micro-/macro-violence, God vs. Satan, Armageddon
T: Christian–Muslim dialogue and concrete local cooperation

[27] **Tripartite Europe, 1995–**
D: Europe confessionally divided Catholic–Protestant/Orthodox/Muslim
P: Yugoslavia escalates Europe trilaterally into conflict
T: Westphalia +: Pan-European institutions up to confederation

[28] **Ecuador–Peru, 1995–**
D: Classical territorial dispute; military seeking legitimacy
P: Setting a pattern of inter-state warfare for Latin America
T: Joint ownership, use of disputed area as peace zone

[29] **Caucasus, 1996–**
D: Three countries/strong minorities; four external powers
P: Endless violence, external meddling, economic penetration
T: Joint peace zone, Caucasian parliament, confederation

[30] **'Comfort Women' (Japan–Korea), 1996–**
D: Patriarchy/imperialism/bellicism syndrome
P: Will be reproduced as long as the syndrome is intact
T: Japan engages in deep self-criticism, uproots the syndrome

[31] **Okinawa, 1996–**
D: US–Japan cooperation using Okinawa as major offshore base
P: Polarizing relations; total destruction in case of war
T: Reducing bases to Japan level; Okinawa as Asian Switzerland

[32] **The Great Lakes Region, 1997–**
D: Mainly projection of German racism, Anglo-French
      tribalism
P: The violence will be reproduced
T: The West shares responsibility; double-ocean confederation

[33] **Hostage Crises, 1997–**
D: Conflict over misery; meta-conflict over use of violence
P: Violence escalation self-sustaining, reproduced by misery
T: All parties disarm and meet in work to reduce misery

[34] **Albania, 1997–**
D: Pyramid schemes to convert fixed into liquid capital
P: Deeper misery and continued violence
T: International commission to investigate; restitution

[35] **Lebanon, 1997–**
D: Violence in deeply divided society when resources run out
P: New destruction when construction has been completed
T: Joint reconstruction, resolution, reconciliation

[36] **Euskal Herria, 1997–**
D: Two countries separating one nation
P: Protracted, endless violence, terrorism and killing
T: Functional independence and French–Spanish
      condominium

[37] **Gibraltar and Ceuta-Melilla, 1997–**
D: Majority and historical rights have different implications
P: Minor, and then major violence
T: Internationalize all three, under Spain–UK–Morocco
      condominium

[38] **Colombia, 1998–**
D: High anomie (deculturation) and atomie (destructuration)
P: Ever-increasing violence and corruption in all groups
T: Intensive reculturation and exemplary zones of peace

[39] Inter-class conflict and globalization, 1998–
D: Bad distribution, low buying power, overproduction
P: Increasing misery, unemployment, capital for speculation
T: Better distribution, securing subsistence all over

[40] Inter-generation conflict and sustainability, 1998–
D: Extreme egoism, short time perspective, high competition
P: Next generation's livelihood compromised, mass migration
T: Fewer people who live longer, 3–4 generation housing, *oikos*

[41] Afghanistan, 2001–
D: Extreme divisiveness and foreign Great Game interventionism
P: This will continue, 'politics as usual' also after 11 September 2001
T: Coalition government, federation, and Central Asia Community

[42] Angola, 2001–
D: Resource driven war with international complicity
P: Diplomatic stagnation and continued warfare
T: Quiet informal diplomacy, humanitarian cease-fire, local power

[43] The Sami nation, 2001–
D: Four countries occupying and exploiting one nation
P: Further exploitation, possibly violent resistance
T: Truth Commission; collective rights, autonomy, confederation

[44] The Christians and the Heathens, 2000–
D: A papal bull in 1493 converts discovery into domination
P: Theology becomes law justifying slavery and colonialism
T: Revocation of the papal bull

[45] The US, the West and the rest
D: The 11 September 2001 attack is retaliation for US violence
P: The reaction will continue the chain of retaliation
T: A massive North–South peace movement to exit from that chain

CHAPTER 2.2

45 Conflicts, 45 Perspectives

Johan Galtung

1. Peace Service: A TRANSCEND Perspective

Diagnosis. Obligatory military service, proposed by Machiavelli in 1505, was first introduced by France in 1793 as the other side of the rights of the citizen: the duty to give their life when called upon by the state to do so. A logical consequence of the military approach to conflict, deeply ingrained in the European tradition, conscription was also a consequence of increasing democratization (participation of the *demos*) for males. Conscription raises a number of questions:

- Is there such a thing as a 'military solution' to a conflict?
- Is there an alternative for those who for any reason say 'no'?
- Could that alternative be a peace, or development, service?
- What would be the precise content of that service?
- How about the female half of the population?

The answer to the first question conditions the answer to the other four, reflecting the bellicist/pacifist divide:

Bellicist: there is no alternative. If CO status is accepted, it is not more attractive than the military service, with risks; they then divide over whether women should be given combat roles.

Pacifist: an alternative is a human right, there should also be a peace/development service open to others, including women.

The state monopoly on violence makes the state not only the organizer of military power, but also of the force to execute (as deserters), persecute and imprison, those who refuse to do military service, or to grant them the right to an alternative. Thus, the whole issue becomes a state vs. citizen issue from a formal point of view, and an issue opening for new ways of energizing peace processes all over from an evolutionary point of view.

Prognosis. The prognosis is positive because of the absurdity in denying young people who want to serve peace the right to do so. (Absurdity: a deep disjunction between avowed goals and reality.) In some countries this may essentially be a question of a sufficient number of conscientious objectors, not only formulating an alternative with general appeal, but backing that approach with a civil disobedience enacting the alternative.

Therapy. From the late 1950s/early 1960s, a 'peace corps', but not in the name only, combining five aspects, is relevant.[1]

- a development service for the most needy in the world community;
- making that service reciprocal, that is, not only from rich to poor countries, having a flow of human and social development services in return for technical services;
- using the service also as a conflict resolution corps of people, young and old, men and women, moving with integrity into conflict arenas, offering their good services as witnesses, facilitators of conflict resolution and reconciliation, social networking and empowerment for peace, peace zones, etc.;
- internationalizing the corps (like United Nations Volunteers), also to avoid using it as propaganda for one country only;
- keeping the service open, for young and old, men and women.

This would not only solve the problem of wasting COs' time and their increasing polarization and marginalization from government, but also mobilize people for alternative, non-violent service for peace as a human right. (1959, 1964)

2a. East–West Conflict, Cold War I: A TRANSCEND Perspective

Diagnosis. The core of this conflict is the inter-state class conflict against the rich, dominant, northwestern corner of Europe, and of the world, the 'First World'; coupled to the intra-state class conflicts of workers against the upper and middle classes; and of the world coloured against the white. In this family of populist uprisings we might count the fascism of Southern Europe; the Nazism of Central Europe; the communism of Eastern Europe/Soviet Union, and the decolonization struggles. The Second World War was used to beat Nazism and fascism; neo-colonialism was used to beat decolonization; and the Cold War to beat the absurd Soviet Union, which ultimately imploded. In this struggle between Northwestern Europe and the Soviet Union over Eastern Europe the Northwest presented the conflict as between democracy/market and dictatorship/plan, not as a world and social class conflict; reducing complexity to a conflict of two parties over one issue. On top of this a potentially devastating meta-conflict over the threat and use of nuclear arms monopolized the attention at the expense of Eastern Europe and ideal society.

Prognosis. The prognosis was *war*, but *not* in the East–West core arena in Europe, with the possible exception of using the two Berlins/Germanies as the battlefield (hence the vast German peace and dissident movements). Displaced wars over Third World territory and allegiance were more likely; Korea and Vietnam, and the near-war over Cuba, being examples. Escalation into the core area, nuclear war and mutual genocide were not impossible. But there was also another prognosis: the collapse of the Soviet Union as an *absurd society* with an intolerable disjunction between myth and reality, and that was what eventually happened.

Therapy. Remedies proposed during the Cold War included:

- *for conflict transformation*, a permanent organization for dialogue and implementation under the auspices of the United Nations in Geneva: *a Security Commission for Europe*, using as a model the UN Economic Commission for Europe (ECE).[2]
- *for the arms race/war threat*: GRIT[3] and defensive defence,[4] based on conventional, para- and nonmilitary components.
- *People's Diplomacy*, also between peace and dissident movements.
  (1967, 1984)

2b. East–West Conflict, Cold War II: A TRANSCEND Perspective

Diagnosis. As mentioned in connection with Cold War I, there is a deeper agenda, rooted in the nineteenth century, now brought into the twenty-first century by the expansion of NATO eastward (adding Poland, the Czech Republic and Hungary, so far) and AMPO, the Japan–US security system, westward. Seen from the centre of the world, the Northwest, the US, the 'Eurasian Continent', is *the* source of geopolitical evil. Latin America is an easily controlled backyard, Africa is insignificant; but Eurasia is the seat of populism, war and terrorism, of billions of coloured people, of other faiths and fundamentalism. West Asia/the Middle East; South Asia with the two new nuclear powers, Central Asia with oil (and US bridge-heads), Southeast Asia with (until recently) booming economies are all key parts of the concept. And so are, indeed, Russia (with Ukraine and Belarus) and China, not to mention the problematic Eurasian peripheries, Korea and the Balkans. 'A global nation with global interests' has its reasons for bringing the alliance systems up to the basic fault-lines: between Catholic/Protestant and Slavic-Orthodox Europe, and between Japan and the rest of Asia. A purely defensive Japan would signal a non-threat. But deep cooperation with the most mobile military power in the world signals the opposite. What matters is the bond to offensive capability, not the defensive posture of the Japanese forces.

The double expansion, establishing 'anchors' on either end of Eurasia, adding the US–Turkey–Israel alliance, is a logical follow-up of the US JCS 570/2 directive under Roosevelt, the 'Base Bible'. A glance at the map informs us that the double anchor expansion is, or can be perceived as, a pincer movement.

Prognosis. There will be a *reactio* of (about) the same size and opposite direction. Russia and China will settle their grievances (e.g. over the Ussuri), share military information, and build a *de facto* alliance. China will reinforce agreements with Pakistan and Russia with India (Kashmir may be settled in the wake of all that). Russia will pick up what the US defines as pariah states – Serbia, Libya, Syria, Iraq, Iran, North Korea – and support them, including in the UN. The whole continent may cohere against the US–NATO–AMPO complex. A minor incident along the highly problematic Poland/Ukraine border or the North and South Korea/Japan complex may easily set in motion large geotectonic aggregates, or at least be grossly magnified geopolitically.

Therapy. It is difficult to imagine any therapies short of: 'Stop it, reverse the decision, promote super-regional, UN, world security, instead.' The solution is not to invite Russia into first-class NATO membership since that would trigger an East Asia Security Community along a White–Yellow fault-line. Nor should China join AMPO, for the same reason. Regional solutions would have to bridge fault-lines, not reinforce them. And that pushes the only viable solution in the direction of world disarmament and UN peacemaking/keeping/building capability with soft military means: Sun Tzu rather than Clausewitz, defensive rather than offensive, non-violent rather than violent, with confidence-building, disengagement zones, systematic use of conflict transformation dialogues for local, regional and global conflicts, like this conflict formation.

The United Nations, with its universal membership, would have to be the key carrier of such initiatives, the problem being that the key actor, the US, can block any significant action with a veto. That confrontation may ultimately lead to another double movement: 'the UN out of the US, the US out of the UN'. (August 1996)

3. Community Race Relations: A TRANSCEND Perspective

Diagnosis. Under this general heading a research project was carried out in Charlottesville, VA, in 1958–60. The research project was a multi-wave panel study of elites in the city, and the major organizations of the segregationists (White Citizens' Councils), of the desegregationists (Human Relations Councils) and of the blacks (NAACP). In addition, a two-wave survey was made of the attitudes of a random sample of the population of the county; more material than anywhere else.

The population was nervous. A Ku Klux Klan cross had been burned. There was a violent meta-conflict in the air superimposed on the root conflict over equal, not separate, citizenship for blacks and whites, according to the Supreme Court Decision of 17 May 1954. The conflict was in fact trilateral, not bilateral. The two white groups differed not only in terms of their stand on the issue (with schools being symbolic of the rest of public space: theatres, toilets, hotels, anything). They had very different relations to the community, enacting the roles of 'locals' and 'cosmopolitans'. The segregationists had deep roots and were more inward-looking; the desegregationists (or, in some cases, even integrationists as they practised the value of togetherness in their private lives) were migrants, often academic, and outward-looking. They legitimized their positions in obvious ways: 'Only those who have roots here are entitled to an opinion,' said one. 'The nation/the world outside moves on; you are being left behind,' said the other. But all of this was verbal and a question of community power. There was no urge anywhere for violence as language or conflict mechanism. But the three parties almost never met. There was no transparency.

Prognosis. With frustration and hatred building up between white segregationists and the black community, the expectation of violence was almost automatic, leading to a growing search among some whites for self-defence, and maybe also for pre-emptive violence. The expectation could develop into a self-fulfilling prophecy, and even more so because of the polarized map of outcomes. With only two possibilities in people's minds: public schools segregated (status quo) vs. public schools desegregated a self-reinforcing dualism arose.

Therapy. Three approaches were suggested:

- Make the situation transparent to the participants, in the media and in meetings, explaining their positions, taking all of them equally seriously, how they had become stuck; but at the same time pointing out that even if there was fear of violence there was no urge for violence anywhere. On the other hand, the mechanisms of self-fulfilling prophecies had to be explained, particularly how exaggerated perceptions could lead to violence.

- These talks included elementary conflict talk, like defining conflict in terms of incompatible goals, not as violence, about how polarization was linked to seeing only two outcomes, how that would play into the hands of the extremists and exacerbate the conflict, the importance of finding something acceptable to both, that outside parties sometimes might see outcomes hidden to the parties to the conflict. This was done in cooperation with capable local journalists to promote conflict literacy.

- A third alternative might be private schools with the advantages (free choice, finding a solution for white extremists) and disadvantages (considerable costs, segregation of private space) of that outcome.

The result was de-escalation, an opening for other positions, and, indeed, desegregation. (June 1960)

4. Cuba: A TRANSCEND Perspective

Diagnosis. The roots of the conflict are much deeper than the current phase: they are found in Spanish colonialism. From the turn of the twentieth century the remnants of the Spanish Empire were included in the second wave of US imperialism (Cuba, Puerto Rico, Guam, Eastern Samoa, the Philippines; the first wave being the conquest of continental US). In a very real way Fidel Castro is a successor to a José Martí fighting a system of bridgehead imperialism, with a tiny, mainly white, upper class delivering goods to an imperial power, together repressing, exploiting and alienating a vast, to a large extent black, lower class. Added to this comes the traumas and destruction of revolutionary and counter-revolutionary violence. There are excessive expectations when a new imperial power replaces the old, as when the US replaced Spain, and when the Soviet Union replaced the US.

The US entered with its three-stage Manifest Destiny programme: first, contiguous US, then the Western Hemisphere (the Monroe Doctrine of 1823, keeping others out as a condition), and, much later, the whole world as 'globalization'.

The Soviet Union entered the conflict as a part of the Cold War logic, adding to the boycott organized by the old imperial power the continuation of Cuban export of the raw (sugar), this time even against the raw (oil) with some other goods thrown in; and encouraged the 'dictatorship of the proletariat' by a single party with local committees – CDR – and general surveillance.

The net result is an island country desperately fighting, with an underdeveloped economy, and a narrow band of freedom of expression, to keep the achievements of the revolution (food, clothing, shelter, health and education for all). The white upper class is in the diaspora (Florida); Cuba is mainly black.

Prognosis. Stability at this unsatisfactory level. There will be neither collapse, nor improvement, takeover neither from inside, nor from outside. One reason for stability is probably the Cuban government's ability to handle these four threats, based on considerable experience.

Therapy. As usual based on very many dialogues from the top to the bottom, inside and outside Cuba:

- *An ever higher level of Cuban economic self-reliance*, a shame that a resource-rich island, with excellent literacy and higher education institutions, has not become more capable of growing all its own food, and creating small-scale industries for the basic means of production, distribution and consumption. There is still an inability to transcend the old pattern of getting all in return for sugar instead of processing the cane in 100 directions. The present situation calls for a maximum of alternative energy conversion, and land and fish farming.

- *An ever higher level of participatory democracy*, including, as in the US, a two-party system. Cuba would only gain from getting countless debates out of private spaces and into the public space, by having, for instance, two socialist parties. The creativity of the population has to find its legitimate expression, inner party discussions are always insufficient. But a white regime and white opposition may not survive democracy in a country with an overwhelmingly black majority.

- *An ever higher level of individuals, organizations, countries counteracting the USA/OAS boycott.* High time to scrap it.

- *An ever higher level of admiration for a regime that insists on basic needs satisfaction as a key part of basic rights.* High time for the world to recognize the significance of this position in spite of other human rights shortcomings.

(April 1973)

5. North–South Conflict:
A TRANSCEND Perspective

Diagnosis. What makes this giant formation a conflict formation is not that some people are rich and some poor, that some people's basic needs are met and others are not; but that some people are poor because others are rich, and vice versa. This is called exploitation (or inequity, a softer term) and is ubiquitous. It explains neither poverty nor wealth. There are many other factors at work, one being hard work, another greed, but a third factor is certainly lack of consideration and exploitation.

Lack of consideration is deeply embedded in economism as an ideology explaining economic growth in terms of a willingness to take risks under conditions only offered by free markets, hoping for a trickle-down effect/distribution, by job-creation.

Under some conditions this happens, particularly at the top of the global economy. But the externalities (side-effects) are usually negative for the poor and positive for the wealthy, like the lack of challenge accruing to the person digging out raw materials for export, and the deep challenge to the person wrestling with problems of processing raw materials. Challenge, training in working together, pollution and depletion, all those asymmetrically distributed side-effects of economic activity, add up to the asymmetric exchange as the solid base on which the Western superiority is built. As the 'science' of economics is its rationale, this is one place where the remedies have to be found: *alternative economics*; a major intellectual challenge. Many people are working on that. In the meantime Western economic globalization continues after the defeat of red and green socialism, for the time being, at the expense of ever-increasing inequality, everywhere. The wealth created cannot even insure rich societies against unemployment, misery and crisis.

Prognosis. There will be economic growth, meaning average upward change in the world, and in many societies; and there will be an ever-increasing disparity between rich and poor countries and rich and poor people in most countries as the ideology of economism (neoliberalism, neoclassicism) gets more firmly rooted in practice. In many parts of the South/Third World this will lead to even more massive misery, violence and migration; in the North it will lead to massive unemployment.

Therapy. Given the limits set by nature the material living standard of the richest people is unattainable for most, and may also be undesirable. But a decent livelihood for all is entirely realistic. The guidelines that are needed include:

- *Alternative economics*: change the focus of economics from growth to meeting the needs of everybody, including the obvious, 'internalizing the externalities', considering all side-effects.
- *Self-reliance I*: stimulate production for basic needs locally, particularly in the fields of food, clothing, shelter, health and education, and beyond necessities into normal consumer goods, internalizing challenges, reducing transportation pollution, using resources better, safeguarding sustainability.
- *Self-reliance II*: beyond that, develop trade with partners at the same level to prevent patterns of dependency, meaning much South–South trade, and cooperation of all kinds.
- *Reciprocal development assistance*: for the same reason, accept development assistance only from partner (countries) willing to accept development assistance in return, including from poor countries that can offer more human and social (as opposed to technical and economic) assistance, building equity.

Much of this will depend on the very uneven capacity of the civil society: the local authorities and the NGOs. (1964, 1978)

6a. Israel–Palestine: A TRANSCEND Perspective

Diagnosis. The conflict is between settler colonialism and indigenous peoples, complicated by the settlers' claim as a Chosen People with a Promised Land. The land, and particular points in space and time, are sacred to both, but to some on either side (fundamentalists) more than to others (moderates). There are diasporas and supporting countries, particularly the US (with a similar story of Chosen People conquering a Promised Land, early in the seventeenth century, drawing on the Jewish archetype) for Israel, very far from a neutral third party.

The Oslo/Wye processes fall short of a peace process (and so did Camp David where the Palestinians were not even present):

1. *Fundamentalists were excluded*, reinserting themselves in the process through acts of violence. They also have peace concepts.
2. *Peace actors/movements on both sides were excluded*, Intifadah, Peace Now were not acknowledged; their action was indispensable.
3. *The US is not a signatory*, even if it is a major actor on the Israeli side, posing as a 'third party'.
4. *Underestimation of polarization inside Palestine and Israel;* overestimation of the extent to which the accords are binding.
5. *An unnecessary amount of secrecy*, no dialogue with public.
6. *Lack of symmetry*: the agreement is between a state and an 'autonomy' lower than for Bantustans in apartheid South Africa.
7. *The Palestinian state not defined*, how would that state relate to Israel, militarily, politically, economically, culturally?
8. *Excessive governmentalism and institutionalism*, the relations between the two sides are not spelt out economically, culturally.
9. *No real effort to weave the two civil societies together.*
10. *An underestimation of the strength of religion* as a code steering people's behaviour, like killing a prime minister, the Hebron Purim massacre, and the fourth, suicidal, stage of *jihad*.
11. *An underestimation of the sacredness of many points in the area for the Jews (Jabutinski)*, only a political/military focus.
12. *An underestimation of the possibility of ecumenical work*, between Jews, Muslims and Christians, emphasizing the positive, gentler aspects of their faiths, turning against harder aspects.

Prognosis. The prognosis today is the same as 50 years ago: oscillation between the structural violence of occupation, exploitation and alienation and the direct violence of bombs and bombing, terror and torture. Also, the probability of escalation of the civil war within Israel between moderates and fundamentalists (with a fundamentalist killing a moderate prime minister, and suicide bombing) is high; and increasing as the 'moment of truth', statehood, is approaching.

Therapy. Four necessary conditions stand out:

1. Symmetry is of the essence, meaning the long overdue and full recognition by all of Palestine, and all of Israel, as states.
2. The conflict cannot be transformed within the narrow confines of today's Israel, but possibly in the context of a long overdue *Conference for Security and Cooperation in the Middle East*–CSCME under UN auspices, Helsinki-type, accommodating the linkages to the US/UK–Iraq conflict and to the Kurdish issue, with full recognition of all states in the region, a Middle East Common Market, arms/oil/water regimes, etc. Neighbouring Arab states might consider ceding some territory to a Palestinian state.
3. There have to be plans beyond autonomy, with a Palestinian state confederating with neighbours, including Israel.
4. There also has to be a concept of a Palestinian-Israeli confederation or even a federal state where the communities learn to live together in peace.

(1964–1971–1993)

The Oslo Accords: From a Flawed Process to a Flawed Outcome

I. Process

1. *Extremists excluded*, meaning Hamas and Likud/Orthodox, the agreement being between PLO and Labour/Secular-Modern; probably related to Norwegian social democrat 'reason is in the middle'. This works in moderate Norway, but not where more than 50 per cent feel excluded. They also have peace concepts, and they will announce themselves (like killing Prime Minister Rabin, or suicide bombs).
2. *Peace actors/movements from both sides excluded, Intifada*, Peace Now, not even acknowledged; yet their action was indispensable.
3. *The US is not a signatory*, even if it is a major actor on the Israeli side, posing as 'third party'. Was Oslo acting for the US?

4. *A general underestimation of polarization inside Palestine and Israel;*
   overestimation of whether the accords are binding.
5. *An unnecessary amount of secrecy,* no dialogue with public.

II. Outcome; Structure

6. *Lack of symmetry:* the agreement does not define two states,
   but a state and an 'autonomy' which in fact is at a lower level
   than for the Bantustans in apartheid South Africa.
7. *Not relational:* the relations between the two sides are not spelt
   out militarily, politically, economically or culturally.
8. *The Palestinian state is not defined:* there are glimpses, but not
   how that state would relate to Israel, militarily, politically, economically or culturally, e.g. as *con*federation (with Jordan?)
9. *Excessive governmentalism and excessive institutionalism,* no real
   effort to weave the two civil societies together.

III. Outcome; Culture

10. *An underestimation, probably related to Norwegian secularism, of*
    the strength of religion as a code guiding people's behaviour,
    like the killing of a prime minister and the Hebron massacre
    at Purim, and the general fourth stage of *jihad.*
11. *An underestimation of the sacredness of many points in the area*
    for the Jews (Jabutinski), only political/economic focus.
12. *An underestimation of the possibility of ecumenical work,* between
    Jews, Muslims and Christians, to emphasize the positive,
    gentle aspects of the faiths and turn against the hard aspects.

These flaws were evident in August/September 1993, and the
repercussions after the White House signing are easily traced. The
counter-argument is that the alternative was no agreement. But is
it obvious that a seriously flawed agreement is better? (September
1993, August 1997)

6b. Israel–Palestine: A TRANSCEND Perspective

Diagnosis. The conflict is a classic conflict between settler colonialism and the indigenous peoples, complicated by the settlers' claim as a Chosen People with a Promised Land. The land, and particular points, are sacred to both, but to some on either side ('fundamentalists') more than to others ('moderates'). There are diasporas and supporting countries.

Prognosis. The prognosis today is the same as 50 years ago: oscillation between the structural violence of occupation, exploitation and alienation and the direct violence of bombs and bombing, terror and torture. In addition, the probability of escalation of the civil war within Israel between moderates and fundamentalists (with one of the latter killing a prime minister of the former) and similar phenomena in Palestine is very high.

Therapy. Two necessary conditions stand out:

1. Symmetry is of the essence, the long overdue and full recognition by all of Palestine and Israel as states.
2. The conflict cannot be transformed within the narrow confines of today's Israel, but possibly in the context of a long overdue *Conference for Security and Cooperation in the Middle East –* CSCME under UN auspices, Helsinki-type, open to the linkages to the US/UK–Iraq conflict and the Kurdish issue, with full recognition of all states in the region, a Middle East Common Market, arms/oil/water regimes, etc. Neighbouring Arab states might consider ceding some territory to a Palestinian state.

The Oslo process falls far short of this:

- *Peace actors/movements on both sides were excluded, Intifada,* and Peace Now were not even acknowledged; yet their action was indispensable.
- *Fundamentalists were excluded,* reinserting themselves in the process through acts of violence. Their peace concepts have to be included in any realistic peace process.
- *Underestimation of polarization inside Palestine and Israel;* overestimation of the extent to which the accords are binding.
- *Lack of symmetry:* the agreement is between a state and an 'autonomy' lower than for Bantustans in apartheid South Africa.

- *The Palestinian state was not defined.* How would that state relate to Israel, militarily, politically, economically, culturally?

A process from autonomy to two states to cooperation?

- *Excessive governmentalism and excessive institutionalism,* no real effort to weave the two civil societies together.
- *Underestimation of the strength of religion* as a code for behaviour, like the killing of a prime minister, the Hebron massacre at Purim, and the general fourth stage of *jihad.*
- *Underestimation of sacredness of certain points for Jews and Arabs* (West Bank, Jerusalem); military/political/economic focus.
- *Underestimation of the possibility of ecumenical work,* between Jews, Muslims and Christians, emphasizing the positive, gentle aspects of the faiths, dialogues with the hard religionists.

(1992)

6c. Israel–Palestine: A TRANSCEND Perspective

Diagnosis. Unfortunately, the prognosis in the February 1999 perspective came true in the second *Intifada* of autumn 2000, and a diagnosis of the seriously flawed 'Oslo Process' (from September 1993, this version was written in August 1997) is at least partly confirmed. The Oslo Process did not die in autumn 2000. It was still-born. The US and Norwegian process managers carry major responsibility for the violence, posing as disinterested third parties, frustrating the Palestinians. The time has come for the UN, EU and Arab states to mediate; though that may be easier than it seems. The time is over for a US policy of fragmented reservations for natives, complete with casinos and duty free shopping as for 'God-chosen' whites in South Africa. Palestinians have to be treated with respect.

Prognosis. One reason for failure was that they knew the process was flawed and preferred failure to parallel civil wars; in Israel as a continuation of the Rabin murder. Both parties know that more parties will have to be involved because an agreement between 'moderates' only hides real issues and will spread so as to include 'extremists'. Sorting this out takes time. But there will be talks, and agreements, at some future time. The two peoples are doomed to coexistence, in turn doomed to be peaceful and both peoples have very long time perspectives for the task.

Images of possible outcomes, not only processes, are needed.

Therapy. The following images have emerged from dialogues:

a. The only point of departure for peace is UNSC Resolution 242 and return to the 4 June 1967 borders with small land exchanges.

Israeli 'non-lethal' bullets kill, but no longer convince.

b. If Israel wants peace, it is obtainable, but by using peace studies rather than security studies as a useful guide:

A basic key to peace is *equal rights*:
Palestinians have the same right to a state as Israelis
Palestinians have the same right to return as Israelis
Palestinians have the same right to a capital in Jerusalem

Another basic key to peace is *equitable cooperation*:
Joint management of Jerusalem as two confederated capitals

Joint efforts to control terrorism and state terrorism
Joint economic ventures based on equal inputs and outputs
Joint peace education with creative conflict resolution
Joint peace journalism with conflict resolution focus
Joint ecumenical focus on peaceful aspects of religions

Another basic key to peace is *a regional cooperative umbrella*:
A Middle East Community of Israel/Arab states/Turkey/Kurds
With regimes for water equity, arms control, return
With free flow of goods/services, persons and ideas; and

Another basic key to peace is *peacekeeping*:
International policing of Jerusalem
International monitors chosen by both sides for inspection
Experiments with joint police, and non-violent, patrolling

c. Recognition of a Palestinian state could be combined with:

Recognition before final agreement on borders
Palestinian citizenship for Israelis and vice versa
Israeli cantons in Palestine and Palestinian in Israel
Egypt and Jordan lease adjacent territory to Palestine

d. Beyond this two-states formula there should be images of a confederation, a federation, a unitary state for the future.

e. Sooner or later a *Truth and Reconciliation* process is needed, combining fact-finding, joint textbooks, healing, closure.

(2000)

6d. Israel/Palestine/Middle East:
A TRANSCEND Perspective

For Israel and Palestine there is no security at the end of this road of violence; only increased violence and insecurity. Israel is now in the most dangerous period of its history: increasingly militarist, fighting unwinnable wars, increasingly isolated and with ever more enemies, exposed to violence, non-violence and boycott from within and without, with the US sooner or later making support conditional on concessions. The basic change in South Africa, from inside and outside, comes to mind:

- Israel's moral capital is rapidly depreciating, is probably negative in most countries, and is slowly changing in the US.
- Israel suffers from a *de facto* military coup, offering the electorate a choice of generals with limited agendas.
- Israeli violence and intransigence mobilize resistance and struggle in the Arab and Muslims worlds, if not in the sense of inter-state warfare, then in the postmodern sense of terrorism against Israeli state terrorism. Highly motivated volunteers willing to enter this struggle are in unlimited supply.
- Sooner or later this will include the 18 per cent of Israeli Arabs.
- Sooner or later this may lead to a massive non-violent struggle – 100,000 Arab women in black marching on Israel.
- An economic boycott of Israeli maybe imposed, as it was against South Africa initiated by NGOs and followed by local authorities and, as with South Africa, may be more important morally than economically.
- Again like for South Africa, US policy may change:

  - *economically:* Israel is becoming a liability, given trade/oil problems with Arab countries no longer willing to see the US as a third party; with imminent boycotts and pressure to disinvest;
  - *militarily:* Israel may commit the US to a highly dubious war, and bases are available elsewhere (Turkey, Kosova, Macedonia);
  - *politically:* Israel is a liability in the UN; the EU and NATO allies may not legitimize violent intervention. The US may prefer a reasonable agreement to supporting a loser (the Shah, Marcos).

Could this peace *package* be more attractive to reasonable people
if the context changes in the way foreseen here?

1. Palestine is recognized as a state following UNSC Res. 242,
   338; with 4 June 1967 borders with small land exchanges.
2. The capital of Palestine is in East Jerusalem.
3. A *Middle East Community* with Israel, Palestine, Egypt, Jordan,
   Lebanon, Syria as full members, with water, arms, trade
   regimes based on multilateral consensus; and an *Organization
   for Security and Cooperation in the Middle East* with a broader
   base.
4. The Community is supported by the EU, Nordic Community
   and ASEAN financially and for institution-building expertise.
5. Egypt and Jordan lease additional land to Palestine.
6. Israel and Palestine become federations with two Israeli
   cantons in Palestine and two Palestinian cantons in Israel.
7. The two neighbouring capitals become a city confederation,
   and host to major regional, UN and ecumenical institutions.
8. The right of return to Israel is accepted in principle, numbers
   to be negotiated within the canton formula.
9. Israel and Palestine have joint and equitable economic
   ventures, joint peace education and joint border patrols.
10. Massive stationing of UN monitoring forces.
11. Sooner or later a Truth and Reconciliation process.

Mediating a peace package should not be a country, or a group of
countries; but a respected person or group of such persons. (August
2001)

7. Cyprus: A TRANSCEND Perspective

Diagnosis. The depth of the conflict is very clear and has a long history. First, the basic incompatibility between:

- *enosis*, union with Greece, for the whole island, for the Greeks;
- *taksim*, independence for the northern part, for the Turks.

This is complicated by the high level of population mix before the violence carried 'ethnic cleansing' in its wake. Second,

- the background of centuries of inter-nation conflict.

One possibility suggested after many dialogues was to introduce Turkish claims to the Dodecanese islands in exchange for *enosis*. But this underestimates Turkish-Cypriot sentiments.

The confrontation in 1974, when a Greek national guard coup in favour of *enosis* was followed one month later by a Turkish military operation for *taksim*, provided an unnecessary proof that the positions were deep. Only Ankara recognized the North.

In 1990 the (Greek) Cypriot government applied for membership of the European Union; in 1995/98 the EU opened negotiations. The original positions are now repeated:

- *enosis*, EU membership for the whole island, for the Greeks;
- *taksim*, in that case a military liberation, for the Turks; unless Cyprus enters as a federation of Greek and Turkish halves.

On top of this comes EU unwillingness to have as a member a country deeply divided. (If this were a general position, both UK and Spanish membership, and to some extent the French, should have been suspended till matters have been solved.)

In addition to the two nations in Cyprus, there are also two mother countries, the EU, and the UN with the 1992 Resolution 789 holding the Turks responsible. Russia came in on the Greek Cypriot side (Orthodox brotherhood) in 1997 with an offer of S-300 missiles for air defence. To the extent that these missiles are seen as not only anti-Turkey but also anti-Israel, the new Middle East alliance US–Turkey–Israel is activated, 'Turkey' meaning secular, anti-Muslim, military Turkey.

The EU has postponed indefinitely the Turkish membership issue. Germany has been associated with that position, possibly because Germany does not want to share economic advantages in Turkey (or in Russia, for that matter) with other EU members; each Turkish former guest worker being an economic bridgehead for Germany.

Prognosis. The possibility of a war is far from negligible; erupting along the European Orthodox–Muslim fault-line (as in Bosnia, Kosovo/a, Macedonia, Chechnya). Turkey is 80 km away, Greece 400 km. And the root conflict, with the inflexible island setting, remains as intractable as ever.

Therapy. The following political measures are sufficient for a solution; they are probably necessary:

1. There is a moratorium on the arms race.
2. The EU admits Turkey after Turkey has settled with the Kurds or before (human rights were also violated in Northern Ireland);
3. EU members and others recognize the Turkish Republic of Northern Cyprus (as they did for Slovenia, in spite of a war).
4. Cyprus becomes a federation with two parts and equal opportunities for both nationalities (like positions in the federal government, right to work and right to settle).
5. UNFICYP is withdrawn after a transition period; the wall is opened for increasingly free flow of persons and goods; and
6. The federal republic becomes an EU member in a symmetric setting, with both mother countries present.

The assumption is that nothing short of symmetry at all levels in and outside Cyprus will bring peace, and that the alternative is a stalemate with occasional wars. (1964–1997)

8. Independence Struggles:
A TRANSCEND Perspective

Diagnosis. Under this general heading a research project was carried out in what was then Southern Rhodesia, partly on the effect of the economic sanctions against the white minority (4 per cent) regime after the Unilateral Declaration of Independence (UDI) in November 1965, and partly on the general strategy of a struggle for independence; in this case against a white settler colonialism with a *mission civilisatrice* complex on top of their obvious economic interests. The conflict was trilateral, the three parties being the white settlers, the black majority (divided, but that was not the focus) and the sanction countries, particularly the UK. The settler goal was status quo through UDI, the goal of the black majority was majority rule, the goal of the UK was to manage that process by making the run-away white regime yield to the 'mother country'.

Prognosis. The prognosis was that the economic sanctions would not suffice to unsettle the regime, partly because both the Republic of South Africa and the white settler regimes in what were then the Portuguese colonies Angola and Mozambique, would come to the assistance, and partly because economic sanctions tend to strengthen the targets and stimulate innovations. But more important was another prognosis: that the black freedom fighters wanted to be the masters, and cause, of their own liberation in a relation which was no longer a UK–White Rhodesia relation. In other words, the freedom fighters would step up their fight rather than wait for the economic sanctions to 'bite'. That fight was a violent guerrilla struggle, not by peaceful means. Economic sanctions were at that time at least less violent, but also almost totally ineffective.

Therapy. The proposal was a struggle for independence through massive non-violence. The other aspect of conflict transformation, creativity, was less important: colonialism, like slavery, is not to be transcended but to be abolished. There is no room for compromise, the only question was how and when minor problems, like the nature of guarantees for settlers who wanted to stay as citizens of Zimbabwe, could be agreed upon.

Top people in white security intimated that what they were most afraid of was precisely massive non-violence, for instance in the form of a non-violent march, particularly by women and children, on the centre of Salisbury (now Harare). They felt they could handle guerrillas, but not massive non-violence.

The reaction of the freedom fighters brought up another aspect of the *conflict over the ownership of liberation*. The struggle for independence is also a struggle for manhood, for self-assertion, if needed through violence, not by 'fighting like women, like Gandhi'. Negotiations also have limitations because they did not cover their degradation as 'the Other' of colonialism, their own plight for generations under white rule. Added to this comes the macho display of prowess as the key to power after the struggle is over, and the black majority prevails.

The same reaction was observed in the Akhali movement for a Sikh Khalistan independent of New Delhi: Singh means lion! And in the Kurdish movement for Kurdish autonomy: the problem was not efficacy and efficiency, but who takes power after the struggle was over, men or women, in a solid patriarchy.

The problem is general. Traditional means of violence were monopolized by the warrior caste. Class and gender survived even if actors changed. With violent popular struggle patriarchy survives. Overcoming repression, violence *and* patriarchy is the challenge. A tall bill, indeed. (1970–1975)

9a. Ulster: A TRANSCEND Outcome Perspective

1. A transitional Anglo-Irish condominium is substituted for the present status for Northern Ireland, with a view to a very high level of autonomy/independence for Ulster after X years. Neither 'UK', nor 'Northern Ireland', convey autonomy.

2. The six counties would constitute Ulster as an entity – actually 6/9 of Ulster – with no internal borders, and could for the period of transition be considered territory of England *and* Ireland. Any resident could opt for English *or* Irish passport. Voting and some other rights in England or Ireland would go with the passport; not excluding voting and other rights in Ulster.

3. Ultimately, the right of Ulsterites to self-rule has to be recognized. The definition of an 'Ulsterite' could be one who defines him/herself as an Ulsterite, not tied to blood quantum, cultural habits or duration of residence. Respect for Ulster, its inhabitants and a sense of homeland would be more basic.

4. A parliament, the Stormont, already exists for the Ulster entity, with a government accountable to the parliament; non-sectarian parties have gradually to be in command.

5. Two assemblies might be elected for and by the Protestant and the Catholic communities, with veto rights in matters relating to their patrimony and local police/courts.

6. There might be a Governing Council with five members, one representative of London, one of Dublin, one of the Protestant community, one of the Catholic community and one of the Ulster Parliament, to guide a process towards ever-increasing autonomy, and to mediate among the communities.

7. Ulster would gradually attain international identity:

   a. an Ulster passport would be recognized, first within the British Isles and the European Union, then in the world; in addition to the British or Irish (EU) passports. Thus, every Ulsterite is entitled to two passports, but may choose only one.

   b. British and Irish currency would be welcomed anywhere.

   c. The euro might have a local version with the same value (an ulster?). To stimulate local economies a discount for deals in the ulster might be considered. Investment in very sophisticated industries and services would be encouraged.

   d. The budget for Ulster would also be based on additional sources of revenue (duties, VAT) as for an EU country, with EU subsidy; monitoring the distribution among the communities.

e. Special treaties would handle the relations to London and Dublin, to be implemented by the Governing Council, with review clauses guaranteeing revision every Y years ($Y = X = 25$?).

f. The entity would be demilitarized, renouncing the right to have a separate army. Its security would be guaranteed by Britain and Ireland together, in cooperation with OSCE and UN.

g. The British Army would be withdrawn, the RUC made non-sectarian, and the IRA/UDF encouraged to disarm bilaterally.

h. The entity would have observer status in the European Union, other European organizations and the UN (like the Swiss).

i. Massive aid from the European Union, other European organizations and the UN could be tuned to a peaceful progress.

j. Independence should not be a priori excluded, provided there is a clear majority in both communities.

k. Some redrawing of some borders should not be a priori excluded, using a voting process at the municipal level similar to the Danish–German model for Schleswig-Holstein 1920.

(June 1997)

9b. Ulster: A TRANSCEND Process Perspective

1. *Giving priority to conflict resolution may make violence dwindle away, giving priority to arms/violence control may encourage violence. In addition, the unresolved conflict may encourage violence.* There are no absolute truths in conflict theory and practice, but this is probably a better rule of thumb than most. To give first priority to violence control ('decommissioning') serves the ball into the court of violent parties that can break any agreement with one bomb (policing is very expensive); moreover, why should they give up their means of violence with no conflict resolution in sight? The parties also worry about their own security. Find exits from a conflict that got stuck, which are acceptable to all parties and reasonably sustainable without violence, and remaining proponents of violence will probably be very few, far between, and easily controlled by softer methods. Give the impression that violence control is the first priority and fronts will harden, and not only among the very few who engage in violence for its own sake.

2. *Let 1,000 dialogues blossom.* That conflict resolution affecting millions in a most basic way is too important to leave to a handful of politicians/diplomats/statesman is a truism in a democracy, and a remnant of feudal phases in our history. The people, the ultimate sovereign in democracies, must also be given a chance in a referendum. But voting does not tap people's creativity. Better, organize dialogues (not debates) everywhere, in small groups, take note of ideas, let them flow together in a Gross National Idea Pool (GNIP), and feed that into the decision-making processes, to the benefit of all.

3. *Give more space in the process to the moderate majority and less to declared Republicans and Unionists.* The moderates carry less negative baggage from the past into the future.

4. *The Orange Order marches will have to come to an end,* or be balanced by 'Green Order' marches. Catholics have to learn to react non-violently and not be so easily provoked.

5. *There is a need for healing, for reconciliation, for closure.* The following may be useful perspectives:

   a. *Encounter groups,* high or low in society, publicly visible or not, where parties that have committed violence against each other actually meet, is one way. They would share experiences and emotions, concerns, fears. There might be elements of restitution and apologies/forgiveness. But above all such groups could very profitably do the following:

- *joint reconstruction*, the parties, together, repairing some material damage rather than leaving it all to construction firms in search of contracts (they may also be needed); helping to heal wounds, rehabilitating the physically and spiritually wounded rather than leaving it all to professionals (also needed).
- *joint resolution*, the parties, together, working out the details of conflict resolution in their area.
- *joint sorrow*, the parties, together, locally or everywhere, setting aside time to mark the tragedy of what happened, as an hour, a day of reflection, also on what could have been done and what needs still to be done to prevent it from recurring.

b. *Personal testimonies.* The victims, including the bereaved, are numerous; their stories should not be forgotten. Their testimonies should be collected and made available, also to deter future generations from doing the same.
c. *A Truth and Reconciliation Commission.* South Africans and other conflict resolution/reconciliation cultures (Polynesian *ho'o pono pono*, Somali *shir*) could assist in the process.

(Glencree, Dublin, August 1997, House of Commons Committee, London, March 1998)

10. Kashmir: A TRANSCEND Perspective

Process. The Simla Accord in 1972 mandated Indo-Pakistan bilateral negotiations, which so far have not delivered peace. If the approach is not wrong but incomplete, add the following:

1. A South Asian Association for Regional Cooperation setting
2. Indo-Pakistan NGO roundtables for dialogue-negotiation
3. Outside mediators, governmental
4. Outside mediators, nongovernmental, individual
5. The United Nations

All could be tried, and simultaneously for synergy effects. If 3 is attempted, big powers with obvious interests in the area, such as US/China (seen as pro-Pakistan) and UK/Russia (seen as pro-India, and then the UK is also the former colonial power) should have the good sense to stay away. So should UNSC as the sum of biases is not likely to be creative and useful.

Outcome. The following is an image of possible outcomes that may one day be acceptable to most parties in the conflict:

A. Differential Centre–Periphery Relations in the Indian Union
For the centre in New Delhi to have the same relations to all states makes sense in a colonial/bureaucratic setting, but guarantees continued violence. That violence should not be construed as a demand for secession/independence when autonomy in some fields is what is asked for. Thus, in Western Europe non-EU countries all cooperate with EU, and two EU members (Denmark and the UK) have autonomy in very important fields. India is twice the size and more complex. Kashmir is not the only part interested in negotiating, say, less federal, more confederal ties: so might Nagaland, and some others. The process will be painful. But 'in strength there is weakness, and in weakness strength'; flexibility will serve them all.

B. Differential yet cohesive policies to the parts of Kashmir
An *undifferentiated policy* for a Kashmir with three/four parts makes sense in a colonial/bureaucratic setting, but guarantees continued violence. That violence should not be construed as a demand for secession/independence when autonomy in some fields may be the solution, ruling out three options:

• full integration with Pakistan (Jamat, Hizbul Mujaheddin);

- full integration with India (the Instrument of Accession);
- independent state of Kashmir (the Hurriyat Conference).

A *differentiated policy* could include the following:

- if Jammu and Ladakh want integration with India, so be it;
- if Azad-Kashmir wants integration with Pakistan, so be it;
- for the Valley: if autonomy and devolution within India on the lines of the 1952 or 1974 constitutional provisions is what is wanted, so be it (the National Conference, Shabbir Shah?).

For cohesiveness the following might be useful:

- Indo-Pakistan transitional condominium for the Valley.
- Indo-Pakistan cooperation in softening the Line of Control (LoC);
- Civil society cooperation across the border/LoC: union of families, cultural cooperation, local economic cooperation – needed everywhere also to overcome the effects of globalization;
- A Greater Kashmir Confederation, with open borders among the parts, economic cooperation, SAARC observer status and representatives in New Delhi and Islamabad.

C. Collateral issues
This does not solve such serious problems as arms merchants/mercenaries wanting profits, military wanting battle, and youth in alienating societies seeing violence/rape not only as 'the best show, but the only show in town'. But they would dwindle away and could also be attacked separately.

(January 1998)

11. Korea: A TRANSCEND Perspective

Diagnosis. Korea is located in the field of force constituted by four big powers: the US and Japan on one side, well established in South Korea even if resented by parts of the population, and China and the Soviet Union/Russia on the other, with complex relations to North Korea. Thus, there is a 2 + 4 formula or a 2 + 2 formula if only the US and China with clear military alliances with one Korea are counted. The crime of dividing a people in 1945 is compounded by the crime of denying the Korea conflict autonomy in this strong field of force. Japan has the complex relation of a very illegitimate colonizer, and the US the trauma of not having won the Korean War. At the same time North Korea has increasingly developed an absurd society with deep disjunction between propaganda and reality, to some extent mirrored in South Korea being caught between a self-image as 'advanced industrial country' and a crisis-hit economy. A high level of general Korean resentment (*han*), combined with missionary complexes, makes the situation even more complicated.

Prognosis. Standard prognoses include collapse of one or the other Korea, the takeover of one by the other, a modified replay of the Korean War of 1950–53. A more valid prognosis: status quo. And then a more optimistic prognosis: there will be a slow move from steps of cooperation via an associative relationship to confederation, then to federation and finally to unification. After 40 years new generations often come into power, with new perspectives on bitter, traumatizing conflicts (Spain 1936–76, Germany 1949–89). 1950–53 should have implied transformation in Korea 1990–93; it did not. Leaders too old? Too Confucian? Lack of autonomy, with both US and China preferring status quo?

Therapy. Four premises might help in a transition:

1. to regard both Koreas as experiencing crises, neither system is perfect, that maybe both Koreas, not one, have given in to single-minded ideologies, leading to too little trade in the North and too much trade in the South, and hence that all-Korean cooperation, including trade, might be useful to both;
2. to talk less about collapse of the two countries, more about the need for some social and political change in both;
3. to talk less about unification of the countries, more about concrete cooperation between them;
4. to talk less about the big/hard military-political issues, more about small/soft economic, social and cultural cooperation.

Concrete examples of cooperation:

- all-Korean cooperation in alternative energy production;
- all-Korean cooperation in ecological agriculture, forestation;
- all-Korean cooperation in fish farming;
- all-Korean cooperation, opening rail and road transportation, in a setting of Euro-Asian cooperation, and the ESCAP plans;
- opening for enormous transit and links to Euro-Asia in general and for a Peace University on rails.

Perspectives on the cooperation:

- direct North–South links between provinces, cities and NGOs;
- moves toward, and not away from, mixed economies are useful;
- cooperation with East Asian neighbours (China, Japan, Vietnam)
- Third parties who can have dialogues with both sides, sounding out ideas without direct negotiations should be used;
- less use of trading X in return for Y, if X is a good idea, like helping North out of famine, then do it unconditionally.
- do not set deadlines, do not touch the military, do not insist on a peace treaty but accumulate many small steps.

(August 1972–May 1998)

12. Pax Pacifica: A TRANSCEND Perspective

Diagnosis. This is a major part of humankind:

In the *Western Pacific*: Russia (Eastern Siberia), Japan, (han-)China, the 'mini Japans/Chinas' of Taiwan, Hong Kong, Singapore, South and North Korea, and the ten ASEAN countries: Vietnam, Laos, Cambodia, Philippines, Indonesia, Brunei, Singapore (again), Malaysia, Thailand and Myanmar/Burma.

In the *Central/South Pacific*: the Pacific Islands in clusters known as Polynesia (with Hawai'i and Tahiti), Melanesia and Micronesia, and the big islands Australia and New Zealand.

In the *Eastern Pacific*: Canada (Yukon and British Columbia), the United States (Alaska, Washington, Oregon and California), Central America (Mexico, Guatemala, El Salvador (Honduras), Nicaragua, Costa Rica, Panama) and South America (Colombia, Ecuador, Peru (Bolivia), Chile).

Counting only the population living on the seaboards of the rim countries we are talking about at least 2 billion, maybe 2.5 billion, human beings; 40–50 per cent of humankind. Of these about 5 million live on the Pacific Islands, a relation of 1:400 or 1:500, indicative of extreme vulnerability to their neighbours; among them four of the big powers today, with very much residual colonialism, some of it even surviving colonialism. Western and Japanese complexes of superiority also survive in the region; as in the French nuclear tests and the South Pacific Commission.

Prognosis. The dynamic diversity of the Pacific Hemisphere can easily spill over into massive violence, against the former or present colonial powers, and among them for 'control' or to prevent control by the others (the Pacific War Japan/China+ from 1931 and Japan/US from December 1941 is still on everybody's mind, not to mention the US/Korea and US/Vietnam Wars). The US–EU–Japan–China–Russia pentagon easily dominates the islands when not tempered by some equitable symbiosis.

Therapy. The forms of peace, the *fa'a pasifika*, would have strong cultural components, celebrating unity-of-humankind, playing on traditional Pacific faiths and other soft religions like Buddhism, Quakerism, Baha'i and the considerable traditions of dialogical and non-violent patterns of conflict resolution.

But it would also address the problems of direct and structural peace, and not only the problems of today but also the past and tomorrow. Thus, there is a need for reconciliation from the horrors of colonialism and the Pacific War. The *karma* approach to traumas, 'we are in it together', of never-ending healing, reparations, apologies can be combined with complete decolonization to restore sovereignty, in part of the contested territories, using formulas like bicameralism and bilingualism.

The area would benefit greatly from massive withdrawal of forward and offensive deployment (the US, Russia, China, Japan within AMPO, North Korea) and, for the US, scrapping JCS 570/2. Denuclearization of the whole area, not only some small islands, would be a great step toward a pacific Pacific. And as to the economic aspect: both *self-reliance I* (do as much as you can yourself) and *self-reliance II* (cooperate with others at the same level, creating no dependencies) would help, with dense networks of affordable communication and transport.

For the future: many more states without armies, conversion to UNPKF for use in nonmilitarized areas, conversion of the rest to purely nonoffensive defence, massive use of creative conflict resolution and a regional forum for the whole area dominated by no big power(s) – a *Pacific Hemisphere Forum*. (April 1989)

13. Hawai'i: A TRANSCEND Perspective

Diagnosis. The classical problem: settler colonialism, with the overthrow of the Hawaiian monarchy in 1893, annexation in 1898 (President McKinley) and the 50th US state in 1959; all illegitimate, from above, at the expense of the Hawaiian people. With more than 50 per cent Hawaiians in the population they would today have been decolonized. But missionary deculturation, diseases ('Acts of God') and land-grabbing reduced them from 800,000 in 1778 to 8,000; today they number 20 per cent, white settlers more like 25 per cent. Most of the rest are East Asians brought in as indentured labour, themselves exploited. The archipelago has been used by the settlers for plantations, tourism and military bases attracting a major Japanese attack. All three industries are today in economic difficulties, leading to major cut-backs.

Prognosis. The obvious prognosis is the protraction of the status quo with the indigenous as second-class citizens in their own land, and settlers' rights prevailing over historical rights. An interesting beginning, however, was made by President Clinton offering in November 1993 'an apology to Native Hawaiians on behalf of the United States for the overthrow of the Kingdom of Hawai'i' (Public Law 103–150). The danger is that this will be followed by the US 'nation-within-a-nation' concept, like the reservations for the Native Americans. That system smacks of South African apartheid some time ago. Apologies, some land restitution, reparations to Native Hawaiians are no longer sufficient (there is also the problem that after Clinton may come a new McKinley, wielding brutal Washington power). Real sovereignty implies control over all eight islands in the archipelago, not only one (Kaho'olawe). And that raises the problem, what happens then to the non-Hawaiians, the majority?

Therapy. One possible solution for a more independent Hawai'i might be a *bicameral legislature*: one ordinary chamber for all citizens regardless of background, and one for Hawaiians only, with a veto over such basic matters as control of sacred time and sacred spaces, the dyad of trauma and glory, allocation of land, control of residence, of foreign relations, language (two administrative languages), and police and court systems for the Hawaiians, administered by themselves. To be achieved by non-violence, and based on a long, complex educational process.

One example would be using the concept of 'sacred time, sacred spaces' to reconquer space and time in an archipelago of sacred spaces (such as burial sites), punctuating the calendar with

Hawaiian sacred time, with their days of glory and trauma, by far outnumbering the *ha'ole* (white) 4 July, 7 December, etc.

Hawai'i could also be reinscribed as Non-Self-Governing Territory and taken through the process defined by the United Nations (a similar case, Kanaky, by the French called Nouvelle Caledonie, was put on the list by the General Assembly December 1986). The sovereignty process can no longer be stopped, the consciousness is too high even with many stages down the road.

A more independent Hawai'i would include, not exclude, non-Hawaiians if they respect basic aspects of Hawaiian culture, such as holism and respect for nature. Increasingly autonomous of Washington, a more independent Hawai'i might have both a strong finance economy and a basic needs oriented self-reliant economy. It would relate to the others in the Polynesian triangle, to the Pacific Rim through the diasporas in Hawai'i, base the security on good relations with all neighbours and no army, and possibly use the bases as staging areas for UN peacekeeping forces. (1993)

14a. The Gulf Conflict 1990–91: A TRANSCEND Perspective

Diagnosis. Much ignorance was needed to be surprised by the Gulf War. Kuwait was an outcome of Western political and economic colonialism; the border was artificial and contested, and many other issues (access to the Gulf, oil fields under the border, currency issues after the Iraq–Iran war) and actors were coupled together in a super-complex conflict. That the US/Bush administration would hit hard and use the war to 'kick the Vietnam syndrome', making war legitimate again in US public opinion, was obvious. In the heat of the conflict all parties reduced the complexity to a 'two parties, one issue' formula, acting out the chosen people, glory and trauma ideas in the US and the Middle East. Key memory: *the Crusades*, and the 1258 Baghdad massacre. The war became the Armageddon enactment of God vs. Satan. There was also the ambiguity over the US Ambassador's statement about not interfering in a conflict between two friendly countries.

Prognosis. Given the linkage to the millennium-old crusades syndrome genocide attempts could be expected, depending on availability of means, this time through bombing and economic sanctions. Given Bedouin values (dignity, courage, honour), and more so the more overwhelming the enemy, Iraq will claim victory.

Therapy. The conflict has to be complexified historically and culturally, bringing in many more parties and goals and issues. As a bilateral conflict essentially between Iraq and US (backed by old UK colonial power traumas, including British use of chemical warfare in Iraq in 1920) no acceptable and sustainable conflict transformation is to be expected. But a *Conference for Security and Cooperation in the Middle East* (CSCME) might one day achieve something like this:

A Twelve-Point Plan for Peace in the Middle East

1. Iraq withdraws from Kuwait, but Kuwait enters negotiations with Iraq over modifications of the northern border of Kuwait.
2. Iraq enters negotiations with the Kurds over human rights and autonomy with a view to sovereignty, and encourages other states in the regions with a Kurdish population to do likewise.
3. Israel recognizes, encourages and helps a Palestinian state as outlined in the PNC 15 November 1988 resolution; Palestine recognizes Israel fully.

4. The Golan Heights revert to Syria; Syria recognizes Israel.
5. All Arab states recognize Israel with non-aggression treaties.
6. The UN, in cooperation with the Arab League, organizes a major UN Peacekeeping Operation, with several hundred thousand police troops, stationed on both sides of borders in the area.
7. All foreign troops are withdrawn not only from Kuwait, but also from Palestine, Lebanon, Saudi Arabia, Turkey, etc.
8. An *arms control regime* is introduced, modelled on the European process, with as its first priority the elimination of weapons of mass destruction in the area, confidence-building measures, inspection on challenge under UN satellite surveillance.
9. A *water regime* is studied and negotiated for the region.
10. An *oil regime*, possibly under UN auspices, bringing oil-importing and oil-exporting countries in permanent dialogue with each other, is studied and negotiated.
11. A *human rights regime* is introduced, moving the countries in the region closer to respect for human rights, democracy and the rule of law.
12. A *Middle East Common Market*, with Israel as full member, is studied and negotiated.

(October 1990)

14b. The Gulf Conflict 1998: A TRANSCEND Perspective

Diagnosis

Iraqi motivations:

- the need for weapons, hence an element of concealment;
- very aggressive, gas Halabja 1988 (UK Summer 1920), Kuwait;
- Bedouin warrior logic: use wars for dignity/courage/honour;
- future of the region and their historical mission at stake.

US/UK motivations:

- to punish Hussein as The Enemy of the People (Orwell, *1984*);
- very aggressive, 310,000 killed in 1991 (International Physicians for the Prevention of Nuclear War), two million by embargo (UNICEF 1,210,000 children, 960,000 adults);
- US/UK warrior logic: win wars to gain status as leaders;
- marking the Middle East as a US/UK sphere of interest.

Conflict Formation: A major war for inspection reasons does not at present have UNSC consent. US/UK have signalled their readiness to go alone contra Iraq, against the UN charter 2(4). US has the support of the new NATO members Czech Republic, Hungary and Poland; and the UK the support of former dependencies, Canada, New Zealand and Australia. In addition, Argentina, Spain and Portugal, Norway and Germany have joined. Kuwait and Oman are used for build-up. Less than half the support last time, and mainly from countries far away.

Prognosis

- Bombing will not achieve the destruction of concealed arms since very small areas are needed, for instance in the mountains. An occupation may, but at least one-tenth the size of Iraq's population would be needed by traditional counts.
- After the bombing inspection will probably be impossible.
- The increase in fundamentalism in Turkey, Saudi Arabia, Syria, Lebanon and Jordan may lead to changes in regimes.
- The Conference of Islamic Countries may emerge as a bloc.

- The Russian–Chinese cooperation/military alliance induced by NATO/AMPO expansion deepens, and may *de facto* include Iraq/Iran.

Therapy. A seven-point plan:

1. Give Russia–China–France and the UNSG more time to negotiate acceptable compromises, soften the language of the inspectors.
2. Accept Iraq's demand, made since 1990, for a dialogue, letting Iraq voice her concerns, including sovereignty. Only very weak people are unwilling to give the other side a voice.
3. Reach a compromise permitting unfettered, representative UNSCOM work against offers on valid points in Iraqi positions.
4. But, a broader agenda is needed, so take steps to organize a *UN Conference on Security and Cooperation in the Middle East* (CSCME), modelled on Helsinki (1973–75), including the Israel/Palestine and Kurdish issues; with Palestinian state and Kurdish autonomies/state not excluded as options. The conference should not be chaired by outside big powers but by somebody from the region, e.g. Jordan.
5. The UN in cooperation with the Arab League, organizes a major UN Peacekeeping Operation in the area, with several hundred thousand troops stationed on either side of critical borders.
6. Regimes for arms control, water, oil and human rights are studied for the whole area.
7. A Middle East Common Market with Israel as a full member is studied and negotiated.

The important point is not to isolate the issue from the rest by defining it as an arms control/inspection/compliance issue alone. There is no way out of the present imbroglio if that narrow conflict logic is accepted. The agenda has to be opened up lest the situation deteriorates even further. (February 1998)

15. The Kurds: A TRANSCEND Perspective

Diagnosis. The Kurds are a nation without a state. Some 25 million Kurds are divided among five states (Turkey, Iraq, Iran, Syria and Armenia), with a considerable diaspora in Europe. Like any other stateless, divided nation they have a yearning not only to come together but to be ruled by their own, *a basic part of the democratic project*. They also form a major part of the vast and complex Middle East conflict syndrome, not only because conflicts over nation/state relations easily spill over into violence in the other five countries, but because a Kurdish state might create a precedent for another key stateless nation in the region, the Palestinians. There are also obvious oil and water issues transcending the Middle East. This may place the Kurds on the opposite side of the US–Turkey–Israel *de facto* alliance even if Iraq is the enemy of all three.

    Prognosis. Protracted, endless violence, terrorism and torture, including export of the violence to Europe and beyond.

    Therapy. The Kurds have a three-stage programme:

1. *human rights* for Kurds in countries dividing the Kurdish nation;
2. *autonomy* within the countries, with Kurdish as one language; and
3. *a Kurdistan*, possibly as a (con)federation of the autonomies, giving the Kurdish nation what they see as their right: a state.

There is nothing extremist in this programme unless one assumes any level of nationalism to be extremist. Should it ever take the form of a unitary Kurdish state, the map of the Middle East would change considerably. The Kurds were until recently basically a nomad nation, and nomads claim a lot of space. What is extremist, however, is the violence of all sides, legitimized by macho, violent cultures in all parts of the conflict formation. In July 1994, at the Rambouillet Conference, TRANSCEND argued (in vain) for a non-violent approach and more women in political leadership positions in the Kurdish struggle, building on the fact that Kurdish women demonstrating and arguing non-violently got the two Kurdish factions in Northern Iraq to stop fighting. One day this may happen on a large scale. But violence is deeply rooted, fed by demands for revenge, honour and male mobility through male acts of courageous violence, keeping women out of politics. The Kurds are also their own enemies. In that they are not alone; this also applies to many of the other parties.

Creative solutions, using Northern Iraq for training in state-building and in complex conflict politics, would include:

- *A Kurdish parliament* abroad, democratically and secretly elected inside the countries. A basic problem is that Kurds seem to prefer naive, even violent, political fights, and have been willingly used by those who pretend to offer them something in return, like the Turks (in return for killing Armenians) and the US (in return for turning against Iran and Iraq).
- *a Kurdish government in exile*, the executive arm of the parliament, with a mandate to organize a pattern of:
- *Dual citizenship*, giving Kurds a passport in addition to what they have in their country of residence, making them mutually recognizable and recognized more of a nation, one day in the future transforming that virtual reality into a real reality, for instance as a confederation of autonomies.

However, there is a condition for all of this to happen, and that applies also to the Kurds: to step down the violence. For those who will not contemplate that on ethical grounds there are military reasons: violence will bring the Kurds nowhere against overwhelming enemies. (December 1990)

16. Japan–US: A TRANSCEND Perspective

Diagnosis. The situation between Japan and the US is serious if the four phases from early Meiji till the Pacific War (1931–45) is a model: 'opening up', then 'Japanese learning enthusiastically', then 'Japan practising what she has learnt by and for herself, with increasing tension', then 'war or warlike activity'. The occupation was the first phase of the post-1945 cycle, the second phase then and right after, the third phase started around 1970, and continues. Will there be a Phase IV?

Exacerbating the situation is the rank incongruence: the US commands more political and military power (*de facto* occupying Japan), and Japan responded for a long period with more economic power (to sell highly demanded products when the yen was not so strong, to buy US property when the yen was strong; underwriting US debt buying US bonds). Both use their comparative advantage, at the expense of the other, increasing the tension. The US no doubt brings up the Pacific War to get more submissiveness from Japan; Japan uses political/military submissiveness to gain more economic access; the US launches economic counter-aggression, manipulating the currency rate, challenging the Japanese formula of lifelong employment and seniority promotion. Highly unstable; with memories of Pearl Harbor and Hiroshima/Nagasaki right under the surface.

Prognosis. The second 'opening–imitation–conflict–war' cycle has stayed for a long time in the third phase (if that is what is going on). No war is in sight, but warlike action might include such measures as deepening and broadening the US *de facto* occupation of Japan through new, expanded, guidelines for the Japan–US security treaty (AMPO), and Japan leaving to the people of Okinawa the struggle for a reduction of the base load.

Therapy. One way out of sour relations could be for the two to interact less, to disentangle. The US could pull out militarily, AMPO could be abrogated, or diluted, not deepened, and both of them could focus on other trade partners; the US more on NAFTA, Japan more on interaction with East Asian partners. Japan should press less for trade across great differences in degree-of-processing, and open for import of processed products from all other countries. The US now makes competitive products; Japan should look for new markets. And when they interact, externalities should be watched carefully lest Japan treats the US like the US treats Latin America. They should recouple, but on a basis of equality and equity.

However, the US has an expanding NAFTA based on US power in the Americas. Japan has nothing similar in East Asia, not so much because the US is popular in Latin America and Japan hated and feared in East Asia because of the Pacific War, as because the US is so much better at handling the traumas created by the US, and Latin America so unable to produce competitive goods. Moreover, Japan has become tied to the US as local appendage. Culturally, historically and geographically Japan's partners would be the other East Asian countries, meaning the Koreas and China (and Vietnam if the criterion is Confucianism/Mahayana Buddhism, and Chinese culture). An East Asian Free Trade Area, EAFTA, later to become an East Asian Community, would be a good alternative to the US; open to NAFTA countries as NAFTA (to some extent) is open to others. The alternative is a Japan lost between East Asia and the US, unable to reconcile with the former and increasingly dumped by the latter. That would make war and warlike responses even more likely. (September 1992)

17. Japan–Russia: A TRANSCEND Perspective

Diagnosis. The Northern Territories/South Kuriles issue derives from history and geography pointing in different directions. The four islands (one is a small archipelago) were discovered in 1634 by the Russians and settled by them. In 1875 Japan got the islands in exchange for Sakhalin. At Yalta, Roosevelt promised the four islands to the Soviet Union if they enter the Pacific War, possibly as a substitute for having to promise them Hokkaido. In 1972 the Soviet Union agreed to the return of Habomai and Shikotan, but ownership of the bigger and southernmost islands Etorofu and Kunashiri is still contested.

The division of Korea had a similar background. Both can serve as typical examples of big powers cutting, dividing and joining together according to their inclinations and interests, with little regard for people, culture, history and geography.

Prognosis. The present situation has lasted more than 50 years and is probably coming to an end. There is no negative prognosis if status quo continues, no war for instance, but a positive prognosis with greatly improved Japan–Russia relations if the issue is solved in a mutually acceptable and sustainable way. Japan and Russia could then enter an escalating cooperation race benefiting all if Russia introduces distributive economies.

Therapy. To find a solution the place to look is not always who settled where and when among the pretenders. To find a solution the meaning of ownership by whom, to whom, might be a better point of departure. The economic and military value of the islands as such to the Soviet Union/Russia seems to be negligible. Quite another matter is the price that might be expected for their return if the islands are used as pawns in return for investment: money, goods, and/or services.

No doubt this approach can be used, and is used, when real estate changes hands. But this is not one of these cases if instead of military or economic values the focus is on the cultural value. Japan cannot claim a long-lasting relationship, but Japan can claim that the islands belong 'naturally' to Japan because of proximity (like Turkey argues about the Dodecanese islands in the Aegean, passing from Turkey to Italy to Greece).

If Japan is seen as the chosen land for the Sun Goddess, *Amaterasu o-mikami*, then the islands take on a higher value. They become priceless because the ground is sacred, not because of possible mineral ores deposits, etc. would be emphasized in a materialistic culture. Such places should be approached with more awe and less money on the mind. The Japanese came close to breaking that rule acquiring property in the US, and the Russians may have done so with the Kuriles/Northern territories. Hence:

- If something has infinite value to the other side, and only finite value to you, give it back because it is the right thing to do. Do not bargain, be generous and you may reap generosity.
- The less you talk, even think of anything in return, the more amply you may be rewarded. The more you haggle, the less you get. The sacred is not approached with profanity.

This could be combined with an intermediary step, *joint sovereignty*, for the two contested islands for a period of X years, after which they will either revert to Japan or remain a condominium (X to be negotiated). The latter would set a useful precedent for territorial conflicts that cannot be decided by self-determination; and does not exclude reciprocal generosity. A great opportunity for the whole world! (June 1991)

18. The Conflict in and over Yugoslavia: A TRANSCEND Perspective

Diagnosis. Standard conflict analysis demands a listing of the key actors and their goals, and of standard fault-lines:

1. *Nature*: the military destruction of nature.
2. *Gender*: general macho attitude, backlash from equality.
3. *Generation*: seeding hatred, revanchism in next generation.
4. *Race:* probably irrelevant, except for some UN troops.
5. *Class*: the under-class revolt against Yugoslav technocrats; and the revolt of the less well-off against the better-off.
6. *Nation*: the Catholic/Orthodox divide (395, 1054) and the Christian/Muslim divide (1096), intersecting in Sarajevo.
7. *Country*: borders from the Nazi occupation +Tito/Djilas.
8. *State/Capital*: the socialism/capitalism controversy.
9. *Capital/Civil Society*: inter-nation, inter-class exploitation.
10. *State/Civil Society*: human rights crimes, killed/wounded and displaced peoples' organizations inside/outside Yugoslavia.

All are relevant, but in particular the nation divides (see table below).

Intersection Sarajevo	Catholic: Croats	Orthodox: Serbs	Muslim: Bosniaks
Inner Circle Bosnia-Herzegovina	Bosnian Croats	Bosnian Serbs	Bosniaks
Middle Circle Yugoslavia	Slovenia Croatia	Serbia Montenegro Macedonia	in Bosnia-Herzegovina; in Kosovo; in Macedonia
Outer Circle Europe	The Vatican Germany-Austria European Union Catholics	Russia + Greece Orthodox	Turkey + Iran/Saudi Muslims
US	US		US (?)

There are three standard hypotheses about the role of nation:

1. age-old unprocessed inter-nation violence and hatred;
2. instrumentalization of that hatred by cynical leaders; and
3. instrumentalization of that instrumentalization by cynical outer circle powers supporting their inner/middle circle people.

Tito's Yugoslavia was no longer able to contain these enormous tensions, with gender and class added to nation. Tito's death in 1980 was a factor, but the death of the Cold War in 1990 was more important since non-alignment had become a major rationale for the Yugoslav construction and one party, the East and later the Soviet Union, had collapsed. The rest is history.

That the Vatican reinforced the Catholic Church by state-building (Slovenia, Croatia) and that Austria took revenge for the First World War and Germany for the Second World War with the same allies and the same enemies was predictable. That the US should support the non-Orthodox was also predictable, but not the strong support for the Albanians in Bosnia-Herzegovina, Kosovo/a and Montenegro, except from a 'what is in it for me' (bases, oil pipelines in return for military/political support) perspective.

Prognosis. Massive alliances vertically in the table, massive, sometimes trilateral, wars horizontally.

Therapy. Massive use of self-determination to define states for Slovenes, Croats, Bosniaks, Serbs, Montenegrins and Macedonians, but at least autonomy for Serbs in Croatia, Serbs and Croats in Bosnia-Herzegovina, Albanians in Serbia and Macedonia. (May 1996)

18a. The Yugoslavia Conflict 1991/95:
A TRANSCEND Perspective

1. **A Conference on Security and Cooperation in Southeast Europe,** CSCSEE-, UN- and OSCE- sponsored, UNSC being too remote, EU too partial, in addition to the London/Geneva conference process. All concerned parties (also sub-state, super-state and non-state) should be invited, with all relevant themes on the agenda; possibly lasting 3–5 years. Outsiders to the region should be present as observers with the right to speak, *there being no disinterested outside states.* One possible long-term goal: *A Southeast European Confederation.*

2. **CSCSEE Working Groups on top priority areas to consider:**

   - *Bosnia-Herzegovina* as a tripartite confederation;
   - *Kosovo/a* as a republic with the same status as for the Serbs in Krajina (not Knin), and with respect for Serbian history;
   - *Macedonia*: a Macedonian confederation should not be ruled out, but can only emerge within a broader setting (1 above).
   - *ex-Yugoslavia*: as long-term goal, a confederation this time.

3. **Increase UNPROFOR ten times, or more, with 50 per cent women**, creating a dense blue carpet to supervise truces and to stabilize the situation. The soldiers must be adequately briefed with police, non-violence and conflict facilitation training, working together with civilian peacekeeping components. Avoid big power participation and powers with a history in the region.

4. **A dense network of municipal solidarity with all parts of ex-Yugoslavia,** for refugees, relief work, reconstruction: *Gemeinde gemeinsam, Cause commune,* Council of Europe.

5. **Let 1,000 local peace conferences blossom,** support local groups with communication hardware, and the *Verona Forum for Peace and Reconciliation on the Territory of Former Yugoslavia.*

6. **International Peace Brigades as hostages for peace**, unarmed foreigners, professionals like doctors (*WHO/*

IPPNW/MSF), working in threatened areas, communicating, dampening violence.

7. **Intensify ecumenical peace work,** building on non-violence and peace traditions in Catholic and Orthodox Christianity and Islam. Challenge hard line religious institutions in the region.

8. **Permanent contact among persons, groups and states working for peace within the state system (1–3), municipal system (4) and civil society system (5–7); let ideas flow**. Have a 'Peace Ladies Conference' parallel to the London/Geneva conference among the warlords; in the Palais des Nations.

9. **Demand professionalism from the media,** less violence and elitism and bias; more focus on common people and peace efforts.

10. **In the spirit of future reconciliation:**

  - *drop the sanctions,* they hit the innocent and harden the conflicts;
  - *drop the War Crimes Tribunal, except as moral individual judgement,* there is no road to the future through revenge and punishment, adding to all the traumas, creating new martyrs;
  - have inside and outside specialists search for *understanding of what went wrong and for positive past and present experiences that can inspire a common, even if more separate, future.*
  - build on the longing of the Yugoslav peoples to come together again, nonetheless, on *bratstvo* (brotherhood) even if it should be with less *jedinstvo* (unity).

(1992)

18b. The Yugoslavia Conflict, 1998:
A TRANSCEND Perspective

1. Old historical processes pitting Orthodox Serbs/Macedonians against Muslim Albanians are picking up new energies at the same time as the region seems unable to arrive at its own solutions.
2. The 'international community' will probably again postpone intervention till the situation is 'ripe', meaning till the violence has come so far that almost any non-war outcome is preferable, meaning that outside powers can dictate the 'peace'.
3. Starting with Kosovo/a, there seem to be five outcomes:

   a. status quo within Serbia, unacceptable to the Albanians
   b. autonomy ('1974 at a higher level')
   c. a Third Republic inside the Federal Republic of Yugoslavia
   d. as a part of a Yugoslav confederation
   e. independence, unacceptable to the Serbs

4. One reasonable prognosis is that a leads to b leads to c leads to d leads to e, possibly jumping some steps (straight to e with foreign military assistance to UCK). If that happens a next prognosis might be unification with Albania and absorption of Western Macedonia ('green transversal'). The next prognosis would be a major Balkan war between Orthodox and Muslim forces, involving Romania, Bulgaria, Greece and Turkey, implying major outside intervention and semi-permanent occupation of Kosovo/a–Macedonia (like in Bosnia at present).
5. An alternative to this scenario might look as follows:

   • Kosovo/a gets status as Third Republic inside FRJ, or a very high level of autonomy. The treaty is made binding for X years ($X = 20$?) after which it is up for review (and a confederation may then be among the options, including Montenegro-Vojvodina?).
   • Protection of Serbian minority rights is ensured also through a Serbian Assembly with veto rights for cultural patrimony (teaching of and in own language, access to sacred sites, etc.).
   • Preventive peacekeeping and international guarantees needed.

6. For Macedonia a productive peace policy might include:

   • a switch from the present passive neutrality (or 'equi-
     distance') to active neutrality in the sense of serving as a
     venue for major conferences on the problems of the
     region;
   • also like Switzerland de-emphasizing nationality by a
     higher level of decentralization and local rule ('can-
     tonization');
   • continuing and stepping up all efforts at cooperation at all
     levels across the divide between Macedonians and
     Albanians;
   • if this does not work a federation should not be excluded.

7. For the region a Balkan Community including Albania, FRJ,
   Romania, Macedonia, Bulgaria, Greece and Turkey (the
   'European part'?) might be capable of accommodating some
   of the tensions, working towards such features found in the
   Nordic and European communities of the 1980s as a common
   market, free flow of goods and services, capital and labour,
   coordinating foreign policies.
8. Nothing of what is mentioned above is overdue, overtaken by
   recent events. But lack of proaction during the 1990s, heeding
   the warnings of the 1980s has been highly irresponsible, leading
   to the current vicious cycles of violent action/reaction.

(June 1998)

18c. The Crisis in and around Kosovo/a: A TRANSCEND Perspective

The illegal NATO war on Serbia has not been conducive to any lasting solution. *The only road is through negotiation*, not *diktat* and, pending that, immediate cessation of the hostilities and atrocities, and agreement on *a massive UN peacekeeping operation.*

For a political solution, consider the points made by former UN Secretary General Pérez de Cuéllar in his correspondence with former German Minister of Foreign Affairs Hans Dietrich Genscher December 1991: *do not favour any party, develop a plan for all of ex-Yugoslavia, make sure that plans are acceptable to minorities.*

In this spirit TRANSCEND suggests:

1. **The United Nations**, which has to learn from its previous failures, **should replace NATO** and assume a peacekeeping role in Former Yugoslavia, including Kosovo/a, with contingents from non-NATO countries. The United Nations will have to *mobilize all its agencies, UNHCR, UNHCHR, UNICEF, WHO, etc. to rebuild Kosovo/a*, and before that, to provide the minimum needs of the people and *the safe return of the refugees.*

2. If the Security Council is paralysed by a US or Russian veto, this gives **the General Assembly and the UN Secretary-General** legitimacy to play an active role in negotiating an end of hostilities. The Secretary-General could be supported in that role by a group of eminent world leaders such as Nelson Mandela, former German President Richard von Weizsäcker and Jimmy Carter. Pressure from world public opinion is necessary.

3. **A Conference on Security and Cooperation in Southeast Europe (CSCSEE)** should be organized, sponsored by the United Nations and the Organization for Security and Cooperation in Europe. The UN Security Council is too remote, the EU and NATO too partial. All concerned parties (also sub-state, super-state and non-state) should be invited, with all relevant themes on the agenda; possibly lasting 3–5 years.

4. The negotiations should aim to establish a **Kosovo/a Zone of Peace Protectorate (KZOPP)** under direct UN Trustee-ship, or if political circumstances preclude this, under an OSCE mandate. It would consist of an *Administrative Office*;

a *Negotiation Task Force* consisting mainly of retired personnel with experience in diplomacy, non-violent conflict resolution, and international negotiations; a *Legal Advisory Unit* to provide legal opinions on various issues to assist in negotiations; *Reconciliation Teams*, consisting of various NGOs and religious organizations, deployed throughout the region to promote reconciliation among conflicting parties, human rights, and peace education; and a *Security Group* of police and peace-keeping forces to train police forces and maintain security. A first step in a multi-year process would include the development of principles and goals to which the parties can agree, the promotion of *Confidence and Security Building Measures*, setting standards regarding self-determination in the zone, peace education, training local police forces in human security and deploying reconciliation teams. Later phases include permanent institution-building.

5. **For a more lasting solution, the similarity between the Serb position in Krajina/Slavonija and the Kosovars in Kosovo/a can be used**. Both ethnic groups form clear majorities in those areas but minorities in Croatia and Serbia as a whole, with 'mother countries' nearby. Refugees, most of them forced to leave, are brought back, and the Kosovars are accorded the same status within Serbia as the Serbs in Krajina/Slavonija. To draw exact borders, each community can join the side its voters prefer, the process used in 1920 to define the Danish–German border. The possibility of Kosovo/a as a third republic in Serbia, with guarantees against seeking independence for a period of perhaps 20 years, and the same for Krajina/Slavonija in Croatia, should not be excluded (nor Vojvodina as a fourth republic). The parallel is not with Bosnia-Herzegovina, which was never a part of Serbia.

6. **For the Southern Balkans, a Balkan Community might be considered**, including Albania, Yugoslavia, Romania, Macedonia, Bulgaria, Greece and Turkey (maybe only the 'European part'). It would allow the Southern Balkan peoples to decide their own fate – economically and politically – supported economically by the European Union, but without meddling by outside big powers. It might be capable of accommodating some of the Orthodox/Muslim tensions, working towards such features found in the Nordic and European communities of the 1980s as a common market, free flow of goods and services, capital and labour, coordination of foreign policies; it might also come up with original and better solutions than the European Union.

7. **A dense network of municipal solidarity with all parts of ex-Yugoslavia,** for refugee/relief work and reconstruction

can be developed. Similar groups in Germany (*'Gemeinde gemeinsam'*) and France (*'Cause commune'*) have been highly successful. The Council of Europe could provide help and advice.

8. **Let 1,000 local peace conferences blossom,** support local groups with communication hardware, elicit and collect people's ideas and present them to the governments.

9. **Intensify ecumenical peace work,** building on peace traditions in Catholic and Orthodox Christianity, and Islam. Challenge hard-line, sectarian religious institutions in the whole region, not only in Yugoslavia.

10. **In the spirit of future reconciliation,** *drop the sanctions,* and have inside and outside specialists search for *understanding of what went wrong, and for positive past and present experiences that can inspire a common future,* such as a Yugoslav confederation of more and smaller parts (somewhat similar to the Swiss cantons, with a high degree of internal autonomy, which have long helped a linguistically and religiously diverse people live in peace). And rather than criminal courts initiate massive reconciliation processes.

(April 1999)

19. Hindu–Muslim Relations: A TRANSCEND Perspective

Diagnosis. What has to be explained in India is not so much the occurrence of violent communal conflict between Hindus and Muslims as its infrequency, especially given that the line drawn by the British (the last Viceroy, Lord Mountbatten) gave Muslim territory to India to secure road access to Kashmir. After the bloodshed accompanying the Partition, Hindu–Muslim peace in India has been the rule rather than violence (but not Indo-Pakistani peace between India and Pakistan). Any explanation would include a high level of tolerance in ecumenical, inclusive (soft) Hinduism, under the condition that others are equally tolerant and respectful of Hinduism. The Islamic invasions of Northern India, from the year 1000, were traumatizing, far from tolerant and respectful. They are not forgotten.

The historicity of the Ayodhya 'Babri Mosque on top of a Ram Temple' is less important than the mobilization of Hindu masses, ending with the demolition of the Mosque on 6 December 1992 and widespread Hindu–Muslim violence in parts of India, paving the way for a fundamentalist party, the BJP, in 1998. The conflict was instrumentalized by cynical leaders, but had solid roots.

Prognosis. What follows later is not easy to predict. This could have been a catalytic event for a civil war to follow with the standard Indian lag, but could also have been the cathartic event instead of that civil war. To gamble on the latter is risky; it would have been better had it not happened. Separation of the communities, even sporadic violence, given the numbers and the proximity involved, could be serious. Remembering the massacre following the invasion of the Sikh Golden Temple and the subsequent assassination of Prime Minister Indira Gandhi in 1984, the prognosis could be ominous.

Therapy. Shortly before the 6 December 1992 confrontation, a committee of four met in Ladnun in Rajasthan: a Hindu, a Tibetan Buddhist (the Dalai Lama), a Jain (Acharya Tulsi) and a Western peace worker (Johan Galtung), in dialogue for a solution. The approaches say perhaps more about their conflict philosophy than about what could be an acceptable/sustainable outcome:

A Hindu view: persuade the parties to postpone any action;
A Buddhist view: compassion of and with all to soften positions;
A Jain view: whatever happens should happen non-violently;

A Western peace worker: an engineering approach, move the mosque 100 metres away from the site, build a Hindu temple on the presumed Ram site, construct a corridor between the two with a room in the middle for inter-communal dialogues.

In other words, Western 'do something!' against Eastern slow-down-the-action, focus on the inner Self and *how*, not *what*. These four perspectives do not exclude each other, and they do not exclude standard approaches like Hindu–Muslim dialogues and local cooperation councils to solve conflicts proactively.

But the deeper issue is whether this was a conflict at all. Did the temple really matter to the parties, or was it a choreographed violent encounter, chosen by the majority, for instance to show who was master in India? Was the temple too concrete a focus, standing for much deeper issues? If the temple issue had not been there, what kind of issue would have come in its place? Thus, could it be like the inclination to discuss technical 'resource issues' (oil, water) when the conflict is over class or the nation/state dialectic in general? A deep, dangerous conflict in search of a manageable discourse?

Un train peut en cacher un autre? (December 1992)

20. Anomie/Atomie and 'Sects': A TRANSCEND Perspective

Diagnosis. Advanced industrial societies, not only in the West, are now entering a postmodern social formation characterized by a high level of dissolution of compelling norms and values (anomie) and of social fabric (atomie). Society becomes a set of isolated individuals steered by the egocentric cost-benefit analysis of the *market*. The computer is an icon, sitting in front of that altar the service. In this society the human search for *meaning* (through compelling norms and values) and *togetherness* (through obliging social relations) will find strong and sometimes unexpected expressions. Typical examples are corruption, criminal gangs low down and high up in society, violence of all kinds, and sect-formation, organizations inside or across the borders of state power with members tied together by strongly shared norms and values and by strong social fabric. Usually entry into the 'sect' is easier than exit, and 'sects' are to some extent societies within societies, even states within states. As such they are resented by state powers fearing not only takeover or the absorption of human/social energy by the sect. Needless to say, nationalism satisfies all these criteria and is a major source of meaning and togetherness.

Prognosis. New, and numerous, groups will form within and across societies as the state becomes a 'failed state', because of anomie/atomie, through violence and corruption, and because of abdication of the state to the market. Nationalism will be on the increase providing both compelling norms and social fabric. States moving from *l'état provident* to *l'état gendarme* will spend much of their energy fighting these new formations, partly with very violent means. The sects will increasingly become similar to underground, clandestine groups under the conditions of foreign occupation. Obedience to sect leadership will be the dominant norm. States often accommodated different types of people; sects will be much more homogeneous.

Therapy. The human rights tradition will protect the freedom of thought and expression of the sectarians, important as much of their critique of contemporary society has validity. The same tradition will also protect their right of assembly. But there is a need for a social contract where 'freedom of expression' and 'freedom of assembly' come together with the 'freedom of non-expression' and 'freedom of disassembly', of exiting. There is a gap here in the human rights tradition. We might think in terms of an SOS system similar to the admirable machinery made available in some places for women battered by their husbands, and children abused by their carers, etc.

But beyond that point the therapy would have to move in a very different direction by counteracting anomie and atomie rather than strengthening the coercive machinery of the state.

Counteracting the absence of compelling values and norms by preaching the old values and norms is probably meaningless and even counterproductive. They may be the values of a dying social formation, and can only be made compelling by returning to that formation. More promising would be a search for new values, and one place not to be overlooked would be 'sects' with something to offer, preferring the term 'movement' to 'sect'. Anything new looks sectarian to start with, but may carry some valid truth.

Counteracting the absence of social fabric presupposes norms of solidarity or reciprocity, abundant in movements and not in gigantic social formations like 'society', 'market'. The state may regulate the movements, but should also learn from them. (August 1993)

21a. Sri Lanka: A TRANSCEND Perspective

Diagnosis. A minority can impose its unitary state on a multinational people, as in the case of Hawai'i. So can a majority, combining democratic and what they see as historical rights. The result has been a catastrophe for the Sinhalas, Tamils and Muslims in Sri Lanka. The conflict in Sri Lanka, with a very high toll in casualties, bereaved, wounded, displaced, material damage, derives essentially from a wrong decision in 1956 – understandable given the definition of British colonialism as the major contradiction – but not excusable. Even less excusable is the inability of the Sinhalese governments simply to retract and give the Tamils not only local autonomy but independence, holding out a confederation as a good second option given the limited size of the island; even if it can be explained in terms of the virulence of the violent meta-conflict touching most families in the three communities. The Sinhalese government even engaged Indian troops in the ill-fated Indian Peacekeeping Force of 1987–90, attempting a 'military solution'; also to prevent Tamils from uniting with mother-land Tamil Nadu.

Prognosis. The prognosis is the continuation of the status quo, meaning protraction, with institutionalization of violence. Both parties have become so accustomed to military offensives and terrorist attacks, to revenge and revenge for the revenge, that the whole of society has become deformed. As in Northern Ireland and the Basque Country popular and media concern is with violence only, which is understandable as anybody can be caught in the crossfire. But any focus on violence and its terrible consequences stands in the way of conflict transformation dialogues. The status quo will one day change to the better. But that day may be far off.

Therapy. One formula, in addition to Tamil secession or a territorial (con)federation, is referred to here as *non-territorial federalism*. Three nations live around each other, with a high level of mixing. They start fighting. The classic idea is secession, or drawing lines somewhere, separating the groups. The problem with such lines is that they may serve as an invitation to engage in 'ethnic cleansing'. Hence, something more creative than drawing lines is needed.

One proposal would be a parliament for each nation with autonomy for the basic concerns of the nation: religion and language, trauma and glory, the sacred points in space and time, police and courts, some of the economy. And a super-parliament for infrastructure, foreign affairs, general security, finance.

This may sound complex. But that complication is a small price to pay to avoid bitter, protracted warfare with its costs not only in dead and wounded and material damage, but in often irreparable psychological damage in terms of individual and family traumas, traumas to the nations and to the country as a whole, and in general a population less capable of handling the next conflict. And nobody has to move: like for Democrats and Republicans voting in US primaries, or the Samis in Nordic countries voting for their Sami Parliament. What is needed is to register and participate; actively, creatively, non-violently.

The three communities in Sri Lanka live around each other with pockets of high density. However, it may very well be too late for creative solutions: the wounds are too deep. In that case it can only be hoped that the Sinhalas will produce a leadership capable of thinking the unthinkable, a Tamil state, and doing the so far undoable; and that the Tamils will join in a giant reconstruction and reconciliation operation. (August 1993)

21b. Sri Lanka: A TRANSCEND Perspective

Here are some points added to the 1993 perspective:

Imagine we work with a conflict formation with six parties in order to break out of the 'Sinhalas vs. Tamils' prison:

1. 'hard' Sinhalas: among them much of the Buddhist clergy
2. 'soft' Sinhalas: among them much of Ariyaratne's *sarvodaya*
3. Muslims (10 per cent of the 18.6 million; 14 per cent Tamils, 76 per cent Sinhalas)
4. Sri Lanka Tamils, with 15,000 'Tigers' facing 150,000 troops and a considerable diaspora with world opinion impact
5. Indian Tamils, in Tamil Nadu (50 million)
6. New Delhi, Hindu India (with large Muslim minority)

The most elementary mistake would be a focus only on 1 + 2 vs. 4, excluding 3 and 5 + 6; 10 per cent of the people and major outside parties. There is more going on, below or above:

4 + 5 vs. 1 + 2 + 6, Tamil secession/union vs. Colombo/New Delhi; 1 + 2 + 3 + 4 vs. 5 + 6, Sri Lanka vs. India, ignoring Big Neighbour. There is a double asymmetry at work: the Sinhalas outnumber the Tamils and the Muslims, but Tamils and Muslims in India by far outnumber the Sinhalas, who have no mother country to turn to.

There are, of course, the old colonial power, the UK, the US and the 'international community', changing the discourse from inter-nation/self-determination to terrorism vs. status quo, possibly with a Tribunal if the Tigers are 'unreasonable'.

With less than 1 per cent participating in the violence but 63,000 killed since 1983 we can assume above half a million bereaved, with deep personal trauma/hatred fuelling the conflict. Policing a determined group using violence for nationalist ends is at worst impossible, at best prohibitively costly. Governments will pursue military solutions with large-scale offensives, pinpoint counter-attacks will deny them that, so will long-term revenge. Such agendas make negotiation/mediation shallow and hollow.

The following is based on dialogues with all six parties:

A. Tripartite non-territorial federalism Tamil–Muslim–Sinhala

The map does not invite ruling with rulers, drawing lines – the Tamils are scattered throughout the island, in addition to the concentrations in the North and the East. Three separate parliaments based on the three constituencies with autonomy in cultural, local economic and legal affairs and a super-parliament for foreign, security and financial affairs might make better sense than 'autonomy' or territorial federalism. Three parties may soften the present polarization. The state would guarantee full human rights for languages and religions, a joint currency and general foreign policy, and possibly no army but a federal and national police/militia in a national rather than territorial EELAM.

B. Functional independence

For both Tamils and Muslims, with the right to associate with Tamils and Muslims in India, with a free flow of people, goods and services and ideas – like the French- and Italian-speaking in Switzerland relate to France and Italy – as one of many nonmilitary approaches to security.

C. SAARC will have to take on umbrella functions

There are some parallels to Kashmir. Hindus and Muslims have mother countries, but not the Ladakh Buddhists. Some of them might agree that it is better to stay together ('The Valley') than join either; yet they want a free flow of people, goods and services and ideas. It might be interesting to combine the two conflicts since the implications are the same: loosening up, more flexibility.

(December 2000)

22. Somalia: A TRANSCEND Perspective

Diagnosis. The postcolonial, Cold War-related devastation of Somalia is not disputed, nor the hunger-related violence. Added to that comes the secondary conflict over the use of Somalia as a laboratory for 'humanitarian assistance', and releasing German funds for UN peacekeeping (as Cambodia was used for Japan). But the major problem is intellectual: Somalia does not fit Western nation-state models as a set of territories administered from a capital, with some autonomy to the provinces of a federation, and very little or no autonomy in a unitary state. Western democracy is based on territorial constituencies and one person-one vote, with majority-takes-all or proportional representation in a national assembly. Somalia looked like a nation-state in the sense of (roughly) one religion and one language. Mogadishu seemed to function like any capital of any nation-state, and when the model did not fit violence was used at the expense of agricultural assistance.

Virtual reality. In reality Somalia can be understood only by seeing the clans as polities; missing in the discourse from the beginning, then introduced, but in a very unfortunate way. The super-clans are the *Darood* (clans: *Dulbahante, Majerteen, Ogaden, Marehan*); *Irir* (clans: *Issak, Hawiye, Isa* and *Godabiirsay*) and *Saab* (*Ahanwayn*). This is a different way of organizing a society, partly territorial, partly by kinship. 'Modern' Westerners may decide this is the wrong way, and wish it away, but kinship is solid. In practice this means less solidarity where it should be according to Western cognitive maps, meaning within the nation-state of Somalia as such; and more solidarity where it should not be, along kinship lines and territory under their command. So the society cracks in unexpected places. And the clan leaders, instead of being honoured, were slotted into an inadequate discourse as 'warlords'. The US/UN spent enormous resources in terms of time, personnel and money hunting for some 13–14 leaders of super-clans, clans and sub-clans instead of doing useful work.

Prognosis. Focus on the 'warlords', like conceiving of Panama in terms of Noriega. Mission failure, of course.

Therapy. If the problem is starvation, 'seeds and tools' would have been a part of the package, combined with medical assistance, administered by agricultural and medical experts; bringing in the supplies by helicopter, bypassing Mogadishu, basing assistance on competent civilian personnel with police for crowd control and order. A UN expert sent to look into the situation in August 1992 reported back to the UN headquarters along such lines and was told that 'this does not fit into our concept'. That concept probably demanded delivery by the military to bolster UN forces, opening for German army participation, like Cambodia was used for and by Japan.

If we now assume that the primary structure of Somalia is:

- as a set of clans rather than a set of territories, and that
- the method of decision-making is dialogue till consensus has been obtained rather than debates leading to a vote/election,

then a better structure for Somalia might be as a set of clans and non-territorial federalism as the clans live around each other. To avoid centralism the presidency of the Council of Heads of Clans (insulted by the West with the term 'warlord') could rotate as in Switzerland, say every half-year (as in the EU), giving each clan visibility, using the very innovative Somali *shir* as a conflict resolution mechanism. (September 1992)

23. The Mayas: A TRANSCEND Perspective

Diagnosis. To the uninformed, the Zapatista uprising in Chiapas in January 1994, at the time of the NAFTA treaty ceding economic power over Mexico to the US and a little more than a year after the marking of the Columbus invasion, came as a surprise. Do such people never read history? How could they imagine that the dreams of the Mayan people could be totally suppressed, in southern Mexico, northern Guatemala, Honduras, in spite of the centuries that have passed since their own decline and the Spanish *conquista*? The Spanish themselves fought the Muslim *khalifat* of Cordoba for 800 years; why do they not attribute similar stamina and dreams to the people they suppressed so brutally? Because 'primitives do not dream'?

What is happening is one more instance in the Americas of what can be called *Columbus in reverse*. There have been many uprisings these 500+ years AC (Anno Columbi). Could there be some hope that the world consciousness has evolved to a point where such problems are not seen merely in terms of much needed land reform, health services, and elementary schools? Or, is the Western concept of linear, irreversible history too strong?

Prognosis. Possibly not. The discourse has oscillated between brutal repression of the uprising and some small concessions, important if enacted, but not touching the heart of the matter: self-determination. The most likely prognosis is, unfortunately, continuation of the revolution-repression cycles of the last five centuries, with most of the world, except conscious, compassionate people's organizations, doing nothing.

Therapy. If this is a nation divided among three countries, then the future may harbour some similarities to the Kurds, including the three-stage formula: human rights–autonomy within countries – (possibly) independence. The latter implies a Mayan nation not only within but across borders, possibly as a (con)federation of autonomies at the state level; the Chiapas being one. And again there is the same tragedy, however heroic, of using violence when non-violence, actively carried out, maybe by women more than men, might give much better results and much more quickly.

There is also the question of creativity. The Mayas are entitled to their state. There could be transition periods with dual citizenship and a joint authority Mexico–Guatemala–Honduras with the United Nations, in cooperation with the Organization of American States, as additional partners. And the measures suggested for the Kurdish situation, elections for a Mayan parliament in exile, a Mayan executive agency granting dual citizenship, might be further down the road if the Mayans do not have the same level of consciousness about their nation as the Kurds. Only one thing is certain: the issue will not disappear.

This does not mean that the countries, such as Guatemala, do not have their own specificity. The line between the 19 Maya communities and the *ladinos* is recognized as basic. But the construction of a civil war as starting in 1961, lasting for 35 years, is misleading: more important were the *conquista*, and the US bombing in 1954 directed against the Arbenz regime. But Spain and the US managed to appear as 'third parties', thereby distorting the discourse, keeping the conflict 'intra-state', suppressing the Mayan linkage. The latter is easy given the general Maya lack of access to world, or even national, media. Which only goes to prove how interesting life becomes with badly informed media: there will always be surprises like Chiapas. (August 1995)

24. Reconciliation Conflicts: A TRANSCEND Perspective

Diagnosis. The 30,000+ killed during the violence in Argentina, not only by the military but also by revolutionary forces, have left deep wounds in the entire society. The problem of healing the wounds from the 1970s has not been solved. The truth is by and large assumed to be known; reconciliation seems distant, partly because of deeply embedded ambivalences.

On the one hand, the military are in a position to block legal processes by arguing that the revolutionary forces also would have to be arraigned into court. That position, blocking judiciary processes, could pave the way for a non-judiciary process. However, given the very strong Christian/juridical tradition of the country, with clear definitions of the 'sinner' and the 'guilty', prescribing the penitence of the sinner and the punishment of the guilty, any process without those elements would be defined by the culture as falling short of the ideal. And reconciliation can hardly be obtained through clear verdicts and sentences. Even if the victims may derive some satisfaction from the pain administered to the perpetrator in the sentence by the court, this may not make it easier for the two to live together in the same society, at present and in the future, or for both of them to live with their own past. But the basic point seems to be that even if a legal process is not a sufficient condition for reconciliation, it may be close to a necessary condition in that type of culture.

Added to this comes the problem of ambivalence. Some of those wanting the military brought to justice may also have wanted the military to intervene against revolutionary violence. Some of the military may also have helped and protected some victims. Some Argentinians may have been on both sides, most on neither. That ambivalence could also pave the way for a non-judiciary process. But the culture may have the upper hand in those issues, effectively blocking reconciliation.

Prognosis. There will be no reconciliation, except maybe for some perpetrators with themselves (and their God) by demanding a trial in Spain, the old mother country (which may use this to win in the struggle with the US in Latin America.)

Therapy. Open dialogue about these issues seems to be the only approach. In Argentinian society much of that dialogue is taking place, not only for their benefit, but for the Western world in general, and for other countries where these processes may be culturally problematic. That dialogue, however, will have to be informed by the many alternatives to the Christian paradigm and the legal paradigm, with elements of apology and restitution added. The problem with the alternatives is that they may come from other cultures and hence be unacceptable in a culture regarding itself as having nothing to learn. This may be truer for the Western periphery than for a Western centre that has as its right and duty to be on the lookout for new approaches. The Polynesian *ho'o pono pono* may not come across under that name, but as a conflict circle, a round-table, a *mesa redonda*. The parties could be invited to tell their story, trying to establish their truths as a point of departure, arriving at an understanding that opens for shared responsibility, and then discuss what each party could do to reconcile, meaning (a) to heal the wounds, (b) to close the book and then, in the end, to display their joint sorrow about what happened and discuss further approaches to reconciliation, all that at the local, the provincial, and the national levels. (December 1995)

25. China: A TRANSCEND Perspective

Diagnosis. That there are (at least) five autonomy movements in the world's most populous and at the same time oldest country (from 221 BC; there are older, but not autonomous countries) is not surprising. Those moves for autonomy are along the periphery, indicative of *han* China overstretching at some point in history (in Hong Kong/Macao others overstretched into a *han* majority). Except for Taiwan autonomy moves are built around non-*han* idioms, faiths, myths and a sense of territorial attachment. Thus, classical conditions for secession, irredentism, and claims for independence, are all present.

Prognosis. The obvious prognosis is the status quo with the Chinese centre controlling *han* and *non-han* peripheries through carrot (clientelism, use of privileges to attract local leaders in Hong Kong), stick (repression in Tibet, Xinjiang and Inner Mongolia) and normative (Taiwan) policies. China works as a super-nation trying to accommodate others with nationality policies similar to Soviet efforts. And with the same weakness: nations want to be self-determining. The power profile differs among the five cases, and over time. A war over Hong Kong with the UK was avoided, a war over Taiwan with the US may still be avoided, but also may not. Military brutality in Tibet, Inner Mongolia and Xinjiang may be stepped up, but the Chinese military can also be brutal in *han* contexts. The more foreign, barbarian powers side with a movement, the more recalcitrant the Chinese. The location of the Tibetan government-in-exile in an India with nuclear weapons, and the deepening linkage between Taiwan and the US–Japan security system counteract reasonable outcomes. Vicious short and long cycles of minor violence are likely.

Therapy. An acceptable, sustainable outcome will go beyond the extremist positions of a *Chinese unitary state* (with the present borders + Taiwan, the 'runaway province') vs. *secession from that unitary state*. In-between are the classics: federations and the looser confederation; outcomes not located in the Chinese past, but coming up frequently in dialogues with the parties. Autonomy in domestic affairs would be guaranteed. In federations foreign/security/finance policies would be common; in confederations they would be coordinated, but with autonomy. One scenario might be federation first, confederation later; the five advancing in step or separately. The underlying philosophy, from Chinese culture, would be Daoist: *in strength weakness, in weakness strength*:

force shows the weakness of the construction, stronger constructions can do without force.

The hurdles to be overcome are considerable. First, the *han* mind-set as the undisputed rulers between the Himalayas, the desert, the tundra and the sea. Will the Chinese be convinced that a looser configuration of *Six Chinas* might also be in their interest? Second, will those who seek independence find that their goals may be better satisfied in a configuration that offers enormous economies of scale and a cultural common ground; yet (in a confederation) offers military-political independence? Third, will all parties agree that the time has come to solve these old Chinese problems jointly, not separately? Fourth, how can the *han* Chinese be protected in the new republics? Separate assemblies?

Tibetans may have to admit that Lamaism was brutal, and that China also has positive aspects; easier for Taiwan, being itself so Chinese. Beijing and Taipei would both have to give up the idea of being the centre of the other, finding confederal equality, with Beijing somewhat more equal than the others. (February 1997)

26. The Christians and the Muslims: A TRANSCEND Perspective

Diagnosis. On 27 November 1095 Pope Urban II made a call for what became known as the First Crusade in the French town of Clermont. In 1291, the Crusades came to an end. But a real declaration of peace has never been made.

Prognosis. The Crusades stand out in history as an example of how religion is used to justify war. Even today collective memories and a crusade mentality persist, defining a 'Gulf Syndrome' with Catholic/Protestant countries against a Muslim country with a major Crusade experience (Baghdad 1258).

Therapy. On 26–27 November 1995, a dialogue was convened at the Swiss Institute for Development in Biel/Bienne, bringing together leading representatives of the Christian and Islamic faiths: Ayatollah, professor Mohammad Taghi Jafari, Tehran; Sheikh Ahmad Kuftarou, Grand Mufti of Syria, Damascus; Nuncio, Archbishop K. J. Rauber, Bern; Metropolit Damaskinos, Bishop of Orthodox Church, Geneva; and scholars and clerics.

Pope John Paul II sent his blessings and a message to the symposium through Cardinal Angelo Sodano, Secretary of State of the Holy See: 'It is opportune to reflect on these events, in order to draw vital lessons for today. His Holiness renews the call of the Second Vatican Council which urged that a sincere effort be made to achieve mutual understanding, so that, for the benefit of all, Christians and Muslims would together preserve and promote peace, liberty, social justice and moral values …'

Communiqué:

The adherents of Islam and Christianity proposed the following to members of their respective faiths and all others:

- to try to understand other religions the way their followers understand themselves, as a condition for true dialogues;
- to develop school material in history, civic education and religious education, particularly material about the two religions, acceptable to all parties;
- not to abuse the freedom of speech when speaking and writing about other religions;
- to work together to identify, develop further and put into practice an inspiring ethic of peace, liberty, social justice,

family values, human rights and dignity, and non-violent forms of conflict resolution;
- to establish permanent inter-religious councils to further mutual respect and understanding;
- to cooperate across religious borders in Bosnia to reconstruct the country;
- to discuss with people in the media more responsible, peace-promoting forms of journalism.

On this day of the ninth centenary of the call for the Crusades, we call upon Christians, Muslims and all others, to go beyond mere tolerance. We must open our hearts and minds to each other. Instead of sensing danger when somebody is different let us be filled with joy at the opportunity to learn, to enrich and be enriched, to live in peace and create peace. Like everything else the two largest religions in the world are also subject to development. While keeping the basic message of devotion let us find new ways, acts and words. It is within the spirit of freedom of interpretation of one's own religion that genuine respect for other religions can evolve. Let the next 900 years and beyond be an era of active peace built in our hearts and our minds, and enacted in our deeds.

(November 1995)

27. Tripartite Europe: A TRANSCEND Perspective

Diagnosis. Two fault-lines cut Europe in three: Protestant/Catholic (also a fault-line, but inactive since 1648 except for Ireland), Slavic-Orthodox and Turko-Muslim. As the fault-lines (Catholic/Orthodox from 1054, and Christian/Muslim from 1095) intersect in Sarajevo, surrounded by Bosnia and Herzegovina, surrounded by Yugoslavia, surrounded by the Balkans this is a major conflict arena by and large with predictable alliances: a Washington/London/Paris/Berlin/Vienna/Rome/Zagreb axis, a Moscow/Belgrade/Skopje/Athens axis and the 'green transversal' Sarajevo/Tirana/Pristina/Tetova/Ankara and onwards.

Another tripartite arena is the Caucasus region, with violent encounters between Slavic-Orthodox and Turko-Muslim forces, the third parties being Georgian/Armenian Christians.

Today most Protestant/Catholic countries are in the European Union, the biggest Slavic-Orthodox in the CIS, and the Turko-Muslim countries also have an organization (ECO): Turkey, six ex-Soviet republics, and Iran, Pakistan and Afghanistan. Should conflicts harden further economic/military/political crystallization would be easy. Oil fuels the conflict.

Prognosis. The order is tripartite, and conflicts where all three have axes to grind with the other two are entirely possible. But wars are between two parties, calling either for alliances or for withdrawal as outsiders or declared neutrals. The Yugoslav catastrophe brought about US intervention to forge a highly unstable Croat-Bosniak federation in Bosnia-Herzegovina, and a Dayton Agreement that does not respect self-determination of the three nations and makes Bosnia-Herzegovina the first NATO protectorate. The Kosovo/a débâcle may eventually lead to a tripartite war with both Serbia and Kosovar/Albanian guerrillas fighting a second NATO protectorate, established against international law (not self-defence, not collective self-defence, not authorized by the Security Council). Who is next?

Escalation by imitation *in* similar European regions (and by extension, *to*) is likely. The formation of Slavic-Orthodox and Turko-Muslim blocs will follow. The culture of violence goes back to brutal, hot-blooded medieval patterns, like in the bloody Irish–English–Scottish interface in Northern Ireland.

Therapy. A Westphalia II in 1998, 1648 + 350 years, bridging the two fault-lines or at least declaring some kind of disengagement, would have been very useful. That did not happen. The logical therapy would be to strengthen the organization that brings all three parts together, the OSCE, with measures to include:

- *militarily*, using OSCE for peacekeeping without threatening East Asia, no extension of NATO up to the two fault-lines, or, if that happens, a 500-kilometre disengagement zone;
- *economically*, using OECD (Organization for Cooperation and Development) in (all of) Europe for equitable trade and growth;
- *politically*, making OSCE a regional UN for Europe, without big power veto and with a real parliament in more permanent session;
- *culturally*, dialogues and cooperation across confession lines; using CE (Council of [almost] Europe) for culture, sport, youth.

In short, use pan-European institutions, not sub-regional EU, NATO or WEU. NATO has been expanded to include two Catholic and one mixed Central European country; troops are watching each other across fatal fault-lines. If Yugoslavia is a meso-cosm of Europe, then what might work in Yugoslavia might work in Europe: smaller units, more homogeneous, woven together (con)federally. The problem: so far nothing of the kind has happened. (October 1996)

28. Ecuador–Peru: A TRANSCEND Perspective

By the classical logic of the state system now celebrating its 350th anniversary since the Treaty of Westphalia, each piece of land, clearly demarcated, belongs to one and only one state. But what if two or more states claim the same piece of land, for instance because there is not only one *divortium aquarum* (watershed) but two, or a possible border river comes and goes? The classical answer is a war to arrive at a 'military solution', and this is what Ecuador and Peru did in 1942, 1981 and 1995, following the 1941 war. Another answer is to have a strong, big state or community of states, take over, as a 'mandate'.

An answer much more in line with an increasingly borderless world would be for the states to administer a disputed territory together as a *condominium*. If both parties have reasonable claims, then rather than dividing the disputed territory define it as joint territory shared by the contestant parties. Rather than fighting it out, the joint territory may be used for cooperative ventures. But exactly what would that mean?

1. The two states could make the '*zona inejecutable*' – where the Rio de Janeiro Protocol from January 1942 did not establish a precise boundary so that the treaty could not be executed – a *bi-national zone*, a *condominium* with both flags.
2. They could establish a protected *natural park* with the help of the IUCN (International Union for the Conservation of Nature) and its Programme on Protected Areas, making the zone more inviolable, in the interest of both peace and the environment. The park would be jointly administered whether a border between the two has been clearly demarcated or not.
3. Camping facilities for youth and others from both countries would fit into a natural park, as they do elsewhere.
4. They could establish *economic zones* for joint ventures inviting companies from both sides. Factories might have to be outside an ecological zone, but administrative facilities could fit in; no major problem in today's electronic world.
5. Troops from the two countries would disengage and withdraw, and procedures would be established for joint security, patrolling, early warning of military movements, etc.
6. Work has to be done adjusting the legal codes to each other, to adjudicate crimes and facilitate cooperation.

In short, two countries with a history of hostility could use conflict creatively to grow together at the disputed point, and at the speed national sentiments would tolerate and demand.

7. But they could go further, internationalizing the zone, retaining bi-national administration and sovereignty as a fallback. Two more flags could come up: the UN and the OAS, alongside the national flags.
8. A compound for negotiating border (and other) disputes would be constructed, for parties from anywhere in the world.
9. UN/OAS peacekeeping troops would internationalize security, using contingents from the two countries, and others.
10. The area could become an international *zone of peace*, and a registry for such zones could be established at the United Nations with emerging rules for a code of conduct. Regional organizations elsewhere (the OAU, OSCE) might be interested in the same constructive approach to border disputes, and follow up using such zones as staging areas for peacemaking and peace-building.

If intergovernmental organizations cooperate, so could international people's organizations from Latin America, giving more substance to an international civil society. (August 1995 and June 1998)

29a. Caucasus: A TRANSCEND Outcome Perspective

Diagnosis. Contrary to what is asserted by many, the situation in the Caucasus is not unique. In a world with about 200 countries and 2,000 nations, but only 20 nation-states, the Caucasus is not the only place where the nations inside states do not appear neatly, side by side, in geographical space, but dwell inside nations dwelling inside nations, in a *matrushka/Chinese boxes* manner. This pattern is particularly frequent in mountainous regions with complex topographies from the Himalayas to the Pyrenees; Bosnia-Herzegovina being another case. Hence, *processes of self-determination come not only in parallel but in series*: (Georgia) separates from a super-state (USSR), is confronted with a nations in its midst (Abkhazia and Ossetia), which in turn may be confronted with sub-sub-nations, etc. in waiting. Even if 'international law', usually an instrument for big power interests, accepts first-order self-determination but not higher orders, the struggle continues. Nor is Russian intervention in its 'sphere of interest' unique; big powers see that as their right and duty. Some countries like to increase their value to the US through oil or investment, incentives. Latin American history may serve as a warning against the latter, and Middle East history against the former strategy based on oil and pipelines. To this we must add a major economic complex: when an empire, the USSR, disintegrates and privatizes, many assets are up for grabs: do they belong to Russia, Georgia or Abkhazia? 'Let the weapons decide' leads to another war, etc. Added to these structural considerations come cultural factors in a *'Caucasian mentality'* with *warrior mentality, chief mentality,* and *victim mentality,* but of course also with the classical five of so many 'traditional/feudal' societies: hospitality, generosity, honour, courage and dignity. *The warrior mentality* leads to a *low threshold for violent action,* the idea that *conflicts are about winning, not about solving* and that *negotiations are about winning, not on solving. The chief/sheikh Mentality* places decisions about war, peace and foreign policy high up, there is nothing people can, or should, do about it. And *the victim mentality,* based on enormous suffering, even genocide, often at the hands of the others leads to a demand for undivided attention and focus on our trauma, including how to deal with the evil-doer. Any idea put forward will either be left uncommented or pushed aside, not necessarily because the idea is bad but because proposals are not essential. Protecting the cognitive and emotional maps is what matters.

The three mentalities combine in the search for the Big Man and for the Big Power, with Russia to the North, Turkey to the West and Iran to the South, and the US everywhere eagerly waiting. *Generally speaking women are less infected by this syndrome than men.* Women have certainly been victims. But they are less convinced than men by warrior and chief mentality. Thus, particularly are proposals put forward by three women Naira Gelashwili (Tbilisi) about a Common Caucasian House for all Caucasian peoples and a Caucasian Civil Society; Ludmila Haroutunian (Erevan) about a Caucasian Confederation with Georgia, Armenia, Azerbaijan; Abkhazia, Ossetia, and Nagorno-Karabakh, and Arzu Abdullayeva (Baku) about dual citizenship.

Prognosis. Big Men with Big Clans will make Big Deals with Big Powers. Oil and cash will flow, building a corrupt class of *nouveaux riches*. People will not be asked, nations will not be respected, only the power of arms and money.

Therapy. *Basically, the key to conflict transformation by peaceful means in the Caucasus lies in Caucasian cooperation, based on democracy and human rights.* With three states and 28 nations any part is too weak to survive alone with four bigger powers pressing. Jointly they complement each other economically and culturally, and could stand up politically against pressure.

But Georgia and Armenia-Azerbaijan have to be transformed: Georgia has to countenance its multinational reality. Any effort to impose Georgian language and history on Abkhazians, Ajaris, Ossetians and others will be resented as much as any Russian effort to do the same with Georgians. Abkhazia, Ajara, (South) Ossetia and others should have been granted linguistic and educational autonomy years ago without passing through wars of nationalism. Georgia and the others might have been saved two wars fuelled by nationalism, but not Georgia's own civil war.

If a country is multinational there is no alternative to symmetry, using Switzerland as a model. Georgia may one day have to translate multinationalism into federalism. And that could also apply to Azerbaijan as a federation with Armenian Nagorno-Karabakh as a part and to Armenia with Azeri Nakitchiwan as another? Might dual passports in all four parts be helpful?

Then proposals at a multilateral, Caucasian level:

1. A *Conference/Organization for Security and Cooperation in the Caucasus (C/OSCC)* might be useful, with a permanent Security Commission under the auspices of the OSCE with good links to the UN, possibly on a pan-Caucasian basis. The basic goal is conflict autonomy, with Caucasians masters in their own house.

2. A *Caucasian Parliament* would sooner or later have to follow, raising such questions as whether the members should be appointed by their state parliaments or elected by popular vote (the two stages in the history of the European Parliament).

3. *The Nordic Council is a useful model* because there are members at different levels: five independent countries (Denmark, Norway, Sweden, Finland and Iceland, full rights), one semi-independent (Greenland), two island groups that are parts of Denmark (Faroe Islands) and Finland (Åland Islands, neutral) and a nation straddling Norway/Sweden/Finland (the Sami). Far from Caucasian complexity but similar and the formula is non-conventional. But having a voice does not mean having a vote.

4. *One model for a Caucasian Parliament would include the three states with full rights, and with their major constituent parts.*

5. *Another model for a Caucasian Parliament might have two houses, one for the three states and one for the (28?) nations,* for articulation of concerns or decision-making, with mechanisms like the US Congress in case of disagreement between the houses.

6. The Nordic case suggests including such issues as abolition of visas, later passports, within the Caucasus, a Caucasian labour market, facilitation of NGO activities, encouragement of joint economic enterprises and reconciliation of parties in conflict.

7. Minorities with grievances should be invited *to raise their concerns at the Caucasian level,* with other Caucasians mediating

8. A special concern of a Caucasian Parliament might be *to look into the possibilities of dual citizenship,* as mentioned one for the state in which a person lives and one for the state of the nation with which he identifies. Special attention would be paid to the problems of double voting, military service and taxation.

9. This cooperation could start *without prejudging the outcome later* as a Council for Cooperation and lead to a common market, a community, a confederation, or even a federation.

(June 1997)

29b. Caucasus: A TRANSCEND Process Perspective

A Peace Zone in the Middle of Caucasus

1. The three biggest Caucasian countries, Armenia, Azerbaijan and Georgia, are so fortunate as to have *a three-countries point, Krasni' Most', in the middle,* sparsely populated, neither lakes nor mountains. Other regions, like the Nordic countries, might wish they had such a point (Denmark and Sweden come close, the three-countries point Norway–Sweden–Finland is more problematic).
2. If each country made available some square kilometres for *a zone of peace, cooperation and development* around this point (while remaining owners of their part) Caucasian cooperation might move from declarations to reality, even quickly.
3. *Culturally,* and that might be a good beginning, the zone could be the site of major cultural festivals, and not only for youth, combining music and singing with dialogues (say, in groups of ten) producing concrete ideas for peace, cooperation and development, giving prizes for the best ideas, handing ideas over to politicians as a gift from the people – all of this in search of UNESCO's goal: peace culture. Permanent exhibitions and ecumenical dialogues might also be considered.
4. *Economically,* the zone, with adequate size, could host a regional airport with good highway connections to the three capitals (thereby also connecting them with each other). International airlines that would not call on the three countries singly might be attracted by a regional facility (in the future a joint Caucasian airline might also be attractive). An economic zone for joint enterprises, particularly in the export sector following Japanese models, could be important.
5. *Militarily,* the zone would be demilitarized or at least devoid of any offensive capability. Training for peace missions by a Caucasian Peacekeeping Force might be worth considering.
6. *Politically,* this might be the neutral ground on which to place Caucasian institutions for functional cooperation in such fields as environment or security (e.g. a C/OSCC, affiliated with the OSCE; or a Caucasian Security Commission in general). Should the region declare itself a community, or even a confederation, then this would be the logical site for a Caucasian Assembly, whether it is with one house (for countries) or two houses (an additional house for nationalities).

7. *The outside world would be invited in as observers,* the four big powers to verify that there is nothing in this concept directed against them. For North Caucasus the three-countries point has no symbolic value; cooperation with that region within a Pan-Caucasian formula might find other venues more appropriate
8. The zone of peace can be used as a first place to practise some important ideas. The danger would be that it becomes the last.

(Galtung and Jacobsen, June 1997)

30. 'Comfort Women': A TRANSCEND Perspective

1. *Japanese Responsibility*

- *Recourse according to international law is very limited,* given the Tokyo Tribunal, the 1952 Peace Treaty and other treaties. The issue was not brought up, other claims were settled. It says a lot about the warrior-macho logic of governments that the suffering of women was outside the responsibility discourse. For individuals recourse must be within old and new domestic law.
- *Recourse according to general moral principles remains open* although with some limitation (thus, Second World War cases would be difficult to argue; the underlying principle probably being whether the victims of non-lethal crimes are still alive).
- *Conclusion: Responsibility for Japan, recourse according to old or new domestic law, and according to moral principles.*

2. *Reconciliation* (GOAL: Peaceful relations in the region)
[2, 1] *The reparation/restitution approach*
TO: Qualified victims (families as successor victims?)
FROM: Japanese People (as successor people); ASIAN WOMEN'S FUND
Japanese government, by facilitating recourse

[2, 2] *The apology/forgiveness approach*
TO: Qualified victims
FROM: Japanese People (as successor people)
Japanese government (as moral successor government), and qualified perpetrators

[2, 3] *The co-dependent origination/*karma *approach*
Question: What went wrong, when? Any victim responsibility?
Goal: Adding victim responsibility to Japanese responsibility
Method: Deep encounters, some of them public, on national television.
Financed by: Japanese government and other sources

[2, 4] *The historical/truth commission approach*
Method: Open all archives for deep history (not only 'facts'); the use of women for 'comfort', and as battlefield for soldiers.

Goal: Learning from history so history does not repeat itself.
Financed by: Japanese government and other sources

[2, 5] *The joint sorrow/healing approach*
Method: Declare a day of mourning; public joint mourning
Goal: sharing the double sorrow, as victim, as perpetrator.
Organized by: Japanese government, with the UN (for 8 March?)

3. *Resolution/Transformation* (GOAL: Preventive, for the future)
[3, 1] In international law, as explicit crime against humanity
[3, 2] In school textbooks, but not only facts, also prevention
[3, 3] Critiquing the warrior/macho myths, and their roots
[3, 4] Critiquing the general war logic, of which this is a part
[3, 5] Alternatives to war, including to the Pacific War 1931–45
Financed by: Japanese government, for a major peace fund

4. *Rehabilitation* (GOAL: Therapeutic, also invisible effects)
[4, 1] Offering rehabilitation (psychotherapy?) for victims
[4, 2] Offering rehabilitation for families
[4, 3] Thinking rehabilitation for those who deny and defend
[4, 4] Improving relations among peoples in East Asia.
Financed by: Japanese government.

(July 1996)

31. Okinawa: A TRANSCEND Perspective

1. Okinawa is an appendix to two powers, Japan and the US, invaded, settled and annexed by Japan (1879); the US as a part of the Pacific War (1945, after 1972 as a base).
2. Okinawans have two mother countries, Japan for many of the Japanese settlers and many of the 'indigenous', and itself, the Ryukyu Islands. Okinawans have two options: some kind of status quo with Japan or some kind of autonomy.
3. Okinawa, Ulster, Hawai'i, Eiffel/Germany, Tahiti, Sicily, North Dakota, Semipalatinsk, Ul Nor have in common their location on the periphery and that they were/are all used as testing and/or stationing/launching areas for major strategic weapons; deflecting military attention away from the centre.
4. We may also talk about second- and third-order outstationing: the US assigns important strategic roles to island countries far away, like Japan and England; they in turn pushing the role on to periphery places like Okinawa and Ulster.
5. People in such periphery areas are being used, even to the point of sacrifice, and the use will be hidden under veils of patriotism, serving the common cause of centre *and* periphery.
6. Thus, Tokyo and Washington have coinciding interests, and as a result 0.6 per cent of Japanese territory has 75 per cent of the US bases territory, occupying about 20 per cent of Okinawan land. At least 10 per cent of that land, in turn, is affected by the 3,000 out of 32,000 land-owners who have leased their property to the US military and do not want to renew the agreements. Tokyo becomes the willing helper of Washington in trying to get some kind of consent from Okinawan authorities and/or land-owners.
7. In the case of Okinawa there are also two other reasons why the US hangs on to its bases. First, there is an historical reason of perhaps minor significance: Commodore Perry, of 'opening Japan' fame, also came to the Ryukyu islands and crowned himself as king. Second and more significantly: Okinawa is the only part of pre-war Japan where the US fought a ground war (with enormous casualties on all three sides, above 200,000 altogether, 14,000 Americans). That victory is in search of a symbol: Okinawa.
8. One argument for autonomy would have as a basis that it is in nobody's interest to be somebody else's appendix, and even more so if essentially used for military purposes. That

argument would be combined with an entirely non-violent approach to autonomy, peaceful, cooperative relations after autonomy, and with precise roles in the world community as bastions of peace.

9. The way out of this dilemma, fraught with violent potential, is what Okinawans have already chosen: non-violence.

10. The problem of security for Okinawa is probably best solved through the following four-pronged formula:

- be neutral, non-aligned (like the Åland Islands), do not become anybody's stationing/launching/training centre;
- develop a strong, nonmilitary, defence capability, belying Napoleon's comment ('But how do they fight, then?', August 1817) to Basil Hall, who reported that they had no arms;
- develop good relations in all directions; make all other parties interested in the survival, not the defeat of Okinawa; develop a capacity for peace/conflict work;
- be as self-reliant economically/ecologically as possible, with a capacity for satisfying own basic needs also in a crisis;
- for Japan a demilitarized Okinawa serving peace would provide more security than a provocative, offensive Okinawa.

(October 1996)

32. Rwanda/The Great Lakes: A TRANSCEND Perspective

Diagnosis. Limiting the Rwanda genocide in 1994 to 'Rwanda' limits the understanding of the conflict and the search for possible remedies. Thus, the racism implicit in a genocide with clear class connotations has roots in German colonialism and '*Rassenkunde*', favouring Tutsis over Hutus (and 'pygmies') for being taller. The Belgian successors to the German colonialists after the First World War favoured the Hutu majority ('numbers over centimetres'). Democracy was 'in'. Western economic investment (France, Belgium) became considerable, and Rwanda-Burundi was seen as symptomatic for the more important Zaire/Congo.

Another aspect is the projection of the European (Anglo-French) tribal feud over linguistic/cultural/economic influence in Africa. Uganda/Tutsi/Bunyamelenge/Kabila anglophiles are pitted against Hutu/Mobutu francophiles, with the Western media traditionally dominated by the French as 'area specialists'. But disasters tend to favour the spread of English as most disasters are managed in English. French/Roman Law is losing ground, it seems, and English/Common Law is pushing westward vigorously.

A third aspect is the role played by development aid, and particularly Swiss aid. Development agencies want success stories and tend to play on dominant groups in society, thereby cementing class relations that may be explosive. The underprivileged see no alternative to violence by revolution or migration and then invasion; the over-privileged see no alternative to pre-emptive violence against the suppressed and the moderates: *genocide*.

Prognosis. If the conditions producing genocide are not rooted out, genocide will be reproduced. If they are in the structure of Rwandan society and a culture of violence, the latter reinforced by a massive genocide traumatizing victims and perpetrators, then the prognosis depends on how much is done to remove the conditions. Tribunals locate the conditions in evil actors. But their removal by execution or imprisonment is unlikely to touch the deeper causes, and also unlikely to reconcile victims and perpetrators and both sides.

Therapy. One point of departure may be to question the availability of any lasting outcome within the narrow confines of Rwanda. Thus, a married couple, deformed by the outside and by themselves, might do well to seek solutions outside the narrow confines of their apartment (note 'apart'). And the solution to Rwanda might be located outside Rwanda.

One possible approach might be *a bi-oceanic confederation* from the Indian to the Atlantic oceans, including Uganda and Tanzania, Rwanda and Burundi, and the two Congos, maybe more countries, trading East–West with Asia and America, as much as North–South. There would be high levels of mobility of people and ideas, goods and services, not confining people with a tradition of enmity to a very limited territory. Japan, with extensive programmes for Africa, could contribute with East–West rail and road infrastructure. New energies could be tapped by doing what the Republic of South Africa has already done: exploiting the bi-oceanic opportunities further South.

It would also be useful if Germany, Belgium, France and Switzerland, the US and UN could assume part of the responsibility, contributing to reconciliation by taking some of that colossal burden off local shoulders. That burden is too big for a small country. Better bring in others, identify causes, have massive programmes in the culture of peace, create a new geopolitical reality, reconcile, mobilizing all forces for peace. (October 1997)

33. Hostage Crises: A TRANSCEND Perspective

The takeover of the Japanese Embassy in Lima, on 17 December 1996 was a conflict with six parties and the following goals:

1. *Tupac Amaru Revolutionary Movement (MRTA)*;

   - release of up to 400 MRTA prisoners,
   - to continue the struggle.

2. *The remaining (about 70) captives*,

   - to be released, unharmed.

3. *The Peruvian government*,

   - not to yield to terrorism, not releasing prisoners,
   - release of the captives, unharmed.

4. *The MRTA prisoners*,

   - to be released,
   - to continue the struggle.

5. *The US government's position*,

   - that nobody yields to terrorism,
   - release of the captives, unharmed.

6. *The Japanese government's position*,

   - release of the captives, unharmed,
   - respect for Japanese ex-territorial premises.

There is also 'Peruvian society' in search of ways to abolish misery, and 'world public opinion' in favour of all the above.

If all parties yield a little and use 'abolition of misery' as the overarching goal, then this could be a golden opportunity:

1. *Tupac Amaru MRTA* disarms and joins the political process in a democratic society, with access to mass media and elections.
2. The *captives* are released, finding ways in which they could contribute to misery abolition.

3. The *Peruvian government* improves the prison conditions, shortens their sentences, accepts MRTA as a non-violent, democratic movement, and steps up misery abolition.
4. The *MRTA prisoners* accept training in the prisons as village workers/social workers, and pledge to disarm.
5. The *US government* makes funding/expertise available for misery abolition projects.
6. The *Japanese government* makes funding/expertise available for misery abolition projects, and holds future Emperor's birthday receptions at multi-exit hotels.

To achieve this four bilateral talks would also be useful:

1. Direct negotiations between the MRTA and Peruvian government.
2. Direct negotiations between the prisoners and the government.
3. Captives and prisoners meet and form joint pressure group.
4. The MRTA and captives conduct dialogues on Peruvian society.

(February 1997)

34. Albania: A TRANSCEND Perspective

Consider these economic, political and military factors:

A *market economy* needs markets and markets need liquid capital. Albanian capital was to a large extent fixed as clan or family houses. To prise that capital loose very high interest rates were promised if the houses were mortgaged or sold and the money was invested in pyramid schemes. Even if there had been sporadic fighting the Albanian arena exploded when family savings disappeared in pyramid banking schemes. Well-informed sources estimate that $2–4 billion was extracted from Albania by Austrian, German, Swiss and US banks.

A *democracy* needs not only elections but also a civil society and an ongoing, unrestrained dialogue. Any election will probably be seen, and not without reasons, as a struggle between power groups for power for themselves, and not for the people. Participation may be very low for lack of support for already suspect politicians. In other words, the June elections may easily turn out like the elections in Haiti.

Pressure can be assumed to come from Italy, demanding in return political backing after Italy has supported Germany in Yugoslavia, France in Algeria and Spain in Morocco. The Italian army has to be given the same chance as 'peacekeeper/enforcer'.

Against this background, consider the following five-point peace plan *for* (not only *in*) Albania:

1. An *International Inquiry into the Banking Activities in Albania,* since the end of the Cold War regime. The commission has to be international and command expertise in the role of international banking, including the World Bank and related institutions. The aim would be not so much to establish any culpability or liability as to understand what happened and who were involved, nationally and internationally.
2. The *question of restitution to the victims* should be raised. If people entered the schemes in good faith, and there was bad faith on the other side, the problem of liability could arise. If not, restitution money might be found somewhere, together with consideration of legal barriers, or at least very clear warnings against similar schemes in the future.
3. Postpone the elections, and organize *round-tables over the future of Albania.* One of them obviously has to be at high levels in Tirana; but equally or more important would be round-tables in each village. Ideas and arguments emerging from such round-

tables (possibly organized and supervised by the OSCE) should be made available to the whole society. After that exercise elections might be more meaningful, including a possible referendum on King Lek's proposal for a monarchy.

4. There is a need for *humanitarian aid*, to old age homes, hospitals, children's homes and other points of direct delivery. Such aid could best be organized from civil society to civil society, involving large groups in Italy and Albania, for instance. There might be a need for protection, in which case an international police force might be considered.

5. *Cancel 'Operation Alba'*; it is ill-conceived from the very beginning. A soldier in full combat gear is not a symbol of humanitarian aid, but of an invasion. Italian leadership is an unfortunate idea, given the memories of Mussolini's invasion 58 years earlier, in April 1939. There is the suspicion of ulterior motives not too different from Mussolini's; motives that might also be attributed to Turkish, ex-Yugoslav and Greek forces.

(April 1997)

35. Lebanon: A TRANSCEND Perspective

Three post-violence tasks are Resolution, Reconstruction and Reconciliation, the three R's, to be taken on together.

Part I: Resolution

1. Lebanon suffers from a double conflict of internal division and external intervention. Foreign powers use Lebanon's weakness. The answer is unification to overcome that division.
2. For unity in a multinational country, divided in two world religions with subdivisions, *unifying themes* are needed:

   - One theme is the *message of conviviality, co-existence between the religions*. For that to happen both confessions have to turn their softer sides to each other, building on old traditions, overcoming the shame of the war.
   - Another theme (also inspired by Switzerland) is Lebanon as a place where *peripheries of world religions find each other rather than being dominated by their centres*.
   - A third theme is *Lebanon as a way of making money, placing Mammon above God and Allah*. But Mammon is a dangerous god to serve punishing with poverty, inequality and injustice: some remain or become poor, inequality spells conflict, and injustice – one community making more money than the other – also spells conflict. The outcome may easily become violence, with the two confessions turning their (very) hard sides to each other.
   - As fourth theme comes *joint suffering and joint shame*, a feeling of having betrayed the three other themes with the war.

3. A more lasting transformation would have to be based on *ever-higher levels of conviviality*. The Declaration of Biel (27 November 1995, commemorating the ninth centenary of the Crusades) contains eight guidelines all of which might be applied to Lebanon:

   - try to understand other people's religion the way they understand it;
   - develop school material acceptable to all parties;
   - do not abuse the freedom of speech when speaking and writing;

- put into practice inspiring ethics of peace, liberty, justice;
- seek ways to promote non-violent forms of conflict resolution;
- establish inter-religious councils for peace and human rights;
- discuss with media people peace-promoting forms of journalism;
- cooperate across religious borders to help reconstruct Bosnia.

4. The problem of class differences and inequality could be addressed by *economic programmes for the underprivileged*, like *grameen* (micro) banks (Bangladesh model), alternative technologies, cooperatives, etc. to produce for own consumption, complementing the market mechanisms through patterns of local self-reliance. To this could be added the artistic dimension that Lebanon does so well. And the problem of injustice can be addressed through rules of parity, *privileging the underprivileged for a period* (Malaysia model).
5. The problem of external intervention can be addressed by developing *strong patterns of conflict autonomy*, depending ever less on outside countries. This would probably presuppose some type of inter-university cooperation to develop a study and training centre for peaceful conflict transformation.

(May 1997)

Part II: Reconstruction

6. The Ministry of the Displaced and the Aïdoun have done work combined with reconciliation that merits the attention of other countries in similar situations, and could have model character. *Study tours, summer camps for people in similar situations in other countries are recommended*, as for Nicaragua–Mozambique. Travel companies should give discounts.
7. *A warning is needed lest reconstruction becomes the new way in which Lebanese make money*, creating a vested interest not only in war economics but also in reconstruction economics. What happens when Lebanon is reconstructed and the bonanza is over? The danger of a new turn of the cycle is obvious: new war, new destruction, new reconstruction, and in the meantime Lebanon more and more indebted and entrepreneurs more enriched.
8. Another approach would take up the Nicaraguan experience of having *former combatants cooperate in the reconstruction of what they destroyed*. Such efforts could be rewarded by the

Ministry with incentives, and by contractors by putting the machinery at their disposal after some training. The thesis would be that joint reconstruction could contribute to reconciliation, through cooperation and joint reflection. That Lebanon may not have had not two, but, say, 17 warring parties is no objection: it makes reconstruction teams larger.

Part III: Reconciliation

9. There will always be a hard nucleus of irreconcilables. One approach is to *work hard with women and youth* less directly involved in the violence, surrounding the irreconcilables with an ocean of conciliation. Above all, empower youth and women by having youth and women committees in all war-torn villages.

10. A basic point is to *make reconciliation visible*, by having the media present examples of former antagonists who cooperate. In general the press has to pay more attention to any reconciliation process and people have to enter more willingly, without being pressed into apologies.

11. Make *a casebook for elementary schools* with 50 (or so) good stories about how to handle conflict without violence, so that the younger generation has a reservoir to draw upon.

12. *Introduce Days of Reflection*, at the local, regional and national level, inviting the population to round-table dialogues. Four or five people, producing five ideas for the three R's would contribute to a Gross National Pool of Ideas (GNPI). The best ideas could be rewarded, the media could make them public.

13. *Introduce more future-directed discourses*, talking less of the past, more about a future with ways of handling conflict non-violently and creatively.

14. *Joint mourning*, as a manifestation of shared sorrow at what happened and promise to reject incitement to violence by leaders who may instrumentalize the situation.

15. *Celebrate Lebanon's small, vibrant, expanding civil society* which can cooperate with both the state and capital for the purpose of strengthening the country, without in any way rejecting the potentials of state and capital for peace.

(May 1997)

36. Euskadi: A TRANSCEND Perspective

1. *The right of the Basques to self-determination is recognized.* The definition of a 'Basque' could be by self-definition as a Basque, tied less to blood quantum or linguistic ability than to cultural identification (*fueros*, *fors*), and a sense of homeland.

2. The three *provincias* and four *provinces* are defined as a Basque entity, *Euskadia*, with no internal border, in the EU, while also continuing for the time being as parts of Spain and of France. Navarra is invited to join or associate itself.

3. *Euskadi* would be trilingual with *Euskara* as official language; Spanish and French also being administrative languages.

4. The present governing organs at the level of the *autonomía* and the *département* (Basque) would continue.

5. A Parliament (*fors*) would be elected for the *Euskadi* entity, with a government responsible to the assembly.

6. There should be assemblies for the Spaniards and the French living in *Euskadi*, with veto rights in matters relating to their patrimony, possibly also local courts and local policing.

7. The *Euskadi* entity could gradually attain a more international personality:

   a. a passport could gradually be recognized, within France/Spain, the EU, the world. Any citizen would, as before, be entitled to French or Spanish (EU) passports;

   b. like the passport, so with voting: as a transition any citizen could have one vote in *Euskadi* and one in Spain or France;

   c. the *euro* might have a *Euskadi* version with the same value (a *euskadi*?). To stimulate local economies a discount for deals in the *euskadi* might be considered;

   d. the budget for *Euskadi* would be based on the joint budget for the *autonomía* and the *département*, with some additional sources of revenue (duties, VAT) as for any EU country, and the same pattern of expenditure;

   e. special treaties would handle relations to Paris and Madrid, with review clauses/revision every N years ($N = 25$?); or when the inexhaustible right to self-determination is exercised;

   f. *Euskadi* would be demilitarized, renouncing the right to have a separate army. Spain and France would guarantee outer security in cooperation with OSCE and the UN;

   g. *Euskadi* would have observer status in the EU, other European organizations, and the UN (like the Swiss);

   h. *Euskadi* gradually develops its own foreign policy;

   i.   dual citizenship *de facto/de jure*, might be considered;

   j.   independence, federation, confederation, association etc. are all options implied by the right of self-determination;

   k. some redrawing of borders might be considered, using voting at the local level, like the Danish–German 1920 model.

  8. The process would at any time keep the outcome open.

  9. A reconciliation process has to be initiated.

10. The process calls for both elite and people participation. A process model: *Andorra*, now an independent UN member.

(May 1997)

37. Gibraltar and Ceuta-Melilla: A TRANSCEND Perspective

1. Whereas history and geography point to integration in Spain and Morocco, self-determination points to the status quo, as Spanish provinces and English colony. Madrid awkwardly changes argumentation from one side of the Mediterranean to the other.
2. The classical approach would be transfer through *conquest* if status quo is neither acceptable, nor sustainable; or acceptance of *adjudication*. Neither one, nor the other solves the problem.
3. When there are good arguments on both sides, some bargain, withdrawal, compromise or transcendence is called for.
4. *Bargain* might be possible if Rabat could offer London X in return for London handing Gibraltar back to Spain and Madrid handing Ceuta-Melilla to Rabat. Finding a good X won't be easy.
5. *Withdrawal*, waiting, 'the time isn't ripe', is an option with time limits: patience may run out. Non-violent marches of some magnitude on the three territories would be difficult to handle.
6. *Compromise* in the sense of dividing territory is also unavailable as an option: the territories are too small.
7. *Transcendence* is called for, and here are some formulas, not mutually exclusive, increasingly distant from status quo [A means return; B could lead to C, then to D, then to E]:

A. *Transfer of sovereignty*: the new Hong Kong formula; the rest unchanged for *X* years (*X* to be negotiated), like the lifetime of present inhabitants. They could have both new passports and territory passports, but no separate international identity.

B. *Joint sovereignty/condominium*: the old Andorra formula. London and Madrid would share administration of Gibraltar; Madrid and Rabat of Ceuta-Melilla. Inhabitants would choose between two passports and voting rights, and also have territory passport and rights; but no separate international identity.

C. *Separate entity in the European Union*, the EU formula. That formula is more available to Gibraltar than to Ceuta and Melilla given that Morocco is a non-member. Status unclear.

D. *Internationalization of the territories*, the Tangier formula, in line with current globalization trends, making all three free ports and exclusive economic zones, in dense cooperation with their neighbours; possibly as joint condominium. Status unclear.

E. *Independence in confederation,* the Nordic formula, with good transport facilities benefiting the Western Mediterranean region. Inhabitants would have passports indicating where they live, and have one local and one confederal vote. The three city-states would constitute an international entity, with membership in the UN. Investment from all over would be invited. The territories might be demilitarized with security guaranteed by the UN and/or UK/Spain/Morocco. As a *zone* or *archipelago of peace* the territories could also become a major convention/conference centre.

(July 1997)

38. Colombia: A TRANSCEND Perspective

Diagnosis I. Some mutually non-exclusive perspectives:

1. An extreme case of *poderes fácticos* (*cleros, latifundistas, militares*) in power, highly hierarchic and exploitative; hence violence from below (guerrillas, FARC/ELN) and counter-violence from above (*para-militares*), in shifting civil war fronts.
2. A two-party system carrying nineteenth-century agendas, incapable of absorbing into public space and debate social democracy, greenism, communism (guerrillas) and fascism (*para-militares*).
3. After the murder of Gaitán on 9 April 1948 a civil war (*'la violencia'*) killing voters for the other party, with impunity.
4. An extreme case of drug trafficking with Colombia as supplier; profits to key power-holders, along violent economic cycles.
5. Public space degenerates into an anarchic battlefield, with corruption, between the private spaces, described in 1–4.
6. US invasion gradually building up to use 4 to stop 1 above unless the Colombian government can do the job for them.

Diagnosis II. The last points can be deepened:

* An extreme case of dissolution of social norms-values-culture for public space behaviour, with impunity for murder: *anomie*.
* An extreme case of dissolution of social fabric, structure, of public space with fragmentation/atomization: *atomie*.

These conditions produce violence, corruption, drug chains (as producer/distributor; consumers in the US), sect-formation, with the violent groups as sects where people find guidance and social fabric. *In short, a total social crisis.*

Prognosis. The dialectic between extreme verticality, and extreme dissolution of public space, culture and structure, makes violence endemic; the prognosis could take violence one step further to the pandemic level. The military/police, being part of public space, are part of the problem rather than of the solution; facilitating rather than impeding the violence of the para-militaries in contexts 1–6 above. The next step may be outside intervention (the US in cooperation with some Latin American countries like using the base in neighbouring Ecuador), against left-wing guerrillas and *narcotráfico*. The outcome could be manifest (Vietnam) or latent (Bosnia today) quagmires.

Therapy. The remedies will depend on the diagnosis chosen. Any remedy based on only one factor is doomed to fail:

1. The *pact paradigm* between governments and guerrillas assumes cohesive cultures (to honour a promise) and structures (to be binding on others); under anomie/atomie this is not the case. In addition, the temptation to see a pact as an end, not as a means. *General point:* **more facts, less pacts**; less faith in pacts.
2. The *multi-party political paradigm* can be counteracted by making elections more ritualistic and parliament less relevant;
3. The *legal paradigm* (more state, police, more punishment) presupposes cohesive structures and cultures in public space;
4. The *war-on-drugs paradigm* is only meaningful if the whole economic cycle with the root causes of demand (anomie/atomie in consumer countries like the US) are effectively confronted (also including chemicals and air transport). One problem is how to find economic substitutes to make peace profitable. Certification of US efforts to remove US causes of drug demand?
5. The *institutional paradigm* intended to provide public space with efficiently and honestly operating institutions is counter-acted by anomie/atomie, including in dubious police/military.
6. The *Plan Colombia paradigm*, leaving the task increasingly to US/OAS, can create long-lasting dependency and colonization.

But this may be patchwork to build a state when the problem is to build a society because of the anomie/atomie complex:

- *Against anomie*: (re-)creating a sense of compelling norms and values; a very challenging task for Church (younger priests?), school and family as major agents of socialization in society. It is a question of (re-)creating the traffic rules in public space, starting with norms like 'Thou shalt not kill' and 'Thou shalt not steal' and values of solidarity with the poor, against the egoistic cost-benefit analysis and materialist individualism of economism. Moral social and world leadership badly needed.
- *Against atomie*: (re-)creating social fabric in public space, weaving a tight web of criss-crossing NGOs of many types, with multiple memberships, not forgetting kinship, friends, workshop and worship, serving as conduits for norms of solidarity. *Then*:

1. Increase the *capacity for handling conflicts* at all social levels, expanding conflict repertoires, using Church, school and

television series once a week for years to combat conflict illiteracy.

2. *Empower women and young people* as conflict/peace workers, training them as mediators (by an *Escuela de Alto Gobierno?*)
3. Introduce *peace and conflict education* in schools, making texts with 50–100 stories of successful non-violent and creative conflict handling available as reference points throughout life.
4. Introduce *peace journalism* in the media, focusing on root conflicts and possible outcomes/processes, less on the violent meta-conflict and who is winning; more on people, less on elites.
5. Build disarmed *peace zones* based on confederations of municipalities and the points mentioned above; upgrade the zones by adding more points; international protection of the zones.
6. For *international peace keeping, with neighbouring countries helping* use Sun Tzu, not Clausewitz military doctrines, police methods, non-violence and mediation; let many of them be women.
7. *'Truth and reconciliation'* along South African rather than Central American lines, using the courts, Church, psychology, television.
8. Conduct business (like coffee) along modern lines with *much higher return to the workers/producers,* cutting out middlemen.
9. Establish *economies of subsistence* (micro-credits, adequate technology, cooperatives, etc.), alongside the growth economy.
10. *Attack pathologies in Colombian culture,* such as machismo and cult of violence, head-on; as part of anti-anomie struggle.
11. Create higher levels of internal security by *retraining police and military for all the tasks mentioned above.*
12. *Use human rights, including the economic, social and cultural rights, as moral guidelines for a vibrant democracy.*

All these to be done parallel/synchronically, not one after the other. (June 1998)

39. Inter-Class Conflict/Globalization: A TRANSCEND Perspective

Diagnosis. In a world where *358 billionaires have more assets than half of humanity* (UNDP), the metaphor 'market' should be questioned. The billionaires (and others) are not only buying and selling, they are also deciding products and factor profiles, thereby changing the life of billions of people (like downsizing through automation).

Globalization means global sharing of the positive and negative consequences of economic growth, with increasing disappearance of national markets, increasing world-wide disparity, and above all increasing displacement of people as ecological, economic, political, military and cultural refugees (one billion on the move by the year 2030? with hardened borders around rich countries). With the mobility (outplacing) of entire companies in search of cheap labour and lower or negative taxes (incentives), state revenues will decrease in many countries.

Privatization takes this one step further by depriving the state also of revenue-creating companies. Ever-increasing productivity leads to downsizing (unemployment) or reduction of working hours (contract). If 1.7 billion earn less than one dollar a day and three billion less than two dollars, we get oversupply/overproduction relative to demand/consumption (80 million cars chasing 60 million buyers). Ever-increasing top–bottom disparity leads to more short-term portfolio investment in search of profit on the top, and more basic needs in search of satisfaction at the bottom, leading to underconsumption at the bottom of use products, and eventually to increasing misery.

The IMF functions like a doctor with only one medicine: increase company autonomy, of the state (privatization, lower taxes, devaluation), of the workers (labour flexibility, contract work), of the country (repatriation of profit), of the public (no subsidies for basic needs, no taxes on luxury products). Credit is made available to such unscrupulous companies, leading to more disparity, misery, free speculation capital and dependence. The net result is *sacrifice of people at the bottom*.

Prognosis. As a result of all of this the crises become self-sustaining, the system will move from one crisis to the other, showing up where the system is weakest, with attention to symptom therapy: preventing crashes on the stock exchanges by building in delays to prevent panics, bailing out foreign firms. A major crash, recession and depression are all highly likely.

Therapy. Massive conflicts call for massive remedies:

- *The reinvention of local authorities*: a major task of a local authority should be to coordinate production for basic needs on a local basis (or in a confederation of LAs) to guarantee that basic needs are met, to internalize externalities and to reduce pollution due to transportation and other factors.
- *The reinvention of the state*: a major task of the state is to coordinate the task of production of normal/luxury goods on a state basis (or in an confederation of states), internalize the externalities, reduce pollution and to be a redistributive agent.
- *The reinvention of the company*: companies have to assume social responsibility, and be rewarded and punished accordingly.
- *The reinvention of civil society*: consumer consciousness must lead to organized preference and organized boycott of companies.
- *The reinvention of the media*: the media should be liberated from corporate interests and state interests and censorship.
- *The invention of global governance*, which would include massive taxation of speculation, and basic needs guarantees for humankind as *global human rights for global citizens*.

(May 1998)

40. Inter-Generation Conflict and Sustainability: A TRANSCEND Perspective

Diagnosis. The conflict between generations is diachronic, through time. Most conflicts are synchronic, and so are the theory and practice of conflicts. Each generation has a goal: its own livelihood. Each generation wants by definition to satisfy its own basic needs. The conflict is obvious: any generation (or, rather, cohort) may compromise the livelihood of succeeding generations through its demand/greed. Concretely:

- *economically*, by polluting and depleting the environment;
- *militarily*, by perpetuating violence through trauma and glory;
- *politically*, by untransformed conflicts and irreversible acts;
- *culturally*, by accepting cultures with such consequences.

The concept of sustainability goes beyond the narrow economic and ecological discourse to a general discourse of handing over a world in good shape, with the environment intact (diverse, symbiotic); people less traumatized by violence and deformed by wishes to prevail through violence; conflicts transformed so they can be handled non-violently and creatively, not blocked by irreversible decisions; and a world culture with that message. Reconciliation processes would be significant in that context.

Prognosis. However, in the world as a whole pollution and depletion are increasing, violence is increasing, the wisdom with which conflicts are handled may be decreasing, and world cultures counteracting these trends are marginalized. The burden of unprocessed problems handed over from one generation to the next is increasing with one exception: better material livelihood for the upper section of humanity. The prognosis is increased violence, mass migration to unsettled areas; the Bible's four horsemen of the Apocalypse: conquest, war, famine, pestilence.

Therapy. What is the therapy for extreme generational egoism and lack of inter-generational solidarity, short time perspectives compromising the next generations' livelihood?

The American Indian adage 'think through the consequences of your acts for the coming seven generations' is excellent, and points to what today is known as future studies. But that will have to be done far beyond the narrow time horizon for most studies of that kind. Moreover, such studies may also serve as a pretext for recklessness, identifying carrying capacities that makes one think that the world is robust enough for an extra load. To be on the safe side insight in tomorrow must be tied to an ethics of diachronic solidarity valid today.

One way of training would be to start with households (*oikos*) with 3–4 generations living close together and people having future generations so near that the solidarity becomes a necessity of daily life. Solidarity would also apply backwards to parents, grandparents, etc., easily forgotten in a one-sided focus on prospective solidarity. Depositing older generations in old age ghettos is incompatible with retrospective solidarity.

Another approach would be to tilt the balance of power in society, and world society, in the direction of categories so far known to be wiser in the sense of being more holistic, more global, more basic needs oriented, with more time perspective. That would point to the older generation, and to women. Women are today getting into and the older generation out of power; the latter trend should be reversed. Beyond and above that we would think in terms of massive education campaigns mobilizing formal and informal education and religious organizations to propagate intergenerational solidarity. (March 1999)

41. Afghanistan: A TRANSCEND Perspective

Diagnosis. The mountains protecting Afghanistan against foreigners, like England and Russia fighting for control (English troops were massacred in Kabul in 1842 leaving only one survivor to tell the story) also divide the country in autonomous parts. The king was overthrown in 1972, followed by a communist coup in 1978, followed by Soviet invasion December 1979 leading to their Vietnam. Gorbachev initiated the withdrawal of troops in 1986, a major factor ending the Cold War. Then came the *Mujahedin* (partly a US construction) and their fight for power, followed by the *Taliban* (partly a Pakistan construction) and their fight for power. Twenty-three years of war have left Afghanistan destitute, the infrastructure partly destroyed, with a war between the Taliban supported by Pakistan, Saudi Arabia, the Emirates, and the Northern Alliance of some nationalities supported by the US, Russia, China, Iran (and India?, the EU?). The Shanghai Alliance of China, Russia and four Central Asian republics is against Islamic militancy, but also aims at trade, investment and stronger security ties in general (against the US?)

Afghanistan is inserted in complex conflict formations:

- the US pincer move expanding NATO eastward and AMPO westward creates a strong Russia–China bond with ties to India–Iran–Iraq;
- the ongoing India–China conflict;
- the ongoing India–Pakistan conflict, particularly over Kashmir;
- the struggle for control over Central Asian oil and pipelines;
- the conflicts with Islamic revival/militancy/fundamentalism;
- UN sanctions because of one member's problem with one person.

Prognosis. Afghanistan will continue to be a battlefield among external powers and their allies among Afghan fractions, at the expense of the Afghan people. The 'humanitarian intervention for US bases' scenario is likely. This is because Afghanistan is weak, not militarily, but fragmented, dependent on foreign aid, with divisive identities, and neighbour quarrels.

Therapy. A four-tier peace policy for Afghanistan includes:

- *A strong Afghan people* with the basic needs for survival, well-being, freedom and identity satisfied through an end to war;

food, housing, clothing, health and education for all; the freedom to choose among competing political actors; and the religious and linguistic identities that are truly theirs.

- A basic needs-oriented Afghanistan must have *a broadly based central government* – after a cease-fire with no winner in the present war – open to, for instance, federal possibilities. A well-planned *Loya Jirga* might provide legitimacy for broadness.

- *A Central-South Asian Community* capable of resisting external pressure must be culturally, economically, politically strong. Cultural strength would derive from an Islam beyond Sunni–Shia divides; economic strength from regional self-reliance; political strength from a community – or Organization for Security and Cooperation in Central-South Asia (OSCCSA) – with the five Central Asian republics, Iran and Pakistan (not more 'impossible' than the European Community was in the late 1940s).

- A UN Security Council with no Muslim but four Christian and a Confucian country as veto powers should seek *cooperation with the Organization of the Islamic Conference (OIC)* for agendas of this type, together with a broadly based Afghan government.

(February 2001)

42. Angola Civil War: A TRANSCEND Perspective

Diagnosis. The current war is largely resource-driven with roots in ethnic, colonial and Cold War conflicts. Patronage structures or autocracies, run by small oligarchies with little or no people participation, provide the central organization on each of the two main sides. Support from the 'international community' is focused on the government side, with a prohibition for contact with the opposition UNITA party, though some evidence exists of CIA support for both sides. Certain controlling interests within each of the major internal and external parties profit from the current war economy. The lack of governance, regulation and taxation results in corruption, high crime rates (including by the police), poverty, empty schools and the spread of infectious diseases.

UNICEF calls Angola the worst country in the world in which to be a child.

The electoral system is modelled on the US two-party system, and very ill-matched to the complexities of Angolan society. Added to this come the UN sanctions, partially effective, partially not, and the landmine situation, globally the highest number in concentration.

Prognosis. Unless there is a break in the political stalemate, the war economy is likely to maintain violence at various levels of intensity for decades. Military resources will finance military expenditures, enriching elites in Angola and in the International Community. Impoverishment will continue, with nutrition, health care and education continuing at substandard levels. In 10–15 years the majority of teachers will have passed on or be too old to teach, resulting in a need to begin basic education from zero. The 'international community' is likely to oppose the substantial action necessary to change the situation by pointing to the lack of political will among the Angolan parties, and stating that the conflict is not 'ripe' for a peace process. Regardless of possible changes of presidential candidate from the government side, the 'winner-take-all' election will serve only to maintain the current conflict situation.

Therapy. Complexity of conflict must be met with complexity of strategic peace confrontation. The political stalemate should be broken through a combination of (1) quiet, informal diplomacy; (2) humanitarian cease-fire for polio eradication; and (3) public information on the wealth accrual in Angolan and international elites by exploiting opportunities in the war economy. Reinvention of the public sphere should include a substantive dialogue to bring about a new electoral system with power sharing more suitable to the Angolan socio-political landscape. Use of natural resources should be structured in accordance with Angola's commitment as a signatory of the International Covenant on Economic, Social and Cultural Rights, with special reference to Article 2. War diamonds and war oil should be monitored and (to the extent possible) traced, with diamonds addressed in the market place and oil by shareholder action. Civil society can be empowered through the creation of zones of peace with resource-sharing regimes in local municipalities. The Catholic Church, as a trusted party, should play a key role in the peacemaking and reconciliation process. (September 2001)

43. The Sami Nation: A TRANSCEND Perspective

Diagnosis. The traditional Sami territory consists of the northern parts of Finland, Sweden, Norway and the northwestern part of Russia. From before the illegal inclusion of their territories by kings and tsars into the four countries, the culture of the Sami people has been systematically destroyed. Superior violent means have been used to eradicate their religion, destroy their traditional communities, exploit the natural resources, impose Christianity, discredit their identity, utilize the population as labour force and prevent any organized resistance. When the uprising in Kautokeino took place in 1854 two leaders were sentenced to death by the Supreme Court. Their crime was to 'with violence and force have worked to eliminate all natural barriers between themselves and the Superiors and that way enforce an equality, which would have destroyed all Civilisation'. Their skulls were brought to University of Oslo for 'scientific studies of lower races' and were not returned for a decent burial until 150 years later.

The exploitations of natural resources are still going on in all four countries without any compensation. The Sami people are not heard when they claim their rights to territory, hunting, natural resources, granted them according to ILO convention 169.

Prognosis. The Sami culture, territory and resources will continue to be exploited by the four occupying states, militaries and international companies. Their culture will be further eroded and end up as exotic items in museums and for exhibitions. A growing number of conscious and determined young Samis will take up violent means in order to put their case on the political agenda in the four states. Secret groups doing spectacular actions could well be found attractive by others and easily recruit more people.

Therapy. A commission of researchers from different disciplines, appointed by UNESCO and the Unrepresented Nations and Peoples' Organization (UNPO) to document all atrocities committed against the Sami peoples since the states started to take control over their territories. The results shall be made public in many ways and the conclusions be a part of the curriculum in schools.

Compensation for abuses of human rights and the exploitation of natural resources shall be invested in a foundation for empowerment of Sami cultures and work for transforming conflicts between Samis and other people living in traditional Sami areas.

Sami parliaments should be established in all four states with a right to veto any exploitation of natural resources within their traditional territories. This should include waterfalls, mining, fishing, oil and gas resources on land, in rivers as well as in the Barents Sea and the respective sectors of the North Atlantic. A group of representatives from the Sami Parliaments, the Nordic Council and OSCE should be set up to monitor the implementation of the veto right and handle conflicts of interpretation.

All military installations and training fields must be removed from the Sami territory and no Samis conscripted.

Respect for all Human Rights of Samis within each of the countries they are living today, with increasing autonomy, opening for the creation of a confederation of Sami autonomies linking Samis in the four countries in which they are living today.

44. The Christians and the Heathens: A TRANSCEND Perspective

Diagnosis. Much of the legitimization underlying such major atrocities as Christian (later called 'Western') conquest (under the name of 'discovery'), colonialism, and imperialism can be found in the papal bull *Inter Caetera* of 4 May 1493 and related documents. It starts praising the 'very dear son/daughter in Christ', *los reyes católicos*, Ferdinand and Isabella (Alexander was Spanish) for spreading the Christian religion so 'that barbarous nations be overthrown and brought to the faith':

> as witnessed with so much glory to the Divine Name in your recovery of the kingdom of Granada from the yoke of the Saracens – you chose our beloved son, Christopher Columbus – to make diligent quest for these remote and unknown mainlands and islands through the sea, where hitherto no one had sailed; and discovered certain very remote islands and even mainlands that hitherto had not been discovered wherein dwell very many peoples living in peace – going unclothed and not eating flesh – disposed to embrace the Catholic faith and be trained in good morals.
>
> ... built a fortress fairly equipped, wherein he has stationed in garrison certain Christians, companions of his, who are to make search for other remote and unknown islands and mainlands. In the islands and countries already discovered are found gold, spices, and very many other precious things ... bring under your sway the said mainlands and islands with their residents and inhabitants and ... bring them to the Catholic World Orders: Old and New faith.

Whereupon he, Alexander VI, assigns to *los reyes catolicos*

> and your heirs and successors, kings of Castile and Leon, forever all rights, jurisdictions, and appurtenances, all islands and mainlands, found and to be found, discovered and to be discovered; – we appoint you lords of them with full and free power *and jurisdiction of every kind* [italics ours].
>
> Let no one, therefore, infringe, or with rash boldness contravene, this our recommendation, exhortation, requisition, gift, grant, assignment, constitution, deputation, decree, mandate, prohibition and will. Should anyone presume to

attempt this, be it known to him that he will incur the wrath of Almighty God and of the blessed apostles Peter and Paul.

In short: the Earth belongs to God, the Pope administers God's will, and delegates to the kings of Spain *all jurisdiction*. The result: legitimation of the hideous reality of colonialism.

Prognosis. As pointed out by Steven T. Newcomb in 'The Evidence of Christian Nationalism in Federal Indian Law: The Doctrine of Discovery', *Review of Law & Social Change*, No. 2 (1993), pp. 303–41, *theology* (Jahveh in *Psalms* 2:8 tells his chosen people through King David: 'I shall give to thee the heathen for thine inheritance, and the uttermost part of the earth for thy possession') becomes *law of the land* ('the principle declared in the fifteenth century as the law of Christendom, that discovery gave title to *assume sovereignty over, and to govern the unconverted natives* of Africa, Asia and North and South America'; Tennessee Supreme Court 1835, 'on the right to coerce obedience').

Therapy. If the violence and the conflicts engendered by it are legitimized by a document, then it is on the revocation of that document that peace and conflict transformation can be built. The papal bull must become as well known as many of its fatal consequences. That revocation should come from the highest Vatican quarters as declarations that annul *Inter Caetera*, and explicitly so, and make it a Christian duty to uproot this type of thinking. (September 2000)

45. The US, the West and the Rest:
A TRANSCEND Perspective

Diagnosis. The world will never be the same again after the terrible attack on the economic US, the military US and on human beings like all of us on 11 September 2001. We embrace the victims of the violence, as with all violence, in profound grief, and express our hope that those responsible will be brought to justice. Violence at this level can be explained only by a very high level of dehumanization of the victims in the minds of the aggressors, often due to a very deep level of unresolved basic conflict. The word 'terrorism' describes the tactics, but like 'state terrorism' only portrays the perpetrator as evil, satanic, and does not go to the roots of the conflict.

The symbolism of targets (the World Trade Center, the Pentagon) and the non-targets (the Capitol or White House) reads like a retaliation for US use of economic power against poor people and poor countries and US use of military power against defenceless people. This calls to mind the 230 or so US military interventions abroad, the near-extermination of native Americans, slavery, the CIA's responsibility for six million killed between 1947 and 1987 according to CIA dissidents, and the 100,000 dying daily at the bottom of an economic system identified by many with US economic, military and political power. Given the millions of victims, not thousands, it has to be expected that this will generate a desire for retaliation somewhere, some time.

The basic dividing line in this conflict is class – of countries and of people. It is not civilization, although the US's sense of mission, of 'manifest destiny', and the Islamic sense of righteousness are parts of it. Right now the confrontations seems to be between the US/West and Arabs/Muslims. But this may simply be because the latter possess more intention and capability than other victims of the enormous US/West violence – direct, structural and cultural – since the Second World War. We should neither underestimate the extent of solidarity in the 'Rest' (of the world), nor the solidarity of the West (with Japan), the world upper class. Because of the strength of these two camps it is crucial to build even stronger solidarity with all victims, everywhere.

In placing the horrendous attack on the US in the context of a cycle of retaliation for US aggression, leading to US retaliation for that retaliation and so on and so forth, there is no element of justification, no excuse, no guilt attribution. There is only deep regret that such chains of violence and retaliation also are parts of human reality. That may also lead us to a desire to break that vicious spiral. But bombing terrorist bases and the countries that host terrorists may also provoke even more retaliation to avenge that violence, and many people may become 'martyrs'.

Prognosis. With talk of crusades from the US, and of the fourth stage of *jihad*, holy war, from Islamic quarters, the world may be heading for the largest violent encounter ever. The first *jihad*, against the Crusades of 1095–1291 lasted 196 years; the Muslims won. The second *jihad*, against Israel, is undecided so far. The third *jihad*, against communism in Afghanistan, ended with Muslim victory, Soviet withdrawal and ultimate collapse. Many of the world's 1.2 billion Muslims, of whom about 3 million live in the US, are willing to die for their beliefs, idolizing martyrdom, expecting to earn a place in paradise.

Therapy. To prevent a slide into a large war with enormous, widespread suffering, the US, everybody, should not rush to action. We need deep self-reflection, identifying the conflicts, the issues, solving them, reconciliation. Dialogue and global education to understand how others think, and to respect other cultures, not debate to defeat others with stronger arguments, can lead the way toward healing and closure.

The enormous global inequality, which denies basic needs to billions while they see a privileged few indulge in luxury and waste, must be overcome, through a peaceful, cooperative world economic system. This will hardly change the mind of terrorist leaders, but will deprive them of the fertile soil of frustrated and angry young people who feel they have nothing to lose, from which they can easily recruit eager followers.

All clergy – Christian and Muslim – need to stress that killing innocent civilians is wrong, blasphemous.

Outside support and the supply of arms to autocratic regimes must stop. People who grow up in a democratic culture – where they can not only vote, but also frequently express their ideas and grievances and are heard, where governments truly represent their people's aspirations – rarely resort to violence. But if all opportunities for change by peaceful means are denied, some feel tempted to resort to violence.

The prolonged wars in the Middle East and many other Third World regions have bred a culture of violence. Transcending those conflicts, finding solutions that bring justice to all parties, is an essential component of a successful strategy against terrorism.

To exit from the cycle of retaliation, the US/West should:

1. Remove all US troops from Arabia, Islam's holy land.
2. Lift the sanctions on Iraq, which hurt mostly children.
3. Accept President Khatami's invitation for an open dialogue.

4. Set up a UN trusteeship in Afghanistan, not US military bases.
5. Set up globalization-free zones in places where people die from globalization because they cannot afford to buy from the market – analogous to the Kyoto Protocol's exemptions for the Third World – and a Marshall-type Plan for the poorest areas of the world, strengthening the local, informal economy with a view to basic needs satisfaction for all.
6. *Reconciliation*: learn from the German approach to the 18 countries they conquered and the two nations they tried to exterminate, the Jews and the Sinta/Roma. Today Germany has reasonable relations with all, and a key element went beyond apologies and compensation to including rewriting of textbooks.

Those who oppose US hegemony should refrain from violence and hold massive, totally non-violent demonstrations, present the facts, and ask for dialogue between people and governments. Washington is sensitive to its own people, and also to allied governments. Like for the cases of slavery and colonialism, massive global injustice is not a problem of force, but a moral problem. Here the underdogs have the upper hand, the more so the more non-violently they conduct the struggle.

We also need mediation by wise and decent people – like Jimmy Carter, Fredrik de Klerk, Nelson Mandela, or the pope. The world needs all the decent, good men and women, right now.

Governments in the West, and also in the South, cannot be relied upon to do this; they are too tied to the US and also afraid of incurring US wrath. But people can, global civil society. What is needed as soon as humanly possible is a massive peace movement, this time North–South. It worked last time, East–West. The future of the world is more than ever in the hands of the only source of legitimacy: people everywhere.

Notes

Chapter 1.1

1. This chapter elaborates on a presentation to the 47th Pugwash Conference on Science and World Affairs, in Lillehammer, Norway, August 1997.
2. John A. Vasquez, *The War Puzzle*, Cambridge: Cambridge University Press Cambridge Studies in International Relations, 1993.
3. Similar characteristics are found in other cultures; what is remarkable in the European–North American case is their culture-defining dominance and the extent to which this ordering of priorities was diffused through colonialism, imperialism and the industrial and technological revolutions of the nineteenth and twentieth centuries.
4. Perhaps the most notable early pioneer in the field was Professor Anatol Rapoport. See, for example, his 'Limits of Individual Rationality', in A. Rapoport, *Origins of Violence*, New York: Paragon, 1989. Cf. also the BBC film *Nice Guys Finish First*, London, 1986.
5. Olof Palme, Independent Commission on Disarmament and Security Issues, *Common Security: A Blueprint for Survival*, New York: Simon and Schuster, 1982.
6. For an in-depth exploration, see C.G. Jacobsen, 'Russia–China: the New "'Strategic Partnership"'', in *European Security*, Autumn 1998; and this volume, chapter 2.2.
7. Including C.G. Jacobsen, *The New World Order's Defining Crises: The Clash of Promise and Essence*, Aldershot: Dartmouth, 1996; and Noam Chomsky, *World Orders Old and New*, New York: Columbia University Press, 1996.
8. Mary B. Anderson, *Do No Harm: Supporting Local Capacities for Peace through Aid*, Cambridge: The Collaborative for Development Action, Inc., 1996.
9. Louis Kriesberg, *Constructive Conflicts: From Escalation to Resolution*, Maryland and Oxford: Rowman & Littlefield, 1998; John Paul Lederach, *Building Peace: Sustainable Reconciliation in Divided Societies*, Washington, D.C.: United States Institute of Peace Press, 1997.
10. See their TFF PressInfo reports, available through the internet at <TFF@transnational.org> or visit <www.transnational.org>.
11. A network of peace researchers and peace workers (*satyagrahi*) from conflict areas around the world working to mobilize and empower local capacities for active peace work; see <www.globalsolidarity.org>.
12. Johan Galtung, *Conflict Transformation by Peaceful Means (The Transcend Method)*, New York: UN Disaster Management Training Programme, 1998 (also available in French, Spanish, Russian, Arabic and Chinese). This is in fact the 'mini-version'; the 'maxi-version'

was published in 1999: for further information, see TRANSCEND web-site: <www.transcend.org>. Johan Galtung, *Peace by Peaceful Means: Peace and Conflict, Development and Civilization*, London, Thousand Oaks and New Delhi: Sage, 1996.

13. See, for example, *Responding to Conflict, Annual Review*, <http://www.respond.org/annual_review.html>.

14. See *The Peace Journalism Option*, Taplow Court Conflict & Peace Courses, January 1988.

15. General Lewis Mackenzie, *Peacekeeper: The Road to Sarajevo*, Vancouver: Douglas, 1993.

16. See, for example, 'Massive Vote-rigging Taints Bosnia Election', *Guardian Weekly*, 29 September 1996.

17. For elaboration, see C.G. Jacobsen, 'Yugoslavia's Successor Wars Reviewed: The Real Lessons for a Not-So-New World Order', *South Slav Journal*, London, Summer 1997; *Review of International Affairs*, Belgrade, July–August 1997; and *The New World Order's Defining Crises*.

18. Noam Chomsky, *Necessary Illusions*, London: Pluto Press, 1993, and *World Orders Old and New*, New York: Columbia University Press, 1994 and (updated) 1996.

19. Jacobsen, 'The Gulf War Revisited: New World Order – or Old?', in *The New World Order's Defining Crises*, pp. 25–34.

20. Chomsky, 'Epilogue: Middle East Diplomacy', in *World Orders Old and New*, pp. 272–98; see also Norman G. Finkelstein, 'Whither the Peace Process?', *New Left Review*, no. 218, 1996.

21. Jacobsen, 'Yugoslavia's Successor Wars', pp. 36–57.

22. Ironically (and perhaps tellingly) those who selectively ascribed extremist black/white judgements and epithets had themselves perpetrated some of history's worst horrors, through colonialism, imperialism, genocides (US policy procured the deaths of more than three times as many Native American peoples as did Nazi death camps; Spanish and others' 'New' or 'heathen' world horrors were no less bestial), deep-seated racism (including, notably, Israeli official and dominant public postures towards Palestinians), sexism, and drives towards global cultural, economic and military domination (Iraqi deaths since 1991: 1.8 million).

23. See, for example, coverage in *The Economist*, 19 April 1997, p. 54.

24. See M.B. Fielden, 'The Geopolitics of Aid: The Provision and Termination of Aid to Afghan Refugees In North Westfrontier Provice, Pakistan', *Political Geography*, Vol. 17, No. 4 (n.d.), pp. 459–87.

25. See A. Mitic, 'The Impact of the Media on Preventive Diplomacy: Three Cases from the Yugoslav Conflict', MA research essay, Norman Paterson School of International Affairs, Carleton University, Ottawa, August 1997; and J. Radosavljevic, 'Reflecting Humanitarian Principles in Complex Humanitarian Emergencies: Case Studies of UNHCR and Oxfam in the Former Yugoslavia', MA research essay. NPSIA, Carleton University, Ottawa, October 1997.

26. This requirement is increasingly accepted; it is, for example, the central principle of the above-mentioned International

Correspondence League, ICL/Praxis for Peace, the new global network of peace researchers and practitioners founded by Kai Frithjof Brand-Jacobsen and Johan Galtung (in 1996) to strengthen active peace work and empower groups and individuals to promote peace through the development of creative and non-violent alternatives to war.

27. The proposals were presented and developed in lectures and seminars, at Tbilisi State University (3 and 4 June 1997), Yerevan State University (7 June 1997) and the private Khazar University in Baku (9 June 1997), at a closed VERTIC-sponsored workshop on Georgia–Abkhaz relations (Tbilisi, 6 June 1997), at a press conference at the Caucasian Institute for Peace, Democracy and Development (Tbilisi, 11 June 1997), and to senior Caucasian government officials and advisers.

28. See, for example, Johan Galtung's 'Northern Ireland: A Transcend Perspective on Outcome and Process', presented to and available from the Glencree Centre for Reconciliation, Ireland, 23 August 1997; and his earlier 'Ecuador and Peru: A Transcend Perspective', available from Transcend web-site at <www.transcend.org>.

29. For elaboration on Russian–Chinese border issues and their resolution, see Jacobsen, 'Russia–China ...'.

30. *The Ottawa Citizen*/Southam Press (with Associated Press files), 21 January 1999.

31. *Le Monde Diplomatique*, May 1999; see also TFF's web-site, at <www.transnational.org> and TRANSCEND's, at <www.transcend.org>.

32. See 'War in the Balkans' analyses, in *Le Monde Diplomatique/Guardian Weekly*, May 1999.

33. 'End "Murderous Bombing"': Pope, Orthodox Leader', *The Ottawa Citizen*, 9 May 1999.

34. James Bissett, 'NATO's Brute Force an Imbecilic Policy', *The Ottawa Citizen*, 17 April 1999.

35. See, for example, 'US Trained Butchers of East Timor', *Guardian Weekly*, 23–29 September 1999; and 'Deathly Silence of the Diplomats', *Guardian Weekly*, 30 October 1994.

36. C.G. Jacobsen, 'Is NATO Prepared to Give Serbia its Heritage Pearls?', *The Globe and Mail* (Toronto), 26 April 1999.

Chapter 1.2

1. In 1948 Israel dealt with the local Arab population through expulsion. By the time of the 1967 war, when Israel conquered the West Bank and Gaza Strip (as well as the Sinai and Golan Heights), expulsion was no longer an option. Instead, encirclement became the toll of Israeli policy, appropriating as much of the resources (especially water) and land as possible while confining the Arab population to reserves. As Finkelstein points out, this was 'the essence of the operative framework of the Oslo process, allowing Israel to retain roughly half the West Bank'. Norman Finkelstein, *Securing*

Occupation: The Real Meaning of the Wye River Memorandum, <normanfinkelstein.com/id66.htm<.

2. At this point leading Israeli officials considered the prospect of full withdrawal. The challenge to Israeli occupation, however, soon receded. As the momentum of the *Intifada* abated, a series of events cascaded to weaken the position of any future Palestinian negotiators. With the Gulf War, implosion of the Soviet Union, open alignment of Arab states with the US and the PLO's declining fortunes, Israel was relieved of the pressure which it had been experiencing and the Palestinians were severely weakened.

3. It was only with Benjamin Netanyahu that this process was made complete. 'By tenaciously claiming that Israel had title to all and Palestinians none of the West Bank, Netanyahu turned *any* withdrawal into an Israeli concession. Who could then expect Israel to "give away" more than 50 per cent of "its" land for peace? Before Netanyahu, full withdrawal in exchange for full peace was the legitimate compromise, Labour's partial withdrawal the illegitimate one; after Netanyahu, partial withdrawal in exchange for full peace became the legitimate compromise, zero withdrawal the illegitimate one. Redefining the poles of the debate with his pugnacious theatrics, Netanyahu has effectively legitimized the Labour Party's rejectionist stance, in the process also managing to "lower," as he put it, "the level of Palestinian expectations". Apart from "extremists", no one any longer speaks about full withdrawal, Indeed, the call for full withdrawal is now equated with the call for zero withdrawal, as pundits condemn the "extremists on both sides".' Finkelstein, *Securing Occupation.*

4. Unless specified otherwise, all statistics and figures referred to in this section are taken from Finkelstein, *Securing Occupation.* A wide range of corroborating evidence and information can be found in the numerous reports of humanitarian organizations and other NGOs operating in the region.

5. Finkelstein, *Securing Occupation.*

6. Noam Chomsky, 'The Middle East Settlement', in *Perspective on Power: Reflections on Human Nature and the Social Order,* Montreal, New York and London: Black Rose Books, 1997, p. 151.

7. See Kai Frithjof Brand-Jacobsen, 'Israel-Palestine: The Need for a Just Peace', 18 October 2000, <www.transcend.org>.

8. See Carl G. Jacobsen with Kai Frithjof-Jacobsen, 'Peacemaking as Realpolitik', chapter 1.1 in this volume.

9. 'The share-out of aid to Bosnia-Herzegovina in 1995/96, with 98 per cent going to the Muslim-Croat Federation, while the largest number of refugees and people in extreme need for basic health care, shelter, and food were in Republika Srpska, which received less than 2 per cent of all international humanitarian development aid, can be seen as a direct result of the "international community's" desire to "punish" the Serbs for their role in the war. As with the sanctions against Iraq, however, the effect of this "punishment" has been an aggravation of the suffering of the people without noticeably affecting the position of the leaders ... Note also: there exists an aid divide

within Republika Srpska, between the east, perceived as being loyal to Karadzic, and the west, identified as more "pro-Western" under Biljana Plavsic (then President of Republika Srpska). Though the *total* number of aid organizations operating in Republika Srpska is still small, the number operating outside the Prijedor/Banja Luka/Doboj region (all in western RS), is infinitesimal, made up mainly of the ICRC/IFRC and some UN agencies.' From Kai Frithjof Brand-Jacobsen, *The Dynamics of War and Peace*, an ICL Report, Ottawa, 1997, p. 18.

10. 'Rambouillet – Imperialism in Disguise', TFF PressInfo No. 55, 16 February 1999, available from <tff@transnational.org>.

11. Ibid.

12. Figures and information provided by the 'Peace Action: End the War Campaign', July 1999.

13. Cf. Barnet Rubin, *The Search for Peace in Afghanistan: From Buffer State to Failed State*, New Haven: Yale University Press, 1995, pp. 97–8.

14. D. Cordovez and S. Harrison, *Out of Afghanistan: The Inside Story of the Soviet Withdrawal*, Oxford: Oxford University Press, 1995, pp. 202, 250.

15. See John Paul Lederach, 'Conflict Transformation in Protracted Internal Crises: The Case for a Comprehensive framework', pp. 215–18 in K. Rupesinghe, ed., *Conflict Transformation*, New York: St. Martin's Press, 1995; see also Lederach's superb *Building Peace: Sustainable Reconciliation in Divided Societies*, Washington, DC: USIP, 1997.

16. For an excellent discussion, see Johan Galtung and Finn Tschudi, this volume, chapter 1.7.

17. See Mohamed Suliman, ed., *Ecology, Politics and Violent Conflict*, London and New York: Zed Books, 1999, p. v.

18. Though this may be more directly true of Catholicism, there are reasons for including it here under Protestantism.

Chapter 1.3

1. Was the fourth plane heading for the CIA in Langley, Virginia? We do not know, but a 'CIA station was lost in attack on Twin Towers' (headline, *International Herald Tribune*, 6 November 2001). 'The station was a base of operations to spy on and recruit foreign diplomats who were stationed at the United Nations' – a statement that should cause an outcry of demands for getting the UN out of the US as soon as possible.

2. The 11 September 2001 attack was massive political violence against people and might be referred to as fascist in content. The 11 September 1973 attack was also political, and also criminal, being directed against a democratically elected regime, and might be referred to as fascist ideologically (Kissinger as Secretary of State felt that the US 'cannot stand by and watch a people voting itself into communism').

3. This suicide form of attack is usually seen as a way of delivering a bomb right on target, which certainly is a valid view. But it could also,

in addition, be seen as a way of committing suicide for people deeply steeped in despair, like those who have suffered or been close to Palestinian refugee camps for three generations. This makes the 'kamikaze' less apt as a metaphor, a comment that also applies to the *tora, tora, tora* attack on Pearl Harbor of 7 December 1941, extremely precise ('surgical', 'smart') with almost no civilian losses ('collateral damage').

4. Sven Lindqvist, of *Exterminate All the Brutes* fame, traces the theme back to the Italian bombing of Arab civilians in the desert of Tripoli in 1911 – in his *A History of Bombing*, London: Granta, 2001. The Italian air command commented that the bombs had a 'wonderful effect on the morale of the Arabs'.

The British bombed Arab towns and villages in Egypt, Iraq, Jordan, Iran and Afghanistan in 1915–20 (gas against civilians, in Iraq, in 1922). Bombing in the colonies was used to kill African, Arab and Asian children, women and men in towns, villages and camps rather than achieving military objectives.

This carried over into the Second World War. Churchill gave the RAF orders to bomb military targets in Germany in May 1940; by June neighbourhoods where industrial workers lived were included. Hitler retaliated in September; by November the RAF was ordered to firebomb 20 German cities (100,000 dead in Hamburg and Dresden). The (in)famous commander, Arthur 'Bomber' Harris, had honed his skills as squadron chief in Iraq in the 1920s (also dropping a 20lb bomb on the palace of the Afghan king).

The Americans preferred precision bombing until the US commander, Curtis LeMay picked up the British techniques and launched the massive firestorm attack on Tokyo, killing 100,000 civilians. In the 1950s LeMay was the commander of an atomic strike force. The civilian 'morale' was the target, neglecting that the bombing, like 11 September, could also engender hatred.

Now there is the doctrine of 'smart bombs', targeted more on infra-structure – in other words killing more civilians, but indirectly through hunger and disease, and more slowly.

5. According to the Yugoslav foreign minister reported by Tim Judah in his book about the war.

6. We shall see, and are told that the methods may not be the same, and may also change when the immediate anger cools off. Iraq, Sudan and Somalia are frequently mentioned, with the Philippines. Ulterior oil motives would point to Iraq.

7. In a comparative 17-nation public opinion survey reported in *Free Inquiry* (Summer 1999): 'the United States turns out to be the *most* religious nation (average ranking = 1.71), followed by Northern Ireland (2.43), the Philippines, Ireland, Poland, Italy, New Zealand, Israel, Austria, Norway, Great Britain, The Netherlands, West Germany, Russia, Slovenia, Hungary, and East Germany' – in other words, on the top the US and Northern Ireland with Protestant majorities (seeing themselves as Chosen Peoples) and Catholic countries, on the bottom former Soviet bloc countries. The United

States, however, is No. 1 in believing in 'Life after Death', 'The Devil' and 'Hell'.

8. *International Herald Tribune*, 31 August 1995. What theocratic position does that entail to the person leading the foreign affairs of a country mandated by God to lead the world?

9. Quoted by Joan Didion in 'God's Country', *The New York Review of Books*, 2 November 2000, p. 70.

10. 'These events have divided the world into two sides – the side of believers and the side of infidels', from his first text on al-Jazeera television, reproduced as 'Hypocrisy Rears its Ugly Head', *Washington Post*, 8 October 2001, p. A12.

11. Another articulation of this DMA syndrome would be hard Marxism, dividing the world into the evil bourgeoisie and the good proletariat, with a violent war called revolution being inevitable.

12. Monroe, MA: Common Courage Press, 2000.

13. Compared with this what bin Laden is accused of is rather paltry: the 1993 bombs in the World Trade Center, the 1998 bombs at the US embassies in Nairobi and Dar es Salaam, the 2000 bomb attack on the US destroyer *Cole* in a Yemen harbour, and 11 September 2001.

14. For bin Laden there is nothing new in this. One of the most important points in his first text is 'Our nation [the Islamic world] has been tasting this humiliation for more than 80 years'. That brings us back to 1920 and before that, almost definitely to the Sykes/Picot treason colonizing, not giving the Arab nation independence in return for their participation in defeating the Muslim Ottoman Empire, bringing them under the rule of infidels. In the *Washington Post* commentary 'this is a reference to the suspension of the Muslim caliphate in 1924', raising some doubts about WP arithmetical aptitude (reproduced in *The Yomiuri Shimbun*, 31 October 2001, p. 16).

15. And so does bin Laden, for the killers in the 11 September attack: 'I pray to God to elevate their status and bless them.'

16. And the magnitude of the three types of violence? A guess:
    direct, overt: six million, with Korea, Vietnam and Indonesia weighing very heavily – all Region I. An element of racism?
    direct covert: former CIA agents estimated that 'at least six million people have died as consequence of U.S. covert operations since World War II', *Guardian Weekly*, 30 December 1987, report from a meeting of CIA dissidents in New York.
    structural: as usual much more. The 100,000 per day estimate gives us in one year three times the total direct violence in 40–50 years.
    The point here is not quarrels about details. We are dealing with mega-violence in all three categories. And it is interesting to compare with the contribution to official development assistance, in principle meeting people's basic needs rather than denying them: the US is at the bottom of a list of 22 countries with 0.10 per cent of the GNP as opposed to what the UN has proposed, 0.70 per cent, and the world leader, Denmark, with 1.01 per cent.

17. New York: Vintage, 1996. On pp. 321–3 McNamara summarizes the errors in eleven points. Many, perhaps most of them, apply to the US punishment attack, like point 4: 'Our misjudgment of friend and foe

alike reflected our profound ignorance of the history, culture and politics of the people in the area, and the personalities and habits of their leaders.'

18. This is a sad token of the instability of US democracy and civil liberties when only three bombs can have that enormous impact on the whole legal structure so laboriously erected over generations.

19. And an excellent Canadian team from MacMaster University, Hamilton under the leadership of Dr Seddiq Veera, as TRANSCEND mission.

20. This would be similar to the huge US base, Camp Bondsteel, 20 km south of Pristina, in Urosevac which the Americans started constructing right after the withdrawal of the Serbian troops; in commentaries related to pipeline corridor VIII.

21. *The Japan Times* reported that the cost of war in Afghanistan may run to $1 billion a month, quoting the costs of the various types of bombs. Of 40 countries in the coalition (not counting the US) only six contribute military equipment: Canada, Australia, Japan, England, France and Germany.

22. The US prefers courts with clear space and time limitations; the ICC has no such limitation, which means that US personnel may be indicted.

23. Much of that has been skilfully collected by Christopher Hitchens and published in his articles in *Harper's Magazine*, February and March 2001 and his book *The Trial of Henry Kissinger*. In an update in *The Nation*, 5 November 2001, p. 9, he mentions that some people say, 'all this was a long time ago'. Hitchens' answer: 'I think that opportunistic, ahistorical objection may now dissolve. The question of international viciousness and the use of criminal violence against civilians is now, so to speak, back on the agenda. It's important that we make our opposition to such conduct both steady and consistent.'

24. A very good example of Muslim critique is Chandra Muzaffar, President of the International Movement for a Just World, based in Malaysia, publishing *Commentary* regularly (see <www.jaling.my/just>). He writes that 'Decent people reject Terrorism and U.S. Bombing' (article in *International Herald Tribune*, 5 November 2001). According to the public opinion data quoted, there must be many decent people in the world.

25. The Saudi royal family, bin Laden and the Taliban are all Wahabbite.

26. At the end of his first text, bin Laden said that people in America will not 'dream of security before we live it in Palestine, and not before all the infidel armies leave the land of Muhammed, peace be upon him'. If bin Laden says 2 + 2 = 4, do we support terrorism by agreeing?

27. According to Jean-Charles Brisard and Guillaume Dasquie, in their *Bin Laden, la verité interdite*, Paris 2001, the key issue in 11 September is oil, a point also discussed by Michael Klare in 'The Geopolitics of War?', *The Nation*, 5 November 2001, pp. 11–15. The US oil politics in the region flows from an accord between Roosevelt and Ibn Saud on a US warship in the Suez Canal after the Yalta meeting in February 1945. 'It is widely believed that Roosevelt gave the King a promise of

US protection in return for privileged American access to Saudi oil – an arrangement that remains in full effect today and constitutes the essential core of the US–Saudi relationship.' For Klare the conflict is between bin Laden and the oil interests of the US leadership, Bush–Cheney–Rice–Evans (Secretary of Commerce)–Abraham (Secretary of Energy) over the be or not to be of the Saudi government and with it 'the US military presence in Saudi Arabia /that/ has steadily increased over the years' (p. 12). The famous $10 million cheque from Prince Walid ibn Talal to the Twin Towers Fund, 'with subsequent statements on US foreign policy' (from ibn Talal's article 'We Want Anti-Terrorism and Peace in the Middle East', *IHT* , 1 November 2001) was an effort to bet on both horses. 'I am glad to see – [that] President George W. Bush has stated his desire to see the establishment of a Palestinian state. Secretary of State Colin Powell has reiterated this view.' But Mayor Giuliani wanted money with no strings attached and returned the cheque and bin Laden wants the end of the Saudis.

28. Among them a former prime minister of Afghanistan and a former prime minister of Pakistan, both refugees in Iran. But a drawn-out mountain-based guerrilla war by the Taliban could also be problematic.

29. Thus, the obvious defence against economic sanctions, a weapon directed against the weak in society – children and the old, the weak and the ill – is more self-reliance at the country level and more self-reliance at the county level. That, of course, does not mean self-sufficiency in normal times, but the capacity for self-sufficiency for basic needs satisfaction in emergencies. Neither Iraq, nor Yugoslavia had planned for this; for Afghanistan the sanctions may have added little to their plight because of low connectedness, except, of course, for the traders.

30. Even if the pope had agreed to stationing of a NATO command in the Vatican (against adequate compensation, of course), it would still have been an act of sacrilege to very many Catholics.

Chapter 1.4

1. John A. Vasquez, *The War Puzzle*, Cambridge: Cambridge University Press Cambridge Studies in International Relations, 1993.

2. See, for example, Anatol Rapoport, 'Limits of Individual Rationality', in *Origins of Violence*, New York: Paragon, 1989; also the BBC film *Nice Guys Finish First*, 1986.

3. Olof Palme, Independent Commission on Disarmament and Security Issues, *Common Security: A Blueprint for Survival*, New York: Simon and Schuster, 1982.

4. See C.G. Jacobsen, 'Sino-Soviet Relations: New Perspectives', in C.G. Jacobsen, ed., *Soviet Foreign Policy: New Dynamics, New Themes*, London: Macmillan, 1989, pp. 148–62; and C.G. Jacobsen, 'Soviet Strategic Policy Since 1945', in C.G. Jacobsen, ed., *Strategic Power: USA/USSR*, London: Macmillan, 1990, pp. 106–20.

5. See The World Bank, *The Simultaneous Evolution of Growth and Inequality*, 1999: 'Globalization appears to increase poverty and inequality ... The costs of adjusting to greater openness are borne exclusively by the poor, regardless of how long the adjustment takes.' And the United States Central Intelligence Agency (CIA) fateful *Global Trends 2015*, 2000 report: 'The rising tide of the global economy will create many economic winners, but it will not lift all boats ... [It will] spawn conflicts at home and abroad, ensuring an even wider gap between regional winners and losers than exists today ... [Globalization's] evolution will be rocky, marked by chronic financial volatility and a widening economic divide ... Regions, countries, and groups feeling left behind will face deepening economic stagnation, political instability, and cultural alienation. They will foster political, ethnic, ideological, and religious extremism, along with the violence that often accompanies it.' Of course, the portrayal of 'globalization' as a 'rising tide' is an ideological device intended to make it appear 'natural', 'unstoppable', 'inevitable'. Part of the neoliberal message that 'there is no alternative' (TINA). While this is patently false – capital-driven globalization is the result of concrete actions and policies put in place by the world's TNCs, IFIs (World Bank, IMF, WTO) and governments and can indeed be reversed, altered, resisted and transcended – it forms part of the core of the neoliberal argument, an attack upon the basic tenets and principles of democracy. Both these reports provide important evidence that capital-driven globalization does indeed deepen and worsen *cultures* and *structures* of violence, increasing the likelihood of violent attacks (including terrorism) and war, and that those implementing these policies were well aware of their impact and ramifications, long before 11 September 2001.

6. Kai Frithjof Brand-Jacobsen, 'Alienation: A Marxian Analysis', Independent Studies thesis, Department of Philosophy, Carleton University, April 1998. With gratitude also to Hillel Ticktin, Editor of *Critique* (Glasgow), for early mentoring into the profound complexities and (still) often startling truths of Marxian analysis and perspective.

7. Brand-Jacobsen, 'Alienation'.

8. 'Global inequalities in human and living standards have reached grotesque proportions'; see [annual] UN Human Development Report, New York: UN, 13 July 1999.

9. See the web-site of *Jubilee South* <http://www.jubileesouth.net/> for excellent documentation and coverage, including the *Dakar Declaration for the Total and Unconditional Cancellation of African and Third World Debt*, and the *South-South Summit Declaration for a Debt-Free Millennium*. See also Dot Keet's excellent *The International Anti-Debt Campaign: An Activist View from 'The South' to Activists in 'The North' ... and the South*, Cape Town: Alternative Information Centre, June 1999, and the work of the International South Group Network (ISGN) <http://www.isgnweb.org/>, Focus on the Global South <http://www.focusweb.org/>, and the Third World Network <http://www.twnside.org.sg/>. The *Accra Declaration* (April 1998)

and the *Tegucigalpa Declaration* (January 1999) by African and Latin American and Caribbean anti-debt campaigners denouncing further debt repayments and calling upon reparations due to countries in the South for the damages inflicted by centuries of slave trade, colonial and neocolonial exploitation are important landmarks in resistance to debt-slavery by organizations and activists across the South. For further details and discussion, see Kai Frithjof Brand-Jacobsen, *The Struggle Continues*, Pluto Press, forthcoming.

10. See, for example, Morris Miller, 'Global Governance to Address the Crises of Debt, Poverty and Environment', in C.G. Jacobsen et al., eds, Canadian Pugwash Group, *World Security: The New Challenge*, Toronto: Science for Peace/Dundurn Press, 1994; and his pioneering *Coping is not Enough: The International Debt Crisis and the Role of the World Bank and IMF*, Chicago: Dow Jones Irwin (then the *Wall Street Journal* imprint), 1986.

11. See ATTAC <http://www.attac.org/> and Halifax Initiative <http://www.web.net/~halifax/> for further details and elaboration.

12. See Walden Bello, Nicola Bullard and Kamal Malhotra, eds, *Global Finance: New Thinking on Regulating Speculative Capital Markets*, London and New York: Zed Books, 2000; and Hans-Peter Martin and Harald Schuman, *The Global Trap: Globalisation & The Assault on Democracy and Prosperity*, London and New York: Zed Books, 1997.

13. See costing calculations in C.G. Jacobsen, *The New World Order's Defining Crises*, Aldershot: Dartmouth, 1996; concluding chapter: 'How to Get There From Here' (note: the tax percentage calculation is a misprint; also: the figure of a grossly underestimated end-of-century extrapolated speculative transactions flow of US$1,000 trillion [US, Canadian and French, not British/German] is juxtaposed to a World Game Institute high estimate of US$255 billion as the annual cost of a comprehensive sustainable development programme – Worldwatch's low estimate of US$124.7 billion would halve the required percentage).

14. Kai Frithjof Brand-Jacobsen, *The Struggle Continues*, forthcoming.

15. On the Marxist concept, see the works of Mihailo Markovic and other Yugoslav writers; Noam Chomsky, *Manufacturing Consent*, the Canadian National Film Board's two-reel video (based on the book of the same title), is representative of his prolific writings on the subject; Metta Spencer, 'How to Enhance Democracy and Discourage Secession', in Jacobsen et al., *World Security: The New Challenge*; Brian Beedham, 'A Better Way to Vote' *The Economist* (150th anniversary essay), 1993; and Brand-Jacobsen, *The Struggle Continues*.

16. See Kai Frithjof Brand-Jacobsen 'American Military Doctrine', in *The Struggle Continues*, Pluto Press, forthcoming. Kennan's exact words are worth noting: 'we have about 50 per cent of the world's wealth but only 6.3 per cent of its population. This disparity is particularly great as between ourselves and the peoples of Asia. Our real task in the coming period is to devise a pattern of relationships which will permit us to maintain this position of disparity without positive detriment to our national security. To do so, we have to dispense

with all sentimentality and day-dreaming; and our attention will have to be concentrated everywhere on our immediate national objectives ... We should cease thinking about vague and unreal objectives such as human rights, the raising of living standards, and democratization. The day is not far off when we are going to have to deal in straight power concepts. The less we are hampered by idealistic slogans the better.' Policy Planning Staff document 23, dated 24 February 1948, classified Top Secret and entitled 'Review of Current Trends: US Foreign Policy', reaffirmed by Schelling and the 1992 Pentagon Papers. More recent figures reveal the same essential structure as 53 years ago. According to the 1992 UN Human Development Report, the richest 20 per cent of humanity, mainly in the North, controls: 82.7 per cent of world GNP; 81.2 per cent of world trade; 94.6 per cent of commercial lending; 80.6 per cent of domestic savings, and 80.5 per cent of research and development. The United States alone, with less than 5 per cent of the world's population consumes about 33 per cent of its resources. In the last ten years, these figures have grown even worse; a division of the world's resources which was termed 'global apartheid' in a 1992 Nobel Peace Institute symposium.

17. Richard Lummis, *Radical Democracy*, Ithaca and London: Cornell University Press, 1996, p. 16.

18. C.G. Jacobsen, *The New World Order's Defining Crises*, Aldershot and Brookfield: Dartmouth, 1996, chapter 6, pp. 110–18; latest figures provided by Dr Morris Miller (telephone conversation, 11 February 1999) – cf. also his seminal *Coping is not Enough: The International Debt Crisis and the Role of the World Bank and the IMF*, Chicago: Dow Jones Irwin, 1986.

19. See Martin Khor, *Globalization and the South: Some Critical Issues*, Penang: Third World Network, 2000, and Jerry Mander and Edward Goldsmith, eds, *The Case against the Global Economy: And for a Turn towards the Local*, San Francisco: Sierra Book Clubs, 1996.

20. With 60 per cent of global food stocks in the hands of private monopolies and 70 per cent of world grain trade carried out by just five TNCs, while TNCs control 40 per cent of the world's total assets and commerce.

21. Though the subsequent enactment of nearly all of the MAI's objectives in bilateral trade treaties and, still later, in the World Trade Organization's Trade-Related Investment Measures (TRIMs) provided still further evidence of the erosion of state power, or rather, the functioning of the state in the interests of capital.

22. See, for example, 'From Market Madness to Recession: a Dangerous New Manifesto for Capitalism', *Le Monde Diplomatique*, 12 October 1998; see also Public Citizens' Global Trade Watch (US), at <http://www.citizen.org/pctrade/tradehome.html>; and, for example, The Council of Canadians <http://www.canadians.org/> and Citizens' Democratic Watch (Canada), at <citizens@bigfoot.com>

23. The basic principle of this was put forward by Kennedy adviser Dean Acheson when he stated to the American Society of International Law that the 'propriety' of a US response to a 'challenge ... [to the] ... power, position, and prestige of the United States ... is not a legal

issue.' A position maintained both before and since by US presidents, military and political leaders, as in Washington's refusal to ratify the International Criminal Court.

24. As per (and therefore reinforcing) established norms, Ottawa's position reflected government/state decision and government-solicited Supreme Court endorsement, with NGO and citizens' participation essentially absent. In view also of other (male-dominated) Supreme Courts' past histories of denying rights to women and minorities, the 'decision-making' process reflected entrenched 'rights' rather than more generic ideals and aspirations.

25. The Summer Peace Institute on 'Peace-building, Globalisation and Social Justice' organized by the Peace Action, Training and Research Institute of Romania (PATRIR) in cooperation with some of the world's leading organizations working for peace-building and social justice for three weeks each July (beginning for the first time in 2002) is an important initiative to build upon this movement, linking the struggles for social justice with those to promote peaceful conflict transformation and peace by peaceful means. An intensive training programme bringing together social activists, peace and development workers, policy makers, diplomats, scholars, academics and politicians from all five continents to discuss and share experiences, ideas, skills and knowledge and working together to come up with strategies and therapy to transform conflicts constructively, the SPI will be an important step in strengthening alliances and social movements across borders to address the challenges facing us today. For more information see <www.transcend.org> or <www.globalsolidarity.org> or write to <training@transcend.org>.

Chapter 1.6

1. See Wolgang Sach's (ed.) superb, *The Development Dictionary: A Guide to Knowledge as Power*, London and New Jersey: Zed Books, 1996.

Chapter 1.7

1. Dollard and Miller, *Frustration and Aggression*, New York: Yale University Press, 1939; L. Berkowitz, 'Frustration and Aggression', *Psychological Bulletin*, 1989, p. 105.

2. It would be unfair to classify the problem-solving workshops of the Yale learning school, the Harvard interactional school and the London communication/human needs school under the a and b corners, failing to take c into account, but not far off the mark. But their rebuttal might be that the TRANSCEND transformation approach is single-mindedly focused on c, which is true, and is why TRANSCEND has eleven other programmes. For a fine analysis, see Tarja Väyrynen, 'Problem-Solving as a Form of Conflict Resolution', Rutherford College, University of Kent, 1992.

3. Johan Galtung, *Conflict Transformation by Peaceful Means*, United Nations, 1998, the 'mini-version', in English, French, Spanish,

Russian, Arabic and Chinese. A 'maxi-version' is forthcoming, available on the TRANSCEND home-page, <www.transcend.org>. For some of the theoretical background, see Johan Galtung, *Peace by Peaceful Means*, London, New Delhi, Thousand Oaks: SAGE, 1996, Part II, particularly chapter 3. For other works, see John Paul Lederach, *Preparing for Peace: Conflict Transformation Across Cultures*, Syracuse, NY: Syracuse University Press, 1995. 'Dialogue' is in neither the contents nor the index. There is a fine comparison of the prescriptive and Lederach's own famous elicitive approach (TRANSCEND is in-between); Mari Fitzduff, *Community Conflict Skills*, third edition, 1998, analyses 'Third Party Roles – Mediation', but 'dialogue' is not found in the detailed Contents (there is no index); and Friedrich Glasl, *Konflikt-Management, Ein Handbuch für Führungskräfte, Beraterinnen und Berater*, Bern: Paul Haupt, 1997. 'Dialogue' is neither in the contents nor in the index.

4. TRANSCEND is today working in and on Chiapas/Guatemala, Colombia, Peru/Ecuador, Northern Ireland, the Basque situation, Gibraltar/Ceuta-Melilla, Yugoslavia, Cyprus, the Middle East, the Kurdish situation, the Caucasus, Afghanistan, Kashmir, China–Tibet–Taiwan, Okinawa, Hawai'i and the Pacific in general, to mention some conflict arenas. See <www.transcend.org>.

5. Good examples include 'common security' (Palme Commission) and 'sustainable development' (Brundtland Commission). TRANSCEND has used 'Middle East Helsinki Process' for the Israel–Palestine and the Gulf conflicts, 'equal right to self-determination' for Yugoslavia, 'condominium', or 'joint sovereignty' or 'bi-national zone' for the Ecuador/Peru border issue, 'Switzerland of East Asia' for Okinawa, '2 + 3' for Korea (meaning the two Koreas with Japan, China and Vietnam, the Mahayana-Buddhist countries), etc.

6. P. Watzlawick, J. Weakland, and R. Fisch, *Change*, New York: W.W. Norton, 1978.

7. This is spelt out in some detail in Galtung, *Peace by Peaceful Means*, Part II, chapter 3.

8. For an excellent exploration of the difference, see Deborah Tannen, *The Argument Culture: Moving From Debate to Dialogue*, New York: Random House, 1998.

9. For a presentation of that spectrum, see Johan Galtung, *After Violence: 3R, Reconstruction, Reconciliation, Resolution*, Geneva: TRANSCEND, 1998; also at <www.transcend.org>.

10. We are grateful to Jim Duffy for suggesting this metaphor.

11. For an exploration of the cognitive collective subconscious, see Galtung, *Peace by Peaceful Means*, Part IV, particularly p. 213, and for an analysis of the emotive collective subconscious see Johan Galtung, *Global Projections of Deep-Rooted U.S. Pathologies*, Fairfax: ICAR, George Mason University, 1996.

12. Silvan S. Tomkins, *Affect, Imagery, Consciousness*, Vol. 2, New York: Springer, 1963, p. 118.

13. Thomas J. Scheff, *Bloody Revenge: Emotions, Nationalism, and War*, Boulder, Colorado: Westview, 1994. Scheff discusses the role played by shame/rage in the origins of the First and Second World Wars.

See also Donald L. Nathanson, *Shame and Pride*, New York: Norton, 1992. This carries further Tomkins' pathbreaking work on emotions.

14. James L. Adams, *Conceptual Blockbusting*, Toronto: McLeod, 1974, may serve as an introduction to creative problem-solving, and since the root of a conflict is an incompatibility we are certainly in the field of problem-solving. His references are: George F. Kneller, *The Art and Science of Creativity*, New York: Holt, Rinehart and Winston, 1965; S. J. Parnes and H. F. Harding, *A Source Book for Creative Thinking*, New York: Scribner's 1962; Arthur Koestler, *The Act of Creation*, New York: Dell, 1967; H. H. Anderson, ed., *Creativity and its Cultivation*, New York: Harper & Row, 1959; Bruner, Goodnow and Austin, *A Study of Thinking*, New York: Wiley, 1957; Sigmund Freud, *On Creativity and the Unconscious*, New York: Harper & Row, 1958; Carl Jung, *Man and His Symbols*, New York: Doubleday, 1964; Lawrence S. Kubie, *Neurotic Distortion of the Creative Process*, New York: Farrar, Strauss and Giroux, 1966; F. Perls, R. Hefferline and P. Goodman, *Gestalt Theory: Excitement and Growth in the Human Personality*, New York: Dell, 1951.

15. See *Serious Creativity*, London: HarperCollins Business, 1998.

16. See Gerard Prunier, 'Somaliland Goes it Alone', *Current History*, May 1998, pp. 225–8; the quote is from p. 227.

17. Thus, see James Scott, *Seeing Like a State: How Certain Schemes to Improve the Human Condition Have Failed*, New Haven: Yale University Press, 1998 (for a review see C. R. Sunstein, 'More is Less', *The New Republic*, 18 May 1998, pp. 32–7).

Chapter 2.1

1. For some details, see my *Nach dem kalten Kriege, Gespräch mit Erwin Koller*, Zürich: Pendo-Verlag, 1993.

2. One attentive observer of my activities was the Swiss secret police, and in their report my work for 'something called the CSCE' in the early 1970s was a major point. In retrospect this seems ridiculous, but not at that time, to extremists on the Right like the Swiss police and their spies among students, receptionists in hotels, etc.

3. In my view time had been ripe for a very long time; it was over-ripe.

4. The Soviet Foreign Minister at the time.

5. The Warsaw Treaty Organization is usually called the 'Warsaw Pact' in the West.

6. Of course, by that time many people had such ideas, and ultimately the CSCE was transformed into the Organization for Security and Cooperation in Europe, OSCE. However, by that time the elites of the Western European countries were deeply immersed in their favourite project, the European Union, gradually taking on the shape of a superpower.

7. See the excellent book by Erich Loest, *Nikolaikirche*, Leipzig: Linden-Verlag, 1995, about the crucial non-violent demonstrations in Leipzig, particularly on 9 October 1995.

NOTES 321

8. Spelt out in some detail in *There Are Alternatives*, Nottingham: Spokesman, 1984, in German, Italian, Spanish, Norwegian, Swedish, Dutch translations; smuggled into the Soviet Union.
9. I would like particularly to mention the late H. Afheldt, Anders Boserup, Dietrich Fischer, Robert Neild.
10. *Environment, Development and Military Activity: Towards Alternative Security Doctrines*, Oslo: Norwegian Universities Press, 1982.
11. Vladimir Petrovsky, who later became Director General of the United Nations Offices in Geneva.

Chapter 2.2

1. See Johan Galtung, *Norske Fredsinitiativ: 20 Forslag* [Norwegian Peace Initiatives: 20 Proposals], Oslo: Pax, 1964, 47pp; and the earlier *Forsvar uten militærvesen* [Defence without the Military], Oslo, 1959, and Norwegian Peace Corps proposals.
2. See Johan Galtung: 'Regional Security Commissions: A Proposal', chapter 6 in Johan Galtung and Sverre Lodgaard, eds., *Co-operation in Europe*, Oslo: Norwegian Universities Press, 1970; pp. 73–83, particularly pp. 77–80. The proposal (p. 77) is 'a *United Nations' system of regional security commissions*, standing in the same relation to the Security Council of the UN (UN Charter, Chapter 8, Articles 52, 53 and 54) as the regional economic commissions (ECE in Geneva for Europe, ECLA in Santiago de Chile for Latin America, ECA in Addis Ababa for Africa and ECAFE in Bangkok for Asia) have to ECOSOC, the Economic and Social Council. Thus, we are suggesting an SCE, SCLA, SCA and SCAFE'. (p. 77, SCAFE would today be SCAP, 'Asia-Pacific').
3. 'Gradual Reciprocated Initiatives in Tension-reduction', by Charles Osgood, in *An Alternative to War and Surrender*, Urbana, University of Illinois Press, 1967; possibly the most important idea coming out of US peace studies during the Cold War.
4. See Johan Galtung, *There Are Alternatives*, Nottingham: Spokesman, 1984, in eight languages, particularly chapter 5.

Index

Compiled by Sue Carlton